The Homeschooler's Book of Lists

Sonya A. Haskins

The Homeschooler's Book of Lists
Copyright © 2007
Sonya A. Haskins

Cover design by Eric Walljasper
Interior design by Brian Brunsting

Published by Bethany House Publishers
11400 Hampshire Avenue South
Bloomington, Minnesota 55438

Bethany House Publishers is a division of
Baker Publishing Group, Grand Rapids, Michigan.

Printed in the United States of America

Library of Congress Cataloging-in-Publication Data

Haskins, Sonya A.
The homeschooler's book of lists : more than 250 lists, charts, and facts to make planning easier and faster / Sonya Haskins.
p. cm.
Summary: "More than 250 useful lists for eight subject areas plus curriculum information, checklists, and helpful Web sites provide homeschool educators with supplemental and enrichment material for elementary-age grade levels"—Provided by publisher.
Includes bibliographical references.
ISBN-13: 978-0-7642-0443-2 (pbk. : alk. paper)
ISBN-10: 0-7642-0443-2 (pbk. : alk. paper)
1. Home schooling—United States. 2. Curriculum planning—United States.
I. Title.

LC40.H373 2007
372.1'04242—dc22

2007023750

In keeping with biblical principles of creation stewardship, Baker Publishing Group advocates the responsible use of our natural resources. As a member of the Green Press Initiative, our company uses recycled paper when possible. The text paper of this book is comprised of 30% post-consumer waste.

The Homeschooler's Book of Lists

For Dr. Linda Woolsey

Thank you for correcting my English

and for believing that I had potential.

SONYA HASKINS and her husband, Chris, have five children who love to travel around the United States doing schoolwork the hands-on way. Sonya always wanted to write books, but she never really planned to be a wife and a mother. As a child, she thought she might be a missionary or be in charge of an orphanage. Over the years, Sonya has used the gifts that drew her to those fields in other ways—parenting foster children, translating Spanish as needed, and taking care of others in need. Now she focuses her time on leading her children to Christ, homeschooling, and trying to be a witness for the Lord through her writing.

Sonya has written extensively on the subject of homeschooling and her work has appeared in magazines such as *Homeschooling Today, Educational Dealer, Pastor's Family, Guideposts for Teens,* and *Physician's Practice Digest.* Sonya is a founding member and the Web site administrator of a local support group for homeschoolers. She enjoys organizing moms' nights out, counseling new homeschoolers, volunteering at various events including book sales, and coordinating other homeschool-related activities. Sonya has a heart for encouraging homeschoolers. She also teaches Spanish, Latin, and an Introduction to Languages class to home-educated students, and she loves discussing etymology (see List #148)! The author of six books, all local bestsellers, Sonya is a popular guest speaker and advocate of home education. She lives in Jonesborough, Tennessee, with her family. You can visit *www.sonyahaskins.com* for Sonya's more detailed biographical sketch and pictures of the author, her family, and their active life as homeschoolers.

Acknowledgments

Many people have helped make this book a reality. People frequently ask, "How do you take care of five children *and* homeschool *and* write books *and* (whatever I happen to be doing that day—or look like I'm doing)...?" The fact is, I don't do it all. Many people make these things happen and I'm the least of them.

First and foremost, I must thank my dear husband for all that he does for our family. He is supportive in all my endeavors, and without his support and his love, I wouldn't be able to do all these things. Also, he is my sweetheart.

When I was in the initial stages of dreaming about this book as a resource for homeschoolers, I received a lot of positive feedback from my friend Lori Keck. Without her encouragement, it may not have become a reality. I am very thankful that she saw the potential and encouraged me to write more.

I would like to thank Rebecca Yarosh, Susan Seaman, Angie Roberts, Juli Hensley, and Tammy Edwards for their comments and suggestions as well as fourteen-year-old homeschooler Rebecca Seaman for her illustrations in the original manuscript. Shelby Edwards provided baby-sitting, for which I'm grateful.

My agent, Les Stobbe, knows how much I appreciate his representation, but I would also like to thank him for being so nice, providing helpful advice, and for having faith in me.

I am also appreciative of the staff at Logan's, Panera Bread, and Golden Corral in Johnson City, Tennessee, for letting me have some "office space" while I waited on my own office. A special thanks goes to Teresa, Chris, Crystal, and Sam.

Finally, I want to thank the editors of Bethany House for taking on this project. I am particularly grateful to Jeff Braun for answering my questions and for working late to make sure this book is just what we wanted it to be. You have done a wonderful job!

Contents

See the beginning of each chapter for the titles and page numbers of specific lists.

Introduction

Like many parents interested in homeschooling, we began by spending lots of money on books, curriculum, and other supplies. Over the past decade, I've tried packaged curriculum, workbooks, read-alouds, and even a bit of "unschooling" at times. No matter what we have used, however, answers to the questions that arise in our household frequently aren't found in the typical books at hand. Our family is blessed to have access to the Internet and large local libraries, but the best answers usually are those I can give within a few minutes—not after an hour of searching online or after our regular trips to the library.

This book is designed to provide parents with important facts and other essential information that will augment *any* education curriculum. You will find details about great people, important dates, famous speeches, renowned works of art, and mathematical formulas. Parents who teach multi-grade levels or subjects will find the book particularly appealing since the lists are designed to provide students with essential information in major academic areas in a manner that is accessible for children of different ages. Parents can use the book to answer questions that otherwise could take several hours per week to research. Then, depending on their age level and abilities, early elementary-age children can memorize portions of the lists (make copies for each of your children), and older children can be responsible for memorizing entire lists.

Finally, another great feature of the book is the inclusion of useful checklists, reading lists, descriptions of homeschool methodologies, and other information exclusively for the parent who teaches at home. Use the lists—make copies of them or just take this book with you to the bookstore or used curriculum fairs to save yourself time and energy. I plan to keep a copy of the book handy any time I might be purchasing homeschool supplies so that I have a record of what I already have, and what I need, right there with me.

God is great and I am thankful He has made this project a reality. It is my wish that this book will make your life easier and enhance your children's education in ways that you never imagined. Use it yourself and hand it over to them every now and then so that they can enjoy reading through the facts and trivia.

Enjoy your children each day and relish every moment of your homeschooling journey. Even through the difficult times, God will be glorified. Please write if you have questions and let me know if you have any comments about the book or would like to schedule a speaking engagement. You can visit my Web site for more information about the book and my family.

Sincerely,
Sonya Haskins
sonya@sonyahaskins.com
www.sonyahaskins.com

1

History and Government

List #1 Important Dates in History

Although there are some wars and "Christian" dates listed here, this is more of a general timeline to use for reference with your studies. Additional dates are included in more specific lists (military conflicts, scientific discoveries, inventions, etc.) throughout the book.

c. 3000 BC	The Sumerian civilization in Mesopotamia; cuneiform writing
c. 3000 BC	The Nile Valley civilization flourishes near Egypt; hieroglyphic writing begins
c. 2530 BC	Great Pyramid, Egypt
c. 2500 BC	Chinese pyramids
c. 2200 BC	Bronze Age
c. 2100 BC	The earliest version of Gilgamesh Epic is recorded (if he was real, Gilgamesh would have lived around 2500 BC)
c. 1190 BC	Trojan War
c. 753 BC	Rome is founded
c. 722 BC	The Assyrians conquer Israel
c. 612 BC	Babylonians and Medes conquer Assyria
605 BC	Nebuchadnezzar becomes king of Babylon
605 BC	The Babylonians invade Judah
586 BC	Babylonian Exile begins
539 BC	The fall of Babylon
516 BC	Jews begin to rebuild the temple
5th century BC	The Parthenon, a temple to Athena, is built in Athens
c. 430 BC	Peloponnesian Wars fought in Greece between the empire of Athens and the Peloponnesian League, led by Sparta
333 BC	Alexander the Great conquers Persian Empire
323 BC	Alexander the Great dies and his empire is divided between his generals, two of whom founded dynasties—the Ptolemy Dynasty in Egypt and the Seleucid Dynasty in Syria and Mesopotamia
2nd century BC	Essene community at Qumran (Dead Sea Scrolls) begins
c. 70 BC	Spartacus, a slave and gladiator, leads an unsuccessful slave revolt against the Roman Republic
30 BC	Cleopatra dies; Rome shifts from a republic to an empire under the rule of Augustus
4 BC	Jesus is born
1st century	Buddhism is introduced in China

List #1 **Important Dates in History** *(continued)*

64	Emperor Nero of Rome persecutes Christians
70	Josephus writes *The Jewish War*
79	Mt. Vesuvius erupts and Pompeii is destroyed
258	The Goths invade Asia Minor
325	The First Council of Nicaea
c. 350	The Emperor Julian rejects Christianity and tries to restore the Roman religion
406	The Franks invade Gaul
447	Attila the Hun takes Rome
453	Attila the Hun dies
455	Vandals plunder Rome (incidentally, this is where the word *vandals* comes from)
476	The fall of the Roman Empire
476 to about 1000	Dark Ages of Europe
5th to 16th centuries	Middle Ages of Europe
541–542	Plague of Justinian–first known pandemic on record; bubonic plague kills about 40% of the Constantinople population
588	The plague spreads through Europe, killing about 25 million people
600–632	Muhammad writes Quran (Koran) and establishes Islam
600	China begins printing books
642	Muslim conquest of North Africa; rapid expansion of the Arab empire
700s–800s	Arabs begin African slave trade
779	The earliest Japanese prints are produced
787	The Second Council of Nicaea
801	Vikings begin selling slaves to Muslims
939	Vietnam gains independence from China
988	Vladimir, the grand prince of Kiev, converts to Christianity
1000	Leif Ericson unknowingly discovers the New World
c. 1100	The Chinese invent gunpowder
1220	Genghis Khan invades central Asia
1264	Mongols invade China and Kublai Khan founds Yuan dynasty
1266	Marco Polo travels to China

List #1 **Important Dates in History** *(continued)*

1330	Bubonic plague pandemic covers Europe and India
1368	The Ming Dynasty rises in China
1450	Johannes Gutenberg invents the printing press
late 1400s	Portuguese explorers add much information about continent of Africa
1492	Columbus sets sail for the Indies and lands on San Salvador
1492	Ferdinand and Isabella drive Moors and Jews out of Spain
1500s	The Spanish conquer civilizations in Central and South America and wipe out several people groups in the New World
1533–1584	Ivan the Terrible rules Russia
1550	Though the Great Wall of China is thought to have been started in the 3rd century to keep out invaders, it is fortified by numerous different rulers for centuries; after the Mongols invade in the 13th century, it becomes even more essential to have adequate protection; after Altan Khan's siege of Beijing in 1550, Ming builds or fortifies most of the existing wall from 1560 to 1640
1558–1603	Elizabethan era of England
1564	Shakespeare is born
1600s	The English, French, and Dutch colonize North America, East and West Indies, and South Africa, enslaving, killing, or evangelizing the native people in the process
18th and 19th centuries	Industrial Revolution
1776–1781	American Revolution
1789	French Revolution
1815	Napoleon is defeated on June 18 at Waterloo
1837–1901	Victorian era of England

Significant dates beyond 1901 are covered in other lists in this book. All dates are based on the Gregorian calendar, introduced in 1582.

List #2 Seven Wonders of the Ancient World

The Great Pyramid of Khufu at Giza, Egypt

The Great Pyramid of Khufu is 756 feet wide and 450 feet high. It is composed of 2.3 million stone blocks, each averaging two and a half tons. The pyramid is perfectly oriented to the points of the compass and each side has a variance of no more than eight inches, which is amazing considering the builders' limited surveying equipment. The pyramid was the tallest building in the world until the nineteenth century. Approximately 4,500 years old, it is the only remaining "wonder" of the Seven Wonders of the Ancient World that still stands.

The Hanging Gardens of Babylon, on the Banks of the Euphrates River

Ancient historian Diodorus recorded that the Hanging Gardens of Babylon were approximately 400 feet wide, 400 feet long, and more than 80 feet high. There are several different accounts regarding the size of the Hanging Gardens, but clearly this green mountain in the desert must have been a wonderful sight. According to stories passed down through ancient historians, the Gardens were built by Nebuchadnezzar II around 600 BC.

The Statue of Zeus at Olympia, Greece

In ancient times, athletes traveled from faraway lands such as Asia Minor, Egypt, and Sicily to compete in the Olympic Games. This event was one of the most important festivals to the Greek people because the Games were held in honor of Zeus, king of their gods. The location of the Games centered around a shrine to Zeus at Olympia. Initially this shrine was modest, but as the Games increased in popularity, the decision was made to erect a new temple containing a majestic statue of Zeus. Construction of the larger temple began between 470 and 460 BC and was completed in 456 BC.

The Temple of Artemis in Ephesus, Greece

The Temple of Artemis was still under construction in 333 BC, when Alexander the Great came to Ephesus. It is believed that this was the first building completely constructed of marble, and it had other unique features as well. Of the approximately 127 columns, 36 had lower portions that were carved with figures in high relief. There were also works of art housed in the temple. According to Pliny, the temple was 425 feet long and 225 feet wide.

List #2 **Seven Wonders of the Ancient World** *(continued)*

The Mausoleum at Halicarnassus Near the Aegean Sea

Mausolus was a leader of the Caria civilization, which at varying times was either friend or foe to the nearby Greek states. Stories differ as to whether Mausolus actually began building the famous Mausoleum of Halicarnassus or if his wife (and sister) Artemisia began building the tomb after his death. It was customary at that time for Caria rulers to marry their own sisters, and it is recorded that Mausolus's death in 353 BC left Artemisia devastated. Whether it was Mausolus or Artemisia who commissioned the project, it is evident that Artemisia invited Greek artists to design the statues and reliefs around and on the tomb. Artemisia died two years after her husband, but work on the magnificent tomb continued, and she was probably buried there with him. It was completed in 350 BC and overlooked the city of Halicarnassus for centuries. Eventually a series of earthquakes before 1400 destroyed the columns, setting off gradual destruction of the tomb. One of the amazing things about the tomb for Mausolus is that it was so grand that people began associating the term *mausoleum* with great tombs, and we retain this word even today.

The Colossus of Rhodes

Rhodes was an island in the Mediterranean Sea. Wars were common in the third century before Christ, and the Rhodians relied on their patron god Helios for blessing in battle and celebrated his name with their victories. The Colossus of Rhodes was built to honor Helios. It stood 120 feet tall with a fifty-foot pedestal. The statue was erected at the entrance of the harbor to the island in 282 BC, but unfortunately it only remained until 226 BC, when an earthquake destroyed it.

The Great Lighthouse at Alexandria on the Island of Pharos in Egypt

Throughout his vast domain, Alexander the Great founded at least seventeen cities that he christened Alexandria. One of the "Alexandria" cities was on the island of Pharos in Egypt. Ptolemy Soter took over rule of Egypt after Alexander's death in 323 BC, but he did not rename the city. Instead, he saw the city develop into a prosperous port area and he authorized the building of the great lighthouse to guide ships into the busy harbor. At the time, it was the second tallest building in the world, ranking behind the Great Pyramid. The lighthouse is thought to have been a great tourist attraction, and it was so popular that the word *Pharos* became the root for the word *lighthouse* in the French (*phare*), Spanish (*faro*), Italian (*faro*), and Romanian (*far*) languages.

List #3 Modern Wonders

Abu Simbel Temple	Egypt
Angkor Wat	Cambodia
The Aztec Temple	Tenochtitlan, Mexico City, Mexico
The Banaue Rice Terraces	Philippines
Borobudur Temple	Indonesia
The Channel Tunnel	Europe (under the channel between Great Britain and France)
The Clock Tower (Big Ben)	London, England
The CN Tower	Toronto, Canada
The Colosseum	Rome, Italy
The Eiffel Tower	Paris, France
The Empire State Building	New York City, New York, USA
The Gateway Arch	St. Louis, Missouri, USA
The Golden Gate Bridge	San Francisco, California, USA
The Great Wall	China
The High Dam	Aswan, Egypt
Hoover Dam	Arizona/Nevada, USA
Itaipú Dam	Brazil/Paraguay
The Leaning Tower	Pisa, Italy
Machu Picchu (Inca city)	Peru
The Mayan Temples	Tikal in Northern Guatemala
The Moai Statues	Rapa Nui (Easter Island), Chile
Mont-Saint-Michel	Normandy, France
Mount Rushmore National Memorial	South Dakota, USA
The Panama Canal	Connects Atlantic and Pacific Oceans in Panama, Central America
The Parthenon	Athens, Greece
Petra, rock-carved city	Jordan
The Petronas Towers	Kuala Lumpur, Malaysia
The Shwedagon Pagoda	Myanmar

List #3 Modern Wonders *(continued)*

The Statue of Cristo Redentor	Rio de Janeiro, Brazil
The Statue of Liberty	New York City, New York, USA
Stonehenge	England
The Suez Canal	Egypt
The Sydney Opera House	Australia
Taj Mahal	Agra, India
The Temple of the Inscriptions	Palenque, Mexico
The Throne Hall of Persepolis	Iran

List #4 Natural Wonders

Angel Falls	Venezuela
The Bay of Fundy	Nova Scotia, Canada
The Grand Canyon	Arizona, USA
The Great Barrier Reef	Australia
Iguaçú Falls	Brazil/Argentina
Krakatoa Island	Indonesia
Mount Everest	Nepal
Mount Fuji	Japan
Mount Kilimanjaro	Tanzania
Niagara Falls	Ontario (Canada) and New York State (USA)
Paricutin Volcano	Mexico
Victoria Falls	Zambia/Zimbabwe

List #5 Pharaohs

A complete list of pharaohs is impossible because the dating systems for Egyptian studies vary. Also, sometimes the pharaohs were known by more than one name, and sometimes the reigns of fathers and sons overlapped, causing confusion about who reigned when. This list will be a good quick reference for world studies or Egyptian studies, or to determine who reigned during a particular era. It is not meant to be exhaustive.

- Early Dynastic or Archaic Period (c. 3150 to 2686 BC)
  - The First Dynasty ruled from c. 3150 to 2890 BC.
  - The Second Dynasty ruled from 2890 to 2686 BC.
- Old Kingdom (2686 to 2181 BC)
  - The Third Dynasty ruled from 2686 to 2613 BC.
  - The Fourth Dynasty ruled from 2613 to 2498 BC and represented the period of pharaohs who commissioned the building of the Great Pyramids.

Sneferu	2613–2589 BC	Sneferu built the Bent Pyramid, which changes angles partway up, and the Red Pyramid, which is the first "true" pyramid.
Khufu	2589–2566 BC	Khufu built the Great Pyramid of Giza, which is the only remaining wonder of the ancient world that still stands.

  - The Fifth Dynasty ruled from 2498 to 2345 BC.
  - The Sixth Dynasty ruled from 2345 to 2181 BC.
- First Intermediate Period—This is the period between the Old Kingdom and the Middle Kingdom (2181 to 2040 BC).
  - The Seventh and Eighth Dynasties ruled from 2181 to 2160 BC.
  - The Ninth Dynasty ruled from 2160 to 2130 BC.
  - The Tenth Dynasty ruled Lower Egypt from 2130 to 2040 BC.
- Middle Kingdom (2055 to 1650 BC).
  - The Eleventh Dynasty ruled Upper Egypt from 2134 to 1991 BC.

Nebhepetre Mentuhotep I	2060–2010 BC	Mentuhotep I gained control of all of Egypt in 2040. This ushered in the period of the Middle Kingdom.

- The Twelfth Dynasty ruled from 1991 to 1802 BC. Many Egyptians consider this the greatest dynasty.

List #5 **Pharaohs** *(continued)*

Senusret III (Sesostris III)	1878–1860 BC	Sesostris III was the most powerful Middle Kingdom pharaoh.
Amenemhat III	1860–1815 BC	
Amenemhat IV	1815–1807 BC	His reign overlapped his father's reign by at least one year.
Sobekneferu	1807–1803 BC	Sobekneferu was a female ruler, which was rare, but not unheard of.

- The Second Intermediate Period (1750 to 1570 BC) marked the end of the Middle Kingdom and the beginning of the New Kingdom. This was a period of disarray in Egypt, with the Hyksos from Asia taking over leadership during the reign of Dudimose I. The Hyksos were eventually forced back to Asia during the Seventeenth Dynasty.
  - The Thirteenth Dynasty ruled from 1803 to 1649 BC.

Sekhemre Khutawy (Sobekhotep)	1803–1799 BC	One interesting note about the rule of Sobekhotep is that several Nile records and papyri verify this reign.
Sedjefakare	c. 1775–c. 1768 BC	The reign of Sedjefakare has been verified on several ancient documents.
Khendjer	c. 1765 BC	We don't know exactly how long he ruled, though it was at least four years, three months.
Sobekhotep III	c. 1755–c. 1751 BC	He ruled for at least four years, two months.

  - The Fourteenth Dynasty ruled from 1705 to c. 1690 BC.
  - The Fifteenth Dynasty was ruled by Bedouins from the Fertile Crescent who came to Egypt and governed the Nile region. They were known as the Hyskos and ruled from 1674 to 1535 BC.
  - The Sixteenth Dynasty ruled from 1663 to c. 1555 BC.
  - The Seventeenth Dynasty ruled from 1650 to 1550 BC and was based in Upper Egypt.

- The New Kingdom spanned the sixteenth century to the eleventh century BC (1550 to 1069 BC). Egyptian armies fought the Hittites during this time and exhibited military dominance abroad, expanding their territories.
  - The Eighteenth Dynasty ruled from 1550 to 1295 BC.

Ahmose I or Ahmosis I	1550–1525 BC	

List #5 **Pharaohs** *(continued)*

Amenhotep I	1525–1504 BC	
Thutmose I	1504–1492 BC	
Thutmose II	1492–1479 BC	
Thutmose III	1479–1425 BC	Thutmose III ruled Egypt for many years, but the early part of his reign was largely controlled by his stepmom Hatshepsut. After she died, Thutmose III began expanding Egyptian rule and is called the "Napoleon of Egypt."
Hatshepsut	1473–1458 BC	She co-ruled with her stepson Thutmose III until her death in 1458 BC. Hatshepsut is only the second known female ruler, and frequently her statues show her as a man.
Amenhotep II	1427–1400 BC	
Thutmose IV	1400–1390 BC	
Amenhotep III	1390–1352 BC	This was a peaceful time for Egypt and it's possible that Amenhotep III led the way for Amenhotep IV's devotion to one god.
Amenhotep IV or Akhenaten	1352–1336 BC	Amenhotep IV believed in and worshiped one god, Aten. This is one of the first known examples of monotheism (worship of one god).
Smenkhkare	1338–1336 BC	He possibly co-reigned with Akhenaten.
Tutankhamun	1336–1327 or 1324 BC	Tutankhamun is one of the most well-known of the kings, particularly since his tomb was discovered largely undisturbed in the Valley of the Kings in 1923.
Horemheb	1323–1295 BC	He previously served as general and advisor to Tutankhamun.

- The Nineteenth Dynasty ruled from 1295 to 1186 BC.

Rameses II (Rameses the Great)	1279–1213 BC	This is the ruler typically associated with Moses and the twelve plagues on Egypt. Rameses II signed a peace treaty with the Hittites in 1258 BC.
Merneptah	1213–1203 BC	A stele, a sort of tombstone, commemorating the accomplishments of Merneptah, mentions the Israelites. While they were mentioned only in passing, it is the earliest known record of the Israelites.

List #5 **Pharaohs** *(continued)*

Twosret	1188–1186 BC	This was a rare female ruler.

- The Twentieth Dynasty ruled from 1185 to 1070 BC.

- The Third Intermediate Period (1069 to 656 BC), also known as the "Libyan Period" due to the rule of a number of dynasties of Libyan origin, marked the end of the New Kingdom. (Notice there is an overlap between the Third Intermediate Period and the Late Period. Some datelines place the Twenty-Fifth Dynasty in the Third Intermediate Period and others place it in the Late Period. We have placed it in the former.)
  - The Twenty-First Dynasty was a weak dynasty that ruled from 1069 to 945 BC. Their influence was limited primarily to Lower Egypt.
  - The Twenty-Second (945 to 729 BC) and Twenty-Third Dynasties (836 to 720 BC) were made up of pharaohs of Libyan origin.
  - There was a Twenty-Fourth Dynasty with only two pharaohs from 732 to 720 BC.
  - The Twenty-Fifth Dynasty was ruled by five pharaohs, according to most experts.

- The Late Period of Egypt extends from 664 to 30 BC, when Egypt became a province of Rome. There were periods of rule by the Nubians, Persians, and Macedonians during this period, which included Dynasties Twenty-Six through Thirty-One.

- The Ptolemaic Period (332 to 30 BC) also overlaps the Late Period (664 to 30 BC). By this time in Egyptian history, rulers from other nations began to set themselves up as Pharaohs. During the Ptolemaic Period, this trend continued when Alexander the Great came to Egypt.
  - The Thirty-Second Dynasty ruled from 332 to 310 BC.

Alexander the Great	332–323 BC	He conquered most of the known world.

  - The Thirty-Third Dynasty ruled from 310 to 30 BC.

Ptolemy I Soter I	305–285 BC	
Ptolemy II Philadelphius	285–246 BC	
Ptolemy III Euergetes I	246–221 BC	

List #5 **Pharaohs** *(continued)*

Ptolemy IV Philopater	221–205 BC	
Ptolemy V Epiphanes	205–180 BC	
Ptolemy VI Philometor	180–145 BC	
Ptolemy VII Neos Philopater	145 BC	
Ptolemy VIII Euergetes II	170–116 BC	
Ptolemy IX Soter II	116–107 BC	
Ptolemy X Alexander I	107–88 BC	
Ptolemy IX Soter II (restored)	88–80 BC	
Ptolemy XI Alexander II	80 BC	
Ptolemy XII Neos Dionysus (Auletes)	80–51 BC	
Cleopatra VII Philopater	51–30 BC	A direct descendant of Ptolemy I Soter, Cleopatra co-ruled with her father and her brothers/husbands; consummated an alliance with Gaius Julius Caesar; had twins with Mark Antony after Caesar's death.
Ptolemy XIII	51–47 BC	
Ptolemy XIV	47–44 BC	
Ptolemy XV Caesarion	44–30 BC	The son of Cleopatra and (most likely) Julius Caesar; his name means "little Caesar."

List #6 Rulers of England

*(Noted are the **dates of rule**, not birth and death dates.)*

House of Normandy

- William I the Conqueror (1066–1087)
- William II Rufus (1087–1100)
- Henry I (1100–1135)
- Stephen (1135–1154)
- Matilda (1141)

House of Plantagenet

- Henry II (1154–1189)
- Richard I (1189–1199)
- John Lackland (1199–1216)
- Henry III (1216–1272)
- Edward I (1272–1307)
- Edward II (1307–1327)
- Edward III (1327–1377)
- Richard II (1377–1399)

House of Lancaster

- Henry IV (1399–1413)
- Henry V (1413–1422)
- Henry VI (1422–1461; 1470–1471)

House of York

- Edward IV (1471–1483)
- Edward V (1483)
- Richard III (1483–1485)

House of the Tudors

- Henry VII (1485–1509)
- Henry VIII (1509–1547)
- Edward VI (1547–1553)
- Jane Grey (1553)
- Mary I (1553–1558)
- Elizabeth I (1558–1603)

House of Stuart

- James I (1603–1625)
- Charles I (1625–1649)
- Charles II (1660–1685)
- James II (1685–1689)
- Mary II (1689)
- William III (1689–1702)
- Anne I (1702–1714)

House of Hanover

- George I (1714–1727)
- George II (1727–1760)
- George III (1760–1820)
- George IV (1820–1830)
- William IV (1830–1837)
- Victoria (1837–1901)
- Edward VII (1901–1910)

House of Windsor

- George V (1910–1936)
- Edward VIII (1936)
- George VI (1936–1952)
- Elizabeth II (1952–present)

House of Capet

- Hugh Capet (987–996)
- Robert II (996–1031)
- Henry I (1031–1060)
- Philip I (1060–1108)
- Louis VI (1108–1137)
- Louis VII (1137–1180)
- Philip II August (1180–1223)
- Louis VIII (1223–1226)
- Louis IX (1226–1270)
- Philip III (1270–1285)
- Philip IV (1286–1314)
- Louis X (1314–1316)
- John I (1316)
- Philip V (1316–1322)
- Charles IV (1322–1328)

House of the Valois

- Philip VI of Valois (1328–1350)
- John II the Good (1350–1364)
- Charles V the Wise (1364–1380)
- Charles VI the Mad (1380–1422)
- Charles VII (1422–1461)
- Louis XI (1461–1483)

House of the Valois *(continued)*

- Charles VIII (1483–1498)
- Louis XII (1498–1515)
- Francis I (1515–1547)
- Henry II (1547–1559)
- Francis II (1559–1560)
- Charles IX (1560–1574)
- Henry IIII (1574–1589)

House of Bourbon

- Henry IV (1589–1610)
- Louis XIII (1610–1643)
- Louis XIV (1643–1715)
- Louis XV (1715–1773)
- Louis XVI (1773–1792)
- Louis XVII (1792–1795)

List #7 Rulers of France

*(Noted are the **dates of rule**, not birth and death dates.)*

Carolingian (Carlovingian) Dynasty

- Pepin the Short (751–768)
- Charlemagne (768–814)
- Louis I the Pious (814–840)
- Charles I the Bald (840–877)
- Louis II the Stammerer (877–879)
- Louis III (879–882)
- Carloman (879–884)
- Charles II the Fat (884–887)
- Eudes (Odo), Count of Paris (888–898)
- Charles III the Simple (893–923)
- Robert I (922–923)
- Rudolf, Duke of Burgundy (923–936)
- Louis IV d'Outremer (936–954)
- Lothair (954–986)
- Louis V the Sluggard (986–987)

Capetian Dynasty

- Hugh Capet (987–996)
- Robert II the Pious (996–1031)
- Henry I (1031–1060)
- Philip I (1060–1108)
- Louis VI the Fat (1108–1137)
- Louis VII the Young (1137–1180)
- Philip II (Philip Augustus) (1180–1223)
- Louis VIII the Lion (1223–1226)
- Louis IX (St. Louis) (1226–1270)
- Philip III the Bold (1270–1285)
- Philip IV the Fair (1285–1314)
- Louis X the Quarreler (1314–1316)
- John I the Posthumous (1316)—a baby who "ruled" for the five days he lived
- Philip V the Tall (1316–1322)
- Charles IV the Fair (1322–1328)

House of Valois

- Philip VI (1328–1350)
- John II the Good (1350–1364)
- Charles V the Wise (1364–1380)
- Charles VI the Well-Beloved (1380–1422)
- Charles VII (1422–1461)
- Louis XI (1461–1483)
- Charles VIII (1483–1498)
- Louis XII the Father of the People (1498–1515)
- Francis I (1515–1547)
- Henry II (1547–1559)
- Francis II (1559–1560)
- Charles IX (1560–1574)
- Henry III (1574–1589)

House of Bourbon

- Henry IV of Navarre (1589–1610)
- Louis XIII (1610–1643)
- Louis XIV the Great (1643–1715)
- Louis XV the Well-Beloved (1715–1774)
- Louis XVI (1774–1792)
- Louis XVII (1793–1795)

The French Revolution leads to abolition of French monarchy and establishment of Republican government, which lasted until First French Empire in 1804.

First Republic

- National Convention (1792–1795)
- Directory (1795–1799)
- Consulate (1799–1804)

Napoléon Bonaparte rules 1799–1804 as country's first consul until he declares himself emperor in 1804.

First Empire

- Napoléon I (1804–1815)

List #7 **Rulers of France** *(continued)*

Restoration of House of Bourbon

- Louis XVIII le Désiré (1814–1824)
- Charles X (1824–1830)

Bourbon-Orleans Line

- Louis Philippe ("Citizen King") (1830–1848)

Second Republic

- Louis Napoléon (1848–1852)

Second Empire

- Napoléon III (Louis Napoléon) (1852–1870)

Third Republic (Presidents)

- Louis Adolphe Thiers (1871–1873)
- Marie E. P. de MacMahon (1873–1879)
- François P. J. Grévy (1879–1887)
- Sadi Carnot (1887–1894)
- Jean Casimir-Périer (1894–1895)
- François Félix Faure (1895–1899)
- Émile Loubet (1899–1906)
- Clement Armand Fallières (1906–1913)
- Raymond Poincaré (1913–1920)
- Paul E. L. Deschanel (1920)
- Alexandre Millerand (1920–1924)
- Gaston Doumergue (1924–1931)
- Paul Doumer (1931–1932)
- Albert Lebrun (1932–1940)

Vichy Government (Chief of State)

- Henri Philippe Pétain (1940–1944)

Provisional Government (Presidents)

- Charles de Gaulle (1944–1946)
- Félix Gouin (1946)
- Georges Bidault (1946–1947)

Fourth Republic (Presidents)

- Vincent Auriol (1947–1954)
- René Coty (1954–1959)

Fifth Republic (Presidents)

- Charles de Gaulle (1959–1969)
- Georges Pompidou (1969–1974)
- Valéry Giscard d'Estaing (1974–1981)
- François Mitterand (1981–1995)
- Jacques Chirac (1995–2007)
- Nicolas Sarkozy (2007–present)

List #8 Rulers of Germany

*(Noted are the **dates of rule**, not birth and death dates.)*

Germany's First Reich

Carolingian (Carlovingian)

- Charles I the Great (771–814)
- Louis I the Pious (814–833)
- Lothar I (833–834)
- Louis I the Pious (restored) (834–840)
- Lothar I (restored) (840–843)
- Louis II the German (843–876)
- Carloman in Bavaria (876–880) with
- Louis the Younger in Saxony (876–882) and
- Charles III the Fat in Swabia (876–887)
- Arnulf (887–899)
- Louis the Child (899–911)

Franconian

- Conrad I (911–919)

The Ottonians

- Henry I the Fowler (919–936)
- Otto I the Great (936–973)
- Otto II (973–983)
- Otto III (983–1002)
- Henry II the Saint (1002–1024)

The Salians

- Conrad II (1024–1039)
- Henry III the Black (1039–1056)
- Henry IV (1056–1106)
- Henry V (1106–1125)
- Lothair I (1125–1137)

House of Hohenstaufen and Welf

- Conrad III (1138–1152)
- Frederick I (1152–1190)
- Henry VI (1169–1197)
- Philip (1198–1208)
- Otto IV (1198–1218)
- Frederick II (1212–1250)
- William of Holland (1247–1256)
- Conrad IV (1237–1254)

Several Houses ruled 1254–1438.

House of Habsburg

- Albrecht II (1438–1439)
- Frederik III (1440–1493)
- Maximilian I (1493–1519)
- Charles V (1520–1556)
- Ferdinand I (1556–1564)
- Maximilian II (1564–1576)
- Rudolf II (1576–1612)
- Matthias (1612–1619)
- Ferdinand II (1619–1637)
- Ferdinand III (1637–1657)
- Leopold I (1657–1705)
- Joseph I (1705–1711)
- Charles VI (1711–1743)
- Charles VII (1743–1745)

House of Lorraine-Habsburg

- Francis I (1742–1765)
- Joseph II (1765–1790)
- Leopold II (1790–1792)
- Francis II (1792–1806)

Confederation of the Rhine

- A Napoleonic creation that was to unite the German states but simply placed them under French rule from 1806–1815.

German Confederation

- Established in 1815 to replace old Holy Roman Empire that Napoleon abolished with Confederation of the Rhine.
- Ruled until 1866.

North German Confederation

- 1866–1871

Germany's Second Reich

- 1871–1918

Modern German States

- First Republic (1918–1933)
- Nationalist Socialist Government (1933–1945); this period is also known as the **Third Reich**.
- People's Republic—East (1949–1990) and
- Federal Republic—West (1949–present)

List #9 Government Types Defined

Absolute monarchy: a system in which the monarch (through election or inheritance) holds absolute power; the monarch, usually a king or queen, is the single ruler and their actions are not restricted

Communist State: ruled by a single political party that declares loyalty to Marxism-Leninism principles

Constitutional monarchy: a form of government where a constitution recognizes a monarch who is elected or born into office through inheritance; sometimes the monarch holds only a ceremonial role rather than executive powers

Jamahiriya: an Arabic term typically translated to "state of the masses"; the term was applied to Libya by Muammar al-Qaddafi, who was trying to equate Libya to republic or kingdom. Libya is the only country to which the term has been applied.

Military dictatorship: governmental system in which the political power rests with the military

Military junta: a military dictatorship that is governed by a junta, or a committee of members of the military regime's senior leadership or sometimes the previous regime's leadership

Parliamentary monarchy: a monarchy that also has a parliament

Parliamentary republic: much like a republic, but the head of state does not have as wide a range of powers because there is also a head of government, typically called a prime minister

Presidential republic (also called congressional system): a governmental system where the executive branch (president) exists and presides separately from the legislature, to which it is not accountable and which it cannot dismiss in normal circumstances

Sacerdotal state: the head of state is also an ecclesiastical leader chosen by a religious body

Semi-constitutional monarchy: a constitution and a monarch, but the monarch may overrule the constitution if he chooses

Semi-presidential republic: a system of government where a president and prime minister are active in the ruling of the country

Semi-presidential state: the president is theoretically the head of the government, but not always so in practice

Stratocracy: the government is ruled directly by the military; similar to a military dictatorship

List #10 Governments Around the World

State	Government
Afghanistan	presidential republic
Albania	parliamentary republic
Algeria	semi-presidential republic
Andorra	parliamentary monarchy
Angola	presidential republic
Antigua and Barbuda	parliamentary monarchy
Argentina	presidential republic
Armenia	presidential republic
Australia	parliamentary monarchy
Austria	parliamentary republic
Azerbaijan	presidential republic
Bahamas, The	parliamentary monarchy
Bahrain	semi-constitutional monarchy
Bangladesh	parliamentary republic
Barbados	parliamentary monarchy
Belarus	presidential republic
Belgium	parliamentary monarchy
Belize	parliamentary monarchy
Benin	presidential republic
Bhutan	absolute monarchy
Bolivia	presidential republic
Bosnia and Herzegovina	presidential republic
Botswana	presidential republic
Brazil	presidential republic
Brunei	absolute monarchy
Bulgaria	presidential republic
Burkina Faso	presidential republic
Burundi	presidential republic
Cambodia	parliamentary monarchy
Cameroon	presidential republic
Canada	parliamentary monarchy
Cape Verde	semi-presidential republic
Central African Republic	presidential republic
Chad	presidential republic
Chile	presidential republic
China, People's Republic of	Communist State

List #10 **Governments Around the World** *(continued)*

State	Government
Colombia	presidential republic
Comoros	presidential republic
Congo, Democratic Republic of the	semi-presidential republic
Congo, Republic of the	presidential republic
Costa Rica	presidential republic
Côte d'Ivoire	presidential republic
Croatia	parliamentary republic
Cuba	Communist State
Cyprus	presidential republic
Czech Republic	parliamentary republic
Denmark	parliamentary republic
Djibouti	presidential republic
Dominica	parliamentary republic
Dominican Republic	presidential republic
Ecuador	presidential republic
Egypt	presidential republic
El Salvador	presidential republic
Equatorial Guinea	presidential republic
Eritrea	parliamentary republic
Estonia	parliamentary republic
Ethiopia	parliamentary republic
Fiji	military dictatorship
Finland	semi-presidential republic
France	semi-presidential republic
Gabon	presidential republic
Gambia	semi-presidential republic
Georgia	presidential republic
Germany	semi-presidential republic
Ghana	presidential republic
Greece	parliamentary republic
Grenada	parliamentary monarchy
Guatemala	presidential republic
Guinea	presidential republic
Guinea-Bissau	presidential republic
Guyana	presidential republic

List #10 **Governments Around the World** *(continued)*

State	Government
Haiti	presidential republic
Honduras	presidential republic
Hungary	parliamentary republic
Iceland	parliamentary republic
India	parliamentary republic
Indonesia	presidential republic
Iran	presidential republic under theocratic tutelage
Iraq	parliamentary republic
Ireland	parliamentary republic
Israel	parliamentary republic
Italy	parliamentary republic
Jamaica	parliamentary monarchy
Japan	parliamentary monarchy
Jordan	semi-constitutional monarchy
Kazakhstan	presidential republic
Kenya	presidential republic
Kiribati	presidential republic
Korea, North	Communist State
Korea, South	presidential republic
Kuwait	semi-constitutional monarchy
Kyrgyzstan	presidential republic
Laos	Communist State
Latvia	parliamentary republic
Lebanon	semi-presidential republic
Lesotho	parliamentary monarchy
Liberia	presidential republic
Libya	Jamahiriya
Liechtenstein	semi-constitutional monarchy
Lithuania	parliamentary republic
Luxembourg	parliamentary monarchy
Macedonia, Republic of	semi-presidential republic
Madagascar	presidential republic
Malawi	presidential republic
Malaysia	parliamentary monarchy
Maldives	presidential republic
Mali	presidential republic

List #10 Governments Around the World *(continued)*

State	Government
Malta	parliamentary republic
Marshall Islands	presidential republic
Mauritania	military junta
Mauritius	parliamentary republic
Mexico	presidential republic
Micronesia, Federated States of	presidential republic
Moldova	semi-presidential republic
Monaco	constitutional monarchy
Mongolia	semi-presidential republic
Montenegro	parliamentary republic
Morocco	semi-constitutional monarchy
Mozambique	presidential republic
Myanmar (Burma)	military junta without representative institutions
Namibia	presidential republic
Nauru	parliamentary republic
Nepal	constitutional monarchy
Netherlands, the	parliamentary monarchy
New Zealand	parliamentary monarchy
Nicaragua	presidential republic
Niger	presidential republic
Nigeria	presidential republic
Norway	parliamentary monarchy
Oman	absolute monarchy
Pakistan	presidential republic
Palau	presidential republic
Panama	presidential republic
Papua New Guinea	parliamentary monarchy
Paraguay	presidential republic
Peru	presidential republic
Philippines	presidential republic
Poland	parliamentary republic
Portugal	parliamentary republic
Qatar	absolute monarchy
Romania	semi-presidential republic
Russia	semi-presidential republic

List #10 Governments Around the World *(continued)*

State	Government
Rwanda	presidential republic
Saint Kitts and Nevis	parliamentary monarchy
Saint Lucia	parliamentary monarchy
Saint Vincent and the Grenadines	parliamentary monarchy
Samoa	parliamentary monarchy
San Marino	parliamentary republic
São Tomé and Príncipe	semi-presidential republic
Saudi Arabia	absolute monarchy
Senegal	presidential republic
Serbia	parliamentary republic
Seychelles	presidential republic
Sierra Leone	presidential republic
Singapore	parliamentary republic
Slovakia	parliamentary republic
Slovenia	parliamentary republic
Solomon Islands	parliamentary monarchy
Somalia	semi-presidential state
South Africa	presidential republic
Spain	parliamentary monarchy
Sri Lanka	semi-presidential republic
Sudan	presidential republic
Suriname	presidential republic
Swaziland	absolute monarchy
Sweden	parliamentary monarchy
Switzerland	parliamentary republic
Syria	presidential republic
Taiwan	presidential republic
Tajikistan	presidential republic
Tanzania	presidential republic
Thailand	constitutional monarchy
Timor-Leste (East Timor)	parliamentary republic
Togo	presidential republic
Tonga	parliamentary monarchy
Trinidad and Tobago	parliamentary republic
Tunisia	presidential republic

List #10 Governments Around the World *(continued)*

State	Government
Turkey	parliamentary republic
Turkmenistan	presidential republic
Tuvalu	parliamentary monarchy
Uganda	presidential republic
Ukraine	semi-presidential republic
United Arab Emirates	semi-constitutional monarchy
United Kingdom	parliamentary monarchy
United States of America	presidential republic
Uruguay	presidential republic
Uzbekistan	presidential republic
Vanuatu	parliamentary republic
Vatican City (Holy See)	sacerdotal state
Venezuela	presidential republic
Vietnam	Communist State
Yemen	presidential republic
Zambia	presidential republic
Zimbabwe	presidential republic

List #11 United States Presidential Election Results

Use this information on election results to help students practice using a key, interpreting a list, and learn about the electoral process and how it has changed over the years. The party key is at the end of this list (p. 52). For more information on the electoral process and election results after 2007, visit the National Archives and Records Administration (NARA) Web site at *www.archives.gov/federal-register/electoral-college/index.html*. There are numerous activities on the Web site that you can use if you want to delve further into the election process. (This list and results are from NARA public documents.)

Election	1789		
President	George Washington [F]		
Main Opponent	John Adams [F]		
Electoral Vote	Winner: 69	Main Opponent: 34	Total/Majority: 69/35
Popular Vote	no record		
Votes for Others	John Jay (9), Robert H. Harrison (6), John Rutledge (6), John Hancock (4), George Clinton (3), Samuel Huntington (2), John Milton (2), James Armstrong (1), Benjamin Lincoln (1), Edward Telfair (1)		
Vice President	John Adams		
Notes	For all intents and purposes, Washington was unopposed for election as president. Under the system then in place, votes for vice president were not differentiated from votes for president.		

Election	1792		
President	George Washington [F]		
Main Opponent	John Adams [F]		
Electoral Vote	Winner: 132	Main Opponent: 77	Total/Majority: 132/67
Popular Vote	no record		
Votes for Others	George Clinton (50), Thomas Jefferson (4), Aaron Burr (1)		
Vice President	John Adams		
Notes	For all intents and purposes, Washington was unopposed for election as president. Under the system then in place, votes for vice president were not differentiated from votes for president.		

Election	1796		
President	John Adams [F]		
Main Opponent	Thomas Jefferson [D-R]		
Electoral Vote	Winner: 71	Main Opponent: 68	Total/Majority: 138/69
Popular Vote	no record		
Votes for Others	Thomas Pinckney (59), Aaron Burr (30), Samuel Adams (15), O. Ellsworth (11), George Clinton (7), John Jay (5), James Iredell (3), S. Johnston (2), George Washington (2), John Henry (2), Charles C. Pinckney (1)		
Vice President	Thomas Jefferson		

List #11 **United States Presidential Election Results** *(continued)*

Election	1800		
President	Thomas Jefferson [D-R]		
Main Opponent	Aaron Burr [D-R]		
Electoral Vote	Winner: 73	Main Opponent: 73	Total/Majority: 138/70
Popular Vote	no record		
Votes for Others	John Adams (65), Charles C. Pinckney (64), John Jay (1)		
Vice President	Aaron Burr		
Notes	Prior to ratification of the 12th Amendment, votes for president and vice president were not listed on separate ballots. Although John Adams ran as Jefferson's main opponent in the general election, running-mates Jefferson and Burr received the same number of electoral votes. The election was decided in the House of Representatives, with 10 state delegations voting for Jefferson, 4 voting for Burr, and 2 making no choice.		

Election	1804		
President	Thomas Jefferson [D-R]		
Main Opponent	Charles C. Pinckney [F]		
Electoral Vote	Winner: 162	Main Opponent: 14	Total/Majority: 176/89
Popular Vote	no record		
Vice President	George Clinton (162)		

Election	1808		
President	James Madison [D-R]		
Main Opponent	Charles C. Pinckney [F]		
Electoral Vote	Winner: 122	Main Opponent: 47	Total/Majority: 175/88
Popular Vote	no record		
Votes for Others	George Clinton (6)		
Vice President	George Clinton (113)		

Election	1812		
President	James Madison [D-R]		
Main Opponent	De Witt Clinton [F]		
Electoral Vote	Winner: 128	Main Opponent: 89	Total/Majority: 217/109
Popular Vote	no record		
Vice President	Elbridge Gerry (131)		

List #11 **United States Presidential Election Results** *(continued)*

Election	1816		
President	James Monroe [D-R]		
Main Opponent	Rufus King [F]		
Electoral Vote	Winner: 183	Main Opponent: 34	Total/Majority: 217/109
Popular Vote	no record		
Vice President	Daniel D. Tompkins (183)		

Election	1820		
President	James Monroe [D-R]		
Main Opponent	John Quincy Adams [N-R]		
Electoral Vote	Winner: 231	Main Opponent: 1	Total/Majority: 235/118
Popular Vote	no record		
Vice President	Daniel D. Tompkins (218)		
Notes	235 electors were appointed, but only 232 votes were cast due to the deaths of electors from Mississippi, Pennsylvania, and Tennessee.		

Election	1824		
President	John Quincy Adams [Coalition]		
Main Opponent	Andrew Jackson [D-R]		
Electoral Vote	Winner: 84	Main Opponent: 99	Total/Majority: 261/131
Popular Vote	Winner: 113,122	Main Opponent: 151,271	
Votes for Others	William H. Crawford (41), Henry Clay (37)		
Vice President	John C. Calhoun (182)		
Notes	John Q. Adams received fewer electoral votes and fewer popular votes than Andrew Jackson, but won the election in the House of Representatives, with 13 state delegations voting for John Q. Adams, 7 voting for Jackson, and 3 voting for Crawford.		

Election	1828		
President	Andrew Jackson [D]		
Main Opponent	John Quincy Adams [N-R]		
Electoral Vote	Winner: 178	Main Opponent: 83	Total/Majority: 261/131
Popular Vote	Winner: 642,553	Main Opponent: 500,897	
Vice President	John C. Calhoun (171)		

List #11 **United States Presidential Election Results** *(continued)*

Election	1832	
President	Andrew Jackson [D]	
Main Opponent	Henry Clay [N-R]	
Electoral Vote	Winner: 219	Main Opponent: 49	Total/Majority: 286/144
Popular Vote	Winner: 701,780	Main Opponent: 484,205	
Votes for Others	John Floyd (11), William Wirt (7)		
Vice President	Martin Van Buren (189)		
Notes	2 electoral votes from Maryland were not cast.		

Election	1836		
President	Martin Van Buren [D]		
Main Opponent	William Henry Harrison [W]		
Electoral Vote	Winner: 170	Main Opponent: 73	Total/Majority: 294/148
Popular Vote	Winner: 764,176	Main Opponent: 550,816	
Votes for Others	Hugh L. White (26), Daniel Webster (14), William P. Mangum (11)		
Vice President	Richard M. Johnson (147)		
Notes	The election for vice president was decided in the Senate, with Johnson receiving 33 votes.		

Election	1840		
President	William Henry Harrison [W]		
Main Opponent	Martin Van Buren [D]		
Electoral Vote	Winner: 234	Main Opponent: 60	Total/Majority: 294/148
Popular Vote	Winner: 1,275,390	Main Opponent: 1,128,854	
Vice President	John Tyler (234)		
Notes	William Henry Harrison died April 4, 1841. He was succeeded by John Tyler.		

Election	1844		
President	James K. Polk [D]		
Main Opponent	Henry Clay [W]		
Electoral Vote	Winner: 170	Main Opponent: 105	Total/Majority: 275/138
Popular Vote	Winner: 1,339,494	Main Opponent: 1,300,004	
Vice President	George M. Dallas (170)		

List #11 **United States Presidential Election Results** *(continued)*

Election	1848		
President	Zachary Taylor [W]		
Main Opponent	Lewis Cass [D]		
Electoral Vote	Winner: 163	Main Opponent: 127	Total/Majority: 290/146
Popular Vote	Winner: 1,361,393	Main Opponent: 1,223,460	
Vice President	Millard Fillmore (163)		
Notes	Zachary Taylor died July 9, 1850. He was succeeded by Millard Fillmore.		

Election	1852		
President	Franklin Pierce [D]		
Main Opponent	Winfield Scott [W]		
Electoral Vote	Winner: 254	Main Opponent: 42	Total/Majority: 296/149
Popular Vote	Winner: 1,607,510	Main Opponent: 1,386,942	
Vice President	William R. King (254)		

Election	1856		
President	James Buchanan [D]		
Main Opponent	John C. Frémont [R]		
Electoral Vote	Winner: 174	Main Opponent: 114	Total/Majority: 296/149
Popular Vote	Winner: 1,836,072	Main Opponent: 1,342,345	
Votes for Others	Millard Fillmore (8)		
Vice President	John C. Breckinridge (174)		

Election	1860		
President	Abraham Lincoln [R]		
Main Opponent	John C. Breckinridge [D]		
Electoral Vote	Winner: 180	Main Opponent: 72	Total/Majority: 303/152
Popular Vote	Winner: 1,865,908	Main Opponent: 848,019	
Votes for Others	John Bell (39), Stephen A. Douglas(12)		
Vice President	Hannibal Hamlin (180)		

List #11 **United States Presidential Election Results** *(continued)*

Election	1864		
President	Abraham Lincoln [R]		
Main Opponent	George B. McClellan [D]		
Electoral Vote	Winner: 212	Main Opponent: 21	Total/Majority: 233/117
Popular Vote	Winner: 2,218,388	Main Opponent: 1,812,807	
Vice President	Andrew Johnson (212)		
Notes	Abraham Lincoln was shot the night of April 14, 1865, and died the next morning. He was succeeded by Andrew Johnson.		

Election	1868		
President	Ulysses S. Grant [R]		
Main Opponent	Horatio Seymour [D]		
Electoral Vote	Winner: 214	Main Opponent: 80	Total/Majority: 294/148
Popular Vote	Winner: 3,013,650	Main Opponent: 2,708,744	
Vice President	Schuyler Colfax (214)		

Election	1872		
President	Ulysses S. Grant [R]		
Main Opponent	Horace Greeley [D-LR]		
Electoral Vote	Winner: 286	Main Opponent: —	Total/Majority: 352/177
Popular Vote	Winner: 3,598,235	Main Opponent: 2,834,761	
Votes for Others	B. Gratz Brown (18), Thomas A. Hendricks (42), Charles J. Jenkins (2), David Davis (1)		
Vice President	Henry Wilson (286)		
Notes	By resolution of the House, 3 votes cast for Greeley were not counted. V.P. Henry Wilson died November 22, 1875.		

Election	1876		
President	Rutherford B. Hayes [R]		
Main Opponent	Samuel J. Tilden [D]		
Electoral Vote	Winner: 185	Main Opponent: 184	Total/Majority: 369/185
Popular Vote	Winner: 4,034,311	Main Opponent: 4,288,546	
Vice President	William A. Wheeler (185)		
Notes	The electoral votes of 4 states were disputed. Congress referred the matter to the Electoral Commission, which gave the decision to Hayes.		

List #11 **United States Presidential Election Results** *(continued)*

Election	1880		
President	James Garfield [R]		
Main Opponent	Winfield S. Hancock [D]		
Electoral Vote	Winner: 214	Main Opponent: 155	Total/Majority: 369/185
Popular Vote	Winner: 4,446,158	Main Opponent: 4,444,260	
Vice President	Chester A. Arthur (214)		
Notes	The vote of Georgia was not cast until December 8, the second Wednesday of December. If they had not been counted, Winfield S. Hancock would only have received 144 votes. James Garfield was shot July 2, 1881, and died September 19, 1881. He was succeeded by Chester A. Arthur.		

Election	1884		
President	Grover Cleveland [D]		
Main Opponent	James G. Blaine [R]		
Electoral Vote	Winner: 219	Main Opponent: 182	Total/Majority: 401/201
Popular Vote	Winner: 4,874,621	Main Opponent: 4,848,936	
Vice President	Thomas A. Hendricks (219)		
Notes	V.P. Thomas A. Hendricks died November 25, 1885.		

Election	1888		
President	Benjamin Harrison [R]		
Main Opponent	Grover Cleveland [D]		
Electoral Vote	Winner: 233	Main Opponent: 168	Total/Majority: 401/201
Popular Vote	Winner: 5,443,892	Main Opponent: 5,534,488	
Vice President	Levi P. Morton (233)		

Election	1892		
President	Grover Cleveland [D]		
Main Opponent	Benjamin Harrison [R]		
Electoral Vote	Winner: 277	Main Opponent: 145	Total/Majority: 444/223
Popular Vote	Winner: 5,551,883	Main Opponent: 5,179,244	
Votes for Others	James B. Weaver (22)		
Vice President	Adlai E. Stevenson (277)		
Notes	People's Party candidate James Weaver received 1,027,329 popular votes for president.		

List #11 **United States Presidential Election Results** *(continued)*

Election	1896		
President	William McKinley [R]		
Main Opponent	William J. Bryan [D-P]		
Electoral Vote	Winner: 271	Main Opponent: 176	Total/Majority: 447/224
Popular Vote	Winner: 7,108,480	Main Opponent: 6,511,495	
Vice President	Garret A. Hobart (271)		
Notes	V.P. Garret A. Hobart died November 21, 1899.		

Election	1900		
President	William McKinley [R]		
Main Opponent	William J. Bryan [D-P]		
Electoral Vote	Winner: 292	Main Opponent: 155	Total/Majority: 447/224
Popular Vote	Winner: 7,218,039	Main Opponent: 6,358,345	
Vice President	Theodore Roosevelt (292)		
Notes	William McKinley was shot September 6, 1901, and died September 14, 1901. He was succeeded by Theodore Roosevelt.		

Election	1904		
President	Theodore Roosevelt [R]		
Main Opponent	Alton B. Parker [D]		
Electoral Vote	Winner: 336	Main Opponent: 140	Total/Majority: 476/239
Popular Vote	Winner: 7,626,593	Main Opponent: 5,082,898	
Vice President	Charles W. Fairbanks (336)		

Election	1908		
President	William H. Taft [R]		
Main Opponent	William J. Bryan [D]		
Electoral Vote	Winner: 321	Main Opponent: 162	Total/Majority: 483/242
Popular Vote	Winner: 7,676,258	Main Opponent: 6,406,801	
Vice President	James S. Sherman (321)		
Notes	V.P. James S. Sherman died October 30, 1912.		

List #11 **United States Presidential Election Results** *(continued)*

Election	1912		
President	Woodrow Wilson [D]		
Main Opponent	Theodore Roosevelt [P]		
Electoral Vote	Winner: 435	Main Opponent: 88	Total/Majority: 531/266
Popular Vote	Winner: 6,293,152	Main Opponent: 4,119,207	
Votes for Others	William H. Taft (8)		
Vice President	Thomas R. Marshall (435)		
Notes	Republican Party candidate Taft received 3,483,922 popular votes for president. After the election, Nicholas Butler was selected to receive the electoral votes from Utah and Vermont due to the death of James S. Sherman.		

Election	1916		
President	Woodrow Wilson [D]		
Main Opponent	Charles E. Hughes [R]		
Electoral Vote	Winner: 277	Main Opponent: 254	Total/Majority: 531/266
Popular Vote	Winner: 9,126,300	Main Opponent: 8,546,789	
Vice President	Thomas R. Marshall (277)		

Election	1920		
President	Warren G. Harding [R]		
Main Opponent	James M. Cox [D]		
Electoral Vote	Winner: 404	Main Opponent: 127	Total/Majority: 531/266
Popular Vote	Winner: 16,153,115	Main Opponent: 9,133,092	
Vice President	Calvin Coolidge (404)		
Notes	Warren G. Harding died August 2, 1923. He was succeeded by Calvin Coolidge.		

Election	1924		
President	Calvin Coolidge [R]		
Main Opponent	John W. Davis [D]		
Electoral Vote	Winner: 382	Main Opponent: 136	Total/Majority: 531/266
Popular Vote	Winner: 15,719,921	Main Opponent: 8,386,704	
Votes for Others	Robert M. LaFollette (13)		
Vice President	Charles G. Dawes (382)		
Notes	Progressive Party candidate LaFollette received 4,822,856 popular votes for president.		

List #11 United States Presidential Election Results *(continued)*

Election	1928		
President	Herbert C. Hoover [R]		
Main Opponent	Alfred E. Smith [D]		
Electoral Vote	Winner: 444	Main Opponent: 87	Total/Majority: 531/266
Popular Vote	Winner: 21,437,277	Main Opponent: 15,007,698	
Vice President	Charles Curtis (444)		

Election	1932		
President	Franklin D. Roosevelt [D]		
Main Opponent	Herbert C. Hoover [R]		
Electoral Vote	Winner: 472	Main Opponent: 59	Total/Majority: 531/266
Popular Vote	Winner: 22,829,501	Main Opponent: 15,760,684	
Vice President	John N. Garner (472)		
Notes	Socialist Party candidate Norman Thomas received 884,781 popular votes for president, but no electoral votes.		

Election	1936		
President	Franklin D. Roosevelt [D]		
Main Opponent	Alfred M. Landon [R]		
Electoral Vote	Winner: 523	Main Opponent: 8	Total/Majority: 531/266
Popular Vote	Winner: 27,757,333	Main Opponent: 16,684,231	
Vice President	John N. Garner (523)		

Election	1940		
President	Franklin D. Roosevelt [D]		
Main Opponent	Wendell L. Wilkie [R]		
Electoral Vote	Winner: 449	Main Opponent: 82	Total/Majority: 531/266
Popular Vote	Winner: 27,313,041	Main Opponent: 22,348,480	
Vice President	Henry A. Wallace (449)		

Election	1944		
President	Franklin D. Roosevelt [D]		
Main Opponent	Thomas E. Dewey [R]		
Electoral Vote	Winner: 432	Main Opponent: 99	Total/Majority: 531/266
Popular Vote	Winner: 25,612,610	Main Opponent: 22,117,617	
Vice President	Harry S. Truman (432)		
Notes	Franklin D. Roosevelt died April 12, 1945. He was succeeded by Harry S. Truman.		

List #11 **United States Presidential Election Results** *(continued)*

Election	1948		
President	Harry S. Truman [D]		
Main Opponent	Thomas E. Dewey [R]		
Electoral Vote	Winner: 303	Main Opponent: 189	Total/Majority: 531/266
Popular Vote	Winner: 24,179,345	Main Opponent: 21,991,291	
Votes for Others	J. Strom Thurmond (39)		
Vice President	Alben W. Barkely (303)		
Notes	State's Rights Party candidate Thurmond received 1,169,021 popular votes for president. Progressive Party candidate Henry A. Wallace received 1,157,172 popular votes for president, but no electoral votes.		

Election	1952		
President	Dwight D. Eisenhower [R]		
Main Opponent	Adlai Stevenson [D]		
Electoral Vote	Winner: 442	Main Opponent: 89	Total/Majority: 531/266
Popular Vote	Winner: 33,936,234	Main Opponent: 27,314,992	
Vice President	Richard M. Nixon (442)		

Election	1956		
President	Dwight D. Eisenhower [R]		
Main Opponent	Adlai Stevenson [D]		
Electoral Vote	Winner: 457	Main Opponent: 73	Total/Majority: 531/266
Popular Vote	Winner: 35,590,472	Main Opponent: 26,022,752	
Votes for Others	Walter B. Jones (1)		
Vice President	Richard M. Nixon (457)		
Notes	An Alabama elector voted for Jones and his running mate.		

Election	1960		
President	John F. Kennedy [D]		
Main Opponent	Richard M. Nixon [R]		
Electoral Vote	Winner: 303	Main Opponent: 219	Total/Majority: 537/269
Popular Vote	Winner: 34,226,731	Main Opponent: 34,108,157	
Votes for Others	Harry F. Byrd (15)		
Vice President	Lyndon B. Johnson (303)		
Notes	Byrd received electoral votes for president from Alabama (6), Mississippi (8), and Oklahoma (1). Thurmond received electoral votes for vice president from Alabama (6) and Mississippi (8). Goldwater received 1 electoral vote for vice president from Oklahoma. John F. Kennedy was assassinated November 22, 1963. He was succeeded by Lyndon B. Johnson.		

List #11 United States Presidential Election Results *(continued)*

Election	1964		
President	Lyndon B. Johnson [D]		
Main Opponent	Barry M. Goldwater [R]		
Electoral Vote	Winner: 486	Main Opponent: 52	Total/Majority: 538/270
Popular Vote	Winner: 43,129,566	Main Opponent: 27,178,188	
Vice President	Hubert H. Humphrey (486)		

Election	1968		
President	Richard M. Nixon [R]		
Main Opponent	Hubert H. Humphrey [D]		
Electoral Vote	Winner: 301	Main Opponent: 191	Total/Majority: 538/270
Popular Vote	Winner: 31,785,480	Main Opponent: 31,275,166	
Votes for Others	George C. Wallace (46)		
Vice President	Spiro T. Agnew (301)		
Notes	American Independent Party candidate Wallace received 9,906,473 popular votes for president.		

Election	1972		
President	Richard M. Nixon [R]		
Main Opponent	George S. McGovern [D]		
Electoral Vote	Winner: 520	Main Opponent: 17	Total/Majority: 538/270
Popular Vote	Winner: 47,169,911	Main Opponent: 29,170,383	
Votes for Others	John Hospers (1)		
Vice President	Spiro T. Agnew (520)		
Notes	Spiro T. Agnew resigned as vice president October 10, 1973. He was succeeded by Gerald R. Ford. Richard M. Nixon resigned as president August 9, 1974. He was succeeded by Gerald R. Ford. V.P. Ford was succeeded by Nelson A. Rockefeller.		

Election	1976		
President	Jimmy Carter [D]		
Main Opponent	Gerald R. Ford [R]		
Electoral Vote	Winner: 297	Main Opponent: 240	Total/Majority: 538/270
Popular Vote	Winner: 40,830,763	Main Opponent: 39,147,793	
Votes for Others	Ronald Reagan (1)		
Vice President	Walter F. Mondale (297)		
Notes	A Washington (State) elector voted for Ronald Reagan.		

List #11 United States Presidential Election Results *(continued)*

Election	1980		
President	Ronald Reagan [R]		
Main Opponent	Jimmy Carter [D]		
Electoral Vote	Winner: 489	Main Opponent: 49	Total/Majority: 538/270
Popular Vote	Winner: 43,904,153	Main Opponent: 35,483,883	
Vice President	George Bush (489)		
Notes	Independent candidate John B. Anderson received 5,719,437 popular votes for president, but no electoral votes.		

Election	1984		
President	Ronald Reagan [R]		
Main Opponent	Walter F. Mondale [D]		
Electoral Vote	Winner: 525	Main Opponent: 13	Total/Majority: 538/270
Popular Vote	Winner: 54,455,075	Main Opponent: 37,577,185	
Vice President	George Bush (525)		

Election	1988		
President	George Bush [R]		
Main Opponent	Michael S. Dukakis [D]		
Electoral Vote	Winner: 426	Main Opponent: 111	Total/Majority: 538/270
Popular Vote	Winner: 48,886,097	Main Opponent: 41,809,074	
Votes for Others	Lloyd Bentsen (1)		
Vice President	James Danforth Quayle (426)		
Notes	A West Virginia elector voted for Bentsen as president and Dukakis as vice president.		

Election	1992		
President	William J. Clinton [D]		
Main Opponent	George Bush [R]		
Electoral Vote	Winner: 370	Main Opponent: 168	Total/Majority: 538/270
Popular Vote	Winner: 44,908,254	Main Opponent: 39,102,343	
Vice President	Albert Gore, Jr. (370)		
Notes	Independent candidate H. Ross Perot received 19,741,065 popular votes for president, but no electoral votes.		

List #11 United States Presidential Election Results *(continued)*

Election	1996		
President	William J. Clinton [D]		
Main Opponent	Bob Dole [R]		
Electoral Vote	Winner: 379	Main Opponent: 159	Total Majority: 538/270
Popular Vote	Winner: 45,590,703	Main Opponent: 37,816,307	
Vice President	Albert Gore, Jr. (379)		
Notes	Reform Party candidate H. Ross Perot received 7,866,284 popular votes for president, but no electoral votes.		

Election	2000		
President	George W. Bush [R]		
Main Opponent	Albert Gore, Jr. [D]		
Electoral Vote	Winner: 271	Main Opponent: 266	Total/Majority: 538/270
Popular Vote	Winner: 50,456,062	Main Opponent: 50,996,582	
Vice President	Richard B. Cheney (271)		
Notes	George W. Bush received fewer popular votes than Albert Gore, Jr., but received a majority of electoral votes. One electoral vote was not cast.		

Election	2004		
President	George W. Bush [R]		
Main Opponent	John F. Kerry [D]		
Electoral Vote	Winner: 286	Main Opponent: 251	Total/Majority: 538/270
Popular Vote	Winner: 60,693,281	Main Opponent: 57,355,978	
Votes for Others	John Edwards (1)		
Vice President	Richard B. Cheney (286)		
Notes	One Minnesota elector voted for John Edwards for both president and vice president. During the counting of the vote in Congress, Rep. Stephanie Tubbs Jones (D-Ohio) and Sen. Barbara Boxer (D-Calif.) raised objections to the Ohio Certificate of Vote alleging that the votes were not regularly given. Both houses voted to override the objection, 74 to 1 in the Senate and 267 to 31 in the House of Representatives.		

Party Key:

[D] = Democrat
[D-LR] = Democrat-Liberal Republican
[D-P] = Democrat-Populist
[D-R] = Democrat-Republican
[F] = Federalist
[N-R] = National-Republican
[P] = Progressive
[R] = Republican
[W] = Whig

List #12 Assassinations/Attempts

Target	Date	Assassin	Comments
Chinese Emperor Qin Shi Huang	210 BC	Jing Ke	Failed assassination attempt
Roman Dictator Gaius Julius Caesar	44 BC	Marcus Junius Brutus	This successful assassination is where we get the phrase *Et tu, Brute?* which means, "And you, Brutus?" In other words, Caesar couldn't believe that his friend Brutus had betrayed him. Supposedly these were the last words of Julius Caesar.
U.S. President Abraham Lincoln	April 14, 1865	John Wilkes Booth	Booth shot Lincoln in the head after entering the presidential box at Ford's Theatre in Washington, D.C. Lincoln died the next day.
U.S. President James Garfield	July 1, 1881	Charles Guiteau	Garfield was shot in the arm and back; he died 79 days later.
U.S. President William McKinley	September 1, 1901	Leon Czolgosz	McKinley was shot twice and died 8 days later.
Former U.S. President Theodore Roosevelt	October 14, 1912	John Schrank	Roosevelt was shot and wounded; the bullet was likely slowed by folded speech papers and a steel eyeglass case in his coat pocket.
Archduke Franz Ferdinand of Austria	June 28, 1914	Gavrilo Princip	Successful; his death led to Austria declaring war on Serbia, actions which triggered World War I.
U.S. President-elect Franklin D. Roosevelt	February 15, 1933	Joseph Zangara, anarchist	When a woman seized Zangara's arm as he shot, the bullet hit and fatally wounded Mayor Anton J. Cermak of Chicago instead of Roosevelt.
Activist Mahatma Gandhi	January 30, 1948	Nathuram Godse	Successful
U.S. President Harry Truman	November 1, 1950	Griselio Torresola and Oscar Collazo, Puerto Rican nationalists	Failed attempt; during this assassination attempt, Torresola was killed, along with a White House policeman, Private Leslie Coffelt.
U.S. President John F. Kennedy	November 22, 1963	Lee Harvey Oswald	Successful
Activist Martin Luther King, Jr.	April 4, 1968	James Earl Ray	Successful

List #12 **Assassinations/Attempts** *(continued)*

Target	Date	Assassin	Comments
U.S. Senator Robert F. Kennedy	June 5, 1968	Sirhan Sirhan	Successful
Alabama Governor George Wallace	May 15, 1972	Arthur Bremer	Wallace was shot and seriously crippled from his injuries.
U.S. President Gerald R. Ford	September 5, 1975	Lynette (Squeaky) Fromme	Failed attempt; a Secret Service agent grabbed a pistol away from Fromme, a follower of Charles Manson, in Sacramento.
U.S. President Gerald R. Ford	September 22, 1975	Sara Jane Moore	Moore fired a revolver at Ford in San Francisco, but the assassination attempt was unsuccessful, partly because a bystander helped deflect the shot.
U.S. President Ronald Reagan	March 30, 1981	John W. Hinckley, Jr.	The president, Press Secretary James Brady, Secret Service agent Timothy J. McCarthy, and Washington, D.C. policeman Thomas Delahanty were all shot and seriously wounded in Washington, D.C.
Pope John Paul II	May 13, 1981	Mehmet Ali Agca	Agca, a Turkish man convicted of murder, who had escaped, shot and wounded the Pope and two bystanders in St. Peter's Square, Rome.
Egyptian President Anwar al-Sadat	October 6, 1981	Khalid Islambouli	Sadat, who had won the Nobel Peace Prize in 1978 for making peace with Israel, was assassinated by religious extremists.
British Prime Minister Margaret Thatcher	October 12, 1984		Four people died, including a member of Parliament, when a bomb was detonated at the Grand Hotel in Brighton, England, during a Conservative Party conference. Prime Minister Thatcher was unharmed.
Chilean President General Augusto Pinochet Ugarte	September 7, 1986	rebels	The president was unharmed when rebels attacked his motorcade.
Egyptian President Hosni Mubarak	June 26, 1995		Four men died, including two Ethiopian police officers, when gunmen tried to kill the Egyptian president in Addis Ababa, Ethiopia.
Israeli Prime Minister Yitzhak Rabin	November 5, 1995	Yigal Amir	Successful; a law student shot the prime minister at a peace rally.

List #12 **Assassinations/Attempts** *(continued)*

Target	Date	Assassin	Comments
Colombian President Ernest Samper Pizano	February 12, 1997		Pizano was unharmed when a bomb exploded on a runway as his plane was getting ready to land.
Tajik President Imamali Rakhmanov	April 30, 1997		A grenade injured Rakhmanov.
Georgian President Eduard A. Shevardnadze	February 9, 1998		Three people died, including a bodyguard and an assailant, when gunmen fired on the Georgian president's motorcade in Tbilisi, Georgia.
Colombian presidential candidate Alvaro Uribe Velez	April 14, 2002		Three bystanders were killed, but Velez was unharmed when a bomb exploded under a parked bus as his motorcade passed by.
French President Jacques Chirac	July 14, 2002	Maxime Brunerie	The French president was unharmed when Brunerie fired at his jeep.
Afghan President Hamid Karzai	September 5, 2002		Unsuccessful
Turkmenistan President Saparmurat Niyazov	November 25, 2002		Unsuccessful
Pakistani President Pervez Musharraf	December 14, 2003		Unsuccessful
Taiwanese President Chen Shui-bian	March 19, 2004		The Taiwanese president received minor injuries when he was shot in his motorcade while campaigning.
Afghan President Hamid Karzai	September 16, 2004		A rocket was fired at the helicopter carrying Karzai, but he was not injured.

List #13 Native American Tribes

Please note: The use of state names or areas here is simply to help students and teachers identify where these tribes lived. Of course in the 1700s there were only tribal regions, and the Native Americans did not think of "owning" the earth or land as we do. They lived where they could provide food for their families. In some cases, notes are made about where these tribes moved after white men came to North America and took over their lands—usually by force or trickery.

Abenaki—eastern Abenaki lived in Maine, east of New Hampshire's White Mountains; western Abenaki lived west of mountains across Vermont and New Hampshire

Algonquian—original tribal areas unknown; but we do know of tribal groups in New York, Pennsylvania, New Jersey, and Delaware

Apache—New Mexico and Arizona

Arapaho—Minnesota, North Dakota, Oklahoma; migrated westward to Colorado, Wyoming, and Kansas after arrival of Europeans

Cayuga—New York State

Cherokee—southern Appalachian mountains

Cheyenne—Great Plains area east of the Rocky Mountains and west of the Mississippi River

Chickasaw—northern Mississippi and Alabama

Chinook—Northwest Pacific Coast

Chippewa—northern United States and southern Canada around shores of Great Lakes

Choctaw—southern Mississippi, but the United States government forced them to cede their lands and move to Oklahoma in 1830s

Comanche—between the Platte and Arkansas rivers in eastern Colorado and western Kansas

Creek—southern Georgia

Delaware—also known as Lenni Lenape or Lenape Indians; originally mid-Atlantic area (New Jersey, Delaware, portions of New York and Pennsylvania); relocated to Oklahoma

Fox—came together with Sauk (Sac) tribes in 1700s when French attempted to wipe them out; originally lived in Michigan and Wisconsin, but were moved to reservations in Oklahoma, Kansas, and Iowa

Huron—St. Lawrence Valley in Quebec

Illinois—Illinois, Indiana, Missouri, Iowa; war in the 1700s nearly wiped out the Illinois Indians

Iroquois—New York State

List #13 **Native American Tribes** *(continued)*

Kickapoo—Michigan and Ohio
Kiowa—southern plains
Mandan—along banks of Missouri River
Massachuset—Boston, Massachusetts, area
Miami—Midwest: Indiana, Illinois, Ohio, Wisconsin
Micmac—Quebec, Newfoundland, Maine
Modoc—northeastern California and central southern Oregon
Mohegan—upstate New York
Mohawk—New York State
Nanticokes—Delaware and Maryland
Narraganset—Massachusetts and Rhode Island
Nez Percé—plains west of the Rocky Mountains
Nipmuc—New England area: Massachusetts, Rhode Island, Connecticut
Onondaga—New York State
Oneida—central New York State and Canada
Ottawa—southern Ontario and Michigan State
Paiute—eastern California, western Nevada, southeast Oregon
Pennacook—northeastern part of Massachusetts
Penobscots—northeastern United States
Pequot—New England area
Potawatomie—Michigan
Powhatan—Virginia
Sauk (Sac)—Michigan and Wisconsin; evidence shows that the Sauk and Fox Indian tribes were related and spoke the same language, but they were independent; the tribes combined to resist French assaults
Seneca—upstate New York
Shawnee—villages ranged from Georgia to New York
Shoshoni—western United States
Sioux—plains of western United States
Wampanoag—southeastern Massachusetts and Rhode Island
Winnebago—northeastern Wisconsin
Wyandot—southern Ontario

List #14 Major Military Conflicts

c. 1190 BC Trojan War
499–479 BC Persian Wars
431–404 BC Peloponnesian War
395–387 BC Corinthian War
334–323 BC Alexander the Great–many wars
274–200 BC Syrian Wars
264–146 BC Punic Wars between Rome and Carthage
215–168 BC Macedonian Wars
209–88 BC Parthian-Seleucid Wars
55–54 BC Julius Caesar's Roman Invasion of Britain
53–51 BC Parthian War of Marcus Licinius Crassus
44–36 BC Sicilian Revolt
44–30 BC Roman Civil War
66–70 First Jewish-Roman War
115–117 Second Jewish-Roman War
535–553 Gothic War in Italy
711–718 Spanish Reconquista
892–936 Korean Civil War
1066 Norman Conquest
1096–1291 Crusades
1218–1222 Mongol invasion of Central Asia
1241–1242 Mongol invasion of Europe
1341–1453 Hundred Years' War
1420–1436 Hussite Wars
1453 Fall of Constantinople
1454–1466 Thirteen Years' War
1455–1485 War of the Roses
1509–1513 Ottoman Civil War
1571 Russo-Crimean War
1775–1783 American Revolutionary War
1792–1802 French Revolutionary Wars
1803–1815 Napoleonic Wars
1804–1806 Serbian Revolt
1811–1812 Korean Revolt
1813–1814 Greek War
1816–1817 Simon Bolivar fights for independence in Venezuela

List #14 **Major Military Conflicts** *(continued)*

1817–1818	Chilean War of Independence
1820–1823	Spanish Civil War
1838	Mormon War
1839–1842	First Opium War
1853–1856	Crimean War
1856–1860	Second Opium War
1861–1865	American Civil War
1897–1900	Boxer Rebellion in China
1898	Spanish-American War
1899–1902	Second Boer War
1899–1913	Philippine-American War
1905	Russian Revolution
1910–1920	Mexican Revolution
1912–1913	Balkan Wars
1914–1918	World War I
1918–1922	Russian Civil War
1939–1945	World War II
1944–1949	Greek Civil War
1945–1949	Chinese Civil War
1950–1953	Korean War
1954–1975	Second Indochina War (Vietnam War)
1990–1991	Gulf War
2001	September 11 terrorists attacks on United States
2003	Second Gulf War

List #15 Ongoing Conflicts

Year Conflict Began	War/Conflict	Location
1964	Colombian armed conflict	Colombia
1969	Philippine civil conflicts	Philippines
1975	Israel vs. Palestine	
1983	Sri Lankan Civil War (Sri Lanka government vs. Tamil Eelam)	Tamil Eelam
1984	Kurdish Separatist Insurgency	Turkey and Kurdistan
1984	Free Papua Movement	Western New Guinea
1987	Second Ugandan Civil War	Uganda
1988	Casamance conflict	Senegal
1988	Somali Civil War	Somalia
1989	Kashmir conflict	Kashmir
1991	Iraqis Sunni vs. Shi'ite and Iraqis vs. Kurds	
1993	Ethnic conflicts in Nagaland	Nagaland, India
1999	Democratic Republic of Congo vs. Uganda, Rwanda, and indigenous rebels	Democratic Republic of Congo
1999	Second Chechen War	Russia
2000	Conflict with the Hmong	Laos
2001	War in Afghanistan	Afghanistan
2001	South Thailand insurgency	South Thailand (region of Pattani)
2002	Ivorian Coast War	Côte d'Ivoire
2003	War in Iraq	Iraq
2003	Balochistan conflict	Pakistan
2003	Central African War: Darfur conflict and Chadian-Sudanese conflict	Sudan/Chad/Central African Republic
2004	Sa'dah conflict	Yemen
2006	Mexican drug war	Mexico
2006	War in Somalia	Somalia

List #16 The Thirteen Original U.S. Colonies

State Order		Year Founded	Founded by	Made a Royal Colony	Accepted as a State
1st	Delaware	1638	Peter Minuit and New Sweden Company; seized by Dutch in 1655; seized by English in 1664; granted to William Penn in 1682		1787
2nd	Pennsylvania	1632	Originally settled by Dutch and Swedes, but William Penn obtained a charter in 1681 from Charles II		1787
3rd	New Jersey	1664	Originally settled by Dutch, but later seized by Lord Berkeley and Sir George Carteret	1702	1787
4th	Georgia	1732	James Edward Oglethorpe; last of 13 original colonies to be settled	1752	1788
5th	Connecticut	c. 1635	Thomas Hooker and Puritans from Massachusetts	1662	1788
6th	Massachusetts	1620	Originally founded as two colonies: one founded by the Pilgrims (Plymouth Colony) in 1620, and the other founded by Massachusetts Bay Colony in 1630, and settled by the Puritans	1691	1788
7th	Maryland	1634	Lord Baltimore; named for Queen Henrietta Maria of England		1788
8th	South Carolina	1663	Originally part of Carolina Colony; 8 nobles with a royal charter from Charles II; was separated from North Carolina in 1711	1729	1778
9th	New Hampshire	1623	John Mason	1679	1788
10th	Virginia	1607	London Company; home to four of first five presidents	1624	1788

List #16 **The Thirteen Original U.S. Colonies** *(continued)*

State Order		Year Founded	Founded by	Made a Royal Colony	Accepted as a State
11th	New York	1624	Originally founded as New Netherland by the Dutch West India Company, but Duke of York seized land in 1664 and renamed it after himself	1685	1788
12th	North Carolina	1653	Virginians and settlers from other colonies	1729	1789
13th	Rhode Island	1636	Roger Williams; first colony to declare independence from England, but last of original 13 colonies to become a state	1663	1790

List #17 Important Dates in the American Revolution

1764 The British pass the Sugar Act (aimed at raising money for the Crown), followed by the Currency Act (prohibiting Americans from printing their own money).

1765 The British pass the Stamp Act. The First Congress of the American Colonies meets in New York.

1767 The British pass the Townshend Acts (levies, or taxes, on glass, lead, paper, paint, and tea). John Dickinson reproduces and distributes "Letters from a Farmer in Pennsylvania to the Inhabitants of the British Colonies," which calls the Townshend Acts unconstitutional.

1769 The Virginia House of Burgesses approves resolutions that denounce British actions of taxing without representation.

1770 Parliament revokes all levies of the Townshend Acts except the tea tax. An exchange of words at the Boston Customs House results in the "Boston Massacre" (three colonists were killed, eight injured, and two of those died later).

1773 Parliament passes the Tea Act (which gives Britain an edge on the tea trade by reducing the tax on imported tea, but not tea obtainable in the Colonies). Colonists rebel by dressing as Native Americans and throwing tea in the Boston Harbor, called the "Boston Tea Party."

1774 The Continental Congress meets in Philadelphia on September 5.

1775 Paul Revere rides, on April 18, to announce the arrival of British reinforcements. Fighting breaks out at Lexington and Concord, Massachusetts, on April 19. The Second Continental Congress meets on May 10. The Battle of Bunker Hill takes place on June 17. Daniel Boone moves to Kentucky.

1776 The Declaration of Independence is accepted by twelve colonies on July 4. On July 9, New York adds its approval of the Declaration, making it part of the original 13 colonies.

1777 The Stars and Stripes flag is adopted by Congress. Washington encamps at Valley Forge for the winter.

List #17 **Important Dates in the American Revolution** *(continued)*

1778 A French-American alliance is solidified and France offers use of their powerful Navy in the U.S. Revolution. The Battle of Monmouth takes place on June 28. The British take Savannah, Georgia.

1779 John Paul Jones, commander of the *BONNE HOMME RICHARD*, refuses to surrender to the British captain of HMS *SERAPIS*, then Jones captures the British ship before his sinks.

1780 Battle of King's Mountain takes place on October 7.

1781 The Colonies adopt the Articles of Confederation. Cornwallis and his British troops surrender at Yorktown on October 19.

1782 The British House of Commons votes on February 27 against further war in America. The British withdraw from Charleston on December 14.

1783 On February 4, England officially declares an end to the war in America. On April 11, Congress officially declares an end to the Revolutionary War.

List #18 Battles of the Revolutionary War

Battle of Lexington and Concord	April 19, 1775
Capture of Fort Ticonderoga	May 11, 1775
Battle of Breed's Hill (Bunker Hill)	June 16, 1775
Siege of Boston	July 1775–March 1776
Battle of Great Bridge	December 9, 1775
Battle of Quebec	December 31, 1775
Battle of Moore's Creek Bridge	February 27, 1776
Battle of Fort Moultrie and Long Island	June 28, 1776
Battle for New York	July/August 1776
Battle of Valcour Bay	October 11, 1776
Battle of Trenton	December 26, 1776
Washington's Retreat through New Jersey	1776
Battle of Princeton	January 3, 1777
Battle of Oriskany	August 6, 1777
Battle of Bennington	August 16, 1777
Battle of Brandywine	September 10, 1777
Battle of Saratoga	September 19,1777
Battle of Germantown	September 22, 1777
Burgoyne Surrender	October 16, 1777
Battle of Monmouth	June 28, 1778
Valley Forge	Winter of 1777/1778
George Rogers Clark and the Battle of Vincennes	February 23, 1779
Battle of Stony Point	July 15, 1779
Battle of Savannah	1779
BONNE HOMME RICHARD vs. HMS *SERAPIS*	September 23, 1779
Siege of Charleston	1779–1780
Battle of Camden	August 16, 1780
Treason of Benedict Arnold	September 21, 1780
Battle of King's Mountain	October 7, 1780
Battle of Cowpens	January 17, 1781
Battle of Guilford Court House	March 15, 1781
Battle of Eutaw Springs	September 8, 1781
Battle of Yorktown	October 6–19, 1781

List #19 History of Slavery in the U.S.

1619 A Dutch ship brought twenty Africans to the colonies and sold them in Jamestown, Virginia, as indentured servants. This is the first record of African slavery in the Colonies.

1642 Marriage between slaves and non-slaves as well as slaves to each other is discouraged through statutes.

1643 Acts are passed stating that runaway slaves will be punished.

1670–1715 Native Americans are exported to other colonies as slaves.

1774 Connecticut and Rhode Island prohibit importation of more slaves.

1776 The Society of Friends (Quakers) abolish slavery among their members, and they later become active in helping abolish slave trade.

1777 The Vermont Constitution prohibits slavery.

1780 The Massachusetts Constitution prohibits slavery. Pennsylvania law allows for gradual emancipation, that slaves born after 1780 will be free on their 28th birthday.

1784 Connecticut and Rhode Island also pass gradual emancipation laws.

1788 Connecticut passes a law prohibiting residents from participating in the slave trade.

1789 The U.S. Constitution is ratified to allow that slavery would end in twenty years.

1793 Eli Whitney invents the cotton gin.

1798–1808 This decade marked the greatest importation ever of African slaves to the United States.

1799 New York passes a gradual emancipation law.

1800 Citizens of the United States are prohibited from exporting slaves.

1804 New Jersey passes a gradual emancipation law.

1807 Great Britain puts an end to their slave trade.

1819 Slave trade is equated to piracy under United States law and is punishable by death.

1820 A pivotal year in the history of slavery. Missouri wants to be admitted as a slave state and eventually is, but only with Maine admitted as a free state. This is known as the Missouri Compromise. President James Monroe orders the first patrols by the United States Navy of the West African coast, where slave capture was abundant. In Jonesborough, Tennessee, Elihu Embree begins publishing *The Emancipator*, the first periodical exclusively devoted to abolishing slavery.

List #19 **History of Slavery in the U.S.** *(continued)*

1827 James Pembroke escapes from slavery in Maryland and becomes a prominent voice in the abolition movement.

1829 David Walker publishes a radical pamphlet, *Appeal to the Coloured Citizens of the World,* attacking slavery. Walker was a free African-American who lived in Boston, and his pamphlet was circulated in ports across the South, probably by free African-American sailors. Walker was killed a year later.

1831 William Lloyd Garrison begins publication of the *Liberator.* Nathaniel "Nat" Turner leads a slave revolt in Southampton, Virginia, killing about sixty whites before local militia gain control.

1833 The Anti-Slavery Society is founded by abolitionists, including William Lloyd Garrison. Connecticut passes the "Black Law," restricting school choice of African-Americans.

1837 The Anti-Slavery Convention of American Women meets in New York City. Women of both races attend. Pennsylvania and Michigan pass legislation that revokes African-Americans' right to vote.

1838 Pennsylvania Hall in Philadelphia is destroyed by a mob against abolitionism, which then goes into African-American neighborhoods to continue the rampage. Authorities do nothing. Joshua R. Giddings is elected to the U.S. House of Representatives. He is the first avowed abolitionist congressman. *A Textbook of the Origin and History of the Colored People* is published by Reverend James W. C. Pennington, who served as minister to the African-American population in Connecticut. The book is the first of its kind.

1839 Captured Africans being brought into slavery revolt on the *AMISTAD* slave ship. The Africans spend the following year in jail, but they are freed in 1841. Theodore Dwight Weld and Angelina and Sarah Grimké compile stories and news reports of the brutalities against slaves. Many of these were reported by slaveholders themselves in Southern newspapers. Weld and the Grimkés reprinted these stories in *American Slavery As It Is.*

1843 Escaped slave Sojourner Truth begins traveling and lecturing for an end to slavery.

1848 Connecticut law completely prohibits slavery.

1854 The Kansas-Nebraska Act repeals the Missouri Compromise of 1820. Now "popular sovereignty" is to determine whether the state is a free state or slave state. This division weakens the traditional two-party system and allows the Republican Party to develop.

List #19 **History of Slavery in the U.S.** *(continued)*

1857	In a very controversial decision, the Supreme Court rules in the *Dred Scott* decision that slaves or descendents of slaves cannot be U.S. citizens. This is a big setback for the abolitionist cause, especially since in five of the original states, free black men had been able to vote since the signing of the Declaration of Independence. As non-citizens, this would no longer be so.
1859	John Brown leads a slave rebellion in Harper's Ferry, Virginia.
1860	After Abraham Lincoln is elected president of the United States, South Carolina secedes from the Union, on December 20.
1861	More states secede from the Union, and in February they form the Confederate States of America. Their Constitution endorses slavery, but prohibits slave trade. After Confederate forces fire upon United States troops at Fort Sumter, President Lincoln commands troops to stop "insurrection" of the South, and the Civil War ensues.
1862	President Lincoln signs the Emancipation Proclamation on September 22, granting freedom to slaves in the South.
1865	Congress passes the 13th Amendment to the Constitution, which abolishes slavery in the United States.
1866	The 14th Amendment defines a citizen as anyone born in the United States (ironically, except for Native Americans) or naturalized to the U.S., thus giving Africans the right to vote.
1875	The Civil Rights Act prohibits discrimination, but this does not apply to schools.
1875	Blanche Kelso Bruce is elected as the first black United States senator, representing Mississippi.
1883	The Civil Rights Act is overturned by the Supreme Court, which rules that the 14th Amendment does not apply to privately owned facilities such as hotels, railroads, and restaurants. This effectively encourages discrimination and leads to "Jim Crow" laws, which require separate facilities for blacks and whites, mostly in the South.
Early 1900s	The Supreme Court begins to repeal Jim Crow laws that had been enacted in many states.
1960	On November 14, five-year-old Ruby Bridges becomes the first black child to enter a white school in Louisiana. She needs federal protection and only one teacher agrees to remain while a black child is enrolled. Barbara Henry teaches Ruby alone for the entire year. The bravery of this young girl and her family paved the way for other children of African descent to begin attending segregated schools across the nation.

List #20 Steps to Creating a Bill and Making It Law

The Federal Legislative Process

1. Any member of Congress can introduce new legislation (a bill). The bill will then be referred to a committee.
2. The committee will determine what action to take next, whether there should be a hearing on the bill or a "markup." A markup is when committee members make changes to the bill.
3. The Committee Chairperson and his or her staff present a Committee Report, which describes the intent of the law, the impact it will have on existing laws and programs, and the position of the majority of committee members.
4. The bill comes before the full body of the House and the Senate for debate, amendment, and final passage. (The Speaker of the House and Majority Leader of the Senate determine if and when this should happen.) Also, the bill can be amended at this point in the House only if permission is obtained from the Rules Committee. The Senate can make amendments (with a majority vote) as long as the general intent of the bill isn't changed.
5. If the House or Senate passes a bill, it is then referred to the other chamber for approval. This chamber must then decide to reject the bill, approve it as received, ignore the bill, or amend it before passing it on.
6. If only minor changes are made to a bill, then it goes back to the original chamber for a concurring vote. If significant changes are made, a conference committee is appointed to reconcile the differences between the two versions of the bill. If this cannot be achieved, the legislation dies. If an agreement is reached and both the House and Senate agree on the conference report, it goes to the next step. If either chamber disapproves of the conference report, the bill dies.
7. Finally, after a conference report has been approved by both chambers (House and Senate), the final version of the bill is sent to the president. If the president approves, he signs the legislation and it becomes law. If Congress is still in session and the president approves the legislation, he can choose to take no action for ten days and the bill will automatically become law. If the president opposes the bill, he can veto it outright, or if Congress has adjourned its second session, the president can choose to do nothing for ten days, which will result in a "pocket veto" and the legislation dies. (A pocket veto is a kind of passive opposition.)
8. If the president vetoes a bill, but the House and Senate still believe it should become law, they can "override the veto." This requires a two-thirds roll call vote of the members who are present. There must be enough members present for a quorum.

List #21 U.S. Government: Legislative Branch

The *Legislative Branch* consists of the United States Congress. Congress is made up of two houses: the upper house (Senate) and the lower house (House of Representatives).

Main roles and powers:

- pass legislation (laws)
- regulate trade
- regulate money
- declare war
- impeach federal officials
- override presidential vetoes (must have 2/3 vote in each house)

Special roles and responsibilities of the *Senate*:

- approve nominations by the president to the federal courts (by majority vote)
- approve nominations by the president to federal positions (by majority vote)
- approve treaties (by 2/3 vote)
- serve as jury in impeachment trials
- select a vice president if the Electoral College fails to do so

Special roles and responsibilities of the *House*:

- originate all spending bills
- serve as prosecution in impeachment trial
- select a president if the Electoral College fails to do so

Requirements, terms of service, and representation of the *Senate*:

- *Term:* Unlimited six-year terms, elected by popular vote. (In the original Constitution, senators were to be elected by the state legislatures, but the Seventeeth Amendment changed this to a popular vote.)
- *Requirements:* Over thirty years old, nine-year citizen of the United States, and a resident of the state they are seeking to represent.
- *Representation:* Each state has two senators.

Requirements, terms of service, and representation of the *House*:

- *Term:* Unlimited two-year terms, elected by popular vote.
- *Requirements:* Over thirty years old, nine-year citizen of the United States, and a resident of the state they are seeking to represent.
- *Representation:* Each state is allowed a number of representatives proportional to its population; the total number of representatives is fixed at 435, and division among the states is determined by a census conducted every ten years. (A census is a population count, which the Constitution requires every ten years.)

List #22 U.S. Government: Executive Branch

The *Executive Branch* consists of the president, the president's advisors, all federal agencies, and their heads.

As *Chief Executive*, the president:

- enforces laws passed by Congress
- issues executive orders
- acts as head of federal bureaucracy and all federal agencies
- nominates judges (including those to the Supreme Court, which require Senate confirmation)
- appoints government officials (some of these require Senate confirmation, some do not)

As *Chief Diplomat/Foreign Policy Director*, the president:

- acts as a representative of the United States to foreign governments
- makes treaties with foreign nations (requires 2/3 vote in Senate to approve)
- extends or withdraws diplomatic recognition of foreign nations

As *Chief Legislator*, the president:

- proposes a federal budget
- recommends proposed laws to Congress
- vetoes legislation passed by Congress
- approves legislation passed by Congress

As *Commander-in-Chief of the Armed Forces*, the president:

- serves as supreme commander of all branches of the United States military
- authorizes use of United States military for up to sixty days (without the approval of Congress or a declaration of war)
- decides whether or not to use nuclear weapons

As *Chief of State*, the president:

- serves as ceremonial head of United States Government

Requirements and terms of service of the *president*:

- *Term:* A maximum of two terms of four years. (Presidents were allowed unlimited terms in the original Constitution, but this was changed with the Twenty-Second Amendment, in 1951.)
- *Requirements:* Over thirty-five years old, a natural-born citizen, and a fourteen-year resident of the United States.

List #23 U.S. Government: Judicial Branch

The *Judicial Branch* is composed of the Supreme Court and all the lower federal courts created by Congress.

Main roles and powers:

- interpret the law
- exercise power of judicial review
- Chief Justice presides over presidential impeachment trials

Requirements and terms of service of the *Judiciary*:

- *Term:* Judges are nominated by the president and approved by the Senate; judges can serve for life; judges can be removed by impeachment proceeding.
- *Requirements:* None specific.

List #24 The Executive Departments

The Executive Branch of the United States government is made up of the president, his advisors, federal agencies, and their heads. These federal agencies are also known as the executive departments and they are the federal government's main operating units. The heads (or leaders) of these fourteen departments form a council of advisors for the president. This council is known as the president's "cabinet," and their departments each have thousands of employees.

In addition to the executive departments listed below, there are numerous other staff organizations that are grouped under the Executive Branch of the government. These include the White House staff, the National Security Council, the Office of Management and Budget, the Council of Economic Advisors, and others.

Department of Agriculture

The United States Department of Agriculture (USDA) is responsible for overseeing food assistance programs, such as food stamps, sponsoring nutrition education programs, and helping farmers and other landowners protect soil, water, forests, and other natural resources. They also help develop foreign markets for U.S. agricultural products, help ensure fair prices, and work to improve farm income.

Department of Commerce

This department is responsible for promoting our nation's international trade, economic growth, and technological advancement.

Department of Defense

The Department of Defense is responsible for all areas that are related to our nation's military security, including overseeing the military forces.

Department of Education

Although schools fall under the responsibility of local governments, the Department of Education serves to address issues of a broader nature, such as raising standards for our students across the nation, involving families in the education of their children, improving teacher standards, etc.

Department of Energy

This department was created in the 1970s during a time when there was growing concern over energy problems. Among other responsibilities, the

List #24 **The Executive Departments** *(continued)*

department is responsible for research and development of energy technology as well as energy conservation and analysis.

Department of Health and Human Services

Most people are probably familiar with this department since more people are directly affected by the programs of this department than any other. Federal health care programs, such as Medicaid, are administered by this department. The Department of Health and Human Services also administers the National Institutes of Health (NIH), which conducts research into diseases, helps prevent the outbreak of communicable diseases, ensures the safety of medicines, oversees programs directed at reducing substance abuse, etc.

Department of Housing and Urban Development

The Department of Housing and Urban Development (HUD) oversees community development programs, helps provide affordable housing for everyone, and makes sure laws do not discriminate against individuals or families seeking housing.

Department of the Interior

This is our nation's main conservation agency, and it is responsible for managing public land and natural resources owned by the federal government. This includes wildlife refuges, wetlands, national fish hatcheries, national parks and monuments, scenic parkways, seashores, riverways, recreation areas, and historic sites.

Department of Justice

The Department of Justice represents our government in legal matters and also provides legal advice to the president and the executive department heads. Several important agencies within the Department of Justice are the Federal Bureau of Investigation (FBI), the Immigration and Naturalization Service (INS), and the Drug Enforcement Administration (DEA).

Department of Labor

This department is responsible for promoting good relationships between workers and employers, helping improve work conditions, promoting the welfare of laborers in the United States, and overseeing workers' rights.

List #24 **The Executive Departments** *(continued)*

Department of State

The Department of State maintains contact with other countries and represents the United States in relationships with these countries; it negotiates with foreign countries and advises the president, who has the ultimate responsibility to formulate and execute foreign policy.

Department of Transportation

Sometimes children wonder who builds all our nation's interstates, who makes sure all the airplanes in the sky don't fly into one another, who makes sure our ports are safe from invaders, etc. The Department of Transportation (DOT) oversees all these transportation related activities through agencies like the Federal Highway Administration, the National Highway Traffic Safety Administration, the Federal Aviation Administration (FAA), and the Maritime Administration.

Department of Treasury

The Department of Treasury has four main responsibilities, but these responsibilities cover a broad spectrum. The department must: formulate policies related to money; serve as a financial agent for our government; provide special law enforcement, such as the Secret Service; and manufacture coins and currency. The department tries to stop the production of counterfeit United States currency. It protects the president and vice president and their families, dignitaries visiting from other countries, and the heads of state. The department also oversees the Customs Service, which controls the flow of goods into the country and taxes such goods as well. One agency in this department that most children have heard of is the IRS, or the Internal Revenue Service. Now perhaps children can understand what some of that money is used for because tax money is used to fund the activities we've described in each of these executive departments.

Department of Veterans Affairs

This relatively new agency was established in 1930 and elevated to the cabinet level in 1989. It is responsible for distributing benefits and services to eligible United States veterans and their dependents.

List #25 Independent Agencies of the Federal Government

While the fourteen executive departments carry the main responsibilities of operating the U.S. federal government, there are numerous independent agencies that play important roles as well. These agencies are still run by the federal government, but they are called "independent agencies" because they are not part of the executive departments.

The Central Intelligence Agency (CIA) oversees intelligence activities and evaluates intelligence information that pertains to national security.

The Environmental Protection Agency (EPA) helps ensure that our water, our air, and our land remain safe by controlling pollution and dealing with issues such as solid waste management, control of pesticides, etc.

The Federal Communications Commission (FCC) gives licenses to radio and television stations; regulates cable, wire, and satellite communications; and oversees regulation intended to keep communication charges reasonable for consumers.

The Federal Emergency Management Agency (FEMA) is in place to respond to natural disasters such as floods, tornadoes, hurricanes, earthquakes, etc. This agency provides funding to help rebuild homes, schools, businesses, and other facilities. It also trains personnel who respond to disasters.

The Federal Reserve Board controls the amount of money in circulation and regulates banking institutions.

The Federal Trade Commission (FTC) seeks to eliminate unfair trade practices and investigates complaints or reports of illegal activities or unfair practices of companies.

The General Services Administration (GSA) oversees child care centers, telecommuting centers, and the federal motor vehicle fleet. Their main responsibility, however, is to purchase, operate, and conduct the sale of federal property, such as buildings and equipment.

The National Aeronautics and Space Administration (NASA) was established in 1958 to run the space program of the United States.

The National Archives and Records Administration (NARA) maintains federal records.

List #25 **Independent Agencies of the Federal Government** *(continued)*

The National Labor Relations Board (NLRB) prevents unfair labor practices and protects employees' rights.

The National Science Foundation (NSF) encourages and supports research and education in science and engineering.

The Office of Personnel Management (OPM) is basically the human resource agency of our federal government.

The Peace Corps, founded in 1961, trains and places volunteers in underdeveloped countries for two years of service. They work to educate the people in health and agriculture as well as other areas. For more information about the Peace Corps or to find out what you can do to help, visit *www.peacecorps.gov*.

The Securities and Exchange Commission (SEC) protects investors who purchase stocks and bonds.

The Small Business Administration (SBA) oversees and protects small business interests.

The Social Security Administration (SSA) pays retirement, disability, and survivors benefits to workers and administers the Supplemental Security Income program.

The United States Agency for International Development (USAID) administers aid and humanitarian assistance to foreign countries in need.

The United States Postal Service is my personal favorite of the agencies because it is operated as an autonomous public corporation. In other words, they bring in as much money through postage costs as they need to operate without taking money through taxes. The money paid for stamps allows the postal service to collect, transport, and deliver the mail as well as operate all the post offices across the country.

List #26 Holidays in the United States

Dates marked with an asterisk are official federal holidays in the United States.

Date	Official Name	Comments
January 1	New Year's Day*	People celebrate the first day of the new year based on the Gregorian calendar. Many count down to midnight on New Year's Eve to welcome in the new year with celebration.
third Monday in January	Martin Luther King Day*	This day is set aside to honor Martin Luther King, Jr., a civil rights leader who was assassinated on April 4, 1968.
January 20, every fourth year (following a presidential election)	Inauguration Day*	Government employees in Washington, D.C., and bordering counties of Maryland and Virginia observe this holiday (as long as it doesn't fall on a Saturday or Sunday) to relieve congestion caused by the inauguration.
February 2	Groundhog Day	Tradition says that if the groundhog sees his shadow on this day midway between the Winter Solstice and the Vernal Equinox, there will be six more weeks of winter. If he doesn't see his shadow, winter will end soon.
third Monday in February	Washington's birthday*	Congress declared Washington's birthday as a federal holiday in 1879, although in 1968 it was changed from February 22 (his actual birthday) to the third Monday in February. We honor Washington on this day, but many people also refer to this as Presidents' Day and take the opportunity to honor all presidents.
the 14th day of Nissan, the first month of the Jewish year (March or April of Gregorian calendar)	Passover	This is an important Jewish festival that commemorates the exodus of the Jews from Egypt and their safe travel through the Red Sea. The name of the festival derives from a specific event in the exodus story, when God instructed Moses to have the Hebrews mark their dwellings with lamb's blood. The firstborn children and livestock of the Egyptians perished, while the Hebrews' families were protected by the blood of the lamb.
the Friday immediately before Easter	Good Friday	Christians recognize Good Friday as the day Jesus Christ was crucified. (It is likely that the name "Good Friday" came from a variation of *Gute Freitag*, which means "Holy Friday." However, it is also possible that the name arose during a time when it was known as "God's Friday" and commoners were not supposed to speak the name of God so they used "Good" instead.)

List #26 **Holidays in the United States** *(continued)*

Date	Official Name	Comments
first Sunday after the first full moon after the vernal equinox (between March 22 and April 25)	Easter	This day commemorates the resurrection of Jesus Christ and is the most important Christian holiday because we recognize Christ's victory over death and the truth of the resurrection for all who believe.
April 14	Pan American Day	Herbert Hoover issued a proclamation in 1931, declaring April 14 Pan American Day. The history actually goes back to 1823 and the Monroe Doctrine, which encouraged a bond between the countries on the American continents. Pan American Day continues to encourage those bonds as flags are flown over government buildings to display solidarity between the nations. Today students also participate in cultural exchange activities.
last Friday in April	Arbor Day	Arbor Day began in 1872 as a way of encouraging settlers to plant trees in the prairie grasses covering the state of Nebraska. The tradition spread and is now celebrated in all 50 states.
May 5	Cinco de Mayo	Though this is officially a Mexican holiday, it is also celebrated in the United States where there are large Hispanic populations. The holiday commemorates the victory of Mexican forces over French forces on May 5, 1862, in Puebla, Mexico.
second Sunday in May	Mother's Day	Mothers are traditionally celebrated in every culture in the world. Common ways to celebrate Mother's Day include taking Mom out for dinner, calling or writing letters to her, and giving her gifts.
third Saturday in May	Armed Forces Day	Personnel serving in one of the five branches of the U.S. Armed Forces (Army, Navy, Marines, Air Force, Coast Guard) are honored on this day with tours of military facilities, parades, and sometimes demonstrations of military activity.
last Monday in May	Memorial Day*	People remember and honor our nation's men and women who have been killed during wartime. This holiday also marks the unofficial beginning of summer.
June 14	Flag Day	This annual observance celebrates the adoption of our flag by the Continental Congress in 1777. The American flag is displayed on public buildings and on many private homes as a symbol of patriotism.

List #26 **Holidays in the United States** *(continued)*

Date	Official Name	Comments
third Sunday in June	Father's Day	Fathers are celebrated with gifts and family activities.
July 4	Independence Day*	We celebrate the signing of our Declaration of Independence. This day is also commonly referred to as the Fourth of July.
fourth Sunday in July	Parents' Day	According to their Web site, this newer holiday was established in 1994 "to celebrate and strengthen the traditional, two-parent family." For more information and how you can honor families on this day, visit *www.parentsday.com*.
August 19	National Aviation Day	First observed in 1939, the goal of this holiday is to recognize and celebrate the contributions of Orville and Wilbur Wright. The holiday is celebrated yearly on Orville's birthday.
first Monday in September	Labor Day*	Labor Day celebrates the achievements of workers and the Labor Union movement itself. This day also marks the unofficial end of summer.
first Sunday after Labor Day	National Grandparents' Day	Established by Marian McQuade, the first Grandparents' Day was declared in 1973 in West Virginia. The goal of the day is to honor grandparents and celebrate the relationship between grandparents and their grandchildren.
September 11	Patriot Day	Established after the terrorist attacks of 2001, Patriot Day commemorates the victims of that day and the horrendous events that occurred.
September 17	Citizenship Day	Native-born and naturalized foreign-born citizens are honored on Citizenship Day, which was signed into law by President Harry S. Truman on February 29, 1952. This day was established to replace I Am an American Day (celebrated in May) and Constitution Day. Constitution Day recognized the official signing of the United States Constitution on September 17, 1787. That date was retained for Citizenship Day.
September 19	International Talk Like a Pirate Day	John Baur and Mark Summers are responsible for starting this day dedicated to celebrating (and talking like!) pirates. It only began in 1995, but has taken off to be a big hit, especially with schoolchildren. Visit their website at *www.talklikeapirate.com* for more information, fun, and games.

List #26 **Holidays in the United States** *(continued)*

Date	Official Name	Comments
first Monday in October	Child Health Day	Established in 1928, parents, families, childcare workers, and child health professionals are all called upon this day to teach children about good health, encourage them to avoid dangerous behaviors, and make good choices in life.
October 6	German-American Day	Recognized yearly on October 6 since 1987, this day recognizes the significant contributions of German-Americans to the culture of the United States.
October 9	Leif Ericson Day	It is likely that Leif Ericson was actually the first European to step onto the North American continent. This day celebrates the Vikings, Ericson, and Nordic heritage.
second Monday in October	Columbus Day*	Since Christopher Columbus is traditionally credited as having discovered the Americas, this day is set aside to honor this great explorer.
October 13	Navy Day	The Continental Congress established the Continental Navy on October 13, 1775. This navy later became the United States Navy, and we now celebrate October 13 as a day to remember our naval heritage, appreciate our navy, and take pride in naval service. Visit *www.history.navy.mil/birthday.htm* for more information.
October 18	Alaska Day	This is a legal holiday in Alaska and celebrates the formal transfer of Alaska's ownership from Russia to the United States on this day in 1867.
October 23	National Mole Day	A mole is a basic measuring unit in chemistry. This day was created in 1991 to foster interest in chemistry and it is celebrated across the United States with chemistry-related activities. For ideas and more information, visit *www.moleday.org*.
November 11	Veterans' Day*	We honor all veterans of the United States Armed Forces on Veterans' Day. There is also a traditional observation of a moment of silence at 11:00 a.m. to remember those who have fought for peace.
fourth Thursday in November	Thanksgiving Day*	This day is traditionally set aside to give thanks to God for the autumn harvest. Since relying on a good autumn harvest no longer particularly means the difference between life and death, many people simply focus on giving thanks to God for all things in life.

List #26 **Holidays in the United States** *(continued)*

Date	Official Name	Comments
November 15	America Recycles Day	America Recycles Day was established in 1997 to promote awareness of the benefits of recycling and to increase participation in recycling programs. This event has grown each year and is a great time for children to begin a recycling commitment. Visit *www.americarecyclesday.org* for more information and how to become involved.
December 7	National Pearl Harbor Remembrance Day	Solemn ceremonies commemorate the day in 1941 when over 2,400 Americans died during the surprise attack on Pearl Harbor.
December 17	Wright Brothers Day	In 1963, Congress approved December 17 each year as Wright Brothers Day to commemorate that day in 1903 when Orville and Wilbur Wright successfully achieved a sustained and controlled flight on the beach near Kitty Hawk, North Carolina.
December 25	Christmas Day*	The birth of Jesus Christ is traditionally observed as December 25, 4 BC, so this day is set aside each year to celebrate Christ's Nativity, or birth.

List #27 Holidays Around the World

You can plan unit studies around the holidays listed here.

Date	Official Name	Country (or Group)	Comments
between January 21 and February 19	Chinese New Year	China	Towns, villages, and cities are decorated with colored lanterns, flower arrangements, and banners as families prepare to celebrate the Chinese New Year with festivities, parades, and fireworks.
January 26	Australia Day	Australia	This is Australia's official national day, commemorating that date in 1788 when Captain Arthur Phillip arrived with his First Fleet at Sydney Cove and set up the Colony of New South Wales.
between February 3 and March 9	Mardi Gras (also known as Shrove Tuesday or Carnival)	United States (and worldwide)	In preparation for a 40-day observance of Lent (a period of reflection and self-denial), Christians participate in parades and merrymaking as their last opportunity for indulgence before Lent.
February 15	Flag Day	Canada	Citizens display the flag of Canada, participate in public ceremonies, and conduct educational programs in schools to commemorate the adoption of the Maple Leaf flag on this date in 1965.
March 8	Motherhood and Beauty Day	Armenia	Armenians have many opportunities to honor women during the four weeks following March 8. Finally, Mother's Day is observed on April 7, when children shower their mothers with gifts.
March 17	Saint Patrick's Day	Ireland (celebrated worldwide, but not as an official holiday)	Saint Patrick (385–461) is one of the patron saints of Ireland. Saint Patrick is remembered each year on the day he died by people in Ireland and around the world. People attend mass, participate in parades, wear shamrocks (three-leaf clovers), wear green, and drink alcohol.
June 11	Davis Day or Miners Memorial Day	Nova Scotia, Canada	Davis Day is observed to remember all the miners killed on the job in coal-mining communities in Nova Scotia.
June 21	National Aboriginal Day	Canada	The diverse cultural backgrounds of the people of Canada are honored.

List #27 **Holidays Around the World** *(continued)*

Date	Official Name	Country (or Group)	Comments
June 24	Fête nationale du Québec ("Quebec National Holiday")	Quebec, Canada	Originally a holiday to honor patron saint John the Baptist, this day is celebrated in Quebec, in other Canadian provinces, and even by those with French-Canadian heritage in the United States as a day of nationalism with parades, concerts, and fireworks.
July 1	Canada Day	Canada	Upper and Lower Canadian colonies united to become a dominion on this day in 1867. Similar to Independence Day in the United States, Canadians celebrate with fireworks, parades, and the display of flags.
first Wednesday in August	Royal St. John's Regatta	St. John's, Newfoundland	This boat race held on Quidi Vidi Lake is the oldest continuously held sporting event—documented back to 1816, and there is evidence that it was held in the 1700s as well.
September 21	Spring Day	Argentina	This day celebrates the beginning of spring and it coincides with another holiday in Argentina called Student's Day. Traditionally, students in all levels of the educational system visit parks, go to beaches, and participate in other activities during a no-school day.
September 26	Dominion Day	New Zealand	New Zealand was granted dominion (or territory) status within the British Empire on this day in 1907, and this is commemorated on its anniversary each year.
November 1 and 2	Day of the Dead	Mexico and other Latin American countries	The deceased are commemorated during two days of festivities that include making offerings for the dead, decorating the graves of deceased family members, and attending festivals. It is no coincidence that this holiday coincides with the Christian celebrations of All Saints Day (November 1) and All Souls Day (November 2).

List #27 **Holidays Around the World** *(continued)*

Date	Official Name	Country (or Group)	Comments
November 5	Guy Fawkes Day	England	In 1605, Guy Fawkes planned an assassination on King James I and the king's leaders for treating Roman Catholics unfairly. Though the plan failed, the day is still celebrated with a straw dummy ("the Guy"), costumes and masks, and a huge bonfire at the end of the day, when they burn the dummies.
November 11	Remembrance Day (Jour du Souvenir)	United Kingdom, Australia, Canada	The sacrifice made by veterans and civilians who died in wars is commemorated on this day.
November 15	Shichi-Go-San	Japan	Children who are seven, five, or three years old are thought to be particularly lucky, so the Japanese people celebrate this very old festival translated "Seven-Five-Three" with worship, praise, and gifts.
December 12	Guadalupe Day	Mexico	About 450 years ago, a poor Indian named Juan Diego is said to have seen the figure of a young Indian woman called Holy Mary of Guadalupe. She instructed Diego to build a shrine on the spot, and after another vision, Diego convinced the bishop that his story was true. The shrine was built, and believers come from all over Mexico to see the Shrine of Our Lady of Guadalupe. Since this is the most important religious holiday in Mexico, even those who can't go to the shrine still celebrate the holiday by taking gifts to churches and reenacting the story of Diego's vision.
December 13	St. Lucia Day	Sweden (Since Lucia was Italian, this day is also celebrated in Italy with bonfires and parades.)	Lucia was a young Christian girl who was martyred by Roman soldiers when she refused to give up her faith. On this holiday, a pretty girl symbolizing Saint Lucia walks down the street in a white dress wearing a wreath of burning candles. Other younger girls carrying candles and boys wearing pointed hats follow. Special cakes are taken to hospitals, homes, offices, and factories.

List #27 **Holidays Around the World** *(continued)*

Date	Official Name	Country (or Group)	Comments
25th day of the Hebrew month of Kislev (around our month of December)	Hanukkah (also known as the Jewish Feast of Lights or Feast of Dedication)	worldwide – Jewish holiday	During this celebration, people exchange gifts and give donations to the poor. One candle is lit per night on a special nine-candlestick candelabrum called a *menorah* until all nine are lit on the last night.
first work day after Christmas Day	Proclamation Day	South Australia	This is a public holiday to commemorate the proclamation of South Australia as a British province, which occurred on December 28, 1836.
December 26	Boxing Day	United Kingdom, Australia, New Zealand, Canada	This holiday may have begun as early as the Middle Ages with the nobility of England presenting gifts in boxes to their servants, but the exact origin is unknown. Boxing Day is celebrated by giving money or other gifts to the needy, orphanages, charitable institutions, and people who work in service jobs.
begins on December 26 and lasts for seven days	Kwanzaa	worldwide – African-American holiday	This holiday was developed in 1966 by Maulana Karenga to celebrate black heritage. Families light candles, discuss the seven principles of black culture, and exchange gifts.

2

Language Arts

Sight Words are words more easily memorized from sight than by phonetically sounding them out. Although the following lists of Sight Words are divided by levels, it is important to note that since all children learn to read at different stages, the levels are only guidelines. Practice reading the following words with your children, and you might also consider using these lists in conjunction with your regular spelling program to make sure your child can spell the words as well as read them. Your child will encounter these words in standardized tests.

List #28 Sight Words—Preschool Level

a
and
away
big
blue
can
come
down
find
for
funny
go
help
here
I
in
is
it
jump
little
look
make
me
my
not
one
play
red
run
said
see
the
three
to
two
up
we
where
yellow
you

List #29 Sight Words—Kindergarten Level

all
am
are
at
ate
be
black
brown
but
came
did
do
door
eat
four
get
good
have
he
into
like
must
new
no
now
on
our
out
please
pretty
ran
ride
saw
say
she
so
soon
that
there
they
this
too
under
want
was
well
went
what
white
who
will
with
yes

List #30 Sight Words—First Grade Level

after
again
an
any
as
ask
by
could
every
father
fly
from
give
giving
had
has
her
him
his
how
just
know
let
live
may
most
mother
move
of
old
once
open
other
over
put
round
some
stop
take
thank
them
then
think
walk
were
when

List #31 Sight Words—Second Grade Level

always	color	green	science	very
around	does	heard	should	wash
because	don't	island	sing	water
become	example	its	sit	which
been	eye	made	sleep	why
before	fast	many	something	wish
best	feather	off	tell	woman
both	first	often	their	women
bread	five	or	these	work
buy	found	pull	those	world
call	gave	read	upon	would
climbed	goes	right	us	write
cold	great	said	use	your

List #32 Sight Words—Third Grade Level

about	draw	hold	myself	small
adjective	drink	hot	never	start
although	earth	hurt	only	ten
answer	eight	if	own	today
better	enough	keep	people	together
bring	fall	kind	piece	try
brought	far	learn	pick	warm
carry	friend	light	seven	watch
clean	full	listen	shall	youth
country	got	long	show	
cut	group	mountain	sign	
done	grow	much	six	

List #33 Sight Words—Fourth Grade Level

action
actually
alive
although
amount
area
blood
cause
central
century
charcoal
chart
check
club
colony
company
condition
court
deal
death
describe
design
disease
eleven
equal
experience
factor
favorite
figure
hospital
include
increase
known
least
length
loud
measure
molecule
national
necessary
noun
oxygen
phrase
property
radio
receive
replace
rhythm
serve
similar
southern
squirrel
straight
subtle
suffix
surely
though
thought
touch
twice
used
usually
view
weight
wheat
whom
young

List #34 Sight Words—Fifth Grade Level

ache
amphibian
antique
audience
bawl
beach
biceps
binoculars
boarder
break
canoes
capital
capitol
conservation
cylinder
deceive
decimal
diagnose
diagonal
dialogue
drought
earthquake
equal
equator
equivalent
exclamation
expedition
expense
extinguish
extraordinary
extrasensory
extraterrestrial
fir
guard
inquire
judicial
knight
loose
microphone
mourn
neighbor
night
nutrient
paraphrase
pause
peace
petition
piece
pour
preamble
prejudice
prospector
punctuation
quail
qualify
quality
quantity
quarrel
quiet
quite
quotation
quotient
request
retract
route
sequence
sketch
sleigh
surround
thermometer
toe
unique
vertebrates
veto
wade
weighed
whether
whole

List #35 The Eight Parts of Speech

Noun A word that names a person, place, or thing (examples: dog, ball, spoon).

Pronoun A word that takes the place of a noun (examples: he, she, we).

Adjective A word that describes a noun (examples: funny, large, nice).

Verb A word that shows action or state of being (examples: work, think, am).

Adverb A word that describes a verb (examples: quickly, slowly, never).

Conjunction A word that joins words or groups of words (examples: and, or, but).

Preposition A word that shows relationship of a noun or pronoun to another word or words in the sentence (examples: with, in, over).

Interjection A word used to express strong emotion (examples: Wow! Great! Oh! Oh no!). *Note that interjections usually appear alone.*

List #36 Other Linguistic Terms

Antonyms Words that have the opposite or nearly the opposite meanings (examples: *big–small; stop–go*).

Collective Noun A word that names a group of people, animals, or things (examples: staff of teachers, pack of wolves, galaxy of stars).

Collocations Words that occur together, especially habitually (examples: *commit* and *crime; pen* and *pencil; socks* and *shoes*).

Heteronym A word spelled like another word, but having a different pronunciation and meaning (examples: *close*–nearby and *close*–to shut).

Homograph A word that is spelled the same as another word, but has a different meaning; the words can have the same or different pronunciations (examples: *tick*–insect and *tick*–the sound a clock makes; *tear*–to pull apart and *tear*–that comes from the eye).

Homophone A word that is pronounced like another word, but has a different meaning whether or not they are spelled the same (examples: *here*–this place, and *hear*–to listen).

Mass Noun A word that has an uncountable substance in the normal sense (examples: furniture, bread, homework; *You would say you have "homework," but not "ten homeworks"*).

Plural Noun More than one of a noun (examples: *tables, houses, foxes, pencils, mice).*

Prefix Letter groups that are added before a base word or before another prefix (examples: *after* added to *noon* gives you *afternoon*; both prefixes *un-* and *re-* help form *unrenewable*).

Proper Noun A noun that names a specific person, place, or thing (examples: Teresa Dugger, Tennessee, or the Statue of Liberty).

Suffix A letter group that is added to the end of a base word (examples: *-ant* can help form words like *servant* or *merchant*; a suffix such as *-er* can help form words such as *wider, smarter,* and *longer*).

Synonyms Words that have similar meanings (examples: *happy, joyous, elated*).

List #37 Capitalization Rules

Rule	Example
Capitalize the pronoun "I."	*I am reading a book.*
Capitalize the first word of sentences.	*Tomorrow we will go to the fair.*
Capitalize the names of specific people, places, events, dates, and documents.	*Rebeccah Yarosh, Soddy-Daisy, Tennessee, the Fourth of July, Wednesday, the Constitution of the United States*
Capitalize names of languages, races, religions, and the names of God.	*Latin, French, African-American, Christianity, Catholicism, Yahweh, Jehovah*
Capitalize titles of respect.	*Dr. Pearson, Judge Hawkins, Mrs. (Dona) Bonnevie*
Capitalize the names of organizations and trade names.	*Wycliffe Bible Translators, Sonlight curriculum, Coca-Cola*
Capitalize the first word of direct quotations.	*Johnny asked, "When are we going to the store?"*
Capitalize important words in the titles of newspapers, magazines, stories, books, etc.	*The Homeschooler's Book of Lists, Window on the World, The Light and the Glory*
Capitalize abbreviations and acronyms.	*U.S., HSLDA, NETHEA*

List #38 Commonly Misspelled Words

These are commonly misspelled words. Students should spend time making sure they know how to spell them accurately. Challenge your child to learn how to spell one of these every few days. Review once every few weeks to be sure he or she has not forgotten previously learned words.

again	dropped	money	their
all right	embarrass	miniature	then
always	every	mischievous	there
amendment	February	morning	they
an	first	mother	they're
and	for	name	things
animals	friend	named	thought
another	friends	occurred	threw
around	frightened	off	through
asked	from	once	to
babies	getting	our	together
beautiful	going	people	too
because	grammar	pretty	tried
before	happening	privilege	two
believe	hear	received	until
bought	heard	rhythm	very
calendar	here	running	wanted
came	him	said	weird
caught	interesting	school	went
children	its	separately	were
clothes	it's	some	when
coming	jumped	something	where
commitment	knew	sometimes	with
conceive	know	started	withhold
course	let's	stopped	woman
cousin	like	surprise	would
decided	little	swimming	Yahweh
didn't	looked	than	you're
different	many	that's	

List #39 Morse Code

A ._	J .___	S ...	1 .____
B _...	K _._	T _	2 ..___
C _._.	L ._..	U .._	3 ...__
D _..	M __	V ..._	4 ...._
E .	N _.	W .__	5 .....
F .._.	O ___	X _.._	6 _....
G __.	P .__.	Y _.__	7 __...
H	Q __._	Z __..	8 ___..
I ..	R ._.		9 ____.
			0 _____

period ._._._	comma __..__	question mark ..__..	colon ___...
apostrophe .____.	hyphen _...._	slash _.._.	semi-colon _._._.
parenthesis _.__._			
underline ..__._			

List #40 Phonetic Alphabet

The phonetic alphabet is used in place of simply saying the letter to avoid confusion by the listener. For instance, some letters that can easily be confused are "D" and "B." Using the phonetic alphabet, "Delta" and "Bravo" can easily be distinguished. This alphabet is primarily used in two-way radio communications.

Alpha	**H**otel	**O**scar	**V**ictor
Bravo	**I**ndia	**P**apa	**W**hiskey
Charlie	**J**uliet	**Q**uebec	**X**ray
Delta	**K**ilo	**R**omeo	**Y**ankee
Echo	**L**ima	**S**ierra	**Z**ulu
Foxtrot	**M**ike	**T**ango	
Golf	**N**ovember	**U**niform	

List #41 Manual Alphabet

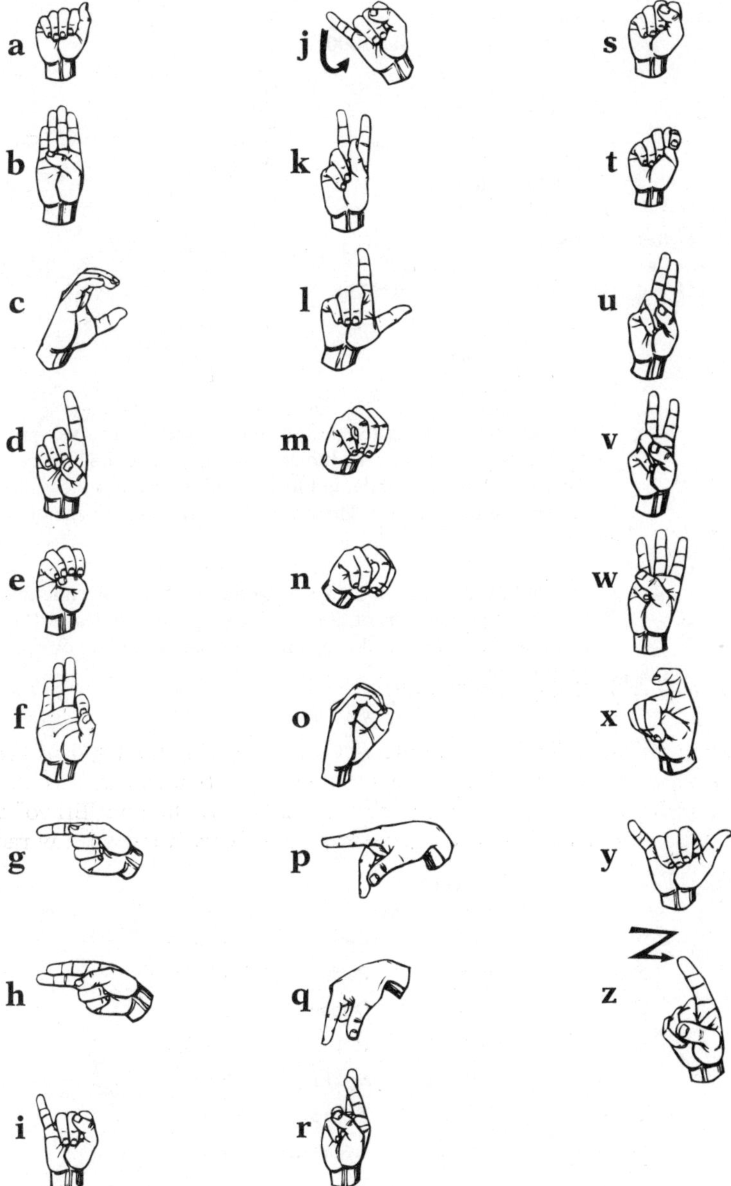

List #42 How to Write a Business Letter (Block Form)

Return address	123 Yucatan Street Johnson City, Tennessee 30901
Date	September 19, 2007
Person to whom the business letter is being addressed	Mr. William Jones President TEACH Educational Corporation 349 Teaching Boulevard New York, New York 08223
Greeting	Dear Mr. Jones:
Body	Thank you for agreeing to read my letter about the proper way to write business letters with a block form. If you use the block format rather than an indented format, all information for the letter should be flush left. The right side of the page does not need to be justified. You should skip a line in between the different sections and also between the paragraphs of the body. Make certain to leave three blank lines between the closing and your name so that you can sign the letter.
Closing	Sincerely,
Signature line	Christopher D. Haskins
Title	Administrative Assistant

List #43 How to Write a Business Letter (Indented Form)

Return address	123 Yucatan Street Johnson City, Tennessee 30901
Date	April 2, 2007
Person to whom the business letter is being addressed	Ms. Carrie Jones Secretary TEACH Educational Corporation 349 Teaching Boulevard New York, New York 08223
Greeting	Dear Ms. Jones:
Body	Thank you for agreeing to read my letter about the proper way to write business letters with an indented format. You can see that one of the biggest differences between this form and the block form is that you should align the left side of your return address, the date, your closing, name, and title with the middle of the page You also indent the paragraphs of the body. The right side of the page still does not need to be justified. Skip a line in between the sections and also between the paragraphs of the body. There is differing consensus about skipping a line between the return address and the date, but this is something up for debate and I chose to add a space for this example. You should still make certain to leave three blank lines between the closing and your name so that you can sign the letter.
Closing	Sincerely,
Signature line	Hannah Grace Haskins
Title	Administrative Assistant

List #44 How to Write a Friendly or Personal Letter

Return address	123 Yucatan Street Johnson City, Tennessee 30901
Date	May 15, 2007
Greeting	Hello, Granny,
Body	I am practicing writing letters. This letter is written in a friendly, or personal, format since you are so special to me. If this were a business letter, I would use a colon after the greeting, but since I know you well and this is a personal letter, I use a comma instead. I could have also used an exclamation point, but only if I were writing about something very exciting, and this is only kind of exciting. Another difference between a friendly letter and a business letter is that I put the date right after my return address. A space can be added for business letters. It is always important to put a return address, though, so that you can write me back. Well, I'd better go. It's bedtime. Please write me soon. I love to receive your letters!
Closing	Love,
Signature line	Daniel

(For personal letters, you can add your signature without typing your name.)

List #45 Writing Ideas

(This list is dedicated to Mia and all the other students who *think* they don't like writing!)

When I talk with parents who are worried about their children's writing abilities, I ask them if their child can verbalize thoughts coherently. Usually the child can. Then I ask what type of writing they are having them do. Too frequently I hear that the parent has assigned book reports, essays, journals, writing workbooks, and so on. You may think, "Well, what's wrong with those things?" Actually, nothing is wrong with those writing activities, but what concerns me is that too many homeschool parents are recreating school at home when it comes to the Language Arts. Homeschoolers have found ways to make science exciting by doing hands-on experiments. We take our youngsters on field trips across the United States to learn about geography and history. Kids help track family finances and do grocery store math. When it comes to the Language Arts, though, particularly writing, we continue to copy the traditional school model.

Listed here (and in the next few lists) are some suggestions that may help your child to have the same enthusiasm for writing that he has for other favorite subjects. Don't make your child do *all* of these. Pick the one that you think would best work for your child (different children in the same family may enjoy different ideas). Explain to your child that you are going to try a different philosophy of writing and get him on board with you. With all of these ideas, you may want to skip the writing assignments for a week or two or even a few. Do the preliminary activities and then begin the writing activities.

Make journals personal. If you want your child to keep a journal, start out by reading some journals of others. There are journals on many topics by many individuals, male and female. Either have your child read some of these or read them out loud to him. If your youngster is interested, read some of your own childhood journals to him and let him ask questions about your history. (This is a great way to discuss your family history at the same time.) Help your child realize that the things he writes in his journal *now* will tell people about his life in 100 years. What does he want his great-great-grandson to know about him? Should he write that he did chores *again* or that he built a fort in the woods with his brothers? There is no right answer. It's for him to decide. After this preliminary "study," give your child a nice journal (or a simple notebook) and let him write in it. Some parents may still feel obligated to schedule a time for journal writing, and some kids may need that extra push, but I highly recommend not checking, grading, or otherwise correctively editing any journal writing that your child might do. This is *personal* writing, and the child should feel free to narrate without fear of being corrected.

List #45 **Writing Ideas** *(continued)*

Get your child a pen pal. Writing letters is a great way for children to practice their writing skills, and it is one thing that most children love to do. It's always fun to receive mail, but you have to be willing to write letters to receive something in return. If you can't find a pen pal among your children's friends, ask a cousin about the same age or a grandparent to be your child's pen pal. There are homeschool groups across the U.S., so you may even be able to find a pen pal while traveling in a different state. (Be wary of Internet pen pal pages and don't let your children correspond with anyone online.) Again, with this type of writing, I highly recommend that you don't edit or correct it. She will be inclined to write more if she knows the letters aren't going to be scrutinized. Your child's letters will be precious to you one day even with all the mistakes (ask the recipient to keep the letters).

Book reports can be useful. See List #47 on Creative Book Report Ideas for ways to encourage your child to think like a writer without being intimidated or frustrated with all the writing requirements.

Be champion of a cause. If your child is concerned about the depletion of natural resources or the deaths of animals at the local shelter, allow her to write letters to the editor or create pamphlets for a cause. She may want to create a community newsletter aimed at making a neighborhood more child-friendly, etc. Whatever calling your child pursues, allow her to use writing for this purpose now. See the next list for more ideas about this.

List #46 Write for a Reason (More Writing Ideas)

Write for a reason. Too frequently I think we forget that even when it comes to writing, God has a specific purpose in mind for each child. The Creator of the Universe made your son or daughter for something great—whether that means he will become a paramedic and save lives, a computer technician who helps us keep the computer operational, a mom who is raising the next generation, or simply a person who is being a tremendous blessing to others. What does your child want to do with his or her life? When considering how to *write for a reason*, ask your child to spend some time in prayer for a day or two and think about what she would most like to do with her life. Most children will come up with something. Whatever it is, there is some way that you can link writing to that job. *Your* job is to begin thinking of every way writing could be related to that line of work. All children want to be a little more grown up. With this writing activity, you can integrate writing and your child's potential career. This will not only help your son or daughter's writing ability, but the research involved in the writing activities will also help prepare him or her for various careers as his or her interests may change over the years. Here are a few examples (some are meant for younger students, some for older students):

Your child says he wants to be a judge when he grows up. So, go ahead and pretend that he is a judge, and each day give him writing assignments that fit that profession. Here are assignments for one week:

- Write a letter to the bar requesting the materials for a new certification.
- Write a newspaper advertisement for a new secretary.
- Write requirements to be a juror in his courtroom.
- Write a note to the office manager requesting office supplies.
- Write an article for the local paper on why judges should be elected/appointed.

Your child says she wants to own her own animal shelter. Great! Have her pretend that she has this business. Give her scenarios each day that she must deal with—in writing. Here are some examples:

- There are not enough funds to take care of the animals. Write an appeal to local citizens to make donations for the shelter.
- Send a notice to the newspaper describing two animals that are available for adoption.
- Write a help-wanted advertisement.

List #46 **Write for a Reason (More Writing Ideas)** *(continued)*

- Complete a grant request. (You can find grant applications online. Find a real one and have your child complete it.)
- Write an article for an animal magazine on why it is important to have your animals spayed.

Your child says he wants to be a policeman. This is a great profession to write about! There is an endless amount of police activity. Here are some ideas:

- For starters, write a three-page essay for a police academy on why you want to be a policeman. This is great incentive for older students to practice writing.
- Write a speeding ticket. (Try to obtain a sample of a real ticket if you can and have your child fill this out. There are actually lots of things to be completed. Allow your child to use your driver's license to complete information correctly.)
- Write a report of a broken window at a local restaurant. (Remember that reports must contain full sentences and complete descriptions of the crime, injury, or activity.)
- Write a report of a lost child.
- Write your future spouse (make up a name) a letter telling her why you want to marry her, but why it may be difficult being married to a policeman. (If your child needs ideas about why, have him interview a policeman. They frequently work long and varied hours, and live with daily stress that comes with a potentially dangerous job.)

Your child says she wants to be "nothing" and so it doesn't matter! Well, even if your child can't think of a single thing she wants to be, there will still be opportunities for writing in her life. Tell her you'll let her be "nothing" (except in God's eyes of course!) and then move forward with the following writing activities that adults still face:

- The local city government is planning to buy all the land around your house and is now turning it into a huge junkyard. Write a letter to the city and county government leaders protesting this purchase.
- You have been denied a loan application for a car, one that you really need to drive to work. Write a letter to the credit bureau requesting a copy of your credit report and another to the bank stating why you think you should qualify.
- You have a new neighbor. Send her a letter of welcome.

List #46 **Write for a Reason (More Writing Ideas)** *(continued)*

- Your grandmother lives in another state. She recently lost a good friend and you would like to comfort her. Write a letter expressing your love for her and your sorrow at her loss.
- Write a letter to the editor of the local newspaper praising the new zoo that recently opened in your area.

Whatever your child wants to do in life, there are ways he or she will need to use writing. If you can't think of some examples, call someone in that field and ask them what sorts of writing they do on a regular basis. Write down all the ideas you can think of and then put these to use in your child's "profession." For additional ideas for various things your child might want to be or do, visit my Web site at *www.sonyahaskins.com* and check out the Write for a Reason link.

List #47 Creative Book Report Ideas

Newspaper	Your child can create a newspaper page (or several pages) about the book. He could have sections for articles, book reviews, obituaries (about the author!), comic strips, sports, etc.
Newscast	Your child (or children) can prepare a newscast about the book. The child can pick out major events in the book and do a short news segment on each major happening—just like they do on the news. There could also be a weather report, interviews (if you have more than one child), etc.
Create a board game	If your child is artistic or creative, he may really enjoy making a board game based on the book. This can actually be very educational and take a lot of time. Give him the supplies, space, time, and support and he may surprise you.
Write a letter to the author	For younger children, they may enjoy writing a letter to the author of the book. This doesn't necessarily have to be a "report" on the book, but it will allow your child the freedom to talk about how he or she feels about the book. When the letter is finished, mail it to the publisher. The author might write back. I know I would!
Allow your child to retell the story to younger siblings	If your child prefers oral reporting, and you're comfortable with that right now, but you still want to hear a synopsis of the book, ask him or her to retell the story to younger siblings.
Make something about the book	If your child likes to make things, let her make little dolls of each of the characters and set up a miniature version of where the book took place.
Make an outline	For skittish writers or those who don't have the ability yet, let them make an outline of the major events in the book and they will be working toward writing papers and essays later.
Skit or play	Even young children can usually act out something they've read. Children also naturally like to perform so developing a skit or play about a book is a great way to present a book report.
Design a computer game	If you have a computer programmer whom you are trying to interest more in reading, allow this young person to develop a computer game based on a book. (Be careful to stress appropriate graphics, etc.) Your child might just develop a great educational supplement to a classic book.

3

Mathematics

List #48 Famous Mathematicians

Archimides	287–212 BC	Greek mathematician, astronomer, philosopher, and physicist; widely regarded as one of the best mathematicians of all time
Aristarchus	c. 300 BC	Greek mathematician who calculated the diameter of Earth with astonishing accuracy and also proposed that the Earth revolves around the sun
Augustin-Louis Cauchy	1789–1857	homeschooled French mathematician who invented the calculus of residues and was one of the first to focus on abstract mathematics
Leonhard Euler	1707–1783	brought us modern trigonometry
Johann Carl Friedrich Gauss	1777–1855	German mathematician who was performing mathematical calculations by the age of three
Joseph-Louis (Comte de) Lagrange	1736–1813	credited with invention of calculus of variations
Gottfried Wilhelm Leibniz	1646–1716	German historian, philosopher, and lawyer who studied mathematics on the side; produced the first calculator able to do multiplication
Sir Isaac Newton	1642–1727	Englishman regarded as the father of calculus
Blaise Pascal	1623–1662	Frenchman who invented the adding machine
Jules Henri Poincaré	1854–1912	produced many mathematical theories and had keen interest in physics
Ptolemy	c. 150	ancient Greek mathematician who studied lunar patterns and said the Earth was the center of the solar system
Pythagoras	c. 530 BC	developed mathematical theory that would influence math forever
Georg Friedrich Bernhard Riemann	1826–1866	proposed “Hypothesis of Riemann’s zeta function,” one of the great unsolved mathematical problems; died relatively young

List #49 Counting by Multiples

2's	3's	4's	5's	10's	20's
2	3	4	5	10	20
4	6	8	10	20	40
6	9	12	15	30	60
8	12	16	20	40	80
10	15	20	25	50	100
12	18	24	30	60	120
14	21	28	35	70	140
16	24	32	40	80	160
18	27	36	45	90	180
20	30	40	50	100	200
22	33	44	55	110	220
24	36	48	60	120	240
26	39	52	65	130	260
28	42	56	70	140	280
30	45	60	75	150	300
32	48	64	80	160	320
34	51	68	85	170	340
36	54	72	90	180	360
38	57	76	95	190	380
40	60	80	100	200	400
42	63	84	105	210	420
44	66	88	110	220	440
46	69	92	115	230	460
48	72	96	120	240	480
50	75	100	125	250	500
52	78	104	130	260	520
54	81	108	135	270	540
56	84	112	140	280	560
58	87	116	145	290	580
60	90	120	150	300	600

List #50 Roman, Arabic, and Ordinal Numerals

Arabic		Roman	Ordinal
1	one	I	first
2	two	II	second
3	three	III	third
4	four	IV	fourth
5	five	V	fifth
6	six	VI	sixth
7	seven	VII	seventh
8	eight	VIII	eighth
9	nine	IX	ninth
10	ten	X	tenth
11	eleven	XI	eleventh
12	twelve	XII	twelfth
13	thirteen	XIII	thirteenth
14	fourteen	XIV	fourteenth
15	fifteen	XV	fifteenth
16	sixteen	XVI	sixteenth
17	seventeen	XVII	seventeenth
18	eighteen	XVIII	eighteenth
19	nineteen	XIX	nineteenth
20	twenty	XX	twentieth
21	twenty-one	XXI	twenty-first
29	twenty-nine	XXIX	twenty-ninth
30	thirty	XXX	thirtieth
40	forty	XL	fortieth
46	forty-six	XLVI	forty-sixth
49	forty-nine	IL	forty-ninth
50	fifty	L	fiftieth
60	sixty	LX	sixtieth
70	seventy	LXX	seventieth
80	eighty	LXXX	eightieth
90	ninety	XC	ninetieth
98	ninety-eight	XCVIII	ninety-eighth
99	ninety-nine	IC	ninety-ninth

List #50 Roman, Arabic, and Ordinal Numerals *(continued)*

Arabic		Roman	Ordinal
100	one hundred	C	one hundredth
200	two hundred	CC	two hundredth
400	four hundred	CD	four hundredth
500	five hundred	D	five hundredth
600	six hundred	DC	six hundredth
900	nine hundred	CM	nine hundredth
1999	one thousand nine hundred ninety-nine	MCMXCIX	one thousand nine hundred ninety-ninth
2000	two thousand	MM	two thousandth
3008	three thousand eight	MMMVIII	three thousand eighth

List #51 Major Fields of Mathematics

abstract algebra
algebra
algebraic geometry
algebraic topology
analysis
analytic geometry
arithmetic
calculus
category theory
combinatorics
computability theory
computational complexity theory
differential equations
differential geometry
fractal geometry
functional analysis
geometry
group theory
information theory
linear algebra
logic
model theory
number theory
numerical analysis
optimization
order theory
probability
proof theory
recursion theory
set theory
statistics
topology
trigonometry
vector calculus

List #52 Geometrical Figures

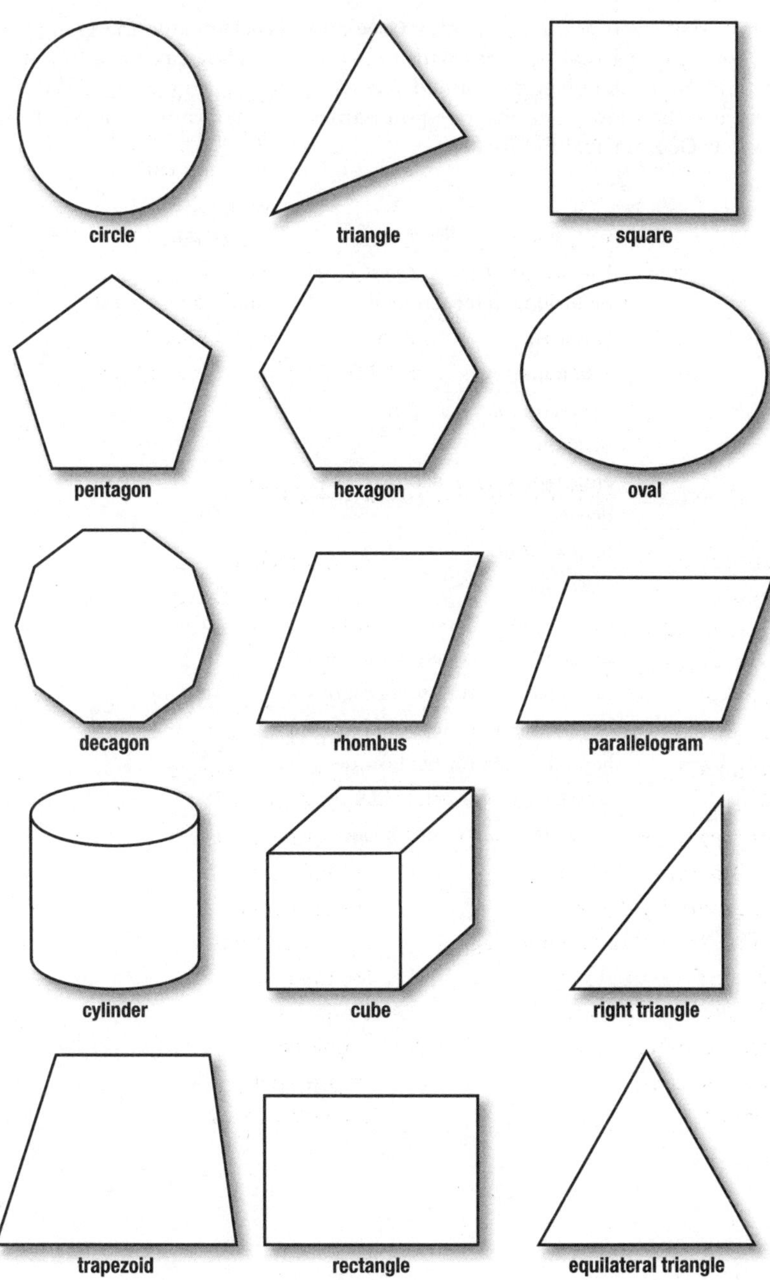

List #53 Names of Polygons

The word *polygon* originates from a Greek word that means "many angles." Polygons are just that—shapes with many angles. They can have few sides or many, but each polygon is named according to the number of sides it has. These are the more common polygon names. (Some are illustrated on the previous Geometrical Figures list.)

Name	Number of Edges
triangle (or trigon)	3
quadrilateral (or tetragon)	4
pentagon	5
hexagon	6
heptagon (*not* septagon)	7
octagon	8
enneagon (or nonagon)	9
decagon	10
hendecagon	11
dodecagon	12
tridecagon (or triskaidecagon)	13
tetradecagon (or tetrakaidecagon)	14
pentadecagon (or quindecagon)	15
hexadecagon (or hexakaidecagon)	16
heptadecagon (or heptakaidecagon)	17
octadecagon (or octakaidecagon)	18
enneadecagon (or enneakaidecagon)	19
icosagon	20

List #54 Measurement Abbreviations

U.S. Customary Measurement System

inch = in.	foot = ft.
feet = ft.	yard = yd.
furlong = fur.	
fluid ounce = fl. oz.	cup = c.
pint = pt.	gallon = gal.
quart = qt.	
ounce = oz.	pound = lb.
ton = T.	
square inches = sq. in.	square feet = sq. ft.
square yards = sq. yd.	acre = A.
cubic inches= cu. in.	cubic feet = cu. ft.
cubic yards = cu. yd.	

Metric System

millimeter = mm	centimeter = cm
decimeter = dm	meter = m
kilometer = km	
milliliter = ml	centiliter = cl
liter = L	
milligram = mg	centigram = cg
gram = g	kilogram = kg
metric ton = t	
square millimeters = mm^2	square centimeters = cm^2
square meters = m^2	hectare = ha
cubic millimeters = mm^3	cubic centimeters = cm^3
cubic decimeters = dm^3	cubic meters = m^3

List #55 Measurement Equivalents

U.S. Customary Measurement System			Metric System		
Length			**Length**		
12 inches	=	1 foot	10 millimeters	=	1 centimeter
3 feet	=	1 yard	10 centimeters	=	1 decimeter
220 yards	=	1 furlong	1000 millimeters	=	1 meter
8 furlongs	=	1 mile	100 centimeters	=	1 meter
			1000 meters	=	1 kilometer
Liquid Capacity			**Liquid Capacity**		
8 fluid ounces	=	1 cup	10 milliliters	=	1 centiliter
2 cups	=	1 pint	1000 milliliters	=	1 liter
16 fluid ounces	=	1 pint			
2 pints	=	1 quart			
32 fluid ounces	=	1 quart			
4 quarts	=	1 gallon			
128 fluid ounces	=	1 gallon			
Weight			**Mass Weight**		
16 ounces	=	1 pound	10 milligrams	=	1 centigram
2000 pounds	=	1 ton	1000 milligrams	=	1 gram
			1000 grams	=	1 kilogram
			1000 kilograms	=	1 metric ton
Area			**Area**		
144 square inches	=	1 square foot	100 square millimeters	=	1 square centimeter
9 square feet	=	1 square yard	10,000 square centimeters	=	1 square meter
4840 square yards	=	1 acre	10,000 square meters	=	1 hectare
Volume			**Volume**		
1728 cubic inches	=	1 cubic foot	1000 cubic millimeters	=	1 cubic centimeter
27 cubic feet	=	1 cubic yard	1000 cubic centimeters	=	1 cubic decimeter
			1,000,000 cubic centimeters	=	1 cubic meter

List #56 Additional Measurement Terms

acre (ac.)
astronomical unit (A.U.)
board foot (bd. ft.)
bolt (bo.)
British thermal unit (BTU)
carat (c)
chain (ch)
decibel (db)
fathom (fm.)
furlong (fur.)
gross (gr.)
hand (hd.)
hertz (Hz)
horsepower (hp)
karat (kt)
knot (kn.)
league (L.)
light-year (ly.)
Mach number
magnum (Mg.)
nautical mile (nm)
pi (π)
pica (pc)
quire (qr.)
ream (rm.)
roentgen (R)
score (sc)
speed of sound
span
township

List #57 Mathematical Formulas

area of a rectangle	$A = lw$ $A = bh$	area equals length times width or base times height
area of a triangle	$A = \frac{1}{2} bh$	area equals one-half the product of the base times the height
area of a circle	$A = \pi r^2$	area equals pi times r squared
area of a square	$A = s^2$	area equals one of the sides squared
area of a parallelogram	$A = bh$	area equals base times height
perimeter of a triangle	$P = l + l + l$	perimeter equals the sum of the lengths of all sides
perimeter of a rectangle	$P = 2l + 2w$	perimeter equals two times the length plus two times the width
diameter of a circle	$D = 2r$	diameter equals two times the radius
circumference of a circle	$C = \pi d$ or $2\pi r$	circumference equals pi times diameter or two times pi times radius
volume of a rectangular solid	$V = lwh$	volume equals length times width times height
volume of a cube	$V = E^3$	volume equals one of the edges to the third power
volume of a pyramid	$V = \frac{1}{3}(blh)$	volume equals one-third of base width times base length times height.
surface of a rectangular solid or cube	$S = 2lw + 2lh + 2wh$	surface area equals two times the length times width plus two times length times height plus two times width times height

List #58 Financial Terms

accounts payable	amounts owed by a business to another business or person for purchases made on credit
accounts receivable	amounts due to a business from other businesses or customers for products or services that they purchased on credit
accumulated depreciation	total amount of depreciation to date that a company has recorded for its fixed assets
asset	anything that has value or future economic value can be an asset
ATM	automated teller machine–where you can make certain bank transactions through a machine without an actual person there
balance sheet	financial statement that lists a company's assets, liabilities, and equity at a particular point in time
bank	a place that loans, safeguards, and helps manage money
benefits	indirect compensation that a company provides to employees; statutory benefits include items such as payroll taxes; discretionary benefits include monetary bonuses, life insurance, vacation time, retirement plans, etc.
budget	an estimation of income and expenses and how you are going to manage that money
cash flow statement	financial statement showing a company's performance in terms of cash generated and spent
change	money you get back after a transaction
cost	what you would pay for something if you bought it
credit card	a plastic card that you can use to secure a debt that will be paid back, typically with interest
currency	money, usually issued by a government, in circulation
debt	a liability; a loan of money, products, or services borrowed from a bank, person, or another company
fiscal year	the 12-month period that constitutes a single year for the company's financial reports and taxes; the fiscal year does not necessarily coincide with the calendar year
fixed assets	tangible assets (land, buildings, machinery, equipment) that are permanent or last a long time
income statement	document that tells how much you have earned
inventory	stock or products that a business has on hand
labor	work

List #58 **Financial Terms** *(continued)*

liability	an obligation (such as a bank loan) a company has obtained to fund the operation of a business
market value	value of an item if it were to pass from an informed seller to an informed buyer, both willing to participate in the transaction
mortgage	a long-term debt or loan obtained for the purpose of purchasing a property in which the property itself is the collateral
net income	amount of income after taxes, insurance, etc.
net sales	sales income minus credit card fees and discounts
overhead	expenses related to operating a business that include items (such as rent, utilities) that are not directly related to providing a service or generating a product
payroll	total wages, not including benefits, paid to employees during a particular time period
salaries	compensation, not including benefits, provided to employees of a company
taxes	money individuals and companies must pay state and federal governments based on the annual income of a person or business

List #59 World Currencies

*On January 1, 1999, the European Monetary Union introduced the euro as the common currency to be used by financial institutions in member countries. As of January 1, 2002, the euro became the sole currency for everyday transactions in member countries, but the countries' native currency is listed here as well.

**The responsible authority is the Bank of the Central African States.

Country	Currency
Afghanistan	afghani
Albania	lek
Algeria	Algerian dinar
Andorra	euro*; French franc; Spanish peseta
Angola	kwanza
Antigua and Barbuda	East Caribbean dollar
Argentina	Argentine peso
Armenia	dram
Australia	Australian dollar
Austria	euro*; Austrian schilling
Azerbaijan	Azerbaijani manat
Bahamas, The	Bahamian dollar
Bahrain	Bahraini dinar
Bangladesh	taka
Barbados	Barbadian dollar
Belarus	Belarusian ruble
Belgium	euro*; Belgian franc
Belize	Belizean dollar
Benin	CFA franc**
Bhutan	ngultrum; Indian rupee
Bolivia	boliviano
Bosnia and Herzegovina	marka
Botswana	pula
Brazil	real
Brunei	Brunei dollar
Bulgaria	lev
Burkina Faso	CFA franc**
Burundi	Burundi franc
Cambodia	riel

List #59 **World Currencies** *(continued)*

Country	Currency
Cameroon	CFA franc**
Canada	Canadian dollar
Cape Verde	Cape Verdean escudo
Central African Republic	CFA franc**
Chad	CFA franc**
Chile	Chilean peso
China, People's Republic of	yuan
Colombia	Colombian peso
Comoros	Comoros franc
Congo, Democratic Republic of the	Congolese franc
Congo, Republic of the	CFA franc**
Costa Rica	Costa Rican colon
Côte d' Ivoire	CFA franc**
Croatia	kuna
Cuba	Cuban peso
Cyprus	Greek Cypriot area: Cypriot pound; Turkish Cypriot area: Turkish lira
Czech Republic	Czech koruna
Denmark	Danish krone
Djibouti	Djibouti franc
Dominica	Eastern Caribbean dollar
Dominican Republic	Dominican peso
Ecuador	U.S. dollar
Egypt	Egyptian pound
El Salvador	Salvadoran colon; U.S. dollar
Equatorial Guinea	CFA franc**
Eritrea	nakfa
Estonia	Estonian kroon
Ethiopia	birr
Fiji	Fijian dollar
Finland	euro*; markka
France	euro*; French franc
Gabon	CFA franc**

List #59 **World Currencies** *(continued)*

Country	Currency
Gambia, The	dalasi
Georgia	lari
Germany	euro*; deutsche mark
Ghana	cedi
Greece	euro*; drachma
Grenada	East Caribbean dollar
Guatemala	quetzal, U.S. dollar, others allowed
Guinea	Guinean franc
Guinea-Bissau	CFA franc**
Guyana	Guyanese dollar
Haiti	gourd
Honduras	Lempira
Hungary	forint
Iceland	Icelandic krona
India	Indian rupee
Indonesia	Indonesian rupiah
Iran	Iranian rial
Iraq	Iraqi dinar
Ireland	euro*; Irish pound
Israel	new Israeli shekel
Italy	euro*; Italian lira
Jamaica	Jamaican dollar
Japan	yen
Jordan	Jordanian dinar
Kazakhstan	tenge
Kenya	Kenyan shilling
Kiribati	Australian dollar
Korea, North	North Korean won
Korea, South	South Korean won
Kuwait	Kuwaiti dinar
Kyrgyzstan	Kyrgyzstani som
Laos	kip
Latvia	Latvian lat
Lebanon	Lebanese pound

List #59 **World Currencies** *(continued)*

Country	Currency
Lesotho	loti; South African rand
Liberia	Liberian dollar
Libya	Libyan dinar
Liechtenstein	Swiss franc
Lithuania	litas
Luxembourg	euro*; Luxembourg franc
Macedonia, Republic of	Macedonian denar
Madagascar	Malagasy franc
Malawi	Malawian kwacha
Malaysia	ringgit
Maldives	rufiyaa
Mali	CFA franc**
Malta	Maltese lira
Marshall Islands	U.S. dollar
Mauritania	ouguiya
Mauritius	Mauritian rupee
Mexico	Mexican peso
Micronesia, Federated States of	U.S. dollar
Moldova	Moldovan leu
Monaco	euro*; French franc
Mongolia	togrog/tugrik
Montenegro	euro*; deutschmark
Morocco	Moroccan dirham
Mozambique	metical
Myanmar (Burma)	kya
Namibia	Namibian dollar; South African rand
Nauru	Australian dollar
Nepal	Nepalese rupee
Netherlands	euro*; Netherlands guilder
New Zealand	New Zealand dollar
Nicaragua	gold cordoba
Niger	CFA franc**
Nigeria	naira

List #59 **World Currencies** *(continued)*

Country	Currency
Norway	Norwegian krone
Oman	Omani rial
Pakistan	Pakistani rupee
Palau	U.S. dollar
Panama	balboa; U.S. dollar
Papua New Guinea	kina
Paraguay	guarani
Peru	nuevo sol
Philippines	Philippine peso
Poland	zloty
Portugal	euro*; Portuguese escudo
Qatar	Qatari rial
Romania	leu
Russia	Russian ruble
Rwanda	Rwandan franc
Saint Kitts and Nevis	East Caribbean dollar
Saint Lucia	East Caribbean dollar
Saint Vincent and the Grenadines	East Caribbean dollar
Samoa	tala
San Marino	euro*; Italian lira
São Tomé and Príncipe	dobra
Saudi Arabia	Saudi riyal
Senegal	CFA franc**
Seychelles	Seychelles rupee
Sierra Leone	leone
Singapore	Singapore dollar
Slovakia	Slovak koruna
Slovenia	tolar
Solomon Islands	Solomon Islands dollar
Somalia	Somali shilling
South Africa	rand
Spain	euro*; Spanish peseta
Sri Lanka	Sri Lankan rupee

List #59 World Currencies *(continued)*

Country	Currency
Sudan	Sudanese dinar
Suriname	Surinamese guilder
Swaziland	lilangeni
Sweden	Swedish krona
Switzerland	Swiss franc
Syria	Syrian pound
Taiwan	New Taiwan dollar
Tajikistan	somoni
Tanzania	Tanzanian shilling
Thailand	baht
Timor-Leste	U.S. dollar
Togo	CFA franc**
Tonga	pa'anga
Trinidad and Tobago	Trinidad and Tobago dollar
Tunisia	Tunisian dinar
Turkey	Turkish lira
Turkmenistan	Turkmen manat
Tuvalu	Australian dollar; *note:* there is also a Tuvaluan dollar
Uganda	Ugandan shilling
Ukraine	hryvnia
United Arab Emirates	Emirati dirham
United Kingdom	British pound
United States of America	U.S. dollar
Uruguay	Uruguayan peso
Uzbekistan	Uzbekistani sum
Vanuatu	vatu
Vatican City (Holy See)	euro*; Italian lira
Venezuela	Bolivar
Vietnam	dong
Yemen	Yemeni rial
Zambia	Zambian kwacha
Zimbabwe	Zimbabwean dollar

List #60 Great Games and Activities

While you don't need to have all of these fabulous games and activities, every homeschool family should have some of these on hand. They can help teach your children academic skills, particularly math, and provide a fun activity for rainy or cold days that prohibit outdoor activities. Games also promote teamwork. Here are some of the best games to build your educational game collection, especially if your children are young.

Monopoly
Operation
Sorry
Mad Libs
Rook
Risk
Othello
Bingo
Dutch Blitz
Boggle
Trivial Pursuit
Yahtzee
Reversi
Clue
Chess
Checkers
Connect Four
Scrabble
Legos
Mille Bornes
Memory
Life
Backgammon
Go
Cranium games, such as Cadoo and Hullabaloo
War
Uno
Twister
Pictionary
Battleship
Chinese Checkers
Mancala
Dominoes
Hungry Hungry Hippos (for younger children)
Playmobil
Lincoln Logs

4

Religion

List #61 Major World Religions

Agnosticism (founded by Thomas Henry Huxley in 1869)

Beliefs and Practices: Agnostics are unconvinced about the existence of deities (gods or God) and are frequently referred to as skeptics.

Atheism

Beliefs and Practices: Atheists do not believe in deities (gods or God) and frequently lean toward secular philosophies in life such as materialism, humanism, etc.

The Baha'i Faith (founded in 1844 by Mirza Husayn' Ali Nuri as a growth from Babism, which was founded by Mirza Ali Muhammad, known as al-Bab)

Sacred or Guiding Text: Bahá u lláh s Kitáb-i-Aqdas (the Most Holy Book)

Beliefs and Practices: The oneness of God, the oneness of humanity, and that all religion has a common foundation. They teach equality of men and women, universal education, and that there should be a federal government system.

Buddhism (founded around 520 BC by Siddhartha Guatama, later known as Buddha or "Enlightened One")

Sacred or Guiding Text: The Pali *Tripitaka* text

Beliefs and Practices: Buddha taught that meditation and faithfulness to moral character would lead one to spiritual enlightenment and truth.

Christianity

Sacred or Guiding Text: The Holy Bible

Beliefs and Practices: God sent His Son Jesus Christ to Earth and Christ died on the cross as a sacrifice for the sins of humankind. Jesus rose again on the third day.

Confucianism (founded by Confucius, a Chinese philosopher who lived in the fifth and sixth centuries BC)

Sacred or Guiding Texts: The *Analects,* a collection of Confucius's sayings and dialogues

Beliefs and Practices: Confucianism emphasizes the relationship between individuals, their families, and society. These relationships are based on *li,* which is proper behavior, and *jen,* which is a sympathetic attitude.

Hinduism (founded about 1500 BC)

Sacred or Guiding Texts: The books of *Ramayana, Vedas,* and *Manu Smriti* (the Memorandum of Manu)

List #61 **Major World Religions** *(continued)*

Beliefs and Practices: Hindus believe in many gods, as well as one great god, Brahman. Followers practice yoga, and the religion includes beliefs and practices from numerous religions in India.

Islam (founded by the prophet Muhammad in the seventh century)

Sacred or Guiding Text: The Koran

Beliefs and Practices: Muslims believe that Muhammad was the last in a long line of prophets that included Adam, Abraham, Moses, and Jesus. Followers also believe that they should uphold the Five Pillars of Islam, including giving alms, prayer five times each day while facing Mecca, and a pilgrimage to Mecca, if possible.

Judaism (founded around 2000 BC by Abraham, Isaac, and Jacob)

Sacred or Guiding Text: The Old Testament, especially the Torah

Beliefs and Practices: Followers teach that the human condition can be improved, that a Messiah will bring paradise, and that Jews should be dedicated to the temple and family life. There are three main groups of Jews: the Orthodox community, which adheres strictly to the Torah; the Reform movement, whose members follow the spirit of the law, observing mostly the ethical content; and the conservative Jews, who follow the laws of the Torah, but they allow for flexibility due to the changes of modern life. (A smaller group includes Reconstructionist Jews, who reject the belief that Jews are God's chosen people, but they do follow the laws of the Torah.)

Shintoism (founded in ancient times in Japan)

Sacred or Guiding Texts: Kojiki and Nihongi (Chronicles of Japan)

Beliefs and Practices: Shinto traditions call for reverence of ancestors, observance of rituals, leading a pure and simple life, and prayer. There is belief in many spiritual beings and gods, known as Kami. There are over 3.5 million followers worldwide.

Taoism (founded in China by Lao-tzu after 604 BC)

Sacred or Guiding Texts: Primarily, the Tao-te Ching and the Chuang-tzu

Beliefs and Practices: Followers are encouraged to seek a simple life and closeness with nature. Followers seek contact with the Tao, or the path of the ever-changing universe, through meditation and simplicity.

Zen Buddhism (founded in about the fifth century by Bodhidharma)

Beliefs and Practices: Strict meditation can lead to sudden enlightenment.

List #62 Major Christian Groups in the United States

Amish/Mennonites (est. 40,000 Amish-Mennonites; est. 180,000 Mennonites)

Beliefs and Practices: The Bible is the sole rule of faith; beliefs are outlined in the Dordrecht Confession of Faith (1632). Mennonite and Amish groups share a common history and belief in simple living, but Mennonites do not separate themselves from society as the Amish do.

Amish and Mennonites come from a Protestant tradition known as Anabaptism (meaning to be baptized again), begun in the sixteenth century. The first Anabaptists separated from the state church because of their belief that a relationship with Christ is an adult choice, and baptism must come out of an adult decision to follow Christ in every aspect of life. In 1693, Jacob Ammann broke away from other Mennonites and his followers became known as the Amish.

Baptist (est. 31 million)

Beliefs and Practices: Authority stems from the Bible. Baptism is by total immersion. Most Baptists shun the use of tobacco or alcoholic beverages.

John Smyth founded the Baptist denomination in England in 1609. Roger Williams began a Baptist church in Rhode Island in 1638.

Catholic Church (est. 50 million)

Beliefs and Practices: Catholics practice seven sacraments: Eucharist (Communion), baptism, confirmation, penance, holy orders, matrimony, and anointing the sick with oil. Worship emphasizes ceremonies and rituals.

The Catholic Church was founded in the first century by the apostle Peter. In 1054, the Eastern Orthodox Church split from the Roman Catholic Church because it rejected the spiritual authority of the bishop of Rome (the Pope).

Church of Christ (est. 1.6 million)

Beliefs and Practices: Authority stems from the Bible as it is written, without embellishment. Rites are not elaborate; baptism is practiced for adults.

The Church of Christ was originally founded by Presbyterians in Kentucky in 1804 and in Pennsylvania in 1809.

Church of England (est. 6,000 in Anglican Orthodox Church in the U.S.)

Beliefs and Practices: The Bible is supreme; the *Book of Common Prayer* is also used. Emphasis is on most essential Christian doctrines. The Church

List #62 **Major Christian Groups in the United States** *(continued)*

of England is part of the Anglican community, represented in the U.S. primarily by the Episcopal Church

When King Henry VIII wanted to divorce one of his wives and the Roman Catholic Church refused, he broke the relationship with the Roman Catholic Church and established the Church of England. When he issued the Act of Supremacy in 1534, he also installed the King of England as head of the Church of England.

Episcopal Church (est. 2.7 million)

Beliefs and Practices: The denomination describes itself as a bridge between Catholicism and Protestant traditions. Worship is based on the Bible and the *Book of Common Prayer*. Baptism of infants is practiced.

The Episcopal Church is an American development of the Church of England. Samuel Seabury was installed as the first bishop in 1784, and the first General Convention was held in 1789.

Lutheran Church (est. 8 million)

Beliefs and Practices: Worship is based on the Bible and the Augsburg Confession, which was written in 1530. Infants are baptized. Members are largely religious and social conservatives.

The Lutheran Church is based on the writings of Martin Luther, who broke away from the Roman Catholic Church between 1517 and 1521, and preached that salvation is through faith; laypeople can read the Bible for themselves without interpretation through church officials. This began the Protestant Reformation. The first Lutheran church in the New World was founded in 1638 in Wilmington, Delaware.

Methodist Church (est. 13.5 million)

Beliefs and Practices: The Bible should be interpreted and followed by tradition and reason. Accepts the baptism of infants or adults.

Reverend John Wesley began preaching throughout England in 1738. He preached that religion should be studied methodically and thus the name "Methodists" came about. In 1784, the Methodist Episcopal Church was founded in the United States. In England, a Wesleyan Methodist Church was established in 1791.

Pentecostal Church (3.5 million)

Beliefs and Practices: Pentecostals believe the Bible is without error. They emphasize the role of the Holy Spirit, speaking in tongues, laying on of hands, and faith healing. Adult baptism is practiced.

List #62 **Major Christian Groups in the United States** *(continued)*

These churches grew out of the "holiness movement" during the early 1900s and attracted many from mainstream Christian denominations. Frequently services are lively, with shouting in the sermons and from those in attendance.

Presbyterian Church (23.2 million)

Beliefs and Practices: Faith is in the Bible; they practice infant baptism. The church has an organized system of clergy and laypeople (presbyters) called the presbytery.

In 1557, John Knox founded the first Presbyterian Church in Scotland. The church had grown out of the Calvinist movement and the Calvinist churches in France and Switzerland. In the New World, the first presbytery was established in 1706 by Francis Makemie, an Irish missionary.

Religious Society of Friends (Quakers) (113,000)

Beliefs and Practices: Quakers are active in social welfare movements. Members refuse to take oaths or bear arms. Quaker meetings usually consist of quiet meditation without ritual or sermon.

In the seventeenth century, George Fox began preaching in England against organized church. He professed a doctrine of the Inner Light, and most Quakers do not define themselves in terms of traditional Christianity. Most Friends practice "plainness," and though many consider Quakers to be Christians, many Quaker beliefs do not fit into traditional Christian categories; some Quakers even consider themselves universalists, agnostics, or atheists.

Seventh-Day Adventist Church (735,000)

Beliefs and Practices: They follow the Bible; the second-coming of Christ is emphasized; adult baptism is practiced. Members shun the use of tobacco and alcoholic beverages.

This denomination grew out of the teachings of William Miller in the 1840s. The church was established in North America in 1863.

United Church of Christ (1.7 million)

Beliefs and Practices: They affirm the Bible as "the authoritative witness to the Word of God" and have roots in the "Covenantal" tradition; infant baptism is accepted.

The General Council of Congregational Churches and the Evangelical and Reformed Churches united in 1957 to form the United Church of Christ.

List #63 Biblical Timeline

c. 2000 BC	Abraham and Sarah
c. 1800 BC	Joseph is taken to Egypt; the Israelites are enslaved in Egypt
c. 1250 BC	Moses and the Exodus from Egypt
c. 1210 BC	Joshua
c. 1120 BC	Judges
c. 1020 BC	Saul
c. 1000 BC	David
c. 965–922 BC	Solomon
c. 931–722 BC	early prophets
c. 732–540 BC	prophecies of Zephaniah, Jeremiah, Habakkuk
c. 536–480 BC	building of second temple; prophecy of Zechariah and Haggai
c. 480 BC	Esther becomes queen of Persia
c. 458 BC	prophet Ezra sent to Judah
c. 444 BC	prophet Nehemiah
c. 397 BC	prophet Malachi
323 BC	Alexander the Great dies
c. 285–246 BC	the Septuagint is translated in Alexandria
c. 200–100 BC	the first books of the Old Testament Apocrypha
c. 168–165 BC	Seleucids are overthrown by Maccabean revolt, led by Mattathias and his sons, Judas (Maccabeus), Jonathan, Simon, John, and Eleazar
63 BC	the Romans invade and violate the temple; Judea becomes a Roman province
37–4 BC	Herod the Great
c. 4 BC	Jesus is born
c. 30	Jesus is crucified
48–64	Paul's letters
c. 68–70	the Dead Sea Scrolls are hidden in the caves above the Dead Sea
c. 70	book of Mark written
c. 80	book of Matthew written
c. 90	books of Luke and John written
c. 80–150	noncanonical gospels are written
325	Council of Nicaea
250–303	Christians suffer persecution under Decius and Diocletian

List #63 **Biblical Timeline** *(continued)*

313	Constantine converts to Christianity
431	Council of Ephesus
451	Council of Chalcedon
525	Dionysius Exiguus, a Scythian monk, leaves us a legacy by creating the Anno Domini (year of our Lord)
600s–735	Saint Bede (later known as Venerable Bede) writes much work about poetry, philosophy, music, religion, and other subjects based on the latest writings of his time; becomes known as the Father of English
900s	the Masoretic text (Hebrew text of the Hebrew Bible) is finalized
1382	John Wycliffe, who believed that the clergy had no special rights and that each man was accountable to God, translates the Bible into Middle English
1456	Gutenberg Bible is printed
c. 1528	William Tyndale begins translating the Scriptures into Early Modern English; martyred on October 6, 1536
1536	King Henry VIII breaks away from the Church of Rome and creates the Church of England
1545–1563	Council of Trent
1549	Book of Common Prayer is published
1560	Geneva Bible is published
1611	King James Bible is published
1648	Westminster Confession written
1700s	John and Charles Wesley begin preaching to common people
1800s	Missionary activities increase around the world and the Bible is translated into many languages
1945	the Nag Hammadi Library is discovered in Egypt (texts dating back to the 3rd and 4th centuries)
1947	the Dead Sea Scrolls are discovered in cliffs along the Dead Sea
1952	Revised Standard Version of the Bible is published
1960	New American Standard Version of the Bible is published
1978	New International Version of the Bible is published
1989	New Revised Standard Version of the Bible is published

List #64 Old Testament Books

	Book	Number of Chapters	Author of the Book
Historical (The first 5 books are called the Pentateuch)	Genesis	50	Moses
	Exodus	50	Moses
	Leviticus	27	Moses
	Numbers	36	Moses
	Deuteronomy	34	Moses
Historical	Joshua	24	not identified
	Judges	21	not identified
	Ruth	4	not identified
	1 Samuel	31	not identified
	2 Samuel	24	not identified
	1 Kings	22	not identified
	2 Kings	25	not identified
	1 Chronicles	29	not identified, possibly Ezra
	2 Chronicles	36	not identified, possibly Ezra
	Ezra	10	Ezra
	Nehemiah	13	not identified, possibly Nehemiah or Ezra
	Esther	10	not identified
Poetic	Job	42	not identified
	Psalms	150	various authors, including David, Solomon, Asaph, Ethan, the sons of Korah
	Proverbs	31	some are written by Solomon
	Ecclesiastes	12	Solomon
	Song of Songs	8	Solomon

List #64 Old Testament Books *(continued)*

	Book	Number of Chapters	Author of the Book
Prophetic	Isaiah	66	Isaiah
	Jeremiah	52	Jeremiah
	Lamentations	5	Jeremiah
	Ezekiel	48	Ezekiel
	Daniel	12	Daniel
	Hosea	14	Hosea
	Joel	3	Joel
	Amos	9	Amos
	Obadiah	1	Obadiah
	Jonah	4	Jonah
	Micah	7	Micah
	Nahum	3	Nahum
	Habakkuk	3	Habakkuk
	Zephaniah	3	Zephaniah
	Haggai	2	Haggai
	Zechariah	14	Zechariah
	Malachi	4	Malachi

List #65 New Testament Books

	Book	Number of Chapters	Author of the Book
Gospels	Matthew	28	Matthew
	Mark	16	Mark
	Luke	24	Luke
	John	21	John
Acts	Acts	28	probably Luke
Epistles	Romans	16	Paul
	1 Corinthians	16	Paul
	2 Corinthians	13	Paul
	Galatians	6	Paul
	Ephesians	6	Paul
	Philippians	4	Paul
	Colossians	4	Paul
	1 Thessalonians	5	Paul
	2 Thessalonians	3	Paul
	1 Timothy	6	Paul
	2 Timothy	4	Paul
	Titus	3	Paul
	Philemon	1	Paul
	Hebrews	13	not identified
	James	5	James
	1 Peter	5	Peter
	2 Peter	3	Peter
	1 John	5	John
	2 John	1	John
	3 John	1	John
	Jude	1	Jude
Prophetic	Revelation	22	John

List #66 Days of Creation

Day 1: God creates the Earth and divides the light from the darkness.

Day 2: God separates the water from the air.

Day 3: God creates the land and plants.

Day 4: God creates the stars and the sun.

Day 5: God creates fish and birds.

Day 6: God creates land animals and man.

God proclaims it all very good.

Day 7: God rests from all His work.

List #67 The Ten Commandments

Exodus 20:1–17

And God spoke all these words: "I am the Lord your God, who brought you out of Egypt, out of the land of slavery.

1. "You shall have no other gods before me."

2. "You shall not make for yourself an idol in the form of anything in heaven above or on the earth beneath or in the waters below. You shall not bow down to them or worship them; for I, the Lord your God, am a jealous God, punishing the children for the sin of the fathers to the third and fourth generation of those who hate me, but showing love to a thousand (generations) of those who love me and keep my commandments."

3. "You shall not misuse the name of the Lord your God, for the Lord will not hold anyone guiltless who misuses his name."

4. "Remember the Sabbath day by keeping it holy. Six days you shall labor and do all your work, but the seventh day is a Sabbath to the Lord your God. On it you shall not do any work, neither you, nor your son or daughter, nor your manservant or maidservant, nor your animals, nor the alien within your gates. For in six days the Lord made the heavens and the earth, the sea, and all that is in them, but he rested on the seventh day. Therefore the Lord blessed the Sabbath day and made it holy."

5. "Honor your father and your mother, so that you may live long in the land the Lord your God is giving you."

6. "You shall not murder."

7. "You shall not commit adultery."

8. "You shall not steal."

9. "You shall not give false testimony against your neighbor."

10. "You shall not covet your neighbor's house. You shall not covet your neighbor's wife, or his manservant or maidservant, his ox or donkey, or anything that belongs to your neighbor."

List #68 Ten Plagues on Egypt

Plague #1: Nile River turned to blood

Plague #2: frogs

Plague #3: gnats

Plague #4: flies

Plague #5: plague on cattle (though *all* the Egyptians' livestock died, including sheep, horses, camels, donkeys, goats, and cattle)

Plague #6: boils

Plague #7: hail

Plague #8: locusts

Plague #9: darkness

Plague #10: death of firstborns

List #69 The Twelve Tribes of Israel

Traditional Division (12 sons of Israel, or Jacob)	Appointed Land in Israel
Asher	Asher
Benjamin	Benjamin
Dan	Dan
Gad	Gad
Issachar	Issachar
Joseph	Judah
Judah	Naphtali
Levi	Simeon
Naphtali	Zebulun
Reuben	Reuben
Simeon	Ephraim
Zebulun	Manasseh

Originally the twelve tribes consisted of the twelve sons of Israel (formerly known as Jacob).

After the land was divided, the tribes of Judah and Benjamin joined to form the Kingdom of Judah. The tribe of Levi, which was assigned religious duty, did not receive tribal land. The remaining tribes are considered the ten lost tribes: Reuben, Simeon, Issachar, Zebulun, Dan, Naphtali, Gad, Asher, Ephraim, and Manasseh.

List #70 Kings of Israel (the Northern Kingdom)

All of the Kings of Israel were wicked. This list shows each king and the approximate period he ruled. Experts do not agree on these periods of rule, so again, these are approximate dates.

Jeroboam I (933–911 BC)	Jehoahaz (820–804 BC)
Nadab (911–910 BC)	Jehoash (Joash) (806–790 BC)
Baasha (910–887 BC)	Jeroboam II (790–749 BC)
Elah (887–886 BC)	Zechariah (748 BC)
Zimri (886 BC)	Shallum (748 BC)
Omri (886–875 BC)	Menahem (748–738 BC)
Ahab (875–854 BC)	Pekahiah (738–736 BC)
Ahaziah (855–854 BC)	Pekah (748–730 BC)
Jehoram (Joram) (854–843 BC)	Hoshea (730–721 BC)
Jehu (843–816 BC)	

List #71 Kings of Judah (the Southern Kingdom)

Only eight of the Kings of Judah worshiped the Lord. They are indicated with an asterisk (*). The periods of reign are approximate.

Rehoboam (933–916 BC)	Jotham* (749–734 BC)
Abijam (915–913 BC)	Ahaz (741–726 BC)
Asa* (912–872 BC)	Hezekiah* (726–697 BC)
Jehoshaphat* (874–850 BC)	Manasseh (697–642 BC)
Jehoram (850–843 BC)	Amon (641–640 BC)
Ahaziah (843 BC)	Josiah* (639–608 BC)
Athaliah (843–837 BC)	Jehoahaz (608 BC)
Joash* (843–803 BC)	Jehoiakim (608–597 BC)
Amaziah* (803–775 BC)	Jehoiachin (597 BC)
Azariah (Uzziah)* (787–735 BC)	Zedekiah (597–586 BC)

List #72 Judges

Othniel	the first judge after Joshua's death	Judges 3:7–11
Ehud	fought the Moabites	Judges 3:12–30
Shamgar	led Israelites against Philistines	Judges 3:31
Deborah	a prophetess who guided Barak to victory over the Canaanites; the only female judge	Judges 4–5
Gideon	defeated Midianites with 300 men	Judges 6–8
Abimelech	the only judge to win leadership through treachery	Judges 9
Tola	judged Israel for 23 years	Judges 10:1–2
Jair	judged Israel for 22 years	Judges 10:3–5
Jepthah	defeated the Ammonites	Judges 10:17–12:7
Ibzan	judged the people for 7 years	Judges 12:8–15
Elon	was a judge for 10 years	Judges 12:8–15
Abdon	ruled for 8 years	Judges 12:8–15
Samson	led Israel 20 years; fought the Philistines and when he was taken prisoner, he brought down the temple, killing himself and many Philistines in the process	Judges 13–16
Eli	a priest; ruled the people from the sanctuary at Gilo	1 Samuel 1:9
Samuel	a barren Hannah conceived Samuel, whom she promised to dedicate to the Lord for all the days of his life; Samuel was the last judge before the kingdom came under Saul's rule	1 Samuel and 2 Samuel

List #73 The Writing Prophets

Prophet	Appox. Date of Composition	Meaning of Prophet's Name	Told Prophecies to or About	Theme of This Book in the Bible	Major Sins Addressed
Obadiah	854–830 BC or 605–586 BC	a servant or worshiper of Yahweh	against Edom	the Day of the Lord; destruction of Edom; the restoration of Israel	Edom is proud and has gloated over Israel's devastation
Joel	830–750 BC	Yahweh is God	Israel, the Northern Kingdom	the Day of the Lord is near; repentance	drunkenness, unfaithfulness, adultery, idolatry
Jonah	800–750 BC	dove	Nineveh (lessons we can all learn from)	God loves all people; God's mercy to those who repent	disobedience to God
Amos	760–750 BC	to carry a load or bear a burden	Israel, Judah, and Benjamin; all nations	social justice; God's imminent judgment/the Day of the Lord is near; God will not abandon His people	social injustices such as oppression of the poor; taking advantage of others to benefit yourself; wanton luxury; corruption
Micah	750–686 BC	who is like the Lord	Samaria, Jerusalem, all nations	judgment and deliverance by God	idolatry, injustice, rebellion, oppression
Isaiah	700–686 BC	Jehovah is my salvation	people of Israel in Judah and Jerusalem	the Savior is coming	rebellion, sacrifices offered without devotion to God, worshiping pagan gods
Hosea	722–721 BC	salvation	Israel, the Northern Kingdom	God's love, grace, forgiveness, and mercy; disloyalty to God is a sin	adultery, sexual immorality, drunkenness

List #73 **The Writing Prophets** *(continued)*

Prophet	Appox. Date of Composition	Meaning of Prophet's Name	Told Prophecies to or About	Theme of This Book in the Bible	Major Sins Addressed
Nahum	663–612 BC	comfort/ consolation	Assyrians, primarily Ninevah	judgment on Nineveh	oppression, cruelty, idolatry, wickedness
Zephaniah	640–609 BC	Yahweh hides	Judah, Jerusalem, all nations and people	God's approaching judgment/the coming of the Day of the Lord	worshiping other gods while pretending to worship Yahweh
Jeremiah	627–586 BC	the Lord is exalted	Judah (southern Kingdom) and Jerusalem	sin will be found out and God will be exalted; Jews disperse; new covenant (Messiah) would come	selfishness, idol worship
Habakkuk	608–604 BC	to embrace	Israel, with implications for everyone	trust God	aggression; greed; pride; encouraging immorality in others
Ezekiel	571 BC	God strengthens	Jews in Babylonian captivity	Judah was destroyed because of people's sin; restoration comes to the faithful	idolatry, rebellion, indifference toward the Lord
Daniel	536 BC	God is my judge	captives in Babylon	God is in control and there is a purpose in difficult circumstances	This book is different by not addressing sins so much as showing how God is in control of everything and we should remain faithful

List #73 **The Writing Prophets** *(continued)*

Prophet	Appox. Date of Composition	Meaning of Prophet's Name	Told Prophecies to or About	Theme of This Book in the Bible	Major Sins Addressed
Haggai	520 BC	festival	Zerubbabel	clear consequences for disobedience	neglecting to build God's House (procrastination to do God's work)
Zechariah	520–480 BC	remembered by Yahweh	Judah	spiritual renewal; God will go to those who seek Him; justice and mercy	living evil ways; lack of good judgment; Joshua had filthy garments
Malachi	c. 432 BC	my messenger	Jerusalem	restore relationship with Yahweh	abuses of priests; proper tithing; marriage to foreigners

List #74 The Twelve Apostles

The word *disciple* is derived from a Greek word that means "learner" or "student." The word *apostle* means "messenger." All the apostles were disciples, but not all disciples were apostles. We can all be disciples of Christ.

The following chart contains the most reliable account of what probably happened to each of the apostles. Some information is found in biblical references. Other written records and oral traditions have allowed stories of the apostles to be passed down through the centuries. While some accounts have been discounted as unreliable, the general consensus is that all but one of the apostles (John) were martyred and possibly John was as well.

Apostle	What happened to him
James, the older brother of John	"He [King Herod] had James, the brother of John, put to death with the sword" (Acts 12:2). He was the first apostle to be martyred.
Philip	It is believed that Philip was martyred at Heliopolis, Phrygia. Reportedly he was severely flogged, imprisoned, and then later crucified.
Matthew, the former tax collector	Killed in Nadabah
James, also known as James the Less	Stoned and clubbed to death in Jerusalem
Judas Iscariot	Judas betrayed Jesus. After the crucifixion, he was replaced by Matthias. Judas hung himself after Jesus was arrested.
Andrew, the brother of Peter	Crucified on an X-shaped cross. This is reportedly the origin of the term *Saint Andrew's Cross*.
Peter (also known as Simon), the brother of Andrew, from Bethsaida	The general consensus is that Peter was crucified, upside down, during the reign of Emperor Nero.
Bartholomew	Bartholomew was present at the Sea of Tiberias when Jesus appeared to some of the disciples. He also witnessed the ascension. Bartholomew was reportedly tortured and crucified in India.
Thomas, also called Didymus, was nicknamed Doubting Thomas	Thomas was reportedly killed with a spear in India.
Simon the Zealot	Simon traveled a lot, and reportedly he was crucified in what we know today as Britain.

List #74 The Twelve Apostles *(continued)*

Apostle	What happened to him
John, younger brother of James	As Jesus asked of him, John took care of Mary after Jesus' crucifixion. He wrote the book of Revelation while he was a prisoner at Patmos. We do not know how he died, but he may be the only apostle who escaped martyrdom.
Thaddeus	Not much is known about this disciple except that he did travel extensively to evangelize. Tradition is that he was martyred, possibly killed by arrows at Mt. Ararat.
Matthias	Matthias was chosen by the apostles to replace Judas Iscariot (recorded in Acts). This brought the number back up to twelve with Judas gone.

List #75 Women of the Bible

Deborah	A prophetess and a judge, Deborah led the people of Israel during war with the Canaanites.
Elizabeth	God blessed the barren woman Elizabeth in her old age by giving her a child, the child who would herald the birth of our Christ.
Esther	Esther was a young Jewish queen in a place where Jews were not particularly welcome. Her Jewish identity was hidden, but we learn that sometimes we have to stand up for what is right even if it means putting our own lives at risk.
Hannah	After praying earnestly for a son and telling the Lord she would dedicate him to the Lord's service, Hannah conceived Samuel. When he was only a few years old, she took him to the temple to live. Hannah's story can show us a lot about love, faith, devotion, and sacrifice.
Jezebel	She was devoted to Baal and lived as such. In addition to her desire to kill the prophet Elijah, Jezebel is largely remembered for her negative influence on Ahab, convincing him to set up idols and murder Naboth.
Leah	As the older daughter, Leah's father wanted her to marry first, so he tricked Jacob into marrying her, even though Jacob had worked seven years to marry Rachel. Leah became mother of six of the twelve tribes of Israel.
Lot's wife	The story of Lot's wife is a great lesson for us not to be constantly looking back at the past, but rather to look ahead toward the future. This story also shows us that obedience should be complete (not even one tiny, quick peek), a good lesson for our children and ourselves.
Martha	While Mary was spending time listening to Jesus, Martha was getting the work done. We can learn from her story that our Lord does want us to "be still" and seek God at times rather than "doing" things that can wait.
Mary	Based on her betrothal to Joseph, Mary was probably only about thirteen years old when she conceived Jesus by the Holy Spirit. She is the mother of Jesus.
Mary Magdala	Mary became one of Jesus' strongest supporters.
Miriam	This young girl is best known for saving her baby brother Moses by keeping watch as he floated downriver in a small reed boat and then seeing him taken in by the Pharaoh's daughter. She then cleverly managed to suggest her own mother as a nurse for Moses.
Rachel	Jacob worked seven years to marry Rachel, but was tricked into taking her older sister first, then had to work seven more years for Rachel—now that's love! She became Jacob's favored wife.

List #75 **Women of the Bible** *(continued)*

Rebekah	Rebekah has some positive characteristics, but overall her story is a lesson in not trying to manipulate situations to suit our own desires, as this is not pleasing to God.
Ruth	This quiet, gentle biblical heroine must have had more pure love in her heart than most of us will ever know. Through her heartache, she continued to love others more than herself.
Sarah	Formerly known as Sarai, this biblical matriarch followed Abraham into an unknown land.
Woman at the well	This outcast was at the well when Jesus came by and spoke with her. She rejoiced in the good news and ran to the city to tell others.

List #76 Children of the Bible

Aaron	Moses' older brother, who served as a spokesman for Moses.
David	Shepherd boy who slayed Goliath with a slingshot; anointed King of Israel by prophet Samuel.
Isaac	At God's command, his father, Abraham, prepared to offer him as a sacrifice to God, but God provided a ram at the last minute; Isaac trusted his father and God.
Ishmael	Abraham and Hagar's son; tormented his brother Isaac to the extent that Abraham had Ishmael and his mother, Hagar, sent away.
Jairus's daughter	Her father was a ruler among the people where he lived; Jairus went to Jesus to ask Him to help his daughter, but someone came to say she had already died. Jesus went to Jairus's house and told the girl to wake up, as though she were only asleep.
Jesus	The Son of God; born in a stable to Mary (a virgin) and Joseph. As a child, Jesus astonished the teachers in the temple with what He knew. When Jesus grew up, He began his public ministry, and then was crucified on a cross for our sins, even though He was sinless.
Joseph	Second youngest son of Jacob; as his favorite son, Jacob gave Joseph a coat of many colors; Joseph's brothers grew jealous of him and initially would not greet him appropriately, then they called him names, then they even plotted to kill him. In the end his brothers sold him into slavery.
Josiah	Became king of Judah when he was only eight years old. Though his father and grandfather were bad and did not worship the Lord God, Josiah had a tender heart and sought the Lord. He was raised in the temple and brought the law of God back to the people.
little children who wanted to come to Jesus	The disciples tried to keep back the little children who wanted to hear Jesus, but Jesus told them to let the little children come to Him. We should all be so persistent and desire Jesus enough to continue to go to Him, even if others discourage us.
Miriam	Moses' older sister; after Moses was placed in the basket in the Nile River, Miriam followed. When Pharoah's daughter found Moses in the basket, Miriam stepped forward and meekly asked if she could find a nurse for the baby.
Moses	Son of Amram and Jochebed; the Pharoah had ordered all young Hebrew boys killed, but Moses' family hid him for a few months and then placed him in a basket in the Nile, praying that God would take care of him. Pharoah's daughter found Moses and decided to raise him herself.

List #76 **Children of the Bible** *(continued)*

Naaman's little slave girl	Naaman had leprosy, and upon the advice of this slave girl, he traveled a long distance to see the prophet Elisha and was cured. She must have been benevolent to have wanted good to come to someone who had put her into slavery; she must have been trustworthy for them to believe her, and she must have been a godly child to have told these people who didn't share her beliefs about a prophet who did share her faith.
Samuel	His mother, Hannah, was childless until the Lord allowed her to become pregnant with Samuel; his name means "asked of the Lord"; taken to the temple when he was still a young boy to be of service to the Lord.
Timothy	It is unclear how old Timothy was when we first hear of him, but apparently he was young enough to consider himself still a child (2 Timothy 3:15). His grandmother's name was Lois; his mother's name was Eunice. They taught him the Word of God when he was young, and he used this knowledge to become a preacher and share the Word with others.
the widow's son	After an extensive drought, Elijah the prophet told the widow to bake him some bread, and he stayed in this household for a time, but the son died. Elijah prayed to God, stretched his body over the boy three times, and the boy came back to life.

List #77 The Lord's Prayer

Matthew 6:9–13

"Our Father in heaven, hallowed be your name, your kingdom come, your will be done on earth as it is in heaven. Give us today our daily bread. Forgive us our debts, as we also have forgiven our debtors. And lead us not into temptation, but deliver us from the evil one."

List# 78 The Beatitudes

Matthew 5:3–12

"Blessed are the poor in spirit,
for theirs is the kingdom of heaven.

Blessed are those who mourn,
for they will be comforted.

Blessed are the meek,
for they will inherit the earth.

Blessed are those who hunger and thirst for righteousness,
for they will be filled.

Blessed are the merciful,
for they will be shown mercy.

Blessed are the pure in heart,
for they will see God.

Blessed are the peacemakers,
for they will be called sons of God.

Blessed are those who are persecuted because of righteousness,
for theirs is the kingdom of heaven.

Blessed are you when people insult you, persecute you and falsely say all kinds of evil against you because of me. Rejoice and be glad, because great is your reward in heaven, for in the same way they persecuted the prophets who were before you."

List #79 The Miracles of Jesus Christ

Healing

- a paralyzed man (Matthew 9:2–8)
- two blind men (Matthew 9:27–31)
- a deaf man (Mark 7:31–37)
- a blind man at Bethsaida (Mark 8:22–25)
- a man blind from birth, at Jerusalem (John 9:1–41)
- a woman who had been crippled for eighteen years (Luke 13:10–17)
- ten people with leprosy (Luke 17:11–19)
- a high fever in Peter's mother-in-law (Matthew 8:14–17)
- the centurion's servant (Matthew 8:5–13)
- Malchus's ear after Peter cut it off with a sword (Luke 22:50–51)
- multitudes (Matthew 4:24)

Nature

- a large catch of fish (Luke 5:1–11)
- calming of the storm on the Sea of Galilee (Matthew 8:23–27)
- the feeding of the 5,000 (Matthew 14:13–21)
- walking on the water (Matthew 14:22–33)
- the feeding of the 4,000 (Matthew 15:32–38)
- money needed to pay taxes obtained from inside a fish (Matthew 17:24–27)
- a fig tree withered (Matthew 21:18–22)

Deliverance From Demon Possession

- a man in the synagogue (Mark 1:21–27)
- a blind and mute man (Matthew 12:22–23)
- two men in the region of the Gadarenes (Matthew 8:28–34)
- a Canaanite woman's daughter (Matthew 15:21–28)
- the epileptic boy (Matthew 17:14–18)

Raising People From the Dead

- Jairus's daughter (Matthew 9:18–25)
- the widow's only son at Nain (Luke 7:11–15)
- Lazarus at Bethany (John 11:1–44)

List #80 The Parables of Jesus Christ

Concerning	Place	Biblical Reference
The Two Debtors	Capernaum	Luke 7:40–48
The Strong Man	Galilee	Matthew 12:25-31 Mark 3:23-29 Luke 11:18–23
The Evil Spirit	Galilee	Matthew 12:43–45 Luke 11:24–26
The Sower	Seashore	Matthew 13:3–9,18–23 Mark 4:3–9,14–20 Luke 8:5–8,11–15
Weeds in the Wheat	Seashore of Galilee	Matthew 13:24–30, 36–43
The Mustard Seed	Seashore of Galilee	Matthew 13:31-32 Mark 4:30–32 Luke 13:18–19
The Growing Seed	Seashore of Galilee	Mark 4:26–29
Yeast	Seashore of Galilee	Matthew 13:33 Luke 13:20–21
Hidden Treasure	Seashore of Galilee	Matthew 13:44
The Pearl	Seashore of Galilee	Matthew 13:45–46
Good and Bad Fish	Seashore of Galilee	Matthew 13:47–50
The Wicked Servant	Capernaum	Matthew 18:21–35
The Good Samaritan	Near Jerusalem	Luke 10:29–37
The Visitor at Midnight	Near Jerusalem	Luke 11:5–10
The Rich Fool	Galilee	Luke 12:16–21
The Unproductive Fig Tree	Galilee	Luke 13:6–9
The Great Banquet	Peraea	Luke 14:15–24
The Lost Sheep	Peraea	Matthew 18:12–14 Luke 15:3–7
The Lost Coin	Peraea	Luke 15:8–10
The Lost Son	Peraea	Luke 15:11–32
The Good Shepherd	Jerusalem	John 10:1–18
The Dishonest Manager	Peraea	Luke 16:1–13
Lazarus and the Rich Man	Peraea	Luke 16:19–31
The Unworthy Servants	Peraea	Luke 17:7–10
The Persistent Widow	Peraea	Luke 18:1–8
Pharisee and Tax Collector	Peraea	Luke 18:9–14

List #80 **The Parables of Jesus Christ** *(continued)*

Concerning	Place	Biblical Reference
Workers in the Vineyard	Peraea	Matthew 20:1–16
The Ten Minas	Jericho	Luke 19:11–27
The Two Sons	Jerusalem	Matthew 21:28–32
Owner of the Vineyard	Jerusalem	Matthew 21:33–44 Mark 12:1–12 Luke 20:9–18
The Wedding Banquet	Jerusalem	Matthew 22:1–14
The Ten Virgins	Mount of Olives	Matthew 25:1–13
The Talents	Mount of Olives	Matthew 25:14–30

List #81 Fruit of the Spirit

The fruit of the Spirit consists of nine biblical attributes that are manifested in every Christian by the Holy Spirit. We can share God's love for others by allowing the Spirit to bear fruit in each of us. Additional Scripture references are listed so that we might memorize verses that speak of attributes we should seek to exhibit in our lives.

Galatians 5:22–23

"But the fruit of the Spirit is love, joy, peace, patience, kindness, goodness, faithfulness, gentleness and self-control. Against such things there is no law."

Love	"And now these three remain: faith, hope and love. But the greatest of these is love" (1 Corinthians 13:13).
Joy	"Nehemiah said, 'Go and enjoy choice food and sweet drinks, and send some to those who have nothing prepared. This day is sacred to our Lord. Do not grieve, for the joy of the Lord is your strength'" (Nehemiah 8:10). "Let us fix our eyes on Jesus, the author and perfecter of our faith, who for the joy set before him endured the cross, scorning its shame, and sat down at the right hand of the throne of God" (Hebrews 12:2).
Peace	"Therefore, since we have been justified through faith, we have peace with God through our Lord Jesus Christ" (Romans 5:1). "May the God of hope fill you with all joy and peace as you trust in him, so that you may overflow with hope by the power of the Holy Spirit" (Romans 15:13).
Patience (longsuffering)	"That you may live a life worthy of the Lord . . . being strengthened with all power according to his glorious might so that you may have great endurance and patience, and joyfully give thanks to the Father" (Colossians 1:10-12). "Be completely humble and gentle; be patient, bearing with one another in love" (Ephesians 4:2).
Kindness (gentleness)	"As servants of God we commend ourselves . . . in purity, understanding, patience and kindness; in the Holy Spirit and in sincere love; in truthful speech and in the power of God; with weapons of righteousness in the right hand and in the left . . . having nothing, and yet possessing everything" (2 Corinthians 6:4, 6-7, 10).
Goodness	"For the fruit of the light consists in all goodness, righteousness and truth" (Ephesians 5:9).

List #81 **Fruit of the Spirit** *(continued)*

Faithfulness	"I pray that out of his glorious riches he may strengthen you with power through his Spirit in your inner being, so that Christ may dwell in your hearts through faith. And I pray that you, being rooted and established in love, may . . . grasp how . . . deep is the love of Christ" (Ephesians 3:16–18).
Gentleness (meekness)	"Be completely humble and gentle; be patient, bearing with one another in love" (Ephesians 4:2).
Self-control (temperance)	"For this very reason, make every effort to add to your faith goodness; and to goodness, knowledge; and to knowledge, self-control; and to self-control, perseverance; and to perseverance, godliness; and to godliness, brotherly kindness; and to brotherly kindness, love" (2 Peter 1:5–7).

List #82 Key Bible Memory Verses

Many parents want their children to memorize Scripture, but they don't know where to begin. Here are some key verses to help you get started. Remember, even very young children can memorize shorter sections or portions of longer passages. Elementary-age children can memorize long passages if they are read aloud to them for several days in a row. I read the selection aloud first (some homeschoolers have the children read the verses aloud), then I read small sections of each verse and have the children repeat after me until we've read the entire selection. Then we go back and say one small part again, such as one verse. We do this for several days, adding more each time. After a couple of weeks on the same selection, the children usually have the verses memorized. Remember, sometimes it takes very small steps to work toward a goal. Don't get discouraged!

Colossians 3:20

Children, obey your parents in everything, for this pleases the Lord.

John 4:24

God is spirit, and his worshipers must worship in spirit and in truth.

Ephesians 6:1–4 *(the first commandment with a promise)*

Children, obey your parents in the Lord, for this is right. Honor your father and mother...that it may go well with you and that you may enjoy long life on the earth. Fathers, do not exasperate your children; instead, bring them up in the training and instruction of the Lord.

1 Corinthians 13

If I speak in the tongues of men and of angels, but have not love, I am only a resounding gong or a clanging cymbal. If I have the gift of prophecy and can fathom all mysteries and all knowledge, and if I have a faith that can move mountains, but have not love, I am nothing. If I give all I possess to the poor and surrender my body to the flames, but have not love, I gain nothing.

Love is patient, love is kind. It does not envy, it does not boast, it is not proud. It is not rude, it is not self-seeking, it is not easily angered, it keeps no record of wrongs. Love does not delight in evil but rejoices with the truth. It always protects, always trusts, always hopes, always perseveres.

List #82 **Key Bible Memory Verses** *(continued)*

Love never fails. But where there are prophecies, they will cease; where there are tongues, they will be stilled; where there is knowledge, it will pass away. For we know in part and we prophesy in part, but when perfection comes, the imperfect disappears. When I was a child, I talked like a child, I thought like a child, I reasoned like a child. When I became a man, I put childish ways behind me. Now we see but a poor reflection as in a mirror; then we shall see face to face. Now I know in part; then I shall know fully, even as I am fully known.

And now these three remain: faith, hope and love. But the greatest of these is love.

Genesis 1

In the beginning God created the heavens and the earth. Now the earth was formless and empty, darkness was over the surface of the deep, and the Spirit of God was hovering over the waters.

And God said, "Let there be light," and there was light. God saw that the light was good, and he separated the light from the darkness. God called the light "day," and the darkness he called "night." And there was evening, and there was morning—the first day.

And God said, "Let there be an expanse between the waters to separate water from water." So God made the expanse and separated the water under the expanse from the water above it. And it was so. God called the expanse "sky." And there was evening, and there was morning—the second day.

And God said, "Let the water under the sky be gathered to one place, and let dry ground appear." And it was so. God called the dry ground "land," and the gathered waters he called "seas." And God saw that it was good.

Then God said, "Let the land produce vegetation: seed-bearing plants and trees on the land that bear fruit with seed in it, according to their various kinds." And it was so. The land produced vegetation: plants bearing seed according to their kinds and trees bearing fruit with seed in it according to their kinds. And God saw that it was good. And there was evening, and there was morning—the third day.

And God said, "Let there be lights in the expanse of the sky to separate the day from the night, and let them serve as signs to mark seasons and days and years, and let them be lights in the expanse of the sky to give light on the earth." And it was so. God made two great lights—the greater light to govern the day and the lesser light to govern the night. He also made the stars. God set them in the expanse of the sky to give light on the earth, to govern the day and the night, and to separate light from darkness. And God saw that it was good. And there was evening, and there was morning—the fourth day.

List #82 **Key Bible Memory Verses** *(continued)*

And God said, "Let the water teem with living creatures, and let birds fly above the earth across the expanse of the sky." So God created the great creatures of the sea and every living and moving thing with which the water teems, according to their kinds, and every winged bird according to its kind. And God saw that it was good. God blessed them and said, "Be fruitful and increase in number and fill the water in the seas, and let the birds increase on the earth." And there was evening, and there was morning—the fifth day.

And God said, "Let the land produce living creatures according to their kinds: livestock, creatures that move along the ground, and wild animals, each according to its kind." And it was so. God made the wild animals according to their kinds, the livestock according to their kinds, and all the creatures that move along the ground according to their kinds. And God saw that it was good.

Then God said, "Let us make man in our image, in our likeness, and let them rule over the fish of the sea and the birds of the air, over the livestock, over all the earth, and over all the creatures that move along the ground." So God created man in his own image, in the image of God he created him; male and female he created them.

God blessed them and said to them, "Be fruitful and increase in number; fill the earth and subdue it. Rule over the fish of the sea and the birds of the air and over every living creature that moves on the ground."

Then God said, "I give you every seed-bearing plant on the face of the whole earth and every tree that has fruit with seed in it. They will be yours for food. And to all the beasts of the earth and all the birds of the air and all the creatures that move on the ground—everything that has the breath of life in it—I give every green plant for food." And it was so.

God saw all that he had made, and it was very good. And there was evening, and there was morning—the sixth day.

John 1:1–7

In the beginning was the Word, and the Word was with God, and the Word was God. He was with God in the beginning. Through him all things were made; without him nothing was made that has been made. In him was life, and that life was the light of men. The light shines in the darkness, but the darkness has not understood it. There came a man who was sent from God; his name was John. He came as a witness to testify concerning that light, so that through him all men might believe.

List #82 **Key Bible Memory Verses** *(continued)*

2 Corinthians 3:17

Now the Lord is the Spirit, and where the Spirit of the Lord is, there is freedom.

John 8:32–36

Then you will know the truth, and the truth will set you free. They answered him, "We are Abraham's descendants and have never been slaves of anyone. How can you say that we shall be set free?"Jesus replied, "I tell you the truth, everyone who sins is a slave to sin. Now a slave has no permanent place in the family, but a son belongs to it forever. So if the Son sets you free, you will be free indeed."

Romans 6:18–23

You have been set free from sin and have become slaves to righteousness. I put this in human terms because you are weak in your natural selves. Just as you used to offer the parts of your body in slavery to impurity and to ever-increasing wickedness, so now offer them in slavery to righteousness leading to holiness. When you were slaves to sin, you were free from the control of righteousness. What benefit did you reap at that time from the things you are now ashamed of? Those things result in death! But now that you have been set free from sin and have become slaves to God, the benefit you reap leads to holiness, and the result is eternal life. For the wages of sin is death, but the gift of God is eternal life in Christ Jesus our Lord.

Hebrews 5:7

During the days of Jesus' life on earth, he offered up prayers and petitions with loud cries and tears to the one who could save him from death, and he was heard because of his reverent submission.

Romans 8:1–17

Therefore, there is now no condemnation for those who are in Christ Jesus, because through Christ Jesus the law of the Spirit of life set me free from the law of sin and death. For what the law was powerless to do in that it was weakened by the sinful nature, God did by sending his own Son in the likeness of sinful man to be a sin offering. And so he condemned sin in sinful man, in order that the righteous requirements of the law might be fully met in us, who do not live according to the sinful nature but according to the Spirit.

Those who live according to the sinful nature have their minds set on what that nature desires; but those who live in accordance with the Spirit have their minds set on what the Spirit desires. The mind of sinful man is death, but the mind controlled by the Spirit is life and peace; the sinful mind is hostile to God. It does not submit to God's law, nor can it do so. Those controlled by the sinful nature cannot please God.

You, however, are controlled not by the sinful nature but by the Spirit, if the Spirit of God lives in you. And if anyone does not have the Spirit of Christ, he does not belong to Christ. But if Christ is in you, your body is dead because of sin, yet your spirit is alive because of righteousness. And if the Spirit of him who raised Jesus from the dead is living in you, he who raised Christ from the dead will also give life to your mortal bodies through his Spirit, who lives in you.

Therefore, brothers, we have an obligation—but it is not to the sinful nature, to live according to it. For if you live according to the sinful nature, you will die; but if by the Spirit you put to death the misdeeds of the body, you will live, because those who are led by the Spirit of God are sons of God. For you did not receive a spirit that makes you a slave again to fear, but you received the Spirit of sonship. And by him we cry, "Abba, Father." The Spirit himself testifies with our spirit that we are God's children. Now if we are children, then we are heirs—heirs of God and co-heirs with Christ, if indeed we share in his sufferings in order that we may also share in his glory.

Genesis 19:15–26

With the coming of dawn, the angels urged Lot, saying, "Hurry! Take your wife and your two daughters who are here, or you will be swept away when the city is punished."

When he hesitated, the men grasped his hand and the hands of his wife and of his two daughters and led them safely out of the city, for the Lord was merciful to them. As soon as they had brought them out, one of them said, "Flee for your lives! Don't look back, and don't stop anywhere in the plain! Flee to the mountains or you will be swept away!"

But Lot said to them, "No, my lords, please! Your servant has found favor in your eyes, and you have shown great kindness to me in sparing my life. But I can't flee to the mountains; this disaster will overtake me, and I'll die. Look, here is a town near enough to run to, and it is small. Let me flee to it—it is very small, isn't it? Then my life will be spared."

He said to him, "Very well, I will grant this request too; I will not overthrow the town you speak of. But flee there quickly, because I cannot do anything until you reach it." (That is why the town was called Zoar.)

By the time Lot reached Zoar, the sun had risen over the land. Then the Lord rained down burning sulfur on Sodom and Gomorrah—from the Lord out of the heavens. Thus he overthrew those cities and the entire plain, including all those living in the cities—and also the vegetation in the land. But Lot's wife looked back, and she became a pillar of salt.

John 11:1–44

Now a man named Lazarus was sick. He was from Bethany, the village of Mary and her sister Martha. This Mary, whose brother Lazarus now lay sick, was the same one who poured perfume on the Lord and wiped his feet with her hair. So the sisters sent word to Jesus, "Lord, the one you love is sick."

When he heard this, Jesus said, "This sickness will not end in death. No, it is for God's glory so that God's Son may be glorified through it." Jesus loved Martha and her sister and Lazarus. Yet when he heard that Lazarus was sick, he stayed where he was two more days.

Then he said to his disciples, "Let us go back to Judea."

"But Rabbi," they said, "a short while ago the Jews tried to stone you, and yet you are going back there?"

Jesus answered, "Are there not twelve hours of daylight? A man who walks by day will not stumble, for he sees by this world's light. It is when he walks by night that he stumbles, for he has no light."

After he had said this, he went on to tell them, "Our friend Lazarus has fallen asleep; but I am going there to wake him up."

His disciples replied, "Lord, if he sleeps, he will get better." Jesus had been speaking of his death, but his disciples thought he meant natural sleep.

So then he told them plainly, "Lazarus is dead, and for your sake I am glad I was not there, so that you may believe. But let us go to him."

Then Thomas (called Didymus) said to the rest of the disciples, "Let us also go, that we may die with him."

On his arrival, Jesus found that Lazarus had already been in the tomb for four days. Bethany was less than two miles from Jerusalem, and many Jews had come to Martha and Mary to comfort them in the loss of their brother. When Martha heard that Jesus was coming, she went out to meet him, but Mary stayed at home.

"Lord," Martha said to Jesus, "if you had been here, my brother would not have died. But I know that even now God will give you whatever you ask."

Jesus said to her, "Your brother will rise again."

List #82 **Key Bible Memory Verses** *(continued)*

Martha answered, "I know he will rise again in the resurrection at the last day."

Jesus said to her, "I am the resurrection and the life. He who believes in me will live, even though he dies; and whoever lives and believes in me will never die. Do you believe this?"

"Yes, Lord," she told him, "I believe that you are the Christ, the Son of God, who was to come into the world."

And after she had said this, she went back and called her sister Mary aside. "The Teacher is here," she said, "and is asking for you." When Mary heard this, she got up quickly and went to him. Now Jesus had not yet entered the village, but was still at the place where Martha had met him. When the Jews who had been with Mary in the house, comforting her, noticed how quickly she got up and went out, they followed her, supposing she was going to the tomb to mourn there.

When Mary reached the place where Jesus was and saw him, she fell at his feet and said, "Lord, if you had been here, my brother would not have died."

When Jesus saw her weeping, and the Jews who had come along with her also weeping, he was deeply moved in spirit and troubled. "Where have you laid him?" he asked.

"Come and see, Lord," they replied.

Jesus wept.

Then the Jews said, "See how he loved him!"

But some of them said, "Could not he who opened the eyes of the blind man have kept this man from dying?"

Jesus, once more deeply moved, came to the tomb. It was a cave with a stone laid across the entrance. "Take away the stone," he said.

"But, Lord," said Martha, the sister of the dead man, "by this time there is a bad odor, for he has been there four days."

Then Jesus said, "Did I not tell you that if you believed, you would see the glory of God?"

So they took away the stone. Then Jesus looked up and said, "Father, I thank you that you have heard me. I knew that you always hear me, but I said this for the benefit of the people standing here, that they may believe that you sent me."

When he had said this, Jesus called in a loud voice, "Lazarus, come out!" The dead man came out, his hands and feet wrapped with strips of linen, and a cloth around his face.

Jesus said to them, "Take off the grave clothes and let him go."

List #82 **Key Bible Memory Verses** *(continued)*

1 John 4:7–21

Dear friends, let us love one another, for love comes from God. Everyone who loves has been born of God and knows God. Whoever does not love does not know God, because God is love. This is how God showed his love among us: He sent his one and only Son into the world that we might live through him. This is love: not that we loved God, but that he loved us and sent his Son as an atoning sacrifice for our sins. Dear friends, since God so loved us, we also ought to love one another. No one has ever seen God; but if we love one another, God lives in us and his love is made complete in us.

We know that we live in him and he in us, because he has given us of his Spirit. And we have seen and testify that the Father has sent his Son to be the Savior of the world. If anyone acknowledges that Jesus is the Son of God, God lives in him and he in God. And so we know and rely on the love God has for us.

God is love. Whoever lives in love lives in God, and God in him. In this way, love is made complete among us so that we will have confidence on the day of judgment, because in this world we are like him. There is no fear in love. But perfect love drives out fear, because fear has to do with punishment. The one who fears is not made perfect in love.

We love because he first loved us. If anyone says, "I love God," yet hates his brother, he is a liar. For anyone who does not love his brother, whom he has seen, cannot love God, whom he has not seen. And he has given us this command: Whoever loves God must also love his brother.

Matthew 4:18–22

As Jesus was walking beside the Sea of Galilee, he saw two brothers, Simon called Peter and his brother Andrew. They were casting a net into the lake, for they were fishermen. "Come, follow me," Jesus said, "and I will make you fishers of men." At once they left their nets and followed him. Going on from there, he saw two other brothers, James son of Zebedee and his brother John. They were in a boat with their father Zebedee, preparing their nets. Jesus called them, and immediately they left the boat and their father and followed him.

Matthew 5:43–48

You have heard that it was said, "Love your neighbor and hate your enemy." But I tell you: Love your enemies and pray for those who persecute you, that you may be sons of your Father in heaven. He causes his sun to rise on the evil and the good, and sends rain on the righteous and the unrighteous.

If you love those who love you, what reward will you get? Are not even the tax collectors doing that? And if you greet only your brothers, what are you doing more than others? Do not even pagans do that? Be perfect, therefore, as your heavenly Father is perfect.

Psalm 8:1–9

O Lord, our Lord, how majestic is your name in all the earth! You have set your glory above the heavens. From the lips of children and infants you have ordained praise because of your enemies, to silence the foe and the avenger. When I consider your heavens, the work of your fingers, the moon and the stars, which you have set in place, what is man that you are mindful of him, the son of man that you care for him? You made him a little lower than the heavenly beings and crowned him with glory and honor. You made him ruler over the works of your hands; you put everything under his feet: all flocks and herds, and the beasts of the field, the birds of the air, and the fish of the sea, all that swim the paths of the seas. O Lord, our Lord, how majestic is your name in all the earth!

Psalm 100:1–5

Shout for joy to the Lord, all the earth. Worship the Lord with gladness; come before him with joyful songs. Know that the Lord is God. It is he who made us, and we are his; we are his people, the sheep of his pasture. Enter his gates with thanksgiving and his courts with praise; give thanks to him and praise his name. For the Lord is good and his love endures forever; his faithfulness continues through all generations.

Psalm 92:1–15

It is good to praise the Lord and make music to your name, O Most High, to proclaim your love in the morning and your faithfulness at night, to the music of the ten-stringed lyre and the melody of the harp. For you make me glad by your deeds, O Lord; I sing for joy at the works of your hands. How great are your works, O Lord, how profound your thoughts!

The senseless man does not know, fools do not understand, that though the wicked spring up like grass and all evildoers flourish, they will be forever destroyed. But you, O Lord, are exalted forever. For surely your enemies, O Lord, surely your enemies will perish; all evildoers will be scattered. You have exalted my horn like that of a wild ox; fine oils have been poured upon

List #82 **Key Bible Memory Verses** *(continued)*

me. My eyes have seen the defeat of my adversaries; my ears have heard the rout of my wicked foes.

The righteous will flourish like a palm tree, they will grow like a cedar of Lebanon; planted in the house of the Lord, they will flourish in the courts of our God. They will still bear fruit in old age, they will stay fresh and green, proclaiming, "The Lord is upright; he is my Rock, and there is no wickedness in him."

Proverbs 16:28

A perverse man stirs up dissension, and a gossip separates close friends.

Psalm 95:1–11

Come, let us sing for joy to the Lord; let us shout aloud to the Rock of our salvation. Let us come before him with thanksgiving and extol him with music and song.

For the Lord is the great God, the great King above all gods. In his hand are the depths of the earth, and the mountain peaks belong to him. The sea is his, for he made it, and his hands formed the dry land.

Come, let us bow down in worship, let us kneel before the Lord our Maker; for he is our God and we are the people of his pasture, the flock under his care.

Today, if you hear his voice, do not harden your hearts as you did at Meribah, as you did that day at Massah in the desert, where your fathers tested and tried me, though they had seen what I did. For forty years I was angry with that generation; I said, "They are a people whose hearts go astray, and they have not known my ways." So I declared on oath in my anger, "They shall never enter my rest."

Psalm 150:1–6

Praise the Lord. Praise God in his sanctuary; praise him in his mighty heavens. Praise him for his acts of power; praise him for his surpassing greatness. Praise him with the sounding of the trumpet, praise him with the harp and lyre, praise him with tambourine and dancing, praise him with the strings and flute, praise him with the clash of cymbals, praise him with resounding cymbals. Let everything that has breath praise the Lord. Praise the Lord.

List #82 **Key Bible Memory Verses** *(continued)*

Matthew 6:5–15

And when you pray, do not be like the hypocrites, for they love to pray standing in the synagogues and on the street corners to be seen by men. I tell you the truth, they have received their reward in full. But when you pray, go into your room, close the door and pray to your Father, who is unseen. Then your Father, who sees what is done in secret, will reward you. And when you pray, do not keep on babbling like pagans, for they think they will be heard because of their many words. Do not be like them, for your Father knows what you need before you ask him.

This, then, is how you should pray:

"Our Father in heaven, hallowed be your name, your kingdom come, your will be done on earth as it is in heaven. Give us today our daily bread. Forgive us our debts, as we also have forgiven our debtors. And lead us not into temptation, but deliver us from the evil one."

For if you forgive men when they sin against you, your heavenly Father will also forgive you. But if you do not forgive men their sins, your Father will not forgive your sins.

Luke 18:9–14

To some who were confident of their own righteousness and looked down on everybody else, Jesus told this parable: "Two men went up to the temple to pray, one a Pharisee and the other a tax collector. The Pharisee stood up and prayed about himself: 'God, I thank you that I am not like other men—robbers, evildoers, adulterers—or even like this tax collector. I fast twice a week and give a tenth of all I get.' But the tax collector stood at a distance. He would not even look up to heaven, but beat his breast and said, 'God, have mercy on me, a sinner.' I tell you that this man, rather than the other, went home justified before God. For everyone who exalts himself will be humbled, and he who humbles himself will be exalted."

James 2:20–24

You foolish man, do you want evidence that faith without deeds is useless? Was not our ancestor Abraham considered righteous for what he did when he offered his son Isaac on the altar? You see that his faith and his actions were working together, and his faith was made complete by what he did. And the scripture was fulfilled that says, "Abraham believed God, and it was credited to him as righteousness," and he was called God's friend. You see that a person is justified by what he does and not by faith alone.

List #82 **Key Bible Memory Verses** *(continued)*

John 15:12–27

My command is this: Love each other as I have loved you. Greater love has no one than this, that he lay down his life for his friends. You are my friends if you do what I command. I no longer call you servants, because a servant does not know his master's business. Instead, I have called you friends, for everything that I learned from my Father I have made known to you. You did not choose me, but I chose you and appointed you to go and bear fruit—fruit that will last. Then the Father will give you whatever you ask in my name. This is my command: Love each other.

If the world hates you, keep in mind that it hated me first. If you belonged to the world, it would love you as its own. As it is, you do not belong to the world, but I have chosen you out of the world. That is why the world hates you. Remember the words I spoke to you: "No servant is greater than his master." If they persecuted me, they will persecute you also. If they obeyed my teaching, they will obey yours also. They will treat you this way because of my name, for they do not know the One who sent me. If I had not come and spoken to them, they would not be guilty of sin. Now, however, they have no excuse for their sin. He who hates me hates my Father as well. If I had not done among them what no one else did, they would not be guilty of sin. But now they have seen these miracles, and yet they have hated both me and my Father. But this is to fulfill what is written in their Law: "They hated me without reason."

When the Counselor comes, whom I will send to you from the Father, the Spirit of truth who goes out from the Father, he will testify about me. And you also must testify, for you have been with me from the beginning.

Ecclesiastes 5:18–20

Then I realized that it is good and proper for a man to eat and drink, and to find satisfaction in his toilsome labor under the sun during the few days of life God has given him—for this is his lot. Moreover, when God gives any man wealth and possessions, and enables him to enjoy them, to accept his lot and be happy in his work—this is a gift of God. He seldom reflects on the days of his life, because God keeps him occupied with gladness of heart.

Ecclesiastes 7:9

Do not be quickly provoked in your spirit, for anger resides in the lap of fools.

List #82 **Key Bible Memory Verses** *(continued)*

Ephesians 4:31

Get rid of all bitterness, rage and anger, brawling and slander, along with every form of malice.

Joel 2:13

Rend your heart and not your garments. Return to the Lord your God, for he is gracious and compassionate, slow to anger and abounding in love, and he relents from sending calamity.

Psalm 5:1–12

Give ear to my words, O Lord, consider my sighing. Listen to my cry for help, my King and my God, for to you I pray. In the morning, O Lord, you hear my voice; in the morning I lay my requests before you and wait in expectation.

You are not a God who takes pleasure in evil; with you the wicked cannot dwell. The arrogant cannot stand in your presence; you hate all who do wrong. You destroy those who tell lies; bloodthirsty and deceitful men the Lord abhors.

But I, by your great mercy, will come into your house; in reverence will I bow down toward your holy temple. Lead me, O Lord, in your righteousness because of my enemies—make straight your way before me.

Not a word from their mouth can be trusted; their heart is filled with destruction. Their throat is an open grave; with their tongue they speak deceit. Declare them guilty, O God! Let their intrigues be their downfall. Banish them for their many sins, for they have rebelled against you.

But let all who take refuge in you be glad; let them ever sing for joy. Spread your protection over them, that those who love your name may rejoice in you. For surely, O Lord, you bless the righteous; you surround them with your favor as with a shield.

Galatians 5:22–23

But the fruit of the Spirit is love, joy, peace, patience, kindness, goodness, faithfulness, gentleness and self-control. Against such things there is no law.

List #82 **Key Bible Memory Verses** *(continued)*

Zephaniah 2:3

Seek the Lord, all you humble of the land, you who do what he commands. Seek righteousness, seek humility; perhaps you will be sheltered on the day of the Lord's anger.

Titus 2

You must teach what is in accord with sound doctrine. Teach the older men to be temperate, worthy of respect, self-controlled, and sound in faith, in love and in endurance.

Likewise, teach the older women to be reverent in the way they live, not to be slanderers or addicted to much wine, but to teach what is good. Then they can train the younger women to love their husbands and children, to be self-controlled and pure, to be busy at home, to be kind, and to be subject to their husbands, so that no one will malign the word of God.

Similarly, encourage the young men to be self-controlled. In everything set them an example by doing what is good. In your teaching show integrity, seriousness and soundness of speech that cannot be condemned, so that those who oppose you may be ashamed because they have nothing bad to say about us.

Teach slaves to be subject to their masters in everything, to try to please them, not to talk back to them, and not to steal from them, but to show that they can be fully trusted, so that in every way they will make the teaching about God our Savior attractive.

For the grace of God that brings salvation has appeared to all men. It teaches us to say "No" to ungodliness and worldly passions, and to live self-controlled, upright and godly lives in this present age, while we wait for the blessed hope—the glorious appearing of our great God and Savior, Jesus Christ, who gave himself for us to redeem us from all wickedness and to purify for himself a people that are his very own, eager to do what is good.

These, then, are the things you should teach. Encourage and rebuke with all authority. Do not let anyone despise you.

Titus 3:1–2

Remind the people to be subject to rulers and authorities, to be obedient, to be ready to do whatever is good, to slander no one, to be peaceable and considerate, and to show true humility toward all men.

List #83 The Plan of Salvation

If you are interested in knowing more about becoming a Christian, or you or your child would like to know more about how to share the story of God's love for us, this is a good list to have. The verses listed would be great for memory verses as well. They will not only remain in your child's heart, but perhaps someday God can use those verses written upon your child's heart as a witness to someone else.*

1. All Are Sinners
"For all have sinned and fall short of the glory of God."

Romans 3:23

2. The Reason All Are Sinners
"Therefore, just as sin entered the the world through one man, and death through sin, and in this way death came to all men, because all sinned."

Romans 5:12

3. The Result of Sin
"For the wages of sin is death, but the gift of God is eternal life in Christ Jesus our Lord."

Romans 6:23

4. God's Love for Sinners
"But God demonstrates his own love for us in this: While we were still sinners, Christ died for us."

Romans 5:8

5. God's Assurance of Salvation
"If you confess with your mouth, 'Jesus is Lord,' and believe in your heart that God raised him from the dead, you will be saved. For it is with your heart that you believe and are justified, and it is with your mouth that you confess and are saved."

Romans 10:9–10

*I asked my pastor and his wife, Art and Bonnie Joyce, for help with this list. They suggested these points, but thought they were from a program called "The Roman Road." While I can't locate its original source and give proper credit, I want to mention it here lest anyone think I "created" it. I didn't! The Lord has placed the right people in my life to help with things like this. Thank you, Art and Bonnie, for your help! I hope many homeschoolers are able to memorize this list and use the information to glorify the Lord. (Adapted to reflect NIV, the version used in the rest of this book.)

5

Science

List #84 Renowned Scientists

Ampère, André Marie	1775–1836	A teacher in Paris, Ampère's name was immortalized in science when it was given to the unit we use to measure electrical current.
Bernouilli, Daniel	1700–1782	Established Bernouilli's principle, which explains why a fixed wing airplane, because of the wing's shape, will stay in the air once it is moving.
Blackwell, Elizabeth	1821–1910	The first woman physician in the United States.
Bohr, Niels Henrik David	1885–1962	Won the Nobel Prize in Physics for his work on the structure of atoms and the radiation that emanates from them.
Born, Max	1882–1970	Won the Nobel Prize in Physics for his research in quantum mechanics.
Boyle, Robert	1627–1691	Boyle is known as the "Father of Modern Chemistry" because he was the first scientist to separate chemistry from alchemy. Boyle also gave the first precise definitions of a chemical element, a chemical reaction, and chemical analysis.
Bruno, Giordano	1548–1600	Burned at the stake for his beliefs, such as that the universe was enormous.
Bunsen, Robert Wilhelm	1811–1899	German scientist who perfected the burner that was originally invented by Michael Faraday, but eventually named after Bunsen. He discovered cesium and rubidium and is considered the founder of modern gas analysis methods.
Burbank, Luther	1849–1926	The thirteenth of fifteen children, Burbank grew up on a farm and received minimal formal education. He experimented with different plants—fruits, flowers, grains, grasses, and vegetables—until he came up with the best variety. Burbank was an amazing pioneer in agricultural science.
Cavendish, Henry	1731–1810	British scientist who is generally credited with discovering hydrogen.
Charles, Jacques Alexander César	1746–1823	French scientist who stated Charles's Law, which states that a rise in temperature expands the volume of gas. He became one of the first balloonists.
Clerk-Maxwell, James	1831–1879	Published *Treatise on Electricity and Magnetism* in 1873. This was his initial contribution to electromagnetic radiation.
Copernicus, Nicolas	1473–1543	An astronomer who contributed the first theories of the sun as the center of the solar system.

List #84 **Renowned Scientists** *(continued)*

Curie, Marie	1867–1934	With her husband, Pierre, and Henri Becquerel, Curie won the 1903 Nobel Prize in Physics for research of radiation. She also won the 1911 Nobel Prize in Chemistry, making her the first woman to win a Nobel Prize and the first person to win the prize twice. Curie was born in Poland and named Marya Sklodowska.
Curie, Pierre	1859–1906	Won the 1903 Nobel Prize in Physics for his research of radiation. Pierre and his wife, Marie, discovered two new elements, radium and polonium, that changed many facets of physics and chemistry. As a child, he was educated at home by his father.
Darwin, Charles	1809–1882	Darwin proposed and advocated the theory of natural selection—that all things have evolved over time into what they are today.
Davy, Sir Humphrey	1778–1829	As a young man, he served as an apprentice to a surgeon and conducted chemical experiments. He later discovered many metals not commonly found in their pure state, such as potassium, sodium, barium, and strontium. His most famous invention, which most likely saved many lives, was a safety lamp for coal miners.
Dulong, Pierre Louis	1785–1838	Dulong was a French chemist who worked with Alexis Petit to establish Dulong and Petit's Law, which states that all chemical elements have approximately the same atomic heat.
Einstein, Albert	1879–1955	German physicist who introduced new concepts to science such as the Theory of Relativity and the Electromagnetic Theory of Light. He won the 1921 Nobel Prize in Physics.
Euclid	c. 300 BC	Greek mathematician who may have written numerous works that are now lost to history. However, his work *Elements* did survive and is used today as a fundamental geometry textbook.
Faraday, Michael	1791–1867	Credited with the discovery of electromagnetic induction in 1821. He also described certain elements and chemical compounds. Faraday was Sir Humphrey Davy's personal assistant at the Royal Society.
Fleming, Alexander	1881–1955	Discovered the enzyme lysyme; his most notable "discovery" was the isolation of penicillin, for which he shared the Nobel Prize in 1945 with Howard Florey and Ernst Chain.
Galen	c. 130–201	Credited with being the first physician to give a diagnosis by taking a person's pulse.

List #84 **Renowned Scientists** *(continued)*

Galileo	1564–1642	Referred to as the "Father of Modern Astronomy," Galileo supported Copernican theories and further developed proof that the sun is the center of the solar system.
Halley, Edmund	1656–1742	An amazing astronomer, geophysicist, mathematician, meteorologist, and physicist who made mostly lunar observations, but contributed much to all fields.
Herschel, Sir John Frederick William	1792–1871	Sir William Herschel's son continued his work in astronomy by discovering numerous nebulae. He was also the first astronomer to use photography.
Herschel, Sir William	1738–1822	Built a reflecting telescope in 1773–74. He proceeded to discover the planet Uranus and uncover other unknown facts about the universe.
Hertz, Gustav Ludwig	1887–1975	Won the 1925 Nobel Prize in Physics for his work and discovery of the impact electrons have on atoms.
Hipparchus	160–125 BC	Ahead of his time with astronomical research, Hipparchus discovered the procession of the equinoxes, determined the length of a solar year, estimated the distances of the sun and the moon from the Earth, invented trigonometry, catalogued 1,080 stars, and fixed the longitudinal and latitudinal geographic positions of various locations.
Hippocrates	460–377 BC	Frequently referred to as the "Father of Medicine," Hippocrates believed that illness had rational explanations. He established a medical school on the Greek island of Cos, and it is likely that he devised the Hippocratic Oath, which states that doctors will "do no harm" to their patients.
Hooke, Robert	1635–1703	Reported that bodies of material can be extended or compressed. Hooke was one of the greatest scientists of the 17th century, though his name has become obscure today. He authored *Micrographia* in 1665, which was a magnificent work of biological studies.
Huygens, Christiaan	1629–1693	Discovered the ring and fourth satellite of Saturn in 1655. In 1657, he created the pendulum clock.
Hypatia	370–415	From the few existing records concerning Hypatia, we know she was a female philosopher and teacher who specialized in mathematics, astronomy, and astrology.
Kelvin, Lord William Thomson	1824–1907	A scientist and inventor, he is most known for his work in thermodynamics, static electricity, and magnetic phenomena.

List #84 **Renowned Scientists** *(continued)*

Kepler, Johann	1571–1630	Most known for his three laws of planetary motion, Kepler's research formed the foundation for Isaac Newton's discoveries.
Leslie, Sir John	1766–1832	A professor at the University of Edinburgh, Leslie invented items such as the differential thermometer, the hygrometer, the pyroscope, and the atmometer.
Lyell, Sir Charles	1797–1875	The eldest of ten children, Lyell left his work as a lawyer and entered geology as a profession. His book *Principles of Geology* established Lyell's importance as a geological theorist.
Mendel, Gregor Johann	1822–1884	Through his studies of heredity, Mendel established that there are dominant and recessive characteristics in living things.
Oppenheimer, J. Robert	1904–1967	Specialized in the study of electron-positron pairs, cosmic rays, and deuteron reactions. He helped devise the nuclear bomb, which brought World War II to an end, but also brought much doubt to Oppenheimer and others about the wisdom of using such devastating devices.
Pasteur, Louis	1822–1895	French chemist who made great advances in the science of microbiology. He developed the process of pasteurization and developed a vaccine for rabies.
Planck, Max	1858–1947	Physicist who entered the University of Munich at the age of 16 and received his doctorate at the age of 21. His doctoral thesis was on the second law of thermodynamics. He received the 1918 Nobel Prize in Physics.
Röntgen, Wilhelm Conrad	1845–1923	Röntgen won the first Nobel Prize in Physics in 1901 for his discovery of Xrays.
Teller, Edward	1908–2003	Known as the "Father of the Hydrogen Bomb," Teller was a Hungarian-born physicist who worked with J. Robert Oppenheimer to develop the first earthbound thermonuclear explosion.
Torricelli, Evangelista	1608–1647	We remember this Italian scientist as the man who invented the "Torricellian tube," which addresses atmospheric pressure. He also helped improve the telescope and the microscope.
Volta, Count Alessandro	1745–1827	This Italian physicist will forever be remembered for giving us the label *volt,* which is used to describe a unit of electric pressure. He developed the theory of current electricity and invented the electric battery.
Watson, James Dewey	b. 1928	An American scientist, he is one of four scientists who discovered the structure of the DNA molecule. Watson, along with two other scientists, was awarded the 1962 Nobel Prize in Physiology or Medicine.

List #85 Significant Scientific Dates and Discoveries

c. 2540 BC	pyramids of Egypt constructed
c. 2000 BC	magnetic attraction discovered by the Chinese
17th century BC	Venus tablet of Ammisaduqa—contained the first known Babylonian astronomical observations
7th century BC	electric attraction discovered by the Greeks
c. 530 BC	Pythagoras develops mathematical theory
3rd century BC	Eratosthenes measures the size of the Earth and the distance to the sun and moon
c. 150 BC	Ptolemy proposes the Earth as the center of the solar system
1220–1235	Robert Grosseteste lays the groundwork foundation for the proper study of science, which eventually leads to the scientific method
Before 1327	English philosopher William of Ockham produces significant works in the areas of logic, physics, and theology
1543	Copernicus states that the Earth revolves around the sun
1543	discoveries of anatomy by Andreas Vesalius, a Belgian physician, help correct misconceptions about the body that had been believed since ancient times and pave the way for modern medicine
1552	Michael Servetus discovers pulmonary circulation
1609	Johannes Kepler, a German mathematician, astrologer, and astronomer, states the first two laws of planetary motion
1610	Galileo Galilei writes *Sidereus Nuncius (Starry Messenger),* which contains telescopic observations of the moon, the stars, and the moons of Jupiter
1614	John Napier uses logarithms for calculation
1628	William Harvey discovers blood circulation
1637	René Descartes establishes scientific method
1643	Evangelista Torricelli invents the mercury barometer
1662	Robert Boyle states one of the "gas laws," which become known as Boyle's law of ideal gas: the product of the pressure and volume of a fixed quantity of gas, as long as it is held at a fixed temperature, is equal to a constant
1665	The first peer-reviewed scientific journal, *Philosophical Transactions of the Royal Society,* is published
1669	Nicholas Steno proposes that fossils are actually organic remains embedded in layers of sediment. This can be considered the beginning of paleontology.
1675	Leibniz and Newton introduce the principles of basic calculus, which strongly influences the development of physics

List #85 **Significant Scientific Dates and Discoveries** *(continued)*

1676	Ole Romer makes the first measurement of the speed of light
1687	Isaac Newton states the laws of motion and law of universal gravitation, the basis for classical physics
1714	Gabriel Fahrenheit invents the mercury thermometer
1745	Ewald Jürgen Georg von Kleist invents the first capacitor, the Leyden jar
1750	Joseph Black describes latent heat
1751	Benjamin Franklin determines that lightning is electrical
1787	Lavoisier determines the law of conservation of mass, which forms the basis for chemistry
1796	Georges Cuvier establishes extinction as a fact
1799	William Smith publishes a geological map of England— the first geological map ever. He also applies stratigraphy for the first time.
1800	Alessandro Volta develops the electric battery
1805	John Dalton devises the atomic theory
1827	Georg Ohm devises Ohm's law of electricity
1838	Matthias Schleiden reports that all plants are made of cells
1843	James Prescott Joule states the law of conservation of energy (or the first law of thermodynamics)
1847	William Morton discovers anesthesia
1848	Lord Kelvin determines the absolute zero of temperature
1859	Charles Darwin and Alfred Wallace introduce the theory of evolution by natural selection
1865	Gregor Mendel states Mendel's laws of inheritance, which becomes the basis for genetics
1869	Dmitri Mendeleev devises a system for organizing the chemical elements—the Periodic Table
1873	James Clerk Maxwell states the theory of electromagnetism
1875	Josiah Willard Gibbs founds chemical thermodynamics
1895	Wilhelm Conrad Röntgen discovers Xrays
1900	Max Planck states Planck's law of black body radiation, which forms the basis for quantum theory
1905	Albert Einstein states the special theory of relativity
1906	Walther Nernst states the third law of thermodynamics
1913	Henry Moseley defines the atomic number
1915	Albert Einstein states the general theory of relativity

List #85 **Significant Scientific Dates and Discoveries** *(continued)*

1927	Werner Heisenberg states the uncertainty principle that applies to quantum mechanics
1927	Georges Lemaître presents the theory of the Big Bang
1929	Edwin Hubble presents Hubble's law of the expanding universe
1943	Oswald Avery proves that DNA (deoxyribonucleic acid) is the genetic material of the chromosome
1947	William Shockley, John Bardeen, and Walter Brattain invent the first transistor
1953	Francis Crick and James Dewey Watson determine the helical structure of DNA, which forms the basis of molecular biology
1965	Leonard Hayflick determines that normal cells only divide a certain number of times. This limit is called the Hayflick limit.
1967	Jocelyn Bell Burnell and Antony Hewish discover the first pulsar
2001	The first draft of the human genome is completed

List #86 Major Inventions

Date	Invention	Inventor/Discoverer (if known)	Nationality
c. 399 BC	catapult	Dionysius the Elder of Syracuse	Greek
c. 250 BC	Archimedian screw, described use of lever, and other inventions	Archimedes	Greek
c. 200 BC	astrolabe (used to determine altitude of stellar objects)		Greek
105	paper (however, papyrus had been used as "paper" in Egypt for many centuries before this)	Ts'ai Lun	Chinese
132	seismometer	Zhang Heng	Chinese
c. 900	gunpowder (used at first to treat skin disorders and later as a weapon)		Chinese
c. 1023	paper money		Chinese
c. 1045	movable type printing	Bi Sheng	Chinese
c. 1050	crossbow		French
1182	magnetic compass		probably Chinese
c. 1202	Hindu-Arabic numbering system	Fibonacci	Italian
1249	gunpowder (wrote formula)	Roger Bacon	English
c. 1250	gun		Chinese
1250	magnifying glass	Roger Bacon	English
1268–1289	eyeglasses	(most likely) Alessandro della Spina and Salvino degli Armati	Italian
late medieval period	sawmill		
1366	scales to use for weighing		

List #86 **Major Inventions** *(continued)*

Date	Invention	Inventor/Discoverer (if known)	Nationality
c. 1400	double-armed catapult	Mariano Taccola	Italian
1420	oil painting	Hubert and Jan van Eyck	Flemish
c. 1450	anemometer (measures speed of wind)	Leon Battista Alberti	Italian
1450	printing press with movable type	Johann Gutenberg	German
1476	England's first printing press and standardization of English language	William Caxton set up England's first printing press and refused to print regional dialect and language variations, so he essentially forced standardization of the English language.	English
1490–1492	globe (earliest globe was called "Nürnberg Terrestrial Globe")	Martin Behaim	German
late 1400s/ early 1500s	water wheel, worm gear (a set of gears with many teeth bearing the pressure), idea of flying machines	Leonardo da Vinci	Italian
1504	pocket watch	Peter Henlein	German
1513	etching	Urs Graf	Swiss/German
1564	"lead" pencil	created after a huge graphite mine was discovered in England (and it was only learned later that graphite consists of carbon, not lead)	English
1589	knitting machine	William Lee	English
1590	compound microscope	Hans and Zacharias Janssen (a father and son team who made eyeglasses)	Dutch
1593	water thermometer	Galileo	Italian
1608	telescope	Hans Lippershey	Dutch
1622	slide ruler	William Oughtred	English
1625	blood transfusion	Jean-Baptiste Denys	French

List #86 **Major Inventions** *(continued)*

Date	Invention	Inventor/Discoverer (if known)	Nationality
1629	steam turbine	Giovanni Branca	Italian
1642	arithmetic machine	Blaise Pascal	French
1643	barometer	Evangelista Torricelli	Italian
1650	air pump	Otto von Guericke	German
1656	pendulum clock	Christiaan Huygens	Dutch
1661	methanol	Robert Boyle	Irish
1663	reflecting telescope	James Gregory (He described it, but never actually made it.)	Scottish
1668	Newtonian telescope	Isaac Newton (Newton improved the design of Lippershey's 1608 telescope.)	English
1671	calculating machine	Gottfried Wilhelm Leibniz	German
1676	universal joint	Robert Hooke	English
1679	pressure cooker	Denis Papin	French
1698	steam pump	Thomas Savery	English
1701	seed drill	Jethro Tull	English
c. 1710	piano	Bartolomeo Cristofori	Italian
1712	steam engine	Thomas Newcomen	British
1714	mercury thermometer	Daniel Gabriel Fahrenheit	German
1717	diving bell	Edmund Halley	English
1725	stereotyping	William Ged	Scottish
1742	Celsius thermometer	Anders Celsius	Swedish
1745	Leyden jar (a condenser)	E. G. von Kleist	German
1752	lightning rod/ conductor	Benjamin Franklin	American
1756	concrete (modern concrete with pebbles)	John Smeaton (Concrete had been used by Assyrians, Babylonians, Egyptians, and Chinese for centuries, but they used different bonding substances.)	British
1758	achromatic lens	John Dollond	British
1759	marine chronometer	John Harrison	British

List #86 **Major Inventions** *(continued)*

Date	Invention	Inventor/Discoverer (if known)	Nationality
1764	spinning jenny	James Hargreaves	British
1768	spinning frame	Richard Arkwright	English
1769	steam engine (with a separate condenser)	James Watt	British
1769	automobile	Nicholas-Joseph Cugnot	French
1774	telegraph (electric)	Georges Louis Lesage	Swiss (though his family was really French and fled to England and then Geneva)
1775	steamship	Jacques Perrier	French
1776	submarine	David Bushnell	American
1779	spinning mule	Samuel Crompton	English
1780	circular saw	Gervinus	German
1782	hot air balloon	Jacques and Joseph Montgolfier	French
1784	bifocal eyeglasses	Benjamin Franklin	American
1784	safety lock	Joseph Bramah	English
1785	chemical bleaching	Claude Berthollet	French
1792	gas lighting	William Murdoch	Scottish
1792	guillotine	Joseph-Ignace Guillotin (He didn't actually *invent* the guillotine—to which an "e" was added—but he did suggest it during this period of public executions and it was used until 1977 in France.)	French
1793	metric system (passed by law in France on August 1, 1793)	French committee of Jean Charles de Borda, Joseph-Louis Comte de Lagrange, Pierre-Simon Laplace, Gaspard Monge, Marie Jean Antoine, Nicholas Caritat	French
1794	cotton gin	Eli Whitney	American
1795	preserving jar (for food)	Nicolas François Appert	French

List #86 **Major Inventions** *(continued)*

Date	Invention	Inventor/Discoverer (if known)	Nationality
1798	interchangeable gun parts	Eli Whitney (Interchangeable parts had been used by clockmakers since the early 1700s, but Whitney successfully applied the principle to gun parts.)	American
1798	lithography	Johann Alois Senefelder	Austrian
1799	sheet paper making machine	Nicholas-Louis Robert	French
1800	electric light bulb	Humphrey Davy	English
1800	electric battery	Alessandro Giuseppe Antonio Volta	Italian
1802	woodworking planer	Joseph Bramah	English
1803	electric refrigerator	Thomas Moore	American
1804	locomotive	Richard Trevithick	English
1806	camera lucida	William Hyde Wollaston	English
1807	conveyor belt	Oliver Evans	American
1810	canning	Nicholas François Appert	French
1813	power loom	William Horrocks (improved Edmund Cartwright's 1785 design)	English
1823	waterproof material	Charles Macintosh	Scottish
1824	cement	Joseph Aspdin	English
1830	sewing machine (not patented)	Barthélemy Thimonnier (His workshop was destroyed by other tailors who feared the new "machine.")	French
1831	electric generator	Michael Faraday	English
1834	harvesting machine	Cyrus Hall McCormick	American
1834	sewing machine (like the 1830 version, it wasn't patented)	Walter Hunt (He didn't want to seek a patent because he feared a new sewing machine would put people out of work.)	American
1835	telegraph (in America)	Samuel Finley Breese Morse	American
1835	revolver	Samuel Colt	American
1835	computer	Charles Babbage	English

List #86 **Major Inventions** *(continued)*

Date	Invention	Inventor/Discoverer (if known)	Nationality
1839	daguerreotype (image on copper—a type of photograph)	Louis-Jacques-Mandé Daguerre	French
1839	photography (on paper)	William Henry Fox Talbot	English
1839	bicycle	Kirkpatrick Macmillan	Scottish
1841	saxophone	Adolphe Sax	Belgian
1843	underground railway	Charles Pearson	English
1845	rubber band	Stephen Perry	English
1845	hydraulic crane	William G. Armstrong	English
1846	sewing machine (first one patented)	Elias Howe	American
1846	rotary printing press	Richard March Hoe	American
1849	safety pin	Walter Hunt	American
1850	dishwasher (wasn't very effective)	Joel Houghton	American
1850	refrigerator	James Harrison and Alexander Twining	American; Australian
1851	mechanical elevator	Elisha Graves Otis	American
1851	Foucault pendulum	Jean Bernard Léon Foucault	French
1852	gyroscope	Jean Bernard Léon Foucault	French
1854	hydraulic elevator	Elisha Graves Otis (Invention was important because it spurred development of skyscrapers.)	American
1855	Bunsen burner	Robert Wilhelm Bunsen	German
1855	steel production	Henry Bessemer	English
1856	synthetic dye	William Henry Perkin	English
1860	lawn mower	Edwin Beard Budding	English
1861	color photography	James Clerk Maxwell	Scottish
1866	telegraph (transatlantic)	William Thompson	English
1867	typewriter	Christopher Latham Sholes	American
1867	pasteurization	Louis Pasteur	French

List #86 **Major Inventions** *(continued)*

Date	Invention	Inventor/Discoverer (if known)	Nationality
1868	tungsten steel	Robert Mushet	English
1868	traffic lights	J. P. Knight	English
1871	pneumatic drill	Samuel Ingersoll	English
1872	electric typewriter	Thomas Edison	American
1873	barbed wire (transformed American western frontier)	Joseph Glidden	American
1876	microphone	Alexander Graham Bell	Scottish
1876	telephone	Alexander Graham Bell	Scottish
1877	phonograph	Thomas Edison	American
1878	electric railway	Ernst Werner von Siemens	German
1879	dry plate method of photography	George Eastman	American
1879	electric lamp	Thomas Edison	American
1880	pendulum seismograph	James Ewing, Thomas Gray, Sir John Milne	British
1882	electric flat iron	Harry W. Seeley	American
1883	automatic machine gun	Sir Hiram Stevens Maxim	English-American
1884	fountain pen	Lewis E. Waterman	American
1884	car (internal combustion)	Gottlieb Daimler	German
1885	adding machine	William Seward Burroughs	American
1885	folding cabinet bed (to save space in small apartments)	Sarah E. Goode (first patent obtained by an African-American woman inventor)	American
1885	petrol engine	Gottlieb Daimler	German
1885	motorcycle	Gottlieb Daimler	German
1886	car (gas-powered)	Karl Friedrich Benz	German
1887	celluloid film	Hannibal Goodwin	American
1888	pneumatic tire	John Boyd Dunlop	Scottish
1888	alternating-current motor	Nikola Tesla	Serbian-American
1888	gramophone record	Emil Berliner	German

List #86 Major Inventions *(continued)*

Date	Invention	Inventor/Discoverer (if known)	Nationality
1889	dishwasher (that worked and was shown at 1893 World's Fair in Chicago)	Mrs. Josephine Garis Cochran	American
1889	photographic film	George Eastman	American
1891	escalator	Jesse Reno	American
1894	automatic loom	J. H. Northrop	English
1894	cinematograph	Auguste and Louis Lumière	French
1894	turbine ship	Charles Parsons	Irish
1895	Xray	Wilhelm Conrad von Röntgen	German
1898	diesel engine	Rudolf Christian Karl Diesel	German
1899	vacuum cleaner	John S. Thurman	American
1899 or 1900	paper clip	Johann Vaaler (a patent clerk who dealt with lots of paperwork!)	Norwegian
1900	push pins	Edwin Moore	American
1900	airship	Graf Ferdinand von Zeppelin	German
1901	radio (originally invented by Serbian-American inventor Nikola Tesla, but frequently credited to Marconi)	Guglielmo Marconi	Italian
1901	vacuum cleaner (electric)	Hubert Cecil Booth	English
1902	windshield wipers	Mary Anderson	American
1903	electrocardiograph	Wilhelm Einthoven	Dutch
1903	airplane	Orville and Wilbur Wright	American
1907	electric washing machine	Alva J. Fisher, introduced by Hurley Machine Company	American
1907	bakelite	Leo Bakeland	American
1911	neon light	Georges Claude	French
1913	stainless steel	Harry Brearly	English

List #86 **Major Inventions** *(continued)*

Date	Invention	Inventor/Discoverer (if known)	Nationality
1913–1914	mass production with assembly line	Henry Ford (Ransome Eli Olds had used a more primitive assembly line in 1901 to manufacture Oldsmobiles.)	American
1924	loudspeaker	Chester Rice and Edward Kellogg	American
1926	television	John Logie Baird	Scottish
1926	liquid fuel rocket	Robert Goddard	American
1932	parking meter	Carlton C. Magee	American
1933	electron microscope	Max Knoll and Ernst Ruska	German
1934	cat's eyes (road reflectors)	Percy Shaw	English
1937	turbo jet	Hans von Ohain and Sir Frank Whittle	German; English
1938	ballpoint pen	László and Georg Biró (brothers)	Hungarian-American
1938	nylon	Wallace Carothers	American
1938	xerography	Chester Carlson	American
1939	helicopter	Igor Ivanovich Sikorsky	Ukrainian-American
1939	atom bomb	Otto Frisch, Niels Bohr, and Rudolf Peierls	Austrian-British; Danish; German
1941	polyethylene terephthalate (a type of polyester used to make everything from soft drink bottles to clothing)	J. R. Whinfield and J. T. Dickson	British
1942	turbo-prop engine	Max Mueller	German
1945	microwave oven	Percy Le Baron Spencer	American
1948	transistor	William Shockley, John Bardeen, and Walter Brattain	British; American; American
1954	solar battery	Gerald Pearson, Calvin Fuller, Daryl Chapin (working for Bell Telephone Company)	American

List #86 **Major Inventions** *(continued)*

Date	Invention	Inventor/Discoverer (if known)	Nationality
1959	hovercraft	Christopher Cockerell	English
1959	microchip (considered one of the most important inventions in history)	Jack St. Clair Kilby and Robert Norton Noyce	American
1960	laser	Charles Townes	American
1966	pocket calculator	Jerry Merryman, James Van Tassel, Jack St. Clair Kilby (working for Texas Instruments)	American
1968	cellular phone	idea conceived by several companies, including NTT (Japanese) and AT&T and Bell Labs (American); also largely developed by Motorola	Japanese; American
1969	"test-tube" baby technique (in vitro fertilization)	Robert Edwards, Patrick Steptoe	English
1969	industrial robot	Victor Scheinman	American
1971	microprocessor	Marcian Edward Ted Hoff	American
1976	space shuttle	NASA	American
1978	TGV high-speed train		French
1979	Walkman	Sony	Japanese
1979	compact disc	Philips and Sony	Dutch; Japanese
1981	personal computer	IBM (designed first commercially successful personal computer)	American
1985	battery-powered vehicle	Clive Sinclair	British
1988	video Walkman	Sony	Japanese
1989	World Wide Web	Sir Timothy Berners-Lee	British
1993	Global Positioning System (GPS)	United States Department of Defense	American

List #86 **Major Inventions** *(continued)*

Date	Invention	Inventor/Discoverer (if known)	Nationality
1995	"wiki" concept (a collaborative Web site that can be edited by anyone with access to it)	Ward Cunningham	American
1996	cloning	first successful at Roslin Institute in Edinburgh, Scotland	Scottish
1997	DVD (Digital Versatile Disk)	several companies—based on patented idea of David Gregg	Gregg was American
1999	Tekno Bubbles	Byron and Melody Swetland	American
2000	Allurion (a prosthetic foot)	Flex-Foot, Inc.	Icelandic
2001	Abiocor Artificial Heart	Abiomed	American
2001	Hy-wire car	General Motors	American

List #87 Fields of Science

Biology
anatomy
astrobiology
biochemistry
bioinformatics
biophysics
biotechnology
botany
cell biology
cladistics
cytology
developmental biology
ecology
entomology
epidemiology
ethology
evolution
evolutionary developmental biology
freshwater biology
genetics
histology
immunology
marine biology
microbiology
molecular biology
morphology
neuroscience
ontogeny
phycology
phylogeny
physical anthropology
physical therapy
physiology
population dynamics
structural biology
taxonomy
toxicology
virology
zoology

Chemistry
analytical chemistry
biochemistry
computational chemistry
electrochemistry
inorganic chemistry
materials science
organic chemistry
physical chemistry
polymer chemistry
quantum chemistry
spectroscopy
stereochemistry
thermochemistry

Earth Sciences
biogeography
cartography
climatology
coastal geography
geodesy
geography
geology
geomorphology
geophysics
geostatistics
glaciology
hydrogeology
hydrology
limnology
meteorology
mineralogy

List #87 **Fields of Science** *(continued)*

oceanography
paleoclimatology
paleontology
petrology
seismology
soil science
topography
volcanology

Physics

acoustics
agrophysics
astrodynamics
astronomy
astrophysics
atomic, molecular, and optical physics
biophysics
computational physics
condensed matter physics
cosmology
cryogenics
dynamics
fluid dynamics
materials physics
mathematical physics
mechanics
nuclear physics
optics
particle physics
plasma physics
polymer physics
solid state
statics
thermodynamics
vehicle dynamics

List #88 Definitions of "-ology" Words

In Greek, *-ology* means "the study of" or "the science of" something. Listed here are the most common -ology words. Not all of these words are related to science, but because a good majority of them are, the list is in this chapter.

Word	Means "the study of . . ." or "the science of . . ."
anthropology	mankind; culture
archaeology	prehistory or historic people and cultures
audiology	hearing
bacteriology	bacteria
biology	life or living matter
cardiology	heart
chronology	time
climatology	climate
cosmology	universe
criminology	crime and criminals
cryptology	codes
cytology	cells
dermatology	skin
ecology	ecosystems
embryology	unborn children in the embryonic stage
entomology	insects
epidemiology	epidemics
ethology	animals in their natural surroundings
etymology	the origins of words
genealogy	family origins; ancestors
geology	the Earth
gerontology	aging and aged people
hemotology	blood
herpetology	reptiles
histology	tissue
hydrology	water
ideology	ideas; a body of doctrine
immunology	immunity; immune systems
meteorology	weather
mineralogy	minerals

List #88 **Definitions of "-ology" Words** *(continued)*

Word	Means "the study of . . ." or "the science of . . ."
morphology	structure of animals and plants
musicology	music
mythology	myths
neurology	nerves
oncology	tumors, including cancer
ornithology	birds
ophthalmology	eyes
paleontology	fossils
pathology	disease
pharmacology	drugs
physiology	living organisms
pomology	fruit
psychology	mind
radiology	radiation
seismology	earthquakes
sociology	society
technology	industrial arts
theology	God
toxicology	poisonous substances
virology	viruses
volcanology	volcanoes and volcanic activity
zoology	animals

List #89 Rainbow Colors

In his early physics experiments, Sir Isaac Newton decided the colors of the rainbow were Red, Orange, Yellow, Green, Blue, Indigo, and Violet. You can remember them as ROY G BIV. (There are actually many other colors in the rainbow, but these are widely accepted.)

List #90 Temperatures

water boils	100° C	=	212° F
water freezes	0° C	=	32° F
normal body temperature	37° C	=	98.6 F

List #91 Periodic Table of Elements

1 H																	2 He
3 Li	4 Be											5 B	6 C	7 N	8 O	9 F	10 Ne
11 Na	12 Mg											13 Al	14 Si	15 P	16 S	17 Cl	18 Ar
19 K	20 Ca	21 Sc	22 Ti	23 V	24 Cr	25 Mn	26 Fe	27 Co	28 Ni	29 Cu	30 Zn	31 Ga	32 Ge	33 As	34 Se	35 Br	36 Kr
37 Rb	38 Sr	39 Y	40 Zr	41 Nb	42 Mo	43 Tc	44 Ru	45 Rh	46 Pd	47 Ag	48 Cd	49 In	50 Sn	51 Sb	52 Te	53 I	54 Xe
55 Cs	56 Ba	*	72 Hf	73 Ta	74 W	75 Re	76 Os	77 Ir	78 Pt	79 Au	80 Hg	81 Tl	82 Pb	83 Bi	84 Po	85 At	86 Rn
87 Fr	88 Ra	**	104 Rf	105 Db	106 Sg	107 Bh	108 Hs	109 Mt	110 Ds	111 Rg	112 Uub	113 Uut	114 Uuq	115 Uup	116 Uuh	117 Uus	118 Uuo
		* Lanthanides	57 La	58 Ce	59 Pr	60 Nd	61 Pm	62 Sm	63 Eu	64 Gd	65 Tb	66 Dy	67 Ho	68 Er	69 Tm	70 Yb	71 Lu
		** Actinides	89 Ac	90 Th	91 Pa	92 U	93 Np	94 Pu	95 Am	96 Cm	97 Bk	98 Cf	99 Es	100 Fm	101 Md	102 No	103 Lr

List #92 Periodic Table of Elements Identification Guide

= Atomic Number S = Symbol Date Disc. = Date the element was discovered

#	S	Name	Atomic Weight	Date Disc.
1	H	Hydrogen	1.0079	1776
2	He	Helium	4.0026	1895
3	Li	Lithium	6.941	1817
4	Be	Beryllium	9.0122	1797
5	B	Boron	10.811	1808
6	C	Carbon	12.0107	ancient
7	N	Nitrogen	14.0067	1772
8	O	Oxygen	15.9994	1774
9	F	Fluorine	18.9984	1886
10	Ne	Neon	20.1797	1898
11	Na	Sodium	22.9897	1807
12	Mg	Magnesium	24.305	1755
13	Al	Aluminum	26.9815	1825
14	Si	Silicon	28.0855	1824
15	P	Phosphorus	30.9738	1669
16	S	Sulfur	32.065	ancient
17	Cl	Chlorine	35.453	1774
18	Ar	Argon	39.948	1894
19	K	Potassium	39.0983	1807
20	Ca	Calcium	40.078	1808
21	Sc	Scandium	44.9559	1879
22	Ti	Titanium	47.867	1791
23	V	Vanadium	50.9415	1830
24	Cr	Chromium	51.9961	1797
25	Mn	Manganese	54.938	1774
26	Fe	Iron	55.845	ancient
27	Co	Cobalt	58.9332	1735
28	Ni	Nickel	58.6934	1751
29	Cu	Copper	63.546	ancient
30	Zn	Zinc	65.39	ancient
31	Ga	Gallium	69.723	1875

List #92 Periodic Table of Elements Identification Guide *(continued)*

#	S	Name	Atomic Weight	Date Disc.
32	Ge	Germanium	72.64	1886
33	As	Arsenic	74.9216	ancient
34	Se	Selenium	78.96	1817
35	Br	Bromine	79.904	1826
36	Kr	Krypton	83.8	1898
37	Rb	Rubidium	85.4678	1861
38	Sr	Strontium	87.62	1790
39	Y	Yttrium	88.9059	1794
40	Zr	Zirconium	91.224	1789
41	Nb	Niobium	92.9064	1801
42	Mo	Molybdenum	95.94	1781
43	Tc	Technetium	98	1937
44	Ru	Ruthenium	101.07	1844
45	Rh	Rhodium	102.9055	1803
46	Pd	Palladium	106.42	1803
47	Ag	Silver	107.8682	ancient
48	Cd	Cadmium	112.411	1817
49	In	Indium	114.818	1863
50	Sn	Tin	118.71	ancient
51	Sb	Antimony	121.76	ancient
52	Te	Tellurium	127.6	1783
53	I	Iodine	126.9045	1811
54	Xe	Xenon	131.293	1898
55	Cs	Cesium	132.9055	1860
56	Ba	Barium	137.327	1808
57	La	Lanthanum	138.9055	1839
58	Ce	Cerium	140.116	1803
59	Pr	Praseodymium	140.9077	1885
60	Nd	Neodymium	144.24	1885
61	Pm	Promethium	145	1945
62	Sm	Samarium	150.36	1879
63	Eu	Europium	151.964	1901
64	Gd	Gadolinium	157.25	1880
65	Tb	Terbium	158.9253	1843

List #92 **Periodic Table of Elements Identification Guide** *(continued)*

#	S	Name	Atomic Weight	Date Disc.
66	Dy	Dysprosium	162.5	1886
67	Ho	Holmium	164.9303	1867
68	Er	Erbium	167.259	1842
69	Tm	Thulium	168.9342	1879
70	Yb	Ytterbium	173.04	1878
71	Lu	Lutetium	174.967	1907
72	Hf	Hafnium	178.49	1923
73	Ta	Tantalum	180.9479	1802
74	W	Tungsten	183.84	1783
75	Re	Rhenium	186.207	1925
76	Os	Osmium	190.23	1803
77	Ir	Iridium	192.217	1803
78	Pt	Platinum	195.078	1735
79	Au	Gold	196.9665	ancient
80	Hg	Mercury	200.59	ancient
81	Tl	Thallium	204.3833	1861
82	Pb	Lead	207.2	ancient
83	Bi	Bismuth	208.9804	ancient
84	Po	Polonium	209	1898
85	At	Astatine	210	1940
86	Rn	Radon	222	1900
87	Fr	Francium	223	1939
88	Ra	Radium	226	1898
89	Ac	Actinium	227	1899
90	Th	Thorium	232.0381	1829
91	Pa	Protactinium	231.0359	1913
92	U	Uranium	238.0289	1789
93	Np	Neptunium	237	1940
94	Pu	Plutonium	244	1940
95	Am	Americium	243	1944
96	Cm	Curium	247	1944
97	Bk	Berkelium	247	1949
98	Cf	Californium	251	1950
99	Es	Einsteinium	252	1952

List #92 **Periodic Table of Elements Identification Guide** *(continued)*

#	S	Name	Atomic Weight	Date Disc.
100	Fm	Fermium	257	1952
101	Md	Mendelevium	258	1955
102	No	Nobelium	259	1958
103	Lr	Lawrencium	262	1961
104	Rf	Rutherfordium	261	1964
105	Db	Dubnium	262	1967
106	Sg	Seaborgium	266	1974
107	Bh	Bohrium	264	1981
108	Hs	Hassium	277	1984
109	Mt	Meitnerium	268	1982
110	Ds	Darmstadtium	271	1994
111	Rg	Roentgenium	272	1994
112	Uub	Ununbium	277	1996
113	Uut	Ununtrium	284	2004
114	Uuq	Ununquadium	289	1998
115	Uup	Ununpentium	299	2004
116	Uuh	Ununhexium	302	2000
117	Uus	Ununseptium	310 est.	*
118	Uuo	Ununoctium	314 est.	2006

*This is the temporary name of an element that is expected to be artificially produced.

List #93 Planets and Their Moons

Planet	Primary Atmospheric Constituents	Moons
Mercury	almost no atmosphere	none
Venus	carbon dioxide, nitrogen	none
Earth	nitrogen, oxygen	1 moon
Mars	carbon dioxide, nitrogen, argon	2 moons: Deimos and Phobos
Jupiter	hydrogen, helium	38 moons; four largest moons are known as the Galilean satellites (after astronomer Galileo Galilei)—Io, Europa, Ganymede, Callisto
Saturn	hydrogen, helium	35 moons; some of the larger, more important moons—Titan (discovered in 1655 by Christiaan Huygens), Iapetus, Rhea, Dione, Tethys, Mimas, and Enceladus, Hyperion, Phoebe
Uranus	hydrogen, helium, methane	27 moons; largest are Oberon and Titania (first discovered by William Herschel in 1787)
Neptune	hydrogen, helium, methane	9 moons; farthest away and largest of Neptune's moons is Triton (discovered by William Lassell in 1846); second largest moon is Proteus, which was discovered by Voyager 2 and was too dark to be seen in 1949, when the third largest moon, Neried, was discovered by Gerard Kuiper
Pluto*	unknown	3 known moons—Hydra, Nix, and Charon

*Pluto has been a controversial planet since its discovery in 1930. It has been listed here for the benefit of those who are unaware that Pluto is no longer considered a planet. The International Astronomical Union (IAU) downgraded Pluto from an official planet to a dwarf planet on August 24, 2006.

For more information about planets, visit *solarsystem.nasa.gov/planets* for some great pictures and additional data.

List #94 History of Space Flights

1957, Oct. 4	Sputnik satellite is launched into space
1957, Nov. 3	Russians launch a dog into space
1958, Dec. 13	monkey dies after a space flight
1959, May 28	monkeys survive a space mission
1959, Sept. 12	Soviets launch a rocket toward the moon
1959, Oct. 26	the world glimpses far side of moon
1960, Mar. 14	a radio telescope makes history by making contact with a satellite 407,000 miles away
1961, Jan. 31	chimp returns safely after a space flight
1961, Apr. 12	Russian cosmonaut Yuri Gagarin is the first human in space and to orbit the Earth; he was in space 1 hour, 48 minutes.
1962, Feb. 20	American spaceman John Glenn orbits the Earth
1962, Apr. 26	first U.S. rocket lands on the moon
1962, Dec. 14	U.S. spacecraft *Music of Spheres* flies by Venus
1963, Jun. 16	Soviets launch the first woman into space
1965, Mar. 18	Russian Alexei Leonov performs first space walk
1965, Mar. 24	space probe crashes into moon, with millions watching on television
1965, Aug. 29	manned Gemini V flight returns to Earth
1966, Feb. 3	Soviets land probe on moon
1966, Jun. 2	first U.S. probe lands on moon
1967, Jan. 27	three astronauts die when Apollo 1 catches fire during a training exercise
1967, Apr. 24	Russian cosmonaut dies in a space crash
1967, May 5	first all-British satellite, Ariel 3, is launched
1967, Oct. 18	Soviets glimpse beneath the clouds of Venus
1967, Oct. 19	U.S. probe flies by Venus
1968, Dec. 24	first astronauts orbit the moon
1969, May 22	Apollo 10 gets a close view of the moon
1969, Jul. 16	Apollo 11 blasts off for the moon
1969, Jul. 20	Neil Armstrong takes first steps on moon
1969, Nov. 19	second Apollo mission lands on the moon
1970, Apr. 14	an explosion damages Apollo 13
1970, Sep. 20	Soviet probe collects rocks from the moon
1971, Feb. 6	man plays golf on the moon

List #94 **History of Space Flights** *(continued)*

1971, Jun. 30	Russian space mission ends in tragedy when crewmen of the Soyuz 11 are asphyxiated upon reentry
1971, Aug. 1	crew of Apollo 15 find rock from birth of moon
1971, Nov. 13	U.S. probe orbits Mars
1972, Apr. 20	Apollo 16 lands safely on the moon after an engine disaster
1972, Dec. 14	the last moon mission returns
1974, Feb. 8	Americans return after an extended stay in space
1976, Jul. 20	pictures of Mars return from Viking ship
1979, Jul. 11	Skylab returns to Earth
1979, Dec. 24	First European-built rocket is launched into space
1980, Nov. 12	Saturn's rings are caught on film
1983, Jun. 24	America's first woman in space, Sally Ride, returns to Earth
1986, Jan. 28	Space shuttle Challenger disintegrates moments after liftoff, killing entire crew, including teacher Christa McAuliffe
1986, Feb. 20	Soviets launch the space station Mir
1988, Sep. 29	U.S. sends a shuttle into space; first mission after Challenger disaster
1989, Aug. 25	Spacecraft Voyager reaches Neptune
1990, Apr. 24	Hubble telescope takes off for space
1990, Aug. 10	NASA space probe Magellan starts mapping Venus
1991, May 18	Helen Sharman becomes Britain's first astronaut launched into space
1995, Jun. 29	U.S. shuttle docks with the Russian space station Mir
1997, Apr. 6	fuel cell defect cuts the space shuttle mission short
1997, Jul. 6	"Mars buggy" starts exploring the Red Planet
1998, Oct. 29	John Glenn orbits Earth in shuttle Discovery, becoming oldest astronaut (age 77)
2001, Apr. 28	California billionaire becomes the first "space tourist," paying money to go to outer space
2003, Feb. 1	Columbia shuttle disintegrates returning into the Earth's atmosphere; all seven crew members die
2003, Oct. 15	China sends its first man into space
2003, Dec. 25	Mars space probe disappears
2004, Jan. 25	NASA rover explores Mars, looking for water

(For additional information, see List #169 Pioneers of Flight.)

List #95 Space Missions

Mission (Country)	Craft	Launch Date	Mission Highlights
Vostok 1 (USSR)	Kedr (Cedar)	April 12, 1961	Cosmonaut Yuri Gagarin becomes the first human in space.
Mercury 3 (USA)	Freedom 7	May 5, 1961	Alan Shepard becomes first American in space during a 15-minute suborbital flight.
Mercury 4 (USA)	Liberty Bell 7	July 21, 1961	The second U.S. suborbital flight, reaches an altitude of 126 miles.
Vostok 2 (USSR)	Orel (Eagle)	August 6, 1961	Gherman Stepanovich Titov is first person to spend an entire day in space.
Mercury 6 (USA)	Friendship 7	February 20, 1962	John Glenn makes first U.S. manned orbital flight at an orbit 100–162 miles from the Earth.
Mercury 7 (USA)	Aurora 7	May 24, 1962	Scott Carpenter makes second U.S. manned orbital flight, which orbits the Earth three times.
Vostok 3 (USSR)	Sokol (Falcon)	August 11, 1962	The Russians make first four-day flight and first "multi-vehicle" flight with Vostok 4.
Vostok 4 (USSR)	Berkut (Golden Eagle)	August 12, 1962	Vostok 4 comes within five miles of Vostok 3, making the first "multi-vehicle" flight.
Mercury 8 (USA)	Sigma 7	October 3, 1962	Walter Schirra orbits the Earth six times during this nine-hour mission.
Mercury 9 (USA)	Faith 7	May 15, 1963	Gordon Cooper pilots the longest and last Mercury mission, totaling 34 hours in space.
Vostok 5 (USSR)	Yastreb (Hawk)	June 14, 1963	Valeri Fyodorovic Bykovsky spends five days in space, the longest time to date.
Vostok 6 (USSR)	Chaika (Seagull)	June 16, 1963	Russian astronaut Valentina Tereshkova becomes the first woman in space.
Voskhod 1 (USSR)	Rubin (Ruby)	October 12, 1964	This mission carries the first space crew, with one pilot and two passengers. The capsule was too crowded for the crew to wear spacesuits and as a result, all suffer from space sickness.
Voskhod 2 (USSR)	Almaz (Diamond)	March 18, 1965	Aleksei Leonov becomes the first person to walk in space.

List #95 **Space Missions** *(continued)*

Mission (Country)	Craft	Launch Date	Mission Highlights
Gemini-Titan 3 (USA)	Molly Brown	March 23, 1965	This is the first manned mission for the Gemini program, which provides more experience for future Apollo missions.
Gemini-Titan 4 (USA)	Gemini 4	June 3, 1965	Edward White becomes the first American to walk in space.
Gemini-Titan 5 (USA)	Gemini 5	August 21, 1965	The crew sets an endurance record of eight days. Gordon Cooper, Jr., becomes the first man to orbit the Earth two separate times. This mission also marks the first use of fuel cells.
Gemini-Titan 7 (USA)	Gemini 7	December 4, 1965	This mission sets yet another endurance record of 14 days and makes the first American rendezvous between two manned spacecraft with Gemini 6. (An interesting fact is that the Gemini 7 is launched first.)
Gemini-Titan 6-A (USA)	Gemini 6	December 15, 1965	Gemini 6 is launched after Gemini 7 and the two make the first space rendezvous.
Gemini-Titan 8 (USA)	Gemini 8	March 16, 1966	Neil Armstrong and David Scott complete the first docking in space between two spacecraft, but when the craft starts spinning uncontrollably, the men are forced to perform the first emergency landing in the U.S. space program.
Gemini-Titan 9-A (USA)	Gemini 9	June 3, 1966	Gemini 9 rendezvouses with a docking target three times, but is unable to complete the docking.
Gemini-Titan 10 (USA)	Gemini 10	July 18, 1966	Gemini 10 reaches a record altitude of 468 miles (752 km). The craft rendezvouses and docks two different Agena targets and Michael Collins performs a two-hour spacewalk.
Gemini-Titan 11 (USA)	Gemini 11	September 12, 1966	Gemini makes the first American autopilot reentry and landing. A new record altitude is made of 850.65 miles. Richard Gordon, Jr., completes two spacewalks.
Gemini-Titan 12 (USA)	Gemini 12	November 11, 1966	In the Gemini's final mission, Buzz Aldrin is outside the vehicle for five and a half hours, the U.S. spacewalk record.

List #95 **Space Missions** *(continued)*

Mission (Country)	Craft	Launch Date	Mission Highlights
Apollo-Saturn (USA)	Apollo 1	January 27, 1967	During a pre-launch test, astronauts Gus Grissom, Edward White, and Roger Chaffee are killed when fire rages through the Apollo 1 at the Kennedy Space Center in Florida.
Soyuz 1 (USSR)	Rubin (Ruby)	April 23, 1967	Cosmonaut Vladimir Komarov launches the Russians' first Soyuz mission. This spacecraft crashes on its return flight to Earth, making Komarov the first fatality on a manned space flight.
Apollo-Saturn 7 (USA)	Apollo 7	October 11, 1968	The first manned flight of the Apollo program includes the first three-man crew for the U.S. Walter Schirra becomes the first man to fly in space three times. The first live television broadcast from space occurs on this mission.
Soyuz 3 (USSR)	Argon	October 26, 1968	First manned flight of the redesigned Soyuz craft. The mission completes a rendezvous with the unmanned Soyuz 2.
Apollo-Saturn 8 (USA)	Apollo 8	December 21, 1968	The crew of Apollo 8 become the first to leave the Earth's gravity and orbit the moon.
Soyuz 4 (USSR)	Amur	January 14, 1969	Soyuz 4 is joined by Soyuz 5 on January 15. After two of the crew make a spacewalk, three return to Earth in the Soyuz 4, and one comes home in the Soyuz 5.
Soyuz 5 (USSR)	Baikal	January 15, 1969	Soyuz 5 is docked by Soyuz 4. Aleksei Yeliseyev and Yevgeny Khrunov transfer over to Soyuz 4, and Boris Volynov returns to Earth alone.
Apollo-Saturn 9 (USA)	Apollo 9 command module: Gumdrop. Lunar module: Spider	March 3, 1969	The crew conducts the first manned test of the lunar module.

List #95 **Space Missions** *(continued)*

Mission (Country)	Craft	Launch Date	Mission Highlights
Apollo-Saturn 10 (USA)	Apollo 10 command module: Charlie Brown. Lunar module: Snoopy	May 18, 1969	This mission is a full dress rehearsal for a lunar landing.
Apollo-Saturn 11 (USA)	Apollo 11 command module: Columbia. Lunar module: Eagle	July 16, 1969	Apollo 11 completes the first manned mission to the lunar surface and on July 20, Neil Armstrong becomes the first human to walk on the moon. Buzz Aldrin joins him 18 minutes later for a two-hour moonwalk.
Soyuz 6 (USSR)	Antei (Anteus)	October 11, 1969	This craft participates in the first simultaneous flight of three manned spacecraft, but they are unable to rendezvous.
Soyuz 7 (USSR)	Buran (Snowstorm)	October 12, 1969	Soyuz 6, 7, and 8 are launched within a day of each other, putting seven cosmonauts in space at the same time for a joint mission. The rendezvous is unsuccessful.
Soyuz 8 (USSR)	Granit (Granite)	October 13, 1969	(See Soyuz 6 and 7.)
Apollo-Saturn 12 (USA)	Apollo 12 command module: Yankee Clipper. Lunar module: Intrepid	November 14, 1969	Apollo 12 makes the second manned lunar landing.
Apollo-Saturn 13 (USA)	Apollo 13 command module: Odyssey. Lunar module: Aquarius	April 11, 1970	A third manned lunar landing is aborted when an explosion occurs on the service module. The mission is still considered successful due to the heroic efforts of many to bring the crew home safely.

List #95 **Space Missions** *(continued)*

Mission (Country)	Craft	Launch Date	Mission Highlights
Soyuz 9 (USSR)	Sokol (Falcon)	June 1, 1970	This eighteen-day flight sets a new endurance record. However, the two astronauts have to be carried from the spacecraft after landing.
Apollo-Saturn 14 (USA)	Apollo 14 command module: Kitty Hawk. Lunar module: Antares	January 31, 1971	Apollo 14 is the third successful lunar landing and an important mission because it returns the U.S. to space after the Apollo 13 accident. The men collect geological data from the moon and Alan Shepard becomes the oldest man in space to that point (at age 47).
Soyuz 10 (USSR)	Granit (Granite)	April 23, 1971	Soyuz 10 is launched four days after Salyut, the first Soviet space station. This was supposed to be the first mission to the space station, but the cosmonauts are unable to properly dock.
Soyuz 11 (USSR)	Yantar (Amber)	June 6, 1971	Three cosmonauts form the first crew of the Salyut 1 space station. They are in orbit for 24 days. Sadly, the mission ends in tragedy when all of the crew die upon reentry due to a valve problem.
Apollo-Saturn 15 (USA)	Apollo 15 command module: Endeavour. Lunar module: Falcon	July 26, 1971	During this fourth successful lunar landing, David Scott and James Irwin become the first astronauts to use a Lunar Roving Vehicle.
Apollo-Saturn 16 (USA)	Apollo 16 command module: Casper. Lunar module: Orion	April 16, 1972	John Young and Charlie Duke visit the previously unexplored lunar highlands, using the Lunar Rover a second time, and collect 213 pounds of moon rocks.
Apollo-Saturn 17 (USA)	Apollo 17 command module: Challenger. Lunar module: America	December 7, 1972	Harrison Schmitt becomes the first "scientist" to fly into space. He and the other astronauts spend three days exploring the moon's surface. Eugene Cernan becomes the last man to walk on the moon (as of 2007) on December 14, 1972.

List #95 **Space Missions** *(continued)*

Mission (Country)	Craft	Launch Date	Mission Highlights
Skylab 1 SL-1 (USA)	Skylab	May 14, 1973	The Skylab Space Station is launched into space by the Saturn 5 rocket so astronauts can spend extended periods in space. The Skylab remains in orbit for six years.
Skylab SL-2 (USA)	Skylab	May 25, 1973	The crew joins the Skylab and make repairs to the lab's meteorite shield, which was damaged during launch. They spend 28 days in space.
Skylab SL-3 (USA)	Skylab	July 23, 1973	The Skylab's second crew performs numerous scientific and medical experiments for 59 days.
Soyuz 12 (USSR)	Urals	September 27, 1973	Using a redesigned spacecraft, this flight furthers the development of manned space craft.
Skylab SL-4 (USA)	Skylab	November 16, 1973	In this the final flight to the Skylab, the astronauts break all previous endurance records by staying in space 84 days, returning safely on February 8, 1974. Skylab itself reenters the Earth's atmosphere in 1979 and breaks up over the Pacific Ocean and Australia.
Soyuz 13 (USSR)	Kavkaz (Caucasus)	December 18, 1973	Soyuz 13 carries the Orion astrophysical observatory, and the crew is able to conduct astronomical observation of stars from the spacecraft.
Soyuz 14 (USSR)	Berkut (Golden Eagle)	July 3, 1974	The astronauts make the first military space station mission and conduct military reconnaissance of the Earth's surface.
Soyuz 15 (USSR)	Dunai (Danube)	August 26, 1974	This mission is aborted due to an electronics failure with the rendezvous mechanism.
Soyuz 16 (USSR)	Buran (Snowstorm)	December 2, 1974	A test flight for the joint flight of Soviet-United States scheduled for July 1975.
Soyuz 17 (USSR)	Zenit (Zenith)	January 11, 1975	The first Soviet civilian mission.
Soyuz 18 (USSR)	Kavkaz (Caucasus)	May 24, 1975	The crew docks with Salyut 4 and spends 62 days in space performing experiments.

List #95 **Space Missions** *(continued)*

Mission (Country)	Craft	Launch Date	Mission Highlights
Apollo-Soyuz Test Project (USA-USSR)	Apollo/Soyuz	July 15, 1975	The first international space mission. The crews successfully dock on July 17, 1975, and transfer between spacecraft several times. They perform scientific experiments and stay docked for two days. This is the last flight for both the Apollo spacecraft and the Saturn 1B rocket.
Soyuz 21 (USSR)	Baikal	July 6, 1976	The two cosmonauts return to Earth early due to physical and mental problems, including psychosis and space sickness. It is possible that toxic gases are at least partly to blame.
Soyuz 22 (USSR)	Yastreb (Hawk)	September 15, 1976	The crew spends eight days photographing the Earth.
Soyuz 23 (USSR)	Rodon	October 14, 1976	The crew returns to Earth early after an electronics failure aborted the docking procedure, and during the emergency landing nearly freezes to death in a lake during a blizzard. Rescuers take hours to get the capsule to shore.
Soyuz 24 (USSR)	Terek	February 7, 1977	The crew conducts the first complete change of cabin atmosphere during this mission.
Soyuz 26 (USSR)	Taimyr	December 10, 1977	Yuri Romanenko and Georgi Grechko receive supplies from another spacecraft and a visiting crew (from Soyuz 27). They set a record flight duration of 96 days.
Soyuz 27 (USSR)	Pamir (Pamirs)	January 10, 1978	The crew docks with the Salyut orbiting station, swaps spacecraft with the crew of Soyuz 26, and returns to Earth after five days.
Soyuz 28 (USSR)	Zenit (Zenith)	March 2, 1978	Czechoslovakian Vladimir Remek becomes the first man in space who is not an American or a Soviet.
Soyuz 29 (USSR)	Foton (Photon)	June 15, 1978	The two cosmonauts set a new endurance record of 136 days in space. They are the second crew of Salyut 6. Two teams of cosmonauts visit Soyuz 29 and the crew members return aboard Soyuz 31.

List #95 **Space Missions** *(continued)*

Mission (Country)	Craft	Launch Date	Mission Highlights
Soyuz 30 (USSR)	Kavkaz (Caucasus)	June 27, 1978	Miroslaw Hermaszewski becomes the first Polish cosmonaut. They dock with Salyut 6, placing the second international crew aboard.
Soyuz 31 (USSR)	Yastreb (Hawk)	August 26, 1978	Sigmund Jaehn becomes the first German astronaut in space. He and Valeri Bykovsky spend a week aboard Salyut 6 performing experiments on materials sciences, observations of Earth, and life sciences.
Soyuz 32 (USSR)	Proton	February 25, 1979	Vladimir Lyakhov and Valeri Ryumin set another endurance record of 175 days in space as the third crew of Salyut 6. Some of their work includes observations with a KT-10 radio telescope. They return aboard Soyuz 34, which had been launched unmanned.
Soyuz 35 (USSR)	Dnepr (Dnieper)	April 9, 1980	Valeri Ryumin and Leonid Popov spend six months in space as the fourth crew of Salyut 6.
Soyuz 36 (USSR)	Orion	May 26, 1980	Bertalan Farkas becomes the first Hungarian in space. He and Valeri Kubasov visit Salyut 6 on their 7-day mission.
Soyuz T-2 (USSR)	Yupiter (Jupiter)	June 5, 1980	In this the first test flight of an improved Soyuz, the new guidance system fails on approach to Salyut 6, but the astronauts are able to dock at Salyut 6 and spend three days with their comrades.
Soyuz 37 (USSR)	Terek	July 23, 1980	Pham Tuan becomes the first Vietnamese in space during a Salyut 6 visit.
Soyuz 38 (USSR)	Taimyr	September 18, 1980	Romanenko Mendez becomes the first Cuban in space during a week-long visit to Salyut 6.
Soyuz T-3 (USSR)	Mayak (Beacon)	November 27, 1980	During this 12-day mission, the cosmonauts make repairs to Salyut 6 in preparation for the fifth crew.
Soyuz T-4 (USSR)	Foton (Photon)	March 12, 1981	Although Salyut 6 has well exceeded its design lifetime, the space station's fifth crew spends 74 days there performing experiments and having guests (fellow cosmonauts, of course).

List #95 **Space Missions** *(continued)*

Mission (Country)	Craft	Launch Date	Mission Highlights
Soyuz 39 (USSR)	Pamir (Pamirs)	March 22, 1981	Zhugderdemidiyn Gurragcha becomes the first Mongolian in space during a 7-day mission to Salyut 6.
STS-1 (USA)	Columbia	April 12, 1981	This is the first flight of the first winged, reusable spacecraft, now known as Space Shuttle.
Soyuz 40 (USSR)	Dnepr (Dnieper)	May 14, 1981	The first Romanian in space, Dumitru Prunariu, spends seven days aboard Salyut 6.
STS-2 (USA)	Columbia	November 12, 1981	The second flight of Shuttle Columbia. Technical problems shorten the mission from five to two days.
STS-3 (USA)	Columbia	March 22, 1982	During the third Shuttle Columbia flight test, astronauts conduct numerous experiments.
Soyuz T-5 (USSR)	Elbrus	May 13, 1982	Anatoli Berezovoy and Valentin Lebedev spend an unprecedented 7 months in space aboard the new space station, Salyut 7.
Soyuz T-6 (USSR)	Pamir (Pamirs)	June 24, 1982	Jean-Loup Chretien becomes the first Frenchman and Western European to go into space aboard a Soviet vehicle. The three cosmonauts spend 7 days aboard Salyut 7.
STS-4 (USA)	Columbia	June 27, 1982	The final Shuttle flight test carries a Department of Defense experiment into orbit.
Soyuz T-7 (USSR)	Dnepr (Dnieper)	August 19, 1982	Serebrov Savitskaya becomes the second woman in space as she and fellow cosmonauts visit Salyut 7 for a 7-day mission.
STS-5 (USA)	Columbia	November 11, 1982	This is the first operational flight of the Space Shuttle and the first manned spacecraft to carry four crew members.
STS-6 (USA)	Challenger	April 4, 1983	In the first flight of Shuttle Challenger, astronauts perform the first spacewalk of the shuttle program.
STS-8 (USA)	Challenger	April 30, 1983	Guion Bluford becomes the first African-American in space. The mission is the first nighttime launch and landing in the Shuttle program.

List #95 **Space Missions** *(continued)*

Mission (Country)	Craft	Launch Date	Mission Highlights
STS-7 (USA)	Challenger	June 18, 1983	Sally Ride becomes the first American woman in space. The crew makes a diverted landing at Edwards Air Force Base.
Soyuz T-9 (USSR)	Proton	June 27, 1983	The crew spends 149 days in space.
STS-9 (USA)	Columbia, Spacelab	November 28, 1983	This is the first six-person crew and the first flight of non-astronauts (for the U. S.). It is also the first flight of the Spacelab science module.
41-B (USA)	Challenger	February 3, 1984	The first untethered spacewalk in history is made using the manned maneuvering unit.
Soyuz T-10 (USSR)	Mayak (Beacon)	February 8, 1984	Three cosmonauts set a new endurance record by spending 8 months aboard Salyut 7, primarily doing medical research.
Soyuz T-11 (USSR)	Yupiter (Jupiter)	April 3, 1984	Rakesh Sharma becomes the first astronaut from India to make a space flight. He and his fellow cosmonauts spend a week aboard Salyut 7.
41-C (USA)	Challenger	April 6, 1984	This mission accomplishes the first capture, repair, and redeployment of a satellite. The astronauts also deploy a long-duration exposure facility (LDEF).
Soyuz T-12 (USSR)	Pamir (Pamirs)	July 17, 1984	Svetlana Savitskaya becomes the first woman to make a spacewalk during this 11-day resupply mission to Salyut 7.
41-D (USA)	Discovery	August 30, 1984	The first flight of the Shuttle Discovery. Three satellites are launched.
41-G (USA)	Challenger	October 5, 1984	First crew of seven. The astronauts deploy the Earth Radiation Budget Satellite. Kathryn Sullivan becomes the first American woman to walk in space.
51-A (USA)	Discovery	November 8, 1984	Two new satellites are launched and two broken satellites are retrieved.
51-C (USA)	Discovery	January 24, 1985	The first classified U.S. Department of Defense Shuttle mission. Astronauts launch defense payload into space.
51-D (USA)	Discovery	April 12, 1985	A communications satellite is deployed.

List #95 **Space Missions** *(continued)*

Mission (Country)	Craft	Launch Date	Mission Highlights
51-B (USA)	Challenger, Spacelab	April 29, 1985	14 experiments are done using Spacelab 3, the first life sciences and space manufacturing Spacelab mission.
Soyuz T-13 (USSR)	Pamir (Pamirs)	June 6, 1985	Two cosmonauts restore the dead Salyut 7 by spending 112 days performing repairs on the space station.
51-G (USA)	Discovery	June 17, 1985	The first tri-national space crew deploys three satellites. Steven Nagel becomes the 100th American in space.
51-F (USA)	Challenger, Spacelab	July 29, 1985	Spacelab 2 carries out experiments in life sciences, plasma physics, astronomy, and solar physics. The mission lasts 8 days.
51-I (USA)	Discovery	August 27, 1985	The astronauts deploy two satellites, then retrieve and repair a third.
Soyuz T-14 (USSR)	Cheget (Tcheget)	September 17, 1985	This represents the first "relief mission" in space history. The crew replaces the crew of Soyuz T-13.
51-J (USA)	Atlantis	October 3, 1985	The first flight of Shuttle Atlantis is the second classified U.S. Department of Defense Shuttle mission.
61-A (USA)	Challenger, Spacelab D1	October 30, 1985	Spacelab D1 carries an 8-person crew and is controlled by the West German Federal Aerospace Research Establishment. It carries out experiments concerning materials processing, communications, and microgravity.
61-B (USA)	Atlantis	November 26, 1985	The crew tests methods for completing assemblies in space. They deploy three satellites.
61-C (USA)	Columbia	January 12, 1986	This mission encounters many problems and has to be shortened. Franklin Chang-Diaz becomes the first Hispanic American in space. This is the second flight of a U.S. congressman, Bill Nelson.
51-L (USA)	Challenger	January 28, 1986	All seven crewmembers are killed when the Challenger explodes 73 seconds after lift-off. Christa McAuliffe was to be the first teacher in space, and millions of schoolchildren watched the launch on television.

List #95 **Space Missions** *(continued)*

Mission (Country)	Craft	Launch Date	Mission Highlights
Soyuz T-15 (USSR)	Mayak (Beacon)	March 13, 1986	The 125-day Soyuz T-15 mission becomes one of the most difficult and successful missions in Soviet space history. Leonid Kizim and Vladimir Solovyov activate the new Mir space station and then transfer over to Salyut 7, where they perform two spacewalks. They fly back to the Mir space station to perform system tests.
Soyuz TM-2 (USSR)	Taimyr	February 6, 1987	Yuri Romanenko and Alexandr Laveykin make up the second resident Mir crew. Romanenko spends 326 days aboard the station, while Laveykin spends 174 days there.
Soyuz TM-3 (USSR)	Vityaz (Knight)	July 22, 1987	Muhammed Ahmed Faris becomes the first Syrian in space as he and his fellow cosmonauts spend 7 days in space. Alexandr Alexandrov replaces Laveykin on the Mir station, spending 160 days in space.
Soyuz TM-4 (USSR)	Okean (Ocean)	December 21, 1987	The third Mir crew completes the first yearlong mission. They perform three spacewalks, and several manufacturing and astronomical experiments. Crewman Anatoli Levchenko dies about eight months later of a brain tumor.
Soyuz TM-5 (USSR)	Rodnik (Spring)	June 7, 1988	The mission features the first Bulgarian in space, Alexandr Alexandrov, who shares the same name as a Soviet cosmonaut.
Soyuz TM-6 (USSR)	Proton	August 29, 1988	Abdul Ahad Mohmand becomes the first space traveler from Afghanistan as he and his fellow cosmonauts visit the Mir station for 7 days. Valery Polyakov, a medical doctor, stays on Mir for 240 days to monitor the health of the resident crew.
STS-26 (USA)	Discovery	September 29, 1988	The U.S. returns to space after the Challenger disaster.
Soyuz TM-7 (USSR)	Donbass (River Don basin)	November 26, 1988	The new crew for the Mir station records the first international spacewalk of a Frenchman and a Soviet. Jean-Loup Chretien returns after 24 days, while the others stay on Mir for 150.

List #95 **Space Missions** *(continued)*

Mission (Country)	Craft	Launch Date	Mission Highlights
STS-27 (USA)	Atlantis	December 2, 1988	This is the third classified Department of Defense Shuttle mission.
STS-29 (USA)	Discovery	March 13, 1989	This mission sends a third tracking and data relay satellite into orbit.
STS-30 (USA)	Atlantis	May 4, 1989	The crew launches the Magellan/Venus Radar Mapper into space.
STS-28 (USA)	Columbia	August 13, 1989	The fourth classified Department of Defense Shuttle mission.
Soyuz TM-8 (USSR)	Vityaz (Knight)	September 6, 1989	This fifth Mir crew spends 166 days in space.
STS-34 (USA)	Atlantis	October 18, 1989	The space probe Galileo is launched on a 5-year mission to Jupiter.
STS-33 (USA)	Discovery	November 22, 1989	This is the fifth Department of Defense Shuttle mission. Frederick Gregory is the first African-American to command a space mission.
STS-32 (USA)	Columbia	January 9, 1990	The crew launches two satellites during their 11 days in space.
Soyuz TM-9 (USSR)	Rodnik (Spring)	February 11, 1990	The Mir's sixth crew spends over 179 days in space.
STS-36 (USA)	Atlantis	February 28, 1990	The sixth classified Department of Defense Shuttle mission.
STS-31 (USA)	Discovery	April 24, 1990	The Hubble Space Telescope is launched.
Soyuz TM-10 (USSR)	Vulkan (Volcano)	August 1, 1990	The seventh Mir crew spends over 131 days in space.
STS-41 (USA)	Discovery	October 6, 1990	The Ulysses solar spacecraft is launched.
STS-38 (USA)	Atlantis	November 15, 1990	The last classified Department of Defense Shuttle mission.
STS-35 (USA)	Columbia	December 2, 1990	The crew performs astronomical experiments with the Astro 1 Spacelab.
Soyuz TM-11 (USSR)	Derbent	December 2, 1990	The first Soviet commercial passenger, Japanese newsman Toyohir Akiyama, spends 7 days in space.
STS-37 (USA)	Atlantis	April 5, 1991	The crew launches the Gamma Ray Observatory.
STS-39 (USA)	Discovery	April 28,1991	An unclassified mission for the Department of Defense.

List #95 **Space Missions** *(continued)*

Mission (Country)	Craft	Launch Date	Mission Highlights
Soyuz TM-12 (USSR)	Ozon (Ozone)	May 18, 1991	Helen Sharman becomes the first British citizen to go into space.
STS-40 (USA)	Columbia	June 5, 1991	The mission of this Spacelab is to study life sciences.
STS-43 (USA)	Atlantis	August 2, 1991	The mission includes a satellite launch and various experimental payloads.
STS-48 (USA)	Discovery	September 12, 1991	The mission launches the Upper Atmosphere Research Satellite.
Soyuz TM-13 (USSR)	Donbass	October 2, 1991	The first Austrian and first Kazakh go to space and spend 7 days aboard Mir.
STS-44 (USA)	Atlantis	November 24, 1991	This unclassified Department of Defense shuttle mission deploys an early warning satellite.
STS-42 (USA)	Discovery	January 22, 1992	This mission features the first International Microgravity Lab.
Soyuz TM-14 (USSR)	Vityaz (Knight)	March 17, 1992	The 11th Mir crew spends the majority of its 145 days in space on Earth resource missions.
STS-45 (USA)	Atlantis	March 24, 1992	This mission carries ATLAS-1 and studies the Earth's atmosphere.
STS-49 (USA)	Endeavour	May 7, 1992	This is the first flight of the orbiter Endeavour. Richard Hieb, Pierre Thuot, and Thomas Akers stay outside the spacecraft longer than any previous U.S. astronauts.
STS-50 (USA)	Columbia	June 25, 1992	This mission has the first U.S. Microgravity Laboratory.
Soyuz TM-15 (USSR)	Rodnik (Spring)	July 27, 1992	The 12th Mir crew mounts the Sofora propulsion module on the Mir complex.
STS-46 (USA)	Atlantis	July 31, 1992	This international crew deploys two satellites, among other activities.
STS-47 (USA)	Endeavour	September 12, 1992	Mark Lee and Jan Davis become the first married couple to fly on the same flight. Mae Jemison becomes the first African-American woman in space. Mamoru Mohri becomes the first Japanese shuttle astronaut. The mission carries the Spacelab J Mission.
STS-52 (USA)	Columbia	October 22, 1992	The crew performs microgravity experiments and launches two satellites.

List #95 **Space Missions** *(continued)*

Mission (Country)	Craft	Launch Date	Mission Highlights
STS-53 (USA)	Discovery	December 2, 1992	A mission for the Department of Defense.
STS-54 (USA)	Endeavour	January 13, 1993	The crew launches a Tracking and Data Relay Satellite.
STS-56 (USA)	Discovery	April 8, 1993	The crew launches an ATLAS-2 satellite.
STS-55 (USA)	Columbia	April 26, 1993	A German Spacelab mission.
STS-57 (USA)	Endeavour	June 21, 1993	The crew recovers the EURECA satellite.
STS-51 (USA)	Atlantis	September 12, 1993	The crew deploys an ATCS satellite.
STS-58 (USA)	Columbia	October 18, 1993	The crew does experiments in the life sciences.
STS-61 (USA)	Endeavour	December 2, 1993	The crew performs the first servicing for the broken Hubble Space Telescope. It is one of the most complex missions to date.
STS-60 (USA)	Discovery	February 3, 1994	The crew performs 11 industry-driven experiments.
STS-62 (USA)	Columbia	March 4, 1994	The crew carries out space technology experiments relevant to the space station.

Additional space flights will not be listed due to "space" constraints. Other flight lists are readily available. The best site the author has found for United States space missions is at *www.spaceflighthistory.com*. They not only have all the information about the flights, crews, missions, etc., but they also have photographs from the missions. Another good Web site, particularly for additional information on the Soviet program, can be found at *www.astronautix.com*.

List #96 Constellations

Constellation	Date discovered and by whom
Andromeda	ancient
Antlia	1763, Lacaille
Apus	1603, Uranometria
Aquarius	ancient
Aquila	ancient
Ara	ancient
Aries	ancient
Auriga	ancient
Boötes	ancient
Caelum	1763, Lacaille
Camelopardalis	1624, Bartsch
Cancer	ancient
Canes Venatici	1690, Hevelius
Canis Major	ancient
Canis Minor	ancient
Capricornus	ancient
Carina	1763, Lacaille
Cassiopeia	ancient
Centaurus	ancient
Cepheus	ancient
Cetus	ancient
Chamaeleon	1603, Keyser and de Houtman
Circinus	1763, Lacaille
Columba	1679, Royer
Coma Berenices	1603
Corona Australis	ancient
Corona Borealis	ancient
Corvus	ancient
Crater	ancient
Crux	1603
Cygnus	ancient
Delphinus	ancient
Dorado	1603, Keyser and de Houtman

List #96 **Constellations** *(continued)*

Constellation	Date discovered and by whom
Draco	ancient
Equuleus	ancient
Eridanus	ancient
Fornax	1763, Lacaille
Gemini	ancient
Grus	1603, Keyser and de Houtman
Hercules	ancient
Horologium	1763, Lacaille
Hydra	ancient
Hydrus	1603, Keyser and de Houtman
Indus	1603, Keyser and de Houtman
Lacerta	1690, Hevelius
Leo	ancient
Leo Minor	1690, Hevelius
Lepus	ancient
Libra	ancient
Lupus	ancient
Lynx	1690, Hevelius
Lyra	ancient
Mensa	1763, Lacaille
Microscopium	1763, Lacaille
Monoceros	1624, Bartsch
Musca	1603, Keyser and de Houtman
Norma	1763, Lacaille
Octans	1763, Lacaille
Ophiuchus	ancient
Orion	ancient
Pavo	1603, Keyser and de Houtman
Pegasus	ancient
Perseus	ancient
Phoenix	1603, Keyser and de Houtman
Pictor	1763, Lacaille
Pisces	ancient
Piscis Austrinus	ancient

List #96 **Constellations** *(continued)*

Constellation	Date discovered and by whom
Puppis	1763, Lacaille
Pyxis	1763, Lacaille
Reticulum	1763, Lacaille
Sagitta	ancient
Sagittarius	ancient
Scorpius	ancient
Sculptor	1763, Lacaille
Scutum	1690, Hevelius
Serpens	ancient
Sextans	1690, Hevelius
Taurus	ancient
Telescopium	1763, Lacaille
Triangulum	ancient
Triangulum Australe	1603, Keyser and de Houtman
Tucana	1603, Keyser and de Houtman
Ursa Major	ancient
Ursa Minor	ancient
Vela	1763, Lacaille
Virgo	ancient
Volans	1603, Keyser and de Houtman
Vulpecula	1690, Hevelius

List #97 The Mohs Scale of Mineral Hardness

German mineralogist Friedrich Mohs came up with a scale in 1812 to help us compare the relative hardness of particular minerals.

Mohs Scale of Hardness

1 **T**alc
2 **G**ypsum
3 **C**alcite
4 **F**luorite
5 **A**patite
6 **F**eldspar
7 **Q**uartz (Amethyst)
6.5–7.5 **G**arnet
7.5 **B**eryl (Emerald)
8 **T**opaz
9 **C**orundum (Ruby and Sapphire)
10 **D**iamond

Some geology students learn a mnemonic to help them remember most of the Mohs Scale. Perhaps this will help your little geologist: "To Get Candy From Aunt Fanny, Quit Teasing Cousin Danny." (Of course, you should point out that this leaves out garnet and beryl.)

6

Animals

List #98 Animal and Plant Classification

Swedish naturalist Carolus Linnaeus (1707–1778) developed the system of classification that we use today for plants and animals. The classification system Linnaeus developed separates plants and animals according to certain physical similarities. The system uses the following seven levels:

Kingdom

Phylum

Class

Order

Family

Genus

Species

List #99 Deadliest Animals

Animal	Human deaths the animal is responsible for per year (worldwide estimate)	How to Reduce the Risk of an Attack
bear	5–10	If you startle a bear, it may attack you, so make plenty of noise as you walk. Do not ever try to approach a bear or bear cub! If you see a bear, back slowly away, but do not run, because a bear can outrun you.
shark	100	Check local beach warnings to make sure there is not a current risk. Heed warnings. Swim in groups, since attacks of individual swimmers are more frequent. Do not do any of the following: swim too far from shore, swim at dusk or dawn (when sharks are most active), swim if you are bleeding, or wear shiny jewelry (can look like fish scales in the water). For more specific advice, see *www.surfrider.org.au/publications/shark_attack_prevent.php*.
jellyfish	100	Wear lightweight protective clothing like "swim skin" or panty hose, which many lifeguards are doing now in Australia and other places where jellyfish stings are common. If you see one jellyfish, beware, because there may be more.
hippopotamus	100–150	Hippos are very territorial. Do not go near them.
elephant	300–500	Stay away from elephants.
crocodile	600–800	In an area where crocodiles may be present, stay out of the water and remain diligent at all times. Do not stroll too close to the water or turn your back to the water.
large cats (tigers, mountain lions, lions)	800	Since mountain lions are going to be the most likely big cat to attack you in the U.S., the advice for preventing an attack is to make yourself look as big as possible (by standing up tall, picking up a branch, raising your arms, etc.) and shout, *Mountain Lion!* or *Cougar!* as loudly as you can. A mountain lion is a big cat, and cats like to chase their prey, so do not turn and run—it will increase your risk of an attack. Be aggressive and defend your position.

List #99 **Deadliest Animals** *(continued)*

Animal	Human deaths the animal is responsible for per year (worldwide estimate)	How to Reduce the Risk of an Attack
scorpion	800–2,000	Do not hike in sandals. In desert areas, always check your shoes (preferably hiking boots) before putting them on, as scorpions like to crawl into small, dark places. Shake out your sleeping bag, folded corners of tents, clothing, etc., before using them.
venomous snakes	50,000	Many snakebites result from snakes being bothered by humans, since snakes don't prey upon humans. Therefore, the best way to avoid a snakebite is to leave snakes alone. Also, when hiking, wear long pants and boots, and stick to the trails.
mosquito	1 million (yes, one *million!*)	Wear clothing when outdoors and use a mosquito repellent on your skin and clothing (mosquitos can also bite through clothes). Dusk and dawn are peak biting hours for many types of mosquitos, so avoid being outside during this time or use extra precautions. (One night we had our little ones out at dusk, and our baby got about fifteen mosquito bites in just over an hour!)

List #100 How to Avoid an Animal Attack

In addition to the precautions listed on the Deadliest Animals list, there are some general things you can do to lessen the risk of an animal attack. Make copies of this for your children to study especially if you will be hiking or camping or participating in other outdoor activities. I was bitten by a water moccasin when I was twelve, and it was no fun! If I had followed one of the rules in this list, it would not have happened. Fortunately, I recovered with no ill effects, but I hope this list saves some other child from harm.

- Always take a friend, relative, or other companion with you on nature outings.
- Bring a cell phone, water, some snacks, and a small first aid kit with you on nature outings.
- Be alert at all times.
- Don't walk around barefoot in areas where you can't see the ground completely or where dangerous animals are known to live. If you're unsure at all, wear shoes when you are outside. (The only outdoor areas we let our children go barefoot are in our own mowed yard and the beach.)
- Use a flashlight if you're walking at night and keep a good look at the ground in front of you to watch out for snakes.
- Keep your yard mowed, trim bushes around your home, and get a domestic cat if snakes are a problem in your area. (The cat will not only try to attack a snake but it will also kill mice, which are a major source of food for snakes.)
- If you are looking under rocks, wood, etc., make sure you lift it up on the side away from you so that any little (or big) critters like snakes, scorpions, etc., can crawl away and you won't be in their direct path. Don't go into caves, crevices, tall grass, or other places where you can't see what's there. Use paths, clearings, mowed lawns, etc., to play, run, and explore. These areas are much safer.
- When camping or even if you just leave some clothing outside for a while, always shake clothes out before putting them back on. Something may have moved in!

List #101 Longest Life Spans

giant tortoise	150 years or more (Galapagos tortoises have been known to live almost 200 years!)
sturgeon	100 years (males typically live 50–60 years, while females can live up to 150 years)
parrot	85 years
eagle	80 years
Indian elephant	77 years
halibut	70 years
clam	60 years
hippopotamus	about 55 years
American alligator	about 58 years
horse	45 years
herring gull	40 years
ostrich	40 years
pigeon	35 years
gorilla	about 35 years, 45 years in captivity

Comparing our life span to animals, it is interesting to note that in the United States, human females have an average life span of 78.81 years, while males have an average life span of 71.83 years. This is drastically lower in some countries.

List #102 Red List Categories (Risks of Extinction)

The International Union for Conservation of Nature and Natural Resources (IUCN) has devised a system to classify species at risk of global extinction. Because the animals appearing on the list change frequently, we have included the definition for each category rather than listing the species that belong in each category. Children hear about animals being extinct or endangered and it is good to know and understand exactly what the implications are for those species, other species, and our whole world. It would be a great idea to take this list with you to zoos, animal sanctuaries, aquariums, and other places where you will be researching animals.

Extinct	A species is extinct when there is certainty beyond a reasonable doubt that the last member of that species has died.
Extinct in the Wild	A species is extinct in the wild when the only living individuals of the species survive in "cultivation," which is captivity in zoos or even in naturalized habitats that are not where the species lived historically.
Critically Endangered	A species is critically endangered when there is a marked decline in the size of the population of the species, the historic geographic area of the species is declining, fragmented, or exists in only one location, or the total population of the species numbers less than 250 mature individuals and a continuing decline of at least 25% within a particular time period. Critically endangered species are at an incredibly high risk of becoming extinct in the wild.
Endangered	Basically, the criteria for endangered species is similar to critically endangered in that there are specific criteria similar to those listed above, but the numbers are not as worrisome as those for the critically endangered. For example, in the criteria for endangered, this category can be applied if the population size falls below 2,500 mature individuals and there is a continuing decline of at least 20% within a particular time period. Endangered species are considered to be at a very high risk of becoming extinct in the wild.
Vulnerable	Vulnerable species are considered at high risk of becoming extinct in the wild. In addition to specific criteria relating to the size of their geographic range and population decline, species are considered vulnerable if there are fewer than 10,000 mature individuals in the wild with a continuing decline of at least 10% within a given time period.
Near Threatened	These species do not qualify for a "threatened" status, but they could in the near future.
Least Concern	These species do not cause concern for possible extinction. Many species fit this category.

List #103 Animals Once Considered Extinct

Genesis 6:19–20 "You are to bring into the ark two of all living creatures, male and female, to keep them alive with you. Two of every kind of bird, of every kind of animal and of every kind of creature that moves along the ground will come to you to be kept alive."

Madeiran land snail—thought to be extinct in early 1990s and listed as extinct on the International Union for Conservation of Nature and Natural Resources (IUCN) Red List in 1996; rediscovered in 1999.

Fernandina rice rat—although officially listed as extinct in 1996, it was discovered again in 1995 (and later in 1997) on the rat's native habitat of Fernandina Island, which is part of the Galapagos Islands.

Ivory-billed woodpecker—thought to be extinct in 1944, but found again in 2004.

Lord Howe Island stick insect—thought to be extinct around 1920 after rats (that eat the insect) were introduced; rediscovered in 2001.

Bavarian pine vole—after a hospital was built on the site of this rodent's native habitat, they were thought to have been extinct and have been listed as such since 1986. It is believed that a population was recently discovered near the German-Austrian border.

Takahe—presumed to be extinct in 1898, but Dr. Geoffrey Orbell, who believed the bird still existed, rediscovered it in 1949. Recommended reading: *Wild South: Saving New Zealand's Endangered Birds* by Rod Morris and Hal Smith (contains a chapter about the Takahe and Dr. Orbell's mission to find them—great inspiration for kids!).

New Zealand storm-petrel—a small seabird presumed extinct and listed as such until it was rediscovered in 2003.

Painted frog—after a lethal skin fungus wiped out amphibian species across Central and South America, the *atelopus ebenoides marinkellei* (painted frog) was last seen in 1995; however, it was discovered again in May 2006 by researchers in deserts of Sarna and Toquilla in eastern Colombia.

Forest owlet—thought to be extinct in the 1800s, but rediscovered in India in 1997 through an interesting chain of events that included theft, deception, investigation, and discovery.

List #103 **Animals Once Considered Extinct** *(continued)*

Woolly flying squirrel—last recorded in 1924 until researchers found some in Pakistan in 1994.

Gilbert's potorro—small marsupial indigenous to Australia that was discovered in 1840 by naturalist John Gilbert, but believed extinct in 1870s, was rediscovered in 1994. A great Web site for additional information is *www.potorro.org*.

Night parrot—native to Australia; believed extinct by early 1900s until one was found dead next to a road in 1990.

New Holland mouse—considered extinct since 1887; rediscovered in 1970; now found only in Victoria, Australia, and is critically endangered.

Edwards' pheasant—first discovered in 1895 in Vietnam; thought to have been extinct since early 1900s, but recently rediscovered in Central Vietnam.

Cuban solenodon—discovered in 1861; in 1970, the species, which is native to Cuba, was thought possibly to be extinct since no specimens had been seen since 1890. A few specimens were captured in 1974 and 1975; the little insectivore is still extremely rare.

Giant Palouse earthworm—first discovered in 1897 by Frank Smith; reportedly can reach a length of three feet. A six-inch specimen was discovered near Palouse, Washington, in 2006, by a graduate student looking for worms.

Madagascar pochard—a bird thought to be extinct since 1991; rediscovered in Madagascar in 2006.

Caatinga woodpecker—initially discovered in 1926 and not seen since then; rediscovered by a Brazilian ornithologist in 2006.

List #104 Birds of North America

Bird watching is a great project for a budding nature enthusiast! Among the groupings of birds listed here, more than 900 species are found in North America. John James Audubon (1785–1851) categorized, drew, described, and painted the birds of America. Visit the Audubon Web site at *www.audu bon.org/bird/BOA/BOA_index.html* to see Audubon's original paintings and learn more about Audubon's work. I highly recommend any of the Audubon Society Field Guides, any of the Peterson field guides, or the *Birds of the World* guide by Colin James Oliver Harrison and Alan Greensmith (published by Dorling Kindersley). All of these books have full-color photographs that make it easier to identify the birds, and the descriptions are written in a manner that children can understand. Also, you can visit my Web site at *www.sonya haskins.com* to print out a more extensive list detailing each species. Use this as a checklist when you go bird watching and add to it each time.

Ducks, Geese, and Swans—131 species worldwide; 61 North American species

Curassows and Guans—50 species worldwide (found only in the Americas); 1 North American specie

Partridges, Grouse, Turkeys, and Old World Quail—180 species worldwide; 16 North American species

New World Quail—32 species worldwide (found only in the Americas); 6 North American species

Loons—5 species worldwide; 5 North American species

Grebes—20 species worldwide; 7 North American species

Albatrosses—21 species worldwide; 8 North American species

Shearwaters and Petrels—75 species worldwide; 24 North American species

Storm-Petrels—21 species worldwide; 12 North American species

Tropic Birds—3 species worldwide; 3 North American species

Boobies and Gannets—8 species worldwide; 5 North American species

Pelicans—8 species worldwide; 2 North American species

Cormorants and Shags—38 species worldwide; 6 North American species

Darters—4 species worldwide; 1 North American specie

Frigate Birds—5 species worldwide; 3 North American species

Bitterns, Herons, and Egrets—61 species worldwide; 17 North American species

Ibises and Spoonbills—33 species worldwide; 4 North American species

Storks—19 species worldwide; 2 North American species

List #104 **Birds of North America** *(continued)*

New World Vultures—7 species worldwide (found only in the Americas); 3 North American species

Flamingos—6 species worldwide; 1 North American specie

Hawks, Kites, and Eagles—233 species worldwide; 28 North American species

Caracaras and Falcons—62 species worldwide; 11 North American species

Rails, Gallinules, and Coots—143 species worldwide; 13 North American species

Limpkins–1 specie, and it's in North America

Cranes—15 species worldwide; 3 North American species

Lapwings and Plovers—66 species worldwide; 17 North American species

Oyster Catchers—11 species worldwide; 2 North American species

Stilts and Avocets—9 species worldwide; 3 North American species

Jacanas—8 species worldwide; 1 North American specie

Sandpipers, Curlews, Stints, Godwits, Snipes, and Phalaropes—86 species worldwide; 65 North American species

Skuas, Gulls, Terns, and Skimmers—108 species worldwide; 54 North American species

Auks, Murres, and Puffins—24 species worldwide; 22 North American species

Pigeons and Doves—308 species worldwide; 18 North American species

Lories, Parakeets, Macaws, and Parrots—335 species worldwide; 8 North American species

Cuckoos, Roadrunners, and Anis—138 species worldwide; 8 North American species

Barn Owls—16 species worldwide; 1 North American specie

Typical Owls—195 species worldwide; 21 North American species

Nightjars—86 species worldwide; 9 North American species

Swifts—98 species worldwide; 9 North American species

Hummingbirds—337 species worldwide; 23 North American species

Kingfishers—94 species worldwide; 3 North American species

Woodpeckers, Sapsuckers, and Flickers—218 species worldwide; 26 North American species

Tyrant Flycatchers—429 species worldwide (found only in the Americas); 45 North American species

Shrikes—31 species worldwide; 3 North American species

Vireos—52 species worldwide; 16 North American species

Jays, Crows, Magpies, and Ravens—120 species worldwide; 21 North American species

List #104 **Birds of North America** *(continued)*

Larks—91 species worldwide; 2 North American species
Swallows and Martins—75 species worldwide; 14 North American species
Chickadees and Titmice—59 species worldwide; 12 North American species
Verdins—1specie, and it's in North America
Bushtits—1 specie, and it's in North America
Nuthatches—24 species worldwide; 4 North American species
Tree Creepers—6 species worldwide; 1 North American specie
Wrens—79 species worldwide; 9 North American species
Dippers—5 species worldwide; 1 North American specie
Bulbuls—130 species worldwide; 1 North American specie
Kinglets—5 species worldwide; 2 North American species
Old World Warblers and Gnatcatchers—300 species worldwide; 12 North American species
Old World Flycatchers—about 400 species worldwide; up to 36 North American species
Thrushes—335 species worldwide; 28 North American species
Babblers—at least 340 species worldwide; 1 North American specie
Mockingbirds and Thrashers—35 species worldwide; 13 North American species
Starlings—125 species, one of which has been introduced to North America
Wagtails and Pipits—54 species worldwide; 11 North American species
Waxwings—3 species worldwide; 2 North American species
Silky-Flycatchers—4 species, and they're in North America
Olive Warbler—1 specie, and it's in North America
Wood Warblers—119 species worldwide; 57 North American species
Banana Quits—1 specie worldwide, and it visits Florida
Tanagers—256 species worldwide; 6 North American species
American Sparrows, Towhees, Juncos, and Longspurs—275 worldwide; 60 North American species
Cardinals, Saltators, and Grosbeaks—43 species worldwide; 13 North American species
Blackbirds, Meadowlarks, Cowbirds, Grackles, and Orioles—98 species worldwide; 25 North American species
Finches—137 species worldwide; 23 North American species
Old World Sparrows—35 species worldwide; 2 North American species

List #105 Pets

At some point, almost every child asks to have a pet. Some children want to keep the frog they just caught in the backyard while others want you to move to a farm and raise horses. We've had numerous sorts of pets, and moms frequently ask which (if any) pets are best for children. If you're considering something other than a cat or dog, here are some things to keep in mind while you make this decision.

Fish	Fish make great pets because you can invest any amount of money you want, from as little as five dollars for a beta fish and a small bowl to hundreds of dollars for a saltwater tank and all the fancy fish to stock it. Even young children enjoy having a fish tank, and there is very little upkeep for the tank itself, but you must remind children to feed the fish on a schedule to avoid overfeeding. Fish are great first pets to help children learn responsibility, the basics of pet care, and also how to deal with loss when a fish dies.
Rodents	Mice and other rodents don't live very long, but they make good pets. One of our favorite pets of all time was a little black and white mouse who loved to run around on our shoulders when we had him out of his cage. Children should be at least elementary age to have pet rodents, though, since they will want to handle the rodent and smaller children might not be as gentle. Children also need to be old enough to clean the cage frequently, at least once per week. Their nails also require trimming occasionally. Rats are intelligent rodents and also make very good pets.
Other small "pocket pets"	Most people consider hamsters and gerbils appropriate pets for children, but hamsters are nocturnal and when children try to play with them during the day, they are prone to bite. You also have this issue with gerbils, but they aren't quite as bad.
Guinea pigs	Guinea pigs are one of my favorite kid-friendly pets. They are absolutely adorable little animals, friendly during the day or night, very versatile, and they don't seem to get as easily stressed as some other pets. Guinea pigs do well in multi-child families, but someone will need to be responsible for cleaning the cage regularly as it can get stinky if left unattended.
Birds	Birds can be great pets to look at and sometimes to interact with, but if a child wants to train the bird, this takes a lot of dedication and patience. Birds can be very messy (cages require frequent cleaning), and you may choose to keep their wings trimmed. They can also live a long time, so make sure the child is ready for a long-term commitment. Birds are a beautiful addition to any home and their music can also be very soothing (or, depending on the bird, irritating), so choose wisely.

List #105 **Pets** *(continued)*

Livestock	Horses, sheep, pigs, cattle, and other livestock are often overlooked as possible animals for pets, but they can actually be very good pets for children, particularly children late elementary age and older. The child will have numerous pet care responsibilities and this can be a good thing if the child can handle them. The drawback to these pets, obviously, is that you must have a suitable sized yard or farm to provide the animal adequate living space. If you do, then a large animal may be perfect.
Rabbits	If you have a calm, gentle, dedicated child who is very interested in rabbits, then this might be an appropriate choice for your child. Rabbits are easily stressed, however, and typically don't do well in homes with other loud animals (such as dogs) or rambunctious children. Rabbit cages require frequent cleaning and their teeth and nails must be trimmed occasionally. In colder climates, you will also need proper winter housing, possibly inside your home. Many families keep rabbits as indoor pets all year.
Poultry	Chickens, geese, and guinea fowl can be good for children who are very interested in the science of having a pet—watching it eat, seeing it grow, learning about egg-laying, etc. Some of these animals can actually become attached to people, and though you can't really sit and "cuddle" them, they make good companions in the yard when they follow you around. Poultry are relatively easy to care for, but you will need to make sure their enclosure is adequate to protect them from predators such as coyotes and foxes.
Reptiles	Due to the increased risk of salmonella, snakes, lizards, turtles, and other reptiles are not recommended as pets, especially for younger children. Our five-year-old had salmonella poisoning once from a turtle and I can assure you that it was very scary. Reptiles are beautiful creatures, but be aware of the danger. If you do allow older children to have a reptile for a pet, make sure they wash their hands each time they come in contact with the animal or the cage.

7

The Human Body

List #106 Human Development Stages

Isaiah 44:2 "This is what the Lord says—he who made you, who formed you in the womb, and who will help you: Do not be afraid, O Jacob, my servant, Jeshurun, whom I have chosen."

zygote	from point of conception (fertilization)
blastocyst	period between conception and embryonic stage
embryo	from 3rd week to end of 8th week of pregnancy
fetus	begins at end of 8th week and continues until childbirth
neonate	newborn (0 to 30 days)
infant	from 1 month to 1 year
toddler	a child from age 1 to 4, though there is some overlap and some may consider a toddler one who toddles and a child who walks a "preschooler"
preschooler	any child not yet of school age (which is usually age 5)
elementary school age	ages 4 to 8 (beginning age may vary depending on compulsory attendance age)
preadolescent	(also known as preteen) ages 9 to 12
adolescent	ages 13–19 (also when a person goes through puberty)
young adult	ages 15–22 (though some charts carry this to age 25)
adult	age 18 (though different charts list this as not starting until 20)
death	may occur at any age, depending on the person

List #107 Twins and More (Fraternal vs. Identical)

Fraternal twins

- develop from two separate eggs fertilized at nearly the same time
- may be two boys, two girls, or a boy and girl
- do not look any more alike than the average brother and sister

Identical twins

- develop from the same fertilized egg
- usually look very much alike, or nearly identical

List #108 Major Organ Systems

System	Organs in the System
circulatory	heart
	blood vessels (arteries, capillaries, veins)
	lymph structures
respiratory	nose
	mouth
	pharynx
	larynx
	trachea
	bronchi
	lungs
nervous	brain
	spinal cord
	nerves
integumentary	skin (surface skin and the underlying structures of the skin, including fat, glands, and blood vessels)
	hair
	nails
	sweat glands
musculoskeletal	muscles
	tendons and ligaments
	bones
	joints
blood	blood cells and platelets
	plasma (the liquid part of blood)
	bone marrow (where blood cells are produced)
	spleen
	thymus

List #108 **Major Organ Systems** *(continued)*

System	Organs in the System
digestive	mouth
	esophagus
	stomach
	small intestine
	large intestine
	liver
	gallbladder
	pancreas (the portion that produces enzymes)
	appendix
	rectum
	anus
endocrine	thyroid gland
	parathyroid glands
	adrenal glands
	pituitary gland
	pancreas (the part that produces insulin)
	stomach (the cells that produce gastrin)
	pineal gland
	ovaries
	testes
urinary/excretory	kidneys
	ureter
	bladder
	urethra
male reproductive organs	penis
	prostate gland
	testes
	vas deferens
	seminal vesicles
female reproductive organs	vagina
	mammary glands
	fallopian tubes
	uterus
	ovaries

List #109 Main Bones in the Skeletal System

Here are the functions of some of these parts of the skeletal system:

skull	provides a built-in helmet for your brain and provides the shape for your face
spinal column	this is your backbone, made up of vertebrae, and holds your body up
ribs	surround and protect your heart and lungs
sternum	connects some of your ribs in front
pelvis	protects your digestive and reproductive organs
humerus, ulna, and radius	make up your arm bones
femur, fibula, and tibia	make up your leg bones
patella	this is your kneecap, which serves as a protective cover over a bent knee

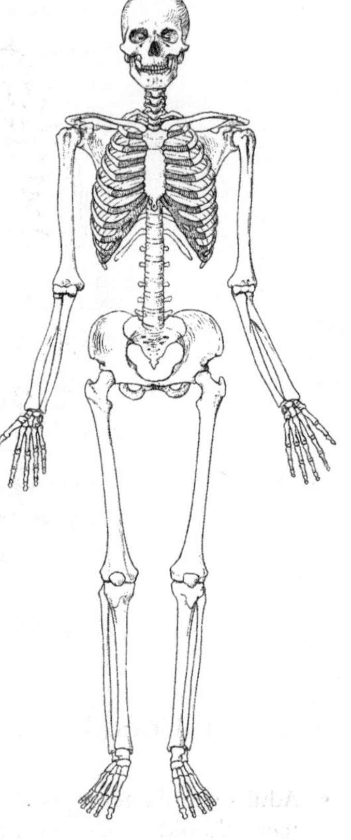

Fast Facts

- An adult has 206 bones.
- The skull is made up of thirty bones.
- An adult's skull is fused together, but a baby's is not. This happens gradually as a baby grows.
- The spine consists of thirty-three vertebrae, bony rings that protect your spinal cord.
- The vertebrae are separated by cartilage, layers of cushion that protect the vertebrae and allow you to bend.
- Three main types of connective tissue: cartilage, tendons, and ligaments.
- Tendons connect muscles to bones and allow the bones to move.

List #110 Human Teeth

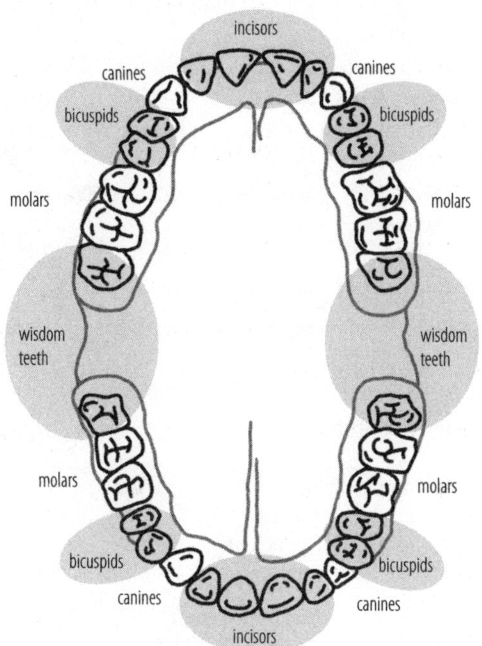

List #111 Good Health Habits

- Adults should get at least eight hours of sleep each night. Children and teens should have at least nine hours of sleep each night.
- Brush your teeth three times every day and floss once every day. Many people don't realize that dental health affects other areas of the body, such as blood flow and the function of the heart.
- Even children can have too many responsibilities, so make sure everyone in your family has some "downtime" each day.
- Avoid stress.
- Wash your hands frequently.
- Eat healthy foods. Avoid fatty foods and don't overindulge or gorge yourself on food.

List #112 Healthy Snacks

- **fruit**: grapes, pineapple, mango, cherries, bananas, oranges, apples, cantaloupe, strawberries, etc.
- **vegetables**: broccoli, celery stalks, cauliflower, baked yams, baked potatoes, any peppers, carrots, etc.
- **bread**: home-baked bread, whole wheat bread, unsweetened cereal (Chex, cornflakes, Cheerios, etc.)
- **dairy**: a slice of American cheese, small blocks of Monterey Jack, cheddar, or mozzarella cheese
- **popcorn**
- **unsweetened fruit juice**
- **shakes made with lowfat milk or mixed fruit and yogurt**

List #113 Food Groups

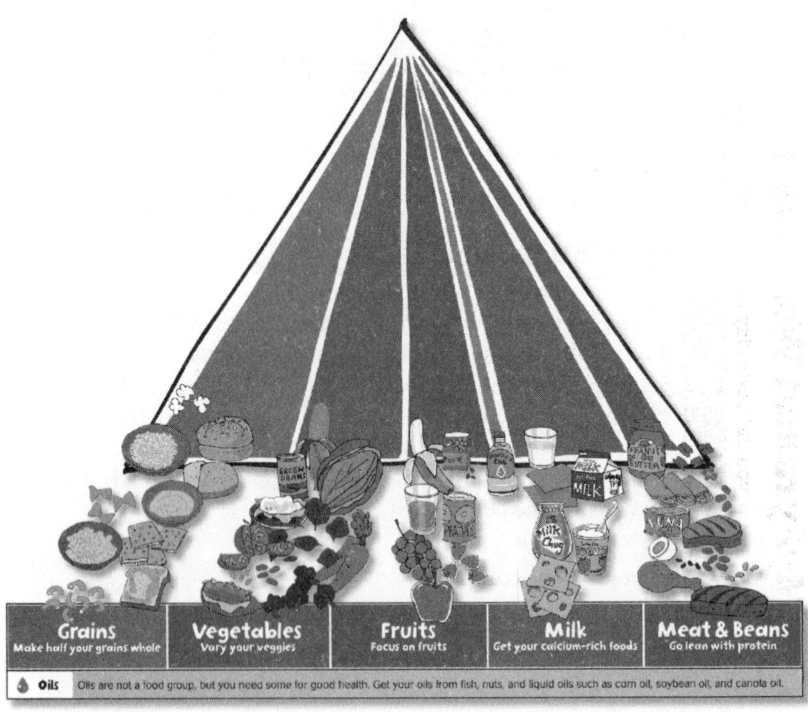

Source: U.S. Department of Agriculture, Food and Nutrition Service (*www.teamnutrition.usda.gov*)

List #114 Food and Activity Goal-Setting Worksheet

MyPyramid Worksheet

Name: ______________________

MyPyramid FOR KIDS

Check how you did yesterday and set a goal to aim for tomorrow

Write In Your Choices From Yesterday	Food and Activity	Tip	Goal (Based On a 1800 Calorie Pattern)	List Each Food Choice In Its Food Group*	Estimate Your Total
Breakfast:	**Grains**	Make at least half your grains whole grains.	**6 ounce equivalents** (1 ounce equivalent is about 1 slice bread, 1 cup dry cereal, or ½ cup cooked rice, pasta, or cereal)		____ ounce equivalents
Lunch:	**Vegetables**	Color your plate with all kinds of great tasting veggies.	**2½ cups** (Choose from dark green, orange, starchy, dry beans and peas, or other veggies).		____ cups
Snack:	**Fruits**	Make most choices fruit, not juice.	**1½ cups**		____ cups
Dinner:	**Milk**	Choose fat-free or lowfat most often.	**3 cups** (1 cup yogurt or 1½ ounces cheese = 1 cup milk)		____ cups
	Meat and Beans	Choose lean meat and chicken or turkey. Vary your choices—more fish, beans, peas, nuts, and seeds.	**5 ounce equivalents** (1 ounce equivalent is 1 ounce meat, chicken or turkey, or fish, 1 egg, 1 T. peanut butter, ½ ounce nuts, or ¼ cup dry beans)		____ ounce equivalents
Physical activity:	**Physical Activity**	Build more physical activity into your daily routine at home and school.	At least **60 minutes** of moderate to vigorous activity a day or most days.		____ minutes

How did you do yesterday? ☐ Great ☐ So-So ☐ Not So Great

My food goal for tomorrow is: ______________________

My activity goal for tomorrow is: ______________________

* Some foods don't fit into any group. These "extras" may be mainly fat or sugar—limit your intake of these.

List #115 Basic First Aid

Every family should have a basic first aid kit available in their home. You should also consider keeping a kit in your vehicle. This is especially handy when you are running errands, participating in outside activities, or traveling. Many places sell prepackaged first aid kits. While these are great, you may want to add a few items of your own. Either way, here are some suggestions for a well-stocked kit in a home with children:

- lots of Band-Aids or other adhesive bandages in various sizes
- burn ointment (over-the-counter or available by prescription)
- scissors
- anti-diarrheal medication
- over-the-counter pain medication, such as Tylenol and Motrin (We keep both brands—or the generic equivalent—available at all times in several different strengths for various ages.)
- necessary prescription medications, such as insulin, an asthma inhaler, heart medication, etc. (I don't keep these in our automobile first aid kit for safety reasons.)
- a list of medication allergies (useful in an accident and you are unable to communicate)
- medium to large sterile dressings to stop bleeding
- antibacterial soap, cleaning agent, or antibiotic towelettes to disinfect an area
- eyewash or eyedrops to flush eyes
- hand sanitizer
- two pairs of disposable gloves (We have never used these within our own family, but if you were helping someone else in an emergency, they might be a good idea.)

Make a list here of other items you would like to keep in your own first aid kit:

____________________ ____________________

____________________ ____________________

____________________ ____________________

____________________ ____________________

____________________ ____________________

____________________ ____________________

List #116 Basic Fire Safety

- Change the batteries in your smoke alarms regularly (at least twice per year).
- Keep a fire extinguisher in your house. (We have one in the kitchen and one in the utility room. If you have a garage, that's another good place to have one.)
- Practice fire drills with your children. Establish a meeting place outside the home and practice at least twice per year. Make sure at least one practice fire drill per year is conducted at night.

List #117 Family Supply Box

We keep our first aid kit in a "family supply box" in our big van. This supply box, which is simply a sturdy plastic tote, has proven invaluable when we've been out longer than expected and run out of diapers or other baby supplies, stayed the night unexpectedly at a relative's house, or had a child get carsick. I would highly recommend that anyone with children under age six consider carrying a family supply box. Here are some suggested items:

- extra diapers and baby wipes
- an extra pair of socks and shoes for each child (an alternate idea is to carry a pair of water shoes for each child, which can serve duty as extra shoes or something to use for impromptu water play)
- an extra change of clothes for each child
- an extra bottle and formula if your child is bottle-fed
- a small container of change and small bills (cash for emergencies)
- a couple of sturdy plastic bags or a small container that can be given to a carsick individual
- a couple of towels and washcloths
- a pair of pajamas for each child
- nonperishable snacks (Having snacks handy also saves money!)
- your first aid kit
- small books, coloring books and crayons, Mad Libs, or other small activity items

8

Geography

List #118 Geography Words

aftershock	a small earthquake that follows a larger earthquake
arid	extremely dry
atlas	a collection of maps bound together in a book
atmosphere	the air; the gaseous area surrounding a heavenly body
barren	not a productive land; not fertile
bay	a body of water that forms an inlet at the coast that is larger than a cove but smaller than a gulf
canyons	deep valleys with steep slopes; often there are streams or rivers flowing through the valley of the canyon
cartographer	a person who creates maps
channel	a chimney or pipelike opening in the top or sides of a volcano through which magma flows up to a vent
climate	the prevailing weather conditions of a region
core	the center of the Earth
crown fire	a fire that burns in the tops of trees
crust	the outer layer of the Earth
cultivation	the act of preparing land for crops or other use
earthquake	a sudden shaking of the earth that can be caused by movement of the Earth's plates, explosions, volcanic eruptions, and other major events on or under the Earth's surface
erosion	a wearing away of the land due to water flow
fault	a crack in the Earth's surface where two plates meet
firebreak	a portion or band of ground that is burned on purpose to remove the fuel for an unwanted fire
flood plain	lowland near rivers or other flood-prone areas
foreshock	a small earthquake that is followed by a larger earthquake
glacier	a mass of ice
grassland	an area of land that consists primarily of various grasses
ground fire	fire burning on the ground or through the understory and not reaching into the tree canopy
gulf	a portion of the ocean or a sea that is partially enclosed by land
highland	an elevated region or plateau
ice cap	a thick cover of ice
iceberg	a large mass of ice that dislodges from a glacier and floats out to sea
lava	melted rock that escapes from a volcano to the Earth's surface

List #118 **Geography Words** *(continued)*

levee	a high bank built of earth, concrete, or even sandbags near the edge of a river to prevent it from flooding nearby land
magma	hot melted rock under the Earth's crust
magma pool	a large pool of magma in the Earth's crust
magnitude	the strength or size of an earthquake
mantle	the middle layer of the Earth
mesa	a land formation that has relatively steep sides, a basically flat top, and is not quite as large as a plateau
natural resource	wealth that comes from nature through forests, water, mineral deposits, etc.
nonrenewable resource	a resource that cannot be recreated once it is used up; examples: oil and coal
nutrients	minerals that help plants grow
oasis	a fertile place, usually with a spring or natural water source, in a desert region
pahoehoe	a Polynesian word scientists use to describe the surface of a smooth lava flow
peninsula	land that is connected by a small portion of land to the mainland, but otherwise surrounded by water; Florida is a peninsula
plate	a section of the Earth's crust that moves slowly across the mantle
plateau	a land with a relatively flat plain that is raised above the adjoining land
prairie	a level portion of land that is typically covered with coarse grass rather than trees; typically associated with land in the Mississippi River valley
renewable resource	a resource that can be regenerated; for example, trees are cut down, but more can be planted; water is also a renewable resource because it comes back through the water cycle
Richter Scale	a scale invented in 1935 by Charles Richter to measure the magnitude of an earthquake
silt	rich soil left on land after floodwaters recede
surface fire	(see "ground fire")
tundra	largely treeless, flat plains areas of the arctic regions of Europe, Asia, and North America
vents	openings at the top of a volcano's channels through which gases and lava escape

List #119 Weather Phenomena

cyclone	a large storm whose winds rotate counterclockwise in the northern hemisphere and clockwise in the southern hemisphere; some people refer to a cyclone as a tornado (but it's technically different)
drought	any extended period of abnormally dry weather
firestorm	a fire that is so large that it creates its own winds, some of which can turn into small tornadoes of fire
flash flood	a flood that occurs quickly and without warning
flood	water that flows onto normally dry land due to overflowing rivers, hurricanes, broken dams, etc.
hurricane	a large storm that starts over the ocean and has winds that swirl in a circular direction
monsoon	although the definition is actually a seasonal wind, we associate this term with the heavy rains it brings with it
seasonal drought	an extended dry period, especially an abnormally dry period, that occurs in certain areas that have a wet/dry climate with periods of rain and periods of dryness
tornado	a violently rotating column of air, often (but not always) visible as a funnel cloud
tsunami	a large ocean wave that can cause damage (sometimes incredible damage) on land; tsunamis are sometimes caused by earthquakes under the ocean floor

List #120 Layers of the Earth

crust	The Earth's crust is the thin, hard outer shell of rock that makes up the topmost layer of the Earth. The crust is anywhere from 3 (ocean) to 37 (continental) miles thick. In relation to the Earth, the thickness would be about the same as the skin on an apple.
mantle	a layer of hot, soft rock located beneath the crust
outer core	composed of liquid iron and nickel
inner core	composed of solid iron and nickel

In addition to these main layers of the Earth, the crust and upper part of the mantle are sometimes divided into three layers, according to their rigidity: the lithosphere, the asthenosphere, and the mesosphere.

List #121 Richter Scale

In 1935, seismologist Charles Richter invented a set of measurements to determine the strength or magnitude of an earthquake.

Magnitude	Description of Damage	Average Occurrences Worldwide
9.0 or greater	Devastating—destruction in areas for several thousand miles	1 every 20 years
8.0 to 8.9	Great—destruction for several hundred miles	1 per year
7.0 to 7.9	Major—destruction in a large area	18 per year
6.0 to 6.9	Strong—damage up to 100 miles away	120 per year
5.0 to 5.9	Moderate—damage to poorly built buildings	800 per year
4.0 to 4.9	Light—damage is not likely, but household items could shake and rattle	6,200 per year
3.0 to 3.9	Minor—usually felt, but little or no damage	49,000 per year
2.9 or lower	Very minor—frequently these quakes aren't even felt by people, but they can be registered on seismographs	9,000 every day

List #122 Fujita Tornado Damage Scale

The Fujita Scale, also known as the F-Scale or Fujita-Pearson Scale, rates a tornado's intensity after it has passed over a particular area and an investigation is conducted to determine with more accuracy the tornado's intensity. Dr. Theodore Fujita invented the scale in 1971.

Category	Wind Speed	Damage
F0	less than 73 mph	**very little damage**; some damage to chimneys, vegetation, tree branches, shallow rooted trees, signs
F1	73–112 mph	**moderate damage**; rooftops torn off, mobile homes slightly damaged, overturned, or pushed off foundations; moving automobiles pushed off road
F2	113–157 mph	**considerable damage**; mobile homes destroyed; roofs torn off structures and walls may collapse; boxcars and automobiles overturned; large trees uprooted or broken; small objects turned into lightweight missiles
F3	158–206 mph	**severe damage**; roofs and walls torn off well-built structures; trains and heavy cars overturned; cars may be thrown a distance; most trees uprooted
F4	207–260 mph	**devastation**; even well-constructed structures leveled; structures with weak foundations blown some distance; automobiles overturned, carried through the air, and thrown some distance
F5	261–318 mph	**near total destruction**; well-built homes lifted off foundation and thrown some distance, where they are busted apart; bark pulled off trees; automobile missiles fly through air over 100 yards
F6	319–379 mph	While the F6 level was present on Dr. Fujita's original wind scale, these types of winds would be almost impossible and have never been observed. If an F6 tornado did occur, the damage would be inconceivable, with large-object missiles, total destruction at eye of storm, and significant damage to surrounding areas.

List #123 Saffir-Simpson Hurricane Scale

Herbert Saffir, a consulting engineer, and Dr. Bob Simpson, director of the National Hurricane Center, developed the Saffir-Simpson Hurricane Scale in 1969 as a more uniform means of predicting damage of an oncoming hurricane and to make comparisons to past hurricanes easier.

Category	Winds	Effects
1	74–95 mph	very little, if any, damage to buildings; main damage to unanchored mobile homes, trees, shrubbery; potential for some coastal flooding and minor damage to piers
2	96–110 mph	minor damage to roofs, doors, and windows; substantial damage to vegetation, trees, plants, mobile homes, small crafts in unprotected anchorages, and piers; coastal areas and low-lying roads flood 2–4 hours before arrival of eye
3	111–130 mph	structural damage to small buildings, residences, and utility buildings; mobile homes destroyed; flooding near coast destroys smaller structures; larger structures can be damaged by floating debris; land continuously lower than five feet above sea level may be flooded for eight or more miles inland
4	131–155 mph	extensive damage to buildings and potential complete roof failure on small residences; major erosion of beach; major damage to structures near shore; land continuously lower than ten feet above sea level may be flooded as far as six miles inland
5	greater than 155 mph	complete roof failure on even larger buildings and complete destruction of smaller buildings; major damage to all structures less than fifteen feet above sea level that are within 500 yards of shoreline; mass evacuation of residential areas within five to ten miles of coast

List #124 Rock Classification

Igneous Rocks	form from molten magma
	divided into two main categories: *plutonic rock* and *volcanic*
	Plutonic rocks form when magma cools and crystallizes slowly within the Earth's crust. It takes a few thousand years for these rocks to cool.
	Volcanic rocks form when magma reaches the Earth's surface as lava or ejections of magma fragments. These rocks cool and solidify in a few days or weeks.
Sedimentary	form by deposits of sediments, organic matter, or chemical precipitates that are compacted and cemented together
	form near the Earth's surface
Metamorphic	form when any type of rock is subjected to different temperature and pressure conditions than those that originally formed the rock
	The temperature and pressure must be higher than those at the Earth's surface to produce the kind of conditions to change the original minerals into other mineral types or different forms of those minerals and thus change the rock's organic composition.

List #125 The Water Cycle

The water cycle is the continuous movement of water around the Earth—over, above, and under the surface. This cycle occurs continuously, powered by solar energy. Throughout the cycle, water changes state—occurring in liquid, solid, and gas forms. Water cycle–related terminology is defined in list #126.

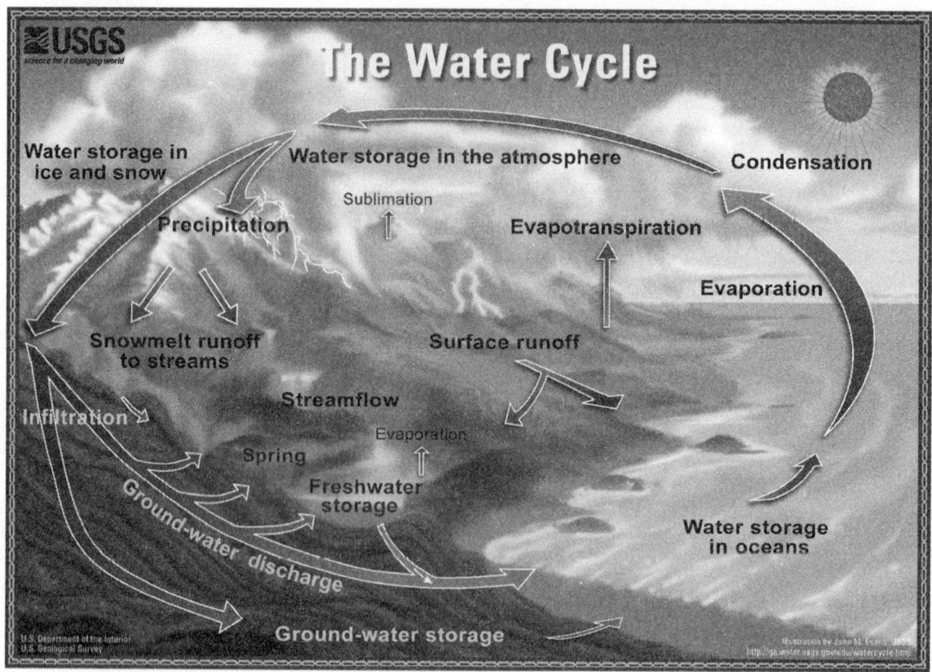

This illustration is by John M. Evans of the United States Geological Survey and is used with permission of the USGS.

List #126 Terms From the Water Cycle

canopy interception	occurs when precipitation falls to the Earth's atmosphere, but is intercepted by tree and plant foliage and then evaporates back to the Earth's atmosphere
condensation	process of water changing from vaporous state to liquid state, which produces clouds and fog
evaporation	process of water transforming from a liquid to a gas state and moving from the Earth's surface to the atmosphere
infiltration	water soaking into the ground
precipitation	water that falls to the Earth's surface; most commonly occurs as rain, but also occurs as sleet, hail, snow, and fog
runoff	water moving across the land to the nearest stream channel
snowmelt	runoff produced by melting snow
sublimation	process of water changing directly from solid to vaporous state
subsurface flow	water that flows underground

List #127 States and Capitals

Order	State	Date Entered Union	State Capital
1	Delaware	December 7, 1787	Dover
2	Pennsylvania	December 12, 1787	Harrisburg
3	New Jersey	December 18, 1787	Trenton
4	Georgia	January 2, 1788	Atlanta
5	Connecticut	January 9, 1788	Hartford
6	Massachusetts	February 6, 1788	Boston
7	Maryland	April 28, 1788	Annapolis
8	South Carolina	May 23, 1788	Columbia
9	New Hampshire	June 21, 1788	Concord
10	Virginia	June 25, 1788	Richmond
11	New York	July 26, 1788	Albany
12	North Carolina	November 21, 1789	Raleigh
13	Rhode Island	May 29, 1790	Providence
14	Vermont	March 4, 1791	Montpelier
15	Kentucky	June 1, 1792	Frankfort
16	Tennessee	June 1, 1796	Nashville
17	Ohio	March 1, 1803	Columbus
18	Louisiana	April 30, 1812	Baton Rouge
19	Indiana	December 11, 1816	Indianapolis
20	Mississippi	December 10, 1817	Jackson
21	Illinois	December 3, 1818	Springfield
22	Alabama	December 14, 1819	Montgomery
23	Maine	March 15, 1820	Augusta
24	Missouri	August 10, 1821	Jefferson City
25	Arkansas	June 15, 1836	Little Rock
26	Michigan	January 26, 1837	Lansing
27	Florida	March 3, 1845	Tallahassee
28	Texas	December 29, 1845	Austin
29	Iowa	December 28, 1846	Des Moines
30	Wisconsin	May 29, 1848	Madison
31	California	September 9, 1850	Sacramento
32	Minnesota	May 11, 1858	St. Paul
33	Oregon	February 14, 1859	Salem

List #127 **States and Capitals** *(continued)*

Order	State	Date Entered Union	State Capital
34	Kansas	January 29, 1861	Topeka
35	West Virginia	June 20, 1863	Charleston
36	Nevada	October 31, 1864	Carson City
37	Nebraska	March 1, 1867	Lincoln
38	Colorado	August 1, 1876	Denver
39	North Dakota	November 2, 1889	Bismarck
40	South Dakota	November 2, 1889	Pierre
41	Montana	November 8, 1889	Helena
42	Washington	November 11, 1889	Olympia
43	Idaho	July 3, 1890	Boise
44	Wyoming	July 10, 1890	Cheyenne
45	Utah	January 4, 1896	Salt Lake City
46	Oklahoma	November 16, 1907	Oklahoma City
47	New Mexico	January 6, 1912	Santa Fe
48	Arizona	February 14, 1912	Phoenix
49	Alaska	January 3, 1959	Juneau
50	Hawaii	August 21, 1959	Honolulu

List #128 State Facts (Key Industries, State Song, etc.)

State	Key Industries	State Song	State Bird	State Tree	State Flower
Alabama	cotton, peanuts	"Alabama" (1931)	yellowhammer (1927)	southern longleaf pine (1949, 1997)	camellia (1959)
Alaska	petroleum, fishing, forestry, tourism	"Alaska's Flag" (1955)	willow ptarmigan (1955)	Sitka spruce (1962)	forget-me-not (1917)
Arizona	copper and mineral production	"Arizona" (1919)	cactus wren (1931)	palo verde (1954)	flower of saguaro cactus (1931)
Arkansas	soybeans, cotton	"Arkansas" (1963)	mockingbird (1929)	pine (1939)	apple blossom (1901)
California	oranges, grapes, wine; computers; tourism; movies and television	"I Love You, California" (1951)	California valley quail (1931)	California redwood (1937, 1953)	golden poppy (1903)
Colorado	skiing, livestock	"Where the Columbines Grow" (1915)	lark bunting (1931)	Colorado blue spruce (1939)	Rocky Mountain columbine (1899)
Connecticut	insurance, submarines	"Yankee Doodle" (1978)	American robin (1943)	white oak (1947)	mountain laurel (1907)
Delaware	chemicals, nylon	"Our Delaware" (1925)	blue hen chicken (1939)	American holly (1939)	peach blossom (1895)
Florida	citrus fruits, tourism	"Swanee River" (1935)	mockingbird (1927)	Sabal palm (1953)	orange blossom (1909)
Georgia	peanuts, peaches, pecans	"Georgia on My Mind" (1922)	brown thrasher (1935)	live oak (1937)	Cherokee rose (1916)
Hawaii	sugar, pineapple; tourism	"Hawaii Ponoi" (1967)	nene (Hawaiian goose) (1957)	kukui (candlenut) (1959)	yellow hibiscus (1988)
Idaho	potatoes	"Here We Have Idaho" (1931)	mountain bluebird (1931)	white pine (1935)	syringe (1931)
Illinois	corn; manufacturing	"Illinois" (1925)	cardinal (1929)	white oak (1973)	violet (1908)

List #128 **State Facts** *(continued)*

State	Key Industries	State Song	State Bird	State Tree	State Flower
Indiana	corn; steel	"On the Banks of the Wabash, Far Away" (1913)	cardinal (1933)	tulip tree (1931)	peony (1957)
Iowa	corn; hogs	"Song of Iowa" (1911)	eastern goldfinch (1933)	oak (1961)	wild rose (1897)
Kansas	cattle; wheat	"Home on the Range" (1947)	western meadowlark (1937)	cottonwood (1937)	sunflower (1903)
Kentucky	tobacco; bourbon whiskey	"My Old Kentucky Home" (1928)	Kentucky cardinal (1926)	tulip poplar (1994)	goldenrod (1926)
Louisiana	cotton, sugarcane; petroleum products	"Give Me Lousiana" (1970)	eastern brown pelican (1958)	bald cypress (1963)	magnolia (1900)
Maine	potatoes, lobster, blueberries	"State of Maine Song" (1937)	chickadee (1927)	white pine tree (1945)	white pine cone and tassel (1895)
Maryland	chickens, dairy products; crabs	"Maryland! My Maryland!" (1939)	Baltimore oriole (1947)	white oak (1941)	black-eyed susan (1918)
Massachusetts	cranberries, clams, oysters, lobsters	"All Hail to Massachusetts" (1966)	chickadee (1941)	American elm (1941)	mayflower (1918)
Michigan	motor vehicles; dairy products, cereal	"My Michigan" (1937)	robin (1931)	white pine (1955)	apple blossom (1897)
Minnesota	oats, corn, soybeans	"Hail, Minnesota" (1945)	common loon or great northern diver (1961)	red pine or Norway pine (1953)	lady slipper (1902)
Mississippi	cotton	"Go, Mississippi" (1962)	mockingbird (1944)	magnolia (1938)	flower or bloom of the magnolia or evergreen magnolia (1952)

List #128 **State Facts** *(continued)*

State	Key Industries	State Song	State Bird	State Tree	State Flower
Missouri	soybeans, corn; lead	"Missouri Waltz" (1949)	bluebird (1927)	flowering dogwood (1955)	hawthorn (1923)
Montana	wheat, barley	"Montana" (1945)	Western meadowlark (1981)	ponderosa pine (1949)	bitterroot (1895)
Nebraska	cattle; corn, wheat, alfalfa; meatpacking	"Beautiful Nebraska" (1967)	Western meadowlark (1929)	cottonwood (1972)	goldenrod (1895)
Nevada	gambling, tourism, mining	"Home Means Nevada" (1933)	mountain bluebird (1967)	single-leaf piñon (1953); bristlecone pine (1987)	sagebrush (1959)
New Hampshire	dairy products; apples, maple syrup	"Old New Hampshire" (1949)	purple finch (1957)	white birch (1947)	purple lilac (1919)
New Jersey	chemicals, pharmaceuticals; nursery plants, tomatoes	*no official song*	eastern goldfinch (1935)	red oak (1950)	purple violet (1913)
New Mexico	cattle; mining	"O Fair New Mexico" (1917)	roadrunner (1949)	piñon pine (1949)	yucca (1927)
New York	publishing, finance, machinery	"I Love New York" (1980)	bluebird (1970)	sugar maple (1956)	rose (1955)
North Carolina	tobacco	"The Old North State" (1927)	cardinal (1943)	pine (1963)	dogwood (1941)
North Dakota	wheat, rye, barley	"North Dakota Hymn" (1947)	western meadowlark (1947)	American elm (1947)	wild prairie rose (1907)
Ohio	soybeans, corn, rubber products	"Beautiful Ohio" (1969)	cardinal (1933)	buckeye (1953)	scarlet carnation (1904)
Oklahoma	petroleum, wheat	"Oklahoma" (1953)	scissor-tailed flycatcher (1951)	redbud (1937)	mistletoe (1893)
Oregon	lumber, fishing, grass seed	"Oregon, My Oregon" (1927)	western meadowlark (1927)	douglas fir (1939)	Oregon grape (1899)

List #128 **State Facts** *(continued)*

State	Key Industries	State Song	State Bird	State Tree	State Flower
Pennsylvania	iron, steel, manufacturing	"Pennsylvania" (1990)	ruffed grouse (1931)	hemlock (1931)	mountain laurel (1933)
Rhode Island	textiles, jewelry	"Rhode Island, It's for Me" (1996)	Rhode Island red hen (1954)	red maple (1964)	violet (1968)
South Carolina	tobacco, cotton	"Carolina" (1911)	Carolina wren (1948)	palmetto tree (1939)	Carolina yellow jessamine (1924)
South Dakota	beef, corn, tourism	"Hail, South Dakota" (1943)	Chinese ring-necked pheasant (1943)	Black Hills spruce (1947)	American pasque (1903)
Tennessee	tobacco, aluminum	7 songs, including "Tennessee Waltz" (1965)	mockingbird (1933)	tulip poplar (1947)	iris (1933)
Texas	petroleum, cotton, chemicals	"Texas, Our Texas" (1929)	mockingbird (1927)	pecan (1919)	bluebonnet (1901)
Utah	mining, tourism	"Utah, We Love Thee" (1953)	California gull (1955)	blue spruce (1933)	sego lily (1911)
Vermont	granite, maple syrup	"These Green Mountains" (2000)	hermit thrush (1941)	sugar maple (1949)	red clover (1894)
Virginia	dairy, tobacco, government	*no state song*	cardinal (1950)	dogwood (1956)	American dogwood (1918)
Washington	apples, cherries, peas, lumber, aircraft	"Washington, My Home" (1959)	willow goldfinch (1951)	western hemlock (1947)	coast rhododendron (1892)
West Virginia	natural gas, coal	3 songs, including "West Virginia Hills" (1963)	cardinal (1949)	sugar maple (1949)	rhododendron (1903)
Wisconsin	paper products	"On, Wisconsin" (1959)	robin (1949)	sugar maple (1949)	wood violet (1949)
Wyoming	coal, cattle, uranium	"Wyoming" (1955)	western meadowlark (1927)	cottonwood (1947)	Indian paintbrush (1917)

List #129 Population Demographics of States

Rank (based on 2005 population)	State (statistics include Puerto Rico and District of Columbia)	Population in 1790	Population in 2005
1	California		36,132,147
2	Texas		22,859,968
3	New York	340,120	19,254,630
4	Florida		17,789,864
5	Illinois		12,763,371
6	Pennsylvania	434,373	12,429,616
7	Ohio		11,464,042
8	Michigan		10,120,860
9	Georgia	82,548	9,072,576
10	New Jersey	184,139	8,717,925
11	North Carolina	393,751	8,683,242
12	Virginia	747,610	7,567,465
13	Massachusetts	378,787	6,398,743
14	Washington		6,287,759
15	Indiana		6,271,973
16	Tennessee	35,691	5,962,959
17	Arizona		5,939,292
18	Missouri		5,800,310
19	Maryland	319,728	5,600,388
20	Wisconsin		5,536,201
21	Minnesota		5,132,799
22	Colorado		4,665,177
23	Alabama		4,557,808
24	Louisiana		4,523,628
25	South Carolina	249,073	4,255,083
26	Kentucky	73,677	4,173,405
27	Puerto Rico		3,912,054
28	Oregon		3,641,056
29	Oklahoma		3,547,884
30	Connecticut	237,946	3,510,297
31	Iowa		2,966,334
32	Mississippi		2,921,088
33	Arkansas		2,779,154

List #129 **Population Demographics of States** *(continued)*

Rank (based on 2005 population)	State (statistics include Puerto Rico and District of Columbia)	Population in 1790	Population in 2005
34	Kansas		2,744,687
35	Utah		2,469,585
36	Nevada		2,414,807
37	New Mexico		1,928,384
38	West Virginia		1,816,856
39	Nebraska		1,758,787
40	Idaho		1,429,096
41	Maine	96,540	1,321,505
42	New Hampshire	141,885	1,309,940
43	Hawaii		1,275,194
44	Rhode Island	68,825	1,076,189
45	Montana		935,670
46	Delaware	59,096	843,524
47	South Dakota		775,933
48	Alaska		663,661
49	North Dakota		636,677
50	Vermont	85,425	623,050
51	District of Columbia		550,521
52	Wyoming		509,294

List #130 Capitals Around the World

Country/Territory	Capital City
Afghanistan	Kabul
Albania	Tirana
Algeria	Algiers
Andorra	Andorra la Vella
Angola	Luanda
Antigua and Barbuda	St. Johns
Argentina	Buenos Aires
Armenia	Yerevan
Australia	Canberra
Austria	Vienna
Azerbaijan	Baku
Bahamas, The	Nassau
Bahrain	Manama
Bangladesh	Dhaka
Barbados	Bridgetown
Belarus	Minsk
Belgium	Brussels
Belize	Belmopan
Benin	Porto-Novo (legislative), Cotonou (administrative)
Bhutan	Thimphu
Bolivia	La Paz (administrative), Sucre (judicial)
Bosnia and Herzegovina	Sarajevo
Botswana	Gaborone
Brazil	Brasilia
Brunei	Bandar Seri Begawan
Bulgaria	Sofia
Burkina Faso	Ouagadougou
Burundi	Bujumbura
Cambodia	Phnom Penh
Cameroon	Yaounde
Canada	Ottawa
Cape Verde	Praia
Central African Republic	Bangui

List #130 **Capitals Around the World** *(continued)*

Country/Territory	Capital City
Chad	N'Djamena
Chile	Santiago
China, People's Republic of	Beijing
Colombia	Bogota
Comoros	Moroni
Congo, Democratic Republic of the	Kinshasa
Congo, Republic of the	Brazzaville
Costa Rica	San Jose
Côte d'Ivoire (Ivory Coast)	Yamoussoukro (official), Abidjan (de facto)
Croatia	Zagreb
Cuba	Havana
Cyprus	Nicosia
Czech Republic	Prague
Denmark	Copenhagen
Djibouti	Djibouti
Dominica	Roseau
Dominican Republic	Santo Domingo
Ecuador	Quito
Egypt	Cairo
El Salvador	San Salvador
Equatorial Guinea	Malabo
Eritrea	Asmara
Estonia	Tallinn
Ethiopia	Addis Ababa
Fiji	Suva
Finland	Helsinki
France	Paris
Gabon	Libreville
Gambia, The	Banjul
Georgia	Tbilisi
Germany	Berlin
Ghana	Accra
Greece	Athens

List #130 **Capitals Around the World** *(continued)*

Country/Territory	Capital City
Grenada	St. George's
Guatemala	Guatemala City
Guinea	Conakry
Guinea-Bissau	Bissau
Guyana	Georgetown
Haiti	Port-au-Prince
Honduras	Tegucigalpa
Hungary	Budapest
Iceland	Reykjavik
India	New Delhi
Indonesia	Jakarta
Iran	Tehran
Iraq	Baghdad
Ireland	Dublin
Israel	Jerusalem
Italy	Rome
Jamaica	Kingston
Japan	Tokyo
Jordan	Amman
Kazakhstan	Astana
Kenya	Nairobi
Kiribati	Bairiki, on the island of Tarawa
Korea, North	Pyongyang
Korea, South	Seoul
Kuwait	Kuwait City
Kyrgyzstan	Bishkek
Laos	Vientiane
Latvia	Riga
Lebanon	Beirut
Lesotho	Maseru
Liberia	Monrovia
Libya	Tripoli
Liechtenstein	Vaduz
Lithuania	Vilnius

List #130 **Capitals Around the World** *(continued)*

Country/Territory	Capital City
Luxembourg	Luxembourg
Macedonia, Republic of	Skopje
Madagascar	Antananarivo
Malawi	Lilongwe
Malaysia	Kuala Lumpur
Maldives	Male
Mali	Bamako
Malta	Valletta
Marshall Islands	Majuro
Mauritania	Nouakchott
Mauritius	Port Louis
Mexico	Mexico City
Micronesia, Federated States of	Palikir
Moldova	Chisinau
Monaco	Monaco
Mongolia	Ulaanbaatar (Ulaan Baatar, aka Ulan Batar, aka Ulan Bator)
Montenegro	Podgorica (administrative capital), Cetinje (capital city)
Morocco	Rabat
Mozambique	Maputo
Myanmar (Burma)	Pyinmana (previously Rangoon)
Namibia	Windhoek
Nauru	Yaren District
Nepal	Kathmandu
Netherlands, The	Amsterdam
New Zealand	Wellington
Nicaragua	Managua
Niger	Niamey
Nigeria	Abuja
Norway	Oslo
Oman	Muscat
Pakistan	Islamabad
Palau	Melekeok on Babelthuap Island (previously Koror)

List #130 **Capitals Around the World** *(continued)*

Country/Territory	Capital City
Panama	Panama City
Papua New Guinea	Port Moresby
Paraguay	Asuncion
Peru	Lima
Philippines	Manila
Poland	Warsaw
Portugal	Lisbon
Qatar	Doha
Romania	Bucharest
Russia	Moscow
Rwanda	Kigali
St. Kitts and Nevis	Basseterre
St. Lucia	Castries
St. Vincent and the Grenadines	Kingstown
Samoa	Apia
San Marino	San Marino
São Tomé and Príncipe	São Tomé
Saudi Arabia	Riyadh
Senegal	Dakar
Serbia	Belgrade
Seychelles	Victoria
Sierra Leone	Freetown
Singapore	Singapore
Slovakia	Bratislava
Slovenia	Ljubljana
Solomon Islands	Honiara
Somalia	Mogadishu
South Africa	Pretoria (administrative), Cape Town (legislative), Bloemfontein (judicial)
Spain	Madrid
Sri Lanka	Colombo
Sudan	Khartoum
Suriname	Paramaribo
Swaziland	Mbabane (adminstrative), Lobamba (legislative)

List #130 **Capitals Around the World** *(continued)*

Country/Territory	Capital City
Sweden	Stockholm
Switzerland	Bern
Syria	Damascus
Taiwan	Taipei
Tajikistan	Dushanbe
Tanzania	Dodoma (previously Dar es Salaam)
Thailand	Bangkok
Timor-Leste (East Timor)	Dili
Togo	Lome
Tonga	Nuku'alofa
Trinidad and Tobago	Port-of-Spain
Tunisia	Tunis
Turkey	Ankara
Turkmenistan	Ashgabat
Tuvalu	Funafuti
Uganda	Kampala
Ukraine	Kiev
United Arab Emirates	Abu Dhabi
United Kingdom	London
United States of America	Washington, D.C.
Uruguay	Montevideo
Uzbekistan	Tashkent
Vanuatu	Port Vila
Vatican City (Holy See)	Vatican City
Venezuela	Caracas
Vietnam	Hanoi
Yemen	Sanaa
Zambia	Lusaka
Zimbabwe	Harare

List #131 Major Mountain Ranges

Mountain Range	Location	Elevation (in feet)
Himalayas	Asia	up to 29,035
Karakorum	central Asia	up to 28,250
Kunlun	central Asia	up to 25,340
Hindu Kush	Pakistan/Afghanistan	up to 25,236
Pamir	central Asia	up to 24,590
Tian Shan	central Asia	up to 24,406
Andes	western South America	up to 22,834
Alps	south central Europe	up to 15,771
Rocky Mountains	western North America	up to 14,431
Pyrenees	southwest Europe between France and Spain	up to 11,168
Apennine Mountains	Italy	up to 9,554
Carpathians/Carpathian Mountains	central and eastern Europe	up to 8,737
Cantabrian Mountains	northern Spain	up to 8,687
Scandinavian Mountains	Scandinavian peninsula	up to 8,098
Appalachian Mountains	eastern North America	up to 6,684
Urals	eastern European Russia and northwest Kazakhstan	up to 5,377
Scottish Highlands	Scotland	up to 4,406

List #132 World Oceans

Pacific Ocean

Atlantic Ocean

Indian Ocean

Arctic Ocean

Southern Ocean (also known as Antarctic Ocean or South Polar Ocean)

- This area of water was given "ocean" status in 2000 by the International Hydrographic Organization, making a total of 5 main ocean divisions.

List #133 Caves and Caverns of the World

Name	Location	Unique Characteristics
Aggtelek Cavern	northern Hungary	a large stalactitic cavern that is about 5 miles long
Altamira Cave	near Santander, Spain	a wonderful cave with Stone Age animal paintings on the roof and walls
Antiparos	on Antiparos island in Greece	contains stalactites up to 20 feet long in dazzling colors and shapes
Blue Grotto	Capri, Italy	a sea cavern made of limestone that was hollowed out through wave action
Carlsbad Caverns	southeast New Mexico	contain large and impressive stalactites and stalagmites
Fingal's Cave	on Island of Staffa, Scotland	has basaltic columns that are almost 40 feet high
Jenolan Caves	New South Wales, Australia	striking stalactitic formations
Kent's Cavern	near Torquay, England	has been the source of much information on Paleolithic humans
Lascaux Cave	southwestern France	prehistoric cave paintings; not open to public
Lubang Nasib Bagus	Sarawak, Malaysia	world's largest cave chamber: 2,300 feet long, 1,480 feet wide, and at least 230 feet high
Luray Caverns	near Luray, Virginia	has large stalactitic and stalagmitic columns of various colors
Mammoth Cave	central Kentucky	longest cave system in the world; 345 miles of irregular subterranean passageways as well as lakes and rivers
Mogao Caves	along old Silk Route in China	492 cells and cave sanctuaries with statues and wall paintings of Buddhists
Peak Cavern or Devil's Hole	Derbyshire, England	2,250 feet into a mountain
Postojna Grotto	Postojna, Slovenia	largest cavern in Europe; beautiful stalactites; a karst cave, which means the irregularly eroded limestone was carved by underground streams
Singing Cave	Iceland	a lava cave
Waitomo Cave	North Island, New Zealand	glowworms on the ceiling make the cave's ceiling look like it has little stars all over it
Wind Cave	in Black Hills of South Dakota	limestone caverns; almost no stalactites or stalagmites
Wyandotte Cave	Crawford County, southern Indiana	limestone cavern with five levels of underground passages

List #134 U.S. National Monuments

Unless otherwise identified, all the places listed here are national monuments and are overseen by the National Park Service. Use the key to identify historic sites, national memorials, etc. If you are planning to travel to several monuments or national parks, you might consider purchasing an Interagency Annual Pass through the National Park Service at *http://store.usgs.gov/pass/* or you can call 1-888-ASK-USGS.

Key:
NHA = National Historic Area
NHS = National Historic Site
NM = National Memorial
NMHS = National Monument and Historic Site
NMP = National Monument and Preserve

Alabama	Russell Cave, Tuskegee Institute NHS, Tuskegee Airmen NHS
Alaska	Admiralty Island, Aniakchak NMP, Cape Krusenstern, Misty Fjords Wilderness, Aleutian World War II NHA
Arizona	Parashant, Canyon de Chelly, Casa Grande Ruins, Chiricahua, Hohokam Pima, Montezuma Castle, Navajo, Organ Pipe, Pipe Spring, Rainbow, Sunset Crater Volcano, Tonto, Tuzigoot, Vermilion Cliffs, Walnut Canyon, Wupatki, Coronado NM, Fort Bowie NHS
Arkansas	Arkansas Post NM, Central High School NHS, Fort Smith NHS
California	Cabrillo, Devil's Postpile, Lava Beds, Muir Woods, Pinnacles, Eugene O'Neill NHS, Fort Point NHS, John Muir NHS, Muir Woods, Rosie the Riveter WWII Home Front NHS, Manzanar NHS, Port Chicago Naval Magazine
Colorado	Bent's Old Fort NHS, Colorado, Dinosaur, Florissant Fossil Beds, Yucca House, Sand Creek Massacre NHS,
Connecticut	Weir Farm NHS
Delaware	Edgar Allan Poe NHS, Fort McHenry, Gloria Dei Church NHS, Hampton NHS, Thaddeus Koscuiszko
District of Columbia	Carter G. Woodson Home NHS, Ford's Theatre NHS, Franklin Delano Roosevelt Memorial, Frederick Douglass NHS, George Mason Memorial, George Washington Memorial Parkway, John Ericsson NM, Korean War Veterans Memorial, Lincoln Memorial, Mary McLeod Bethune Council House NHS, National World War II Memorial, Old Post Office Tower, Pierce Mill, Pennsylvania Avenue NHS, Sewall-Belmont House NHS, The Old Stone House, Thomas Jefferson Memorial, Vietnam Veterans Memorial, Washington Monument
Florida	Castillo de San Marcos, Fort Matanzas, De Soto NM, Fort Caroline NM
Georgia	Fort Frederica, Ocmulgee, Fort Pulaski, Andersonville NHS, Jimmy Carter NHS, Martin Luther King Jr. NHS
Hawaii	Puukohola Heiau NHS, USS Arizona Memorial

List #134 **U.S. National Monuments** *(continued)*

Idaho	Craters of the Moon NMP, Hagerman Fossil Beds, Minidoka Internment
Illinois	Lincoln Home NHS
Indiana	Lincoln Boyhood
Iowa	Effigy Mounds, Herbert Hoover NHS
Kansas	Brown V Board of Education NHS, Fort Larned NHS, Fort Scott NHS, Nicodemus NHS
Kentucky	Abraham Lincoln Birthplace NHS
Louisiana	Poverty Point, Cane River National Heritage Area
Maine	Saint Croix Island International Historic Site
Maryland	Fort McHenry NM and HS, Clara Barton NHS, Hampton NHS, Harmony Hall, Thomas Stone NHS
Massachusetts	Appalachian NST, Blackstone River Valley National Heritage Corridor, Boston African American NHS, Essex National Heritage Area, Frederick Law Olmsted NHS, John F. Kennedy NHS, Longfellow NHS, Salem Maritime NHS, Saugus Iron Works NHS, Springfield Armory NHS
Michigan	Motor Cities National Heritage Area
Minnesota	Pipestone, Grand Portage
Missouri	George Washington Carver, Harry S. Truman NHS, Jefferson National Expansion Memorial, Ulysses S. Grant NHS
Montana	Little Bighorn Battlefield, Grant-Kohrs Ranch NHS
Nebraska	Agate Fossil Beds, Scotts Bluff, Homestead National Monument of America
Nevada	Lehman Caves
New Hampshire	Saint-Gaudens NHS
New Jersey	Ellis Island, Edison NHS
New Mexico	Aztec Ruins, Bandelier, Capulin Volcano, El Malpais, El Morro, Fort Union, Gila Cliff Dwellings, Petroglyph, Salinas Pueblo Missions, White Sands
New York	African Burial Ground Designation, Castle Clinton, Eleanor Roosevelt NHS, Ellis Island, Erie Canalway National Heritage Corridor, Federal Hall NM, Fort Stanwix, Statue of Liberty, General Grant NM, Governors Island, Hamilton Grange NM, Home of Franklin D. Roosevelt NHS, Lower East Side Tenement Museum NHS, Martin Van Buren NHS, Sagamore Hill NHS, Saint Paul's Church NHS, Theodore Roosevelt Birthplace NHS, Theodore Roosevelt Inaugural NHS, Vanderbilt Mansion NHS
North Carolina	Wright Brothers NM, Fort Raleigh NHS, Carl Sandurg Home NHS
North Dakota	Fort Union Trading Post NHS, Knife River Indian Villages NHS

List #134 **U.S. National Monuments** *(continued)*

Ohio	Mound City Group, Perry's Victory & International Peace Memorial, William Howard Taft NHS, National Aviation Heritage Area, James A. Garfield NHS, First Ladies NHS, David Berger NM
Oklahoma	Fort Smith NHS, Oklahoma City NM, Washita Battlefield NHS
Oregon	John Day Fossil Beds, Oregon Caves, Fort Vancouver NHS
Pennsylvania	Allegheny Portage Railroad NHS, Deshler-Morris House, Edgar Allan Poe NHS, Eisenhower NHS, Flight 93 NM, Friendship Hill NHS, Gloria Dei Church NHS, Hopewell Furnace NHS, Johnstown Flood NM, Oil Region NHA, Steamtown NHS, Thaddeus Kosciuszko NM
Rhode Island	Roger Williams NM, Touro Synagogue NHS
South Carolina	Charles Pinckney NHS, Fort Moultrie, Fort Sumter, Ninety Six NHS
South Dakota	Jewel Cave, Mount Rushmore NM, Minuteman Missile NHS
Tennessee	Andrew Johnson NHS
Texas	Alibates Flint Quarries, Chamizal NM, Fort Davis NHS, Palo Alto Battlefield NHS
Utah	Cedar Breaks, Dinosaur, Golden Spike NHS, Hovenweep, Natural Bridges, Rainbow Bridge, Timpanogos Cave
Virgin Islands	Buck Island Reef, Christiansted NHS, Virgin Islands Coral Reef
Virginia	Arlington House – Robert E. Lee Memorial, Booker T. Washington, Cape Henry Memorial, Claude Moore Colonial Farm, George Washington Birthplace, Green Springs National Historic District, Jamestown NHS, Lyndon Baines Johnson Memorial Grove on the Potomac, Maggie L. Walker NHS
Washington	Fort Vancouver NHS, Whitman Mission NHS, Mount Saint Helens National Volcanic Monument
Wyoming	Devils Tower, Fort Laramie NHS, Fossil Butte

List #135 U.S. National Parks

Unless otherwise identified, all the places listed here are national parks and are overseen by the National Park Service. Use the key to identify national historic parks, preserves, and other great places. If you are planning to travel to several parks, you might consider purchasing an Interagency Annual Pass through the National Park Service at *http://store.usgs.gov/pass/* or you can call 1-888-ASK-USGS.

Key:

NB = National Battlefield
NBP = National Battlefield Park
NBS = National Battlefield Site
NHA = National Heritage Area
NHC = National Heritage Corridor
NHP = National Historic Park
NHPP = National Historic Park & Preserve
NHT = National Historic Trail
NL = National Lakeshore
NMP = National Military Park
NP = National Preserve
NPP = National Park and Preserve
NR = National River
NRE = National Reserve
NRA = National Recreation Area
NRRA = National River & Recreation Area
NS = National Seashore
NSR = National Scenic Riverway
NST = National Scenic Trail
WSR = Wild & Scenic River

Alabama	Little River Canyon, Horseshoe Bend NMP
Alaska	Bering Land Bridge, Denali NPP, Gates of the Arctic NPP, Glacier Bay NPP, Katmai NPP, Kenai Fjords, Kobuk Valley, Lake Clark NPP, Noatak NP, Wrangell-St. Elias NPP, Yukon-Charley Rivers NP, Klondike Gold Rush NHP, Sitka NHP
American Samoa	National Park of American Samoa
Arizona	Saguaro, Petrified Forest NP, Tumacácori NHP, Lake Mead NRA
Arkansas	Hot Springs, Pea Ridge NMP, Buffalo NR, Trail of Tears NHT
California	Channel Islands, Death Valley, Joshua Tree, Kings Canyon, Lassen Volcanic, Mojave NP, Redwood, Sequoia, Yosemite, California NHT, Golden Gate NRA, Juan Bautista de Anza NHT, Old Spanish NHT, Point Reyes NS, Pony Express NHT, San Francisco Maritime NHP, Santa Monica Mountains NRA, Whiskey NRA
Colorado	Black Canyon of the Gunnison, Great Sand Dunes NPP, Mesa Verde, Rocky Mountain, California NHT, Curecanti NRA, Old Spanish NHT, Pony Express NHT, Santa Fe NHT
Connecticut	Appalachian NST, Quinebaug & Shetucket Rivers Valley NHC
Delaware	Assateague Island NS, Chesapeake Bay Gateways Network, Greenbelt Park, Independence NHP, New Jersey Coastal Heritage Trail Route, New Jersey NRE

List #135 **U.S. National Parks** *(continued)*

District of Columbia	Captain John Smith Chesapeake NHT, Chesapeake & Ohio Canal NHP, Chesapeake Bay Gateways Network, Constitution Gardens, Kenilworth Park & Aquatic Gardens, National Mall & Memorial Parks, Potomac Heritage NST
Florida	Big Cypress NP, Biscayne, Dry Tortugas, Everglades, Canaveral NS, Gulf Islands NS, Timucuan Ecological & Historic Preserve
Georgia	Appalachian NST, Augusta Canal National Heritage Area, Chattahoochee River NRA, Chickamauga & Chattanooga NMP, Cumberland Island NS, Kennesaw Mountain NBP, Trail of Tears NHT
Hawaii	Haleakala, Hawaii Volcanoes, Ala Kahakai NHT, Kalaupapa NHP, Kaloko-Honokohau NHP, Pu'uhonua O Honaunau NHP
Idaho	California NHT, City of Rocks NR, Lewis & Clark NHT, Nez Perce NHP, Oregon NHT, Yellowstone
Illinois	Lewis & Clark NHT, Mormon Pioneer NHT, Trail of Tears NHT
Indiana	George Rogers Clark NHP, Indiana Dunes NL
Iowa	Mormon Pioneer NHT, Lewis & Clark NHT
Kansas	California NHT, Lewis & Clark NHT, Oregon NHT, Pony Express NHT, Santa Fe NHT, Tallgrass Prairie NP
Kentucky	Mammoth Cave, Big South Fork NRRA, Cumberland Gap NHP, Trail of Tears NHT
Louisiana	New Orleans Jazz NHP, Jean Lafitte NHPP, El Camino Real de Los Tejas NHT, Cane River Creole NHP
Maine	Acadia, Appalachian NST, Maine Acadian Culture, Roosevelt Campobello International Park
Maryland	Antietam, Appalachian NST, Assateague Island NS, Baltimore-Washington Parkway, Captain John Smith Chesapeake NHT, Chesapeake & Ohio Canal NHP, Chesapeake Bay Gateways Network, George Washington Memorial Parkway, Glen Echo, Greenbelt Park, Monocacy NB, Oxon Cove Park & Oxon Hill Farm, Piscataway Park, Potomac Heritage NST, Suitland Parkway
Massachusetts	Adams NHP, Boston NHP, Boston Harbor Islands NRA, Cape Cod NS, Lowell NHP, Minute Man NHP, New Bedford Whaling NHP
Michigan	Isle Royale, Keweenaw NHP, North Country NST, Pictured Rocks NL, Sleeping Bear Dunes NL
Minnesota	Voyageurs, Mississippi NRRA, North Country NST
Mississippi	Brices Cross Roads NBS, Gulf Islands NS, Natchez NHP, Natchez Trace Parkway, Natchez Trace NST, Tupelo NB, Vicksburg NMP
Missouri	California National Historic Trail, Lewis & Clark NHT, Oregon NHT, Ozark NSR, Pony Express NHT, Santa Fe NHT, Trail of Tears NHT, Wilson's Creek NB

List #135 **U.S. National Parks** *(continued)*

Montana	Glacier, Big Hole NB, Bighorn Canyon NRA, Lewis & Clark NHT, Nez Perce NHP, Yellowstone
Nebraska	Pony Express NHT, Oregon NHT, Niobrara NSR, Mormon Pioneer NHT, Lewis & Clark NHT, California NHT
Nevada	Great Basin, California NHT, Death Valley, Lake Mead NRA, Old Spanish NHT, Pony Express NHT
New Hampshire	Appalachian NST
New Jersey	Appalachian NST, Delaware NSR, Delaware Water Gap NRA, Gateway NRA, Great Egg Harbor River, Lower Delaware National Wild and Scenic River, Morristown NHP, New Jersey Coastal Heritage Trail Route, New Jersey Pinelands NR
New Mexico	Carlsbad Caverns, Chaco Culture NHP, El Camino Real de Los Tejas NHT, El Camino Real de Tierra Adentro NHT, Old Spanish NHT, Pecos NHP, Santa Fe NHT
New York	Women's Rights NHP, Upper Delaware Scenic & Recreational River, Saratoga NHP, North Country NST, National Parks of New York Harbor, Hudson River Valley NHA, Gateway NRA, Fire Island NS, Chesapeake Bay Gateways Network
North Carolina	Great Smoky Mountains, Appalachian NST, Blue Ridge Parkway, Blue Ridge NHA, Cape Hatteras NS, Cape Lookout NS, Guilford Courthouse NMP, Moores Creek NB, Overmountain Victory NHT, Trail of Tears NHT
North Dakota	Theodore Roosevelt, Lewis & Clark NHT, North Country NST
Ohio	Cuyahoga Valley, Dayton Aviation Heritage NHP, Hopewell Culture NHP, North Country NST
Oklahoma	Trail of Tears NHT, Santa Fe NHT, Chickasaw NRA
Oregon	Crater Lake, California NHT, Lewis & Clark NHT, Lewis & Clark NHP, Nez Perce NHP, Oregon NHT
Pennsylvania	Appalachian NST, Chesapeake Bay Gateways Network, Delaware NSR, Delaware & Lehigh NHC, Delaware Water Gap NRA, Fort Necessity NB, Gettysburg NMP, Lackawanna Heritage Valley, Lower Delaware National WSR, North Country NST, Path of Progress National Heritage Tour Route, Potomac Heritage NST, Rivers of Steel NHA, Schuylkill River Valley NHA, Upper Delaware Scenic & Recreational River, Valley Forge NHP
Rhode Island	Blackstone River Valley NHC
South Carolina	Congaree, Cowpens NB, Kings Mountain NMP, Overmountain Victory NHT, South Carolina NHC
South Dakota	Badlands, Lewis & Clark NHT, Missouri NRR, Wind Cave

List #135 **U.S. National Parks** *(continued)*

Tennessee	Appalachian NST, Big South Fork NRRA, Fort Donelson NB, Great Smoky Mountains, Natchez Trace Parkway, Obed WSR, Overmountain Victory NHT, Shiloh NMP, Stones River NB, Tennessee Civil War NHA, Trail of Tears NHT
Texas	Amistad NRA, Big Bend, Big Thicket NP, El Camino Real de Los Tejas NHT, El Camino Real de Tierra Adentro NHT, Guadalupe Mountains, Lake Meredith NRA, Lyndon B. Johnson NHP, Padre Island NS, Rio Grande WSR, San Antonio Missions NHP
Utah	Arches, Bryce Canyon, California NHT, Canyonlands, Capitol Reef, Glen Canyon NRA, Mormon Pioneer NHT, Old Spanish NHT, Pony Express NHT, Zion
Vermont	Appalachian NST, Marsh-Billings-Rockefeller NHP
Virgin Islands	Salt River Bay NHP and Ecological Preserve, Virgin Islands
Virginia	Appalachian NST, Appomattox Court House NHP, Assateague Island NS, Blue Ridge Parkway, Captain John Smith Chesapeake NHT, Cedar Creek & Belle Grove NHP, Chesapeake Bay Gateways Network, Colonial NHP, Fredericksburg & Spotsylvania NMP, George Washington Memorial Parkway, Great Falls Park, Green Springs, Manassas NBP, Overmountain Victory NHT, Petersburg NB, Prince William Forest Park, Richmond NBP, Shenandoah, Theodore Roosevelt Island Park, Wolf Trap National Park for the Performing Arts, Yorktown National Cemetery
Washington	Ebey's Landing NHP, Klondike Gold Rush-Seattle Unit NHP, Lake Chelan NRA, Lake Roosevelt NRA, Lewis & Clark NHT, Mount Rainier, Nez Perce NHP, North Cascades, Olympic, Ross Lake NRA, San Juan Island NHP
West Virginia	Appalachian NST, Bluestone NSR, Chesapeake & Ohio Canal NHP, Chesapeake Bay Gateways Network, Gauley River NRA, Harpers Ferry NHP, New River Gorge National River, Wheeling NHA
Wisconsin	Apostle Islands NL, Ice Age NST, North Country NST, Saint Croix NSR
Wyoming	Bighorn Canyon NRA, California NHT, Grand Teton, John D. Rockefeller Jr Memorial Parkway, Mormon Pioneer NHT, Oregon NHT, Pony Express NHT, Yellowstone

List #136 Major Rivers of the World

Name of River	Length (miles)	Continent
Nile	4,180	Africa
Amazon	3,912	South America
Yangtze	3,602	Asia
Ob	3,459	Asia
Huang Ho	2,900	Asia
Yenisei	2,800	Asia
Parana	2,795	South America
Irtish	2,758	Asia
Zaire	2,716	Africa
Amur	2,704	Asia
Lena	2,652	Asia
Mackenzie	2,635	North America
Niger	2,600	Africa
Mekong	2,500	Asia
Mississippi	2,348	North America
Missouri	2,313	North America

9

Foreign Language

List #137 Common Greek and Latin Roots

Greek Roots

Root	Meaning	Examples
aero	air	aerodynamics, aerobics, aerate, aeronautics
ast	star	astronaut (*ast* combined with *naut*, meaning "star sailor"), astronomy, asteroid
biblio	book	Bible, bibliography, bibliophile, bibliomania
bio	life	biography, biology, biopsy, biological
chron	time	chronology, chronological, chronicle, synchronize
cosm	universe	cosmos, cosmopolitan, microcosm, cosmic
cycl	circle, ring	cycle, bicycle, cyclone, recycle
gen	birth, race	generation, generate, regeneration, genealogy
geo	earth	geology, geological, geometry, geologist, geode
gram	written or drawn	diagram, telegram, grammar, monogram
graph	written or drawn	graph, telegraph, photograph, biography, autograph
meter	measure	thermometer, diameter, centimeter, millimeter, barometer
morph	shape	metamorphoses, morph, morphing, amorphous

Latin Roots

Root	Meaning	Examples
acer	sharp, keen	eager, acrid, eagerly, vinegar
amor	love, desire	amateur, amiable, amour, enamor
cadere	to fall	accident, cadence, parachute, casuality
defendere	to defend	defend, defendant, fence
fortis	strong, brave	comfortable, comforter, effort, force, fortification
fortuna	fortune, chance	fortunate, misfortune, fortune
gaudeo	be glad, rejoice	enjoy, gaudy, rejoice, joyful
heres	heir, princess	heir, heirloom, inheritance
labor	work, toil	labor, laborer, laboratory, collaborate
navigare	to sail	navigate, navigator, navy, circumnavigate, naval
sacer	sacred	sacrament, sacred, sacrilege, consecrate

There are literally thousands of English words of Greek or Latin origin. There are only a handful listed here to show you how you can study words with a similar derivative and to interest your student in language roots.

List #138 Foreign Origins of English Words

Many words of foreign origin are commonly used in English speech, but the ones listed here are those most likely to be encountered by the elementary- or junior-high-age student. For further exploration of foreign words, show your students how to find the etymology (origin) of a word in the dictionary and then encourage them to find their own words of foreign origin. Ask students why one country might have had need for a particular word (such as *yam*) when other countries did not need the word until later.

African Words

- banana
- cola
- gnu
- mumbo jumbo
- safari
- yam
- zombie

Arabic Words

- admiral
- alcohol
- alfalfa
- algebra
- artichoke
- assassin
- caravan
- coffee
- cotton
- magazine
- monsoon
- sherbet
- sofa
- zero

Australian / Aboriginal Words

- boomerang
- dingo
- kangaroo
- koala

Chinese Words

- gung ho
- kumquat
- kung fu
- soy
- tea
- tofu
- typhoon
- yen

Czech Words

- robot

Dutch Words

- bush
- cole slaw
- cookie
- drill
- pickle
- skate
- sketch
- sled
- slim
- sloop
- stove
- wagon
- yacht

East Indian Words

- bungalow
- cashmere
- cheetah
- juggernaut
- jungle
- khaki
- loot
- pajamas
- shampoo
- shawl
- thug
- veranda

French Words

- attorney
- authority
- ballet
- bizarre
- boulevard
- bouquet
- brochure
- cadet
- carousel
- charity
- chef
- clergy
- coroner
- crime
- debris
- depot
- detour
- essay
- exposé
- fiancé
- fiancée
- garage
- gourmet
- government
- judge
- jury
- liberty
- mayor
- migraine
- minister
- morgue
- pastor
- public
- rebel
- religion
- résumé
- traitor
- treasurer
- troop
- trophy
- vague
- verdict

German Words

- delicatessen
- diesel
- ecology
- Fahrenheit
- frankfurter
- Gestapo
- gesundheit
- hamburger
- kaput
- loaf
- sauerkraut
- strudel

Greek Words

- hieroglyph
- (also see list #137)

Hebrew Words

- bar mitzvah
- kosher
- menorah
- shalom
- shekel

Hungarian Word

- goulash

Irish Words

- brat
- galore

List #138 **Foreign Origins of English Words** *(continued)*

Italian Words

- allot
- attitude
- balcony
- bandit
- banister
- bologna
- bronze
- cannon
- carnival
- casino
- cavalry
- cello
- colonel
- confetti
- duel
- fiasco
- finale
- ghetto
- gondola
- incognito
- infantry
- influenza
- jeans
- macaroni
- malaria
- pasta
- pastel
- piano
- relief
- spaghetti
- torso
- trio
- volcano
- wig

Japanese Words

- bonsai
- futon
- judo
- jujitsu
- kamikaze
- karate
- ninja
- origami
- samuri
- sayonara
- sushi
- tsunami
- tycoon

Lapp Word

- tundra

Latin Words

- (see list #137)

Malay Words (Malaysia and Indonesia)

- amuck
- gingham
- ketchup
- gong

Native American Words

- chipmunk
- pow wow
- skunk
- totem
- wigwam

Polynesian Words

- aloha
- hula
- taboo

Portuguese Words

- commando
- marmalade

Russian Words

- cosmonaut
- czar
- Kremlin
- mammoth
- parka
- sputnik

Sanskrit Words

- karma
- nirvana
- yoga

Spanish Words

- adobe
- albino
- alfalfa
- amigo
- armada
- avocado
- bronco
- burro
- cafeteria
- canoe
- canyon
- chocolate
- corral
- coyote
- fiesta
- hurricane
- mesa
- mosquito
- patio
- poncho
- potato
- ranch
- rodeo
- sierra
- silo
- tobacco
- tomato
- tornado
- tortilla

Turkish Words

- sherbet
- shish kebab
- yogurt

Yiddish Words

- bagel
- klutz
- pastrami

List #139 Origin of Names of Days of the Week

Sunday	Originated from Latin *dies solis*, which means "sun's day" (the name of an ancient Roman holiday). The day was also known as *Dominica* ("the Day of God") in Latin and it was this root that carried into the Romance languages' words for Sunday: *dimanche* (French), *domingo* (Spanish), and *domenica* (Italian).
Monday	Originated from Anglo-Saxon word *monandaeg*, meaning "the moon's day," or the day which was sacred to the moon.
Tuesday	Originated as a dedication to the Norse god of war, Tiw. The Romans dedicated this day to their god of war, Mars, thus the Romance languages' words for Tuesday: *mardi* (French), *martes* (Spanish), and *martedi* (Italian).
Wednesday	Originally a day to honor Odin, the Scandinavian king of gods and the god of war, transformed to "Wodan's day." Romans called it *dies Mercurii* in honor of their god Mercury; then the other Romance languages used similar words: *mercredi* (French), *miércoles* (Spanish), and *mercoledi* (Italian).
Thursday	Named in honor of the Norse god Thor ("Thor's day," which was Torsdag in Norse). If you look at the etymology, you see the similarity to Germanic languages: *Donnerstag* (German), *donderdag* (Dutch), and *torsdag* (Swedish). Romans named the day after Jove or Jupiter, the supreme god of the Romans, and it was called *dies Jovis*. The root from Latin for Romance languages is obvious: *jeudi* (French), *jueves* (Spanish), and *giovedi* (Italian).
Friday	Named in honor of the Norse god Frigg; thus the Old High German word was *frigedag*, which eventually became Friday for us. Romans named this day for Venus, and it was called *dies veneris* in Latin; in other Romance languages, the day became *vendredi* (French), *viernes* (Spanish), and *venerdi* (Italian).
Saturday	Called *dies Saturni* (Saturn's Day) in Latin, in honor of the Roman god Saturn.

List #140 Origin of Names of Months of the Year

January	Named after the Roman god Janus, the god of doorways or beginnings and endings, and called *Januarius* in Latin.
February	Named after the old Italian god Februus or from the Latin word *februa*, which signified purification festivals in Rome during that month.
March	The first month of the Roman year, this month was named after the Roman god of war, Mars.
April	Originally called *Aprilis*, which originated from *aperire*, meaning "to open," it is possible that this month was named for the opening of buds that occurs in April.
May	Though uncertain, it is possible that the name comes from Maiesta, who was the Roman goddess of honor and reverence.
June	Named in honor of Juno, Roman goddess of women and childbirth.
July	Originally called *Quintilis* (fifth month), this month was renamed *Julius* in 44 BC after the assassination of Julius Caesar, this month being the one in which he was born.
August	Originally called *Sextilis* (sixth month), this month was renamed in honor of the first Roman emperor Augustus.
September	From *septem*, which means seven in Latin; this was the seventh month of the Roman calendar.
October	From *octo*, which means eight in Latin; this was the eighth month of the Roman calendar.
November	From *novem*, which means nine in Latin; this was the ninth month of the Roman calendar.
December	From *decem*, which means ten in Latin; this was the tenth month of the Roman calendar.

List #141 Origin of Animal Names

The origins listed here of animal names include the word or words that directly influenced the English name of that particular animal. The date following the origin is the date of the first recorded use in English.

Many of the words in other languages, however, were also derived from another language. For example, we get "alligator" from the Spanish words *el lagarto* (the lizard), but the Spanish words were derived from the Latin words *ille* (that) and *lacertus* (lizard).

Activity ideas: Find pictures of each animal and make sure the student can identify them. Have students also memorize the etymology (origin) of the names and look up the words to find out if there was another language of influence. Have students then identify on a map where each animal name originated and discuss the native habitat of each animal. Discuss questions like why "bear" and "cat" were introduced to English before 1000, but animal names like "alligator" and "canary" didn't come to English until the 1500s (the age of exploration).

alligator	from Spanish *el lagarto*, meaning "the lizard"; 1560–70
bear	from Middle English *be(a)re* or *beor(e)*; before 1000
canary	from Spanish *Canaria*, meaning the Canary Islands; 1585–95
cat	from Middle English *cat* or *catte*; before 900
chicken	from Middle English *chiken*; before 950
chipmunk	from *chitmunk*, which was from the Odawa (a Native American language) word *jidmoonh*, which means "red squirrel"; 1825–35
cockatoo	from Dutch *kaketoe*; 1610–20
coyote	from Mexican Spanish *coyote* and Nahuatl *coyotl*; 1825–35
dog	from Middle English *dogge*; before 1050
elephant	from Latin *elephantus*; 1250–1300
fish	from Middle English *fis(c)h* or *fyssh*; before 900
flamingo	from Portuguese *flamengo* and Spanish *flamenco*; 1555–65
giraffe	from French *giraffe*; 1585–95
hippopotamus	from Greek *hippopotamus*, meaning "riverine horse"; 1555–65
horse	from Old English *hors*; before 900
iguana	from Spanish that came from Caribbean *iwana*; 1545–55
jaguar	from Portuguese *jaguara*; 1595–1605
kangaroo	from an Australian Aboriginal language; 1770
lemur	from Latin *lemures*, meaning "ghosts"; 1790–1800
lizard	from Middle English *liserd*; 1350–1400; originated from Latin *lacerta*

List #141 **Origin of Animal Names** *(continued)*

moose	from Natick (a Native American language) *moos*; 1595–1605
opossum	from Powhatan (a Native American language) *apasum*, meaning "white dog-like animal"
orangutan	from pidgin Malay *orang* (meaning "man") and *hutan* (meaning "wilderness" or "jungle"); 1690–1700
ostrich	from Middle English *ostrice* or *ostriche*; 1175–1225
penguin	from Welsh *pen gwyn*, meaning "white head"; 1570–80
puma	from Quechua (a Native American language)
scorpion	from Middle English, but the word was taken from the Greek *skorpios*; 1175–1225
skunk	from Massachusett (a Native American language) *squunck*; 1625–35

List #142 Comparison of Animal Names

English	German	French	Spanish	Italian	Swedish	Yiddish
cat	Katze	chat	gato	gatto	katt	kats
cow	Kuh	vache	vaca	vacca	ko	ku
dog	Hund	chien	perro	cane	hund	hunt
fish	Fisch	poisson	pescado	pesce	fisk	fish
frog	Frosch	grenouille	rana	rana	groda	zhabe
horse	Pferd	cheval	caballo	cavallo	häst	ferd
pig	Schwein	cochon	cerdo	porco	gris	khazer
rabbit	Kaninchen	lapin	conejo	coniglio	kanin	kinigl
snake	Schlange	serpent	serpiente	culebra	orm	shlang
turtle	Schildkröte	tortue	tortuga	tartaruga	sköldpadda	tsherepakhe
zebra	Zebra	zèbra	cebra	zebra	sebra	zebra

If your child enjoys the study of languages and word origins, called *etymology,* consider purchasing a *Webster's Third New International Dictionary and Seven Language Dictionary* by Merriam-Webster. The dictionary comes in a three-volume set, and the last volume lists various words in seven languages so you can cross-reference words, try to guess the original word, etc. This book is a great resource for etymology students.

List #143 Origin of Food Names

Origins of common food names are listed here. The date following the origin is the date of the first recorded use in English. The meaning of the word may have been different at that time and, of course, most words were in existence in the spoken language long before their first recorded written usage in the English language.

biscuit	from the Middle English *bysquyte,* which was from French *biscuit,* which literally meant "twice cooked"; 1300–50
cake	from Middle English *kechel,* meaning "little cake," which came from Old Norse *kaka* and German *Kuchen,* which means "cake"; 1200–50
casserole	from the French meaning "ladle-like pan," which was from the Old Provençal word *cassa,* meaning "large spoon"; 1700–10
hominy	from Powhatan (a Native American language) *uskatahomen*; 1620–30
pasta	from Italian, which came from the Late Latin word *pasta,* meaning "dough"; 1870–75
pecan	from Algonguian languages (Illinois *pakani* and Ojibwe *bagaan*), meaning "nut";1765–75
persimmon	from Powhatan (a Native American language) *pasimenan*, meaning "dried fruits"; 1612
pizza	from Italian *pizza,* which came from the Greek words *pétea*, meaning "bran," and *petítes*, meaning "bran bread"; 1930–35
potato	from several different languages, possibly Taino *batata* (means "sweet potato") and Quechua *papa* (means "potato") and Spanish *patata,* which means "white potato"; 1545–55
ravioli	from Italian *raviolo,* meaning "little turnip"; 1835–45
sandwich	a word of unique origin, reportedly created after John Montagu, the fourth Earl of Sandwich, wanted some meat put between bread for a quick snack; 1755–65
spaghetti	from Italian *spaghetto,* which is a diminutive form of *spago* or "little rope"; *spago* derived from the Late Latin word *spacus,* meaning "twine"; 1885–90
squash	from Narragansett (a Native American language) *askútasquash*, meaning "some little thing eaten raw"; 1555–65

List #144 Geographical Words of Native American Origin

Alabama	may come from the Choctaw word, meaning "thicket-clearers" or "vegetation-gatherers"
Alaska	comes from the Aleut word that means "great land," "mainland," or "shore"
Arizona	from Indian word *Arizonac*, meaning "little spring" or "young spring"
Arkansas	from the Quapaw (Sioux Indian) word *acansa*, meaning "downstream place" or "south wind"
Chesapeake	from Algonquian word *Chesepioc*, meaning "great shellfish bay"
Chicago	from Algonquian word *Checagou*, meaning "place of the wild onion or garlic" or "garlic field"
Connecticut	from the Mohican word *Qiunnehtukqut*, meaning "beside the long tidal river"
Illinois	from the Algonquian word that means "tribe of superior men"
Indiana	means "land of Indians"
Iowa	"this is the place" or "the beautiful land"
Kansas	may be from a Sioux word meaning "people of the south wind," though I think it is more likely that this word is a mutated version of the Spanish word *cansar*, which means "to molest, stir up, or harass"
Kentucky	from Iroquoian word *kentahten*, meaning "land of tomorrow"
Manhattan	from an Algonquian word, believed to mean "isolated thing in water"
Massachusetts	named after the Massachusett tribe, meaning "at or about the great hill"
Michigan	from *Michigana*, meaning "great or large lake"
Milwaukee	from Algonquian, believed to mean "a good spot or place"
Minnesota	from a Dakota word meaning "sky-tinted water"
Mississippi	a combination of Native American words that mean "Father of Waters"—a Chippewa word, *mici zibi*, which means "great river" and an Algonquin word, *messippi*
Missouri	named after the Missouri tribe; means "town of the large canoes"
Nebraska	from Oto word meaning "flat water"
Niagara	named after an Iroquoian town that was called "Ongiaahra"
North Dakota	from Sioux word meaning "allies"
Ohio	from Iroquoian word meaning "great river"
Oklahoma	from two Choctaw words that together mean "red people"
Pensacola	from Choctaw word meaning "hair" and "people"

List #144 **Geographical Words of Native American Origin** *(continued)*

Roanoke	from Algonquian word that means "shell money"
Saratoga	it is thought that this word is from a Mohawk word that means "springs (of water) from the hillside"
South Dakota	from Sioux word meaning "allies"
Sunappee (a lake in New Hampshire)	from a Pennacook word meaning "rocky pond"
Tahoe	from Washo word meaning "big water"
Tennessee	most likely from Cherokee word *Tanasi*, which was the name of a prominent Cherokee town in southeast Tennessee before Native Americans were forced to leave the area in 1800s
Texas	Caddo Tribe reportedly used word *tayshas* when greeting Spanish explorers, and this word was changed to "Tejas" to indicate the area and later to "Texas"; the word originally meant "friends"
Utah	named after Ute tribe, which means "people of the mountains"
Wisconsin	uncertain origin, but possibly from an Algonquian word that means "long river"
Wyoming	from Lenape word *Maughwauwane*, which means "great plains"

List #145 Similar Words in Seven Languages

English	German	Yiddish	Swedish	French	Spanish	Italian
spring	der Frühling	friling	vår	le printemps	la primavera	la primavera
summer	der Sommer	zumer	sommar	l'été	el verano	l'estate
fall	der Herbst	harbst	host	l'automne	el otoño	l'autunno
winter	der Winter	vinter	vinter	l'hiver	el invierno	l'inverno
January	Januar	Yanuar	januari	Janvier	enero	gennaio
February	Februar	Februar	februari	Février	febrero	febbraio
March	März	Marts	mars	Mars	marcho	marzo
April	April	April	april	Avril	abril	aprile
May	Mai	May	maj	Mai	mayo	maggio
June	Juni	Yuni	juni	Juin	junio	giugno
July	Juli	Yuli	juli	Juillet	julio	luglio
August	August	Oygust	augusti	Août	agosto	agosto
September	September	September	september	Septembre	septiembre	settembre
October	Oktober	Oktober	oktober	Octobre	octubre	ottobre
November	November	November	november	Novembre	noviembre	nobembre
December	Dezember	Detsember	december	Décembre	diciembre	dicembre
Sunday	Sonntag	zuntik	söndag	Dimanche	Domingo	domenica
Monday	Montag	montik	mändag	Lundi	Lunes	lunedì
Tuesday	Dienstag	dinstik	tisdag	Mardi	Martes	martedì
Wednesday	Mittwoch	mitvokh	onsdag	Mercredi	Miércoles	mercoledì
Thursday	Donnerstag	donershtik	torsdag	Jeudi	Jueves	giovedì
Friday	Freitag	fraytik	fredag	Vendredi	Viernes	venerdì
Saturday	Samstag	shabes	lördag	Samedi	Sabado	sabato
one	eins	eyns	en, ett	un	uno	uno
two	zwei	tsvey	två	deux	dos	due
three	drei	drey	tre	trois	tres	tre
four	vier	fir	fyra	quatre	cuatro	quattro
five	fünf	finf	fem	cinq	cinco	cinque
six	sechs	zeks	sex	six	seis	sei
seven	sieben	zibn	sju	sept	siete	sette
eight	acht	akht	åtta	huit	ocho	otto
nine	neun	nayn	nio	neuf	nueve	nove

List #145 Similar Words in Seven Languages *(continued)*

English	German	Yiddish	Swedish	French	Spanish	Italian
ten	zehn	tsen	tio	dix	diez	dieci
eleven	elf	elf	elva	onze	once	undici
twelve	zwölf	tsvelf	tolv	douze	doce	dodici
thirteen	dreizehn	draytsn	tretton	treize	trece	tredici
fourteen	vierzehn	fertsn	fjorton	quatorze	catorce	quattordici
fifteen	fünfzehn	fuftsn	femton	quinze	quince	quindici
sixteen	sechzehn	zekhtsn	sexton	seize	dieciseis	sedici
seventeen	siebzehn	zibetsn	sjutton	dix-sept	diecisiete	diciassette
eighteen	achtzehn	akhtsn	arton	dix-huit	dieciocho	diciotto
nineteen	neunzehn	nayntsn	nitton	dix-neuf	diecinueve	diciannove
twenty	zwanzig	tsvantsik	tjugo	vingt	veinte	venti
thirty	dreißig	draysik	trettio	trente	treinta	trenta
forty	vierzig	fertsik	fyrtio	quarante	cuarenta	quaranta
fifty	fünfzig	fuftsik	femtio	cinquante	cincuenta	cinquanta
sixty	sechzig	zekhtsik	sextio	soixante	sesenta	sessanta
seventy	siebzig	zibetsik	sjuttio	soixante-dix	setenta	settanta
eighty	achtzig	akhtsik	åttio	quatre-vingts	ochenta	ottanta
ninety	neunzig	nayntsik	nittio	quatre-vingt-dix	noventa	novanta
hundred	hundert	hundert	hundra	cent	cien	cento
million	Million	milyon	miljon	million	millón	milione
red	rot	royt	röd	rouge	rojo	rosso
yellow	gelb	gel	gul	jaune	amarillo	giallo
green	grün	grin	grön	vert	verde	verde
blue	blau	bloy	blå	bleu	azul	azzurro
black	Schwarz	shvarts	svart	noir	negro	nero
white	weiß	vays	vit	blanc	blanco	bianco
brown	braun	broyn	brun	brun	café	marrone
orange	orange	oranzh	orange	orange	anaranjado	arancione
purple	lila	lila	purpurfärgad	pourpre	púrpura	violetto
pink	rosa	rozeve	skär	rose	rosa	rosa
father	der Vater	foter	fa(de)r	le père	el padre	il padre
mother	die Mutter	muter	mo(de)r	la mère	la madre	la madre
son	der Sohn	zun	son	le fils	el hijo	il figlio

List #145 **Similar Words in Seven Languages** *(continued)*

English	German	Yiddish	Swedish	French	Spanish	Italian
daughter	die Tochter	tokhter	dotter	la fille	la hija	la figlia
brother	der Bruder	bruder	bro(de)r	le frère	el hermano	il fratello
sister	die Schwester	shvester	syster	la soeur	la hermana	la sorella
grandfather	der Grossvater	zeyde	far-fa(de)r; mor-fa(de)r	le grand-père	el abuelo	il nonno
grandmother	die Grossmutter	bobe	far-mo(de)r; mor-mo(de)r	la grand-mère	la abuela	il nonna
uncle	der Onkel	feter	far-bro(de)r; mor-bro(de)r	l'oncle	el tío	il zio
aunt	die Tante	mume	faster; moster	la tante	la tía	la zia
cousin	der Vetter	shvesterkind	kusin	le cousin/ la cousine	el primo/ la prima	il cugino/ la cugina

List #146: Common Foreign Words and Phrases Used in English

All students should become familiar with foreign phrases commonly used in English writing, particularly in novels, newspapers, and magazines. The phrases listed here have been selected because they are the ones your child is most likely to encounter and also they should be relatively easy for your child to understand and put into use appropriately. You might introduce one new phrase per week and then encourage your student(s) to use the phrase in the correct context as much as possible.

French Phrases

a la carte: ordering individual items off a menu
a la mode: in fashion or (alternate meaning) served with ice cream
au contraire: on the contrary
au revoir: until we meet again; good-bye
bon appetit: good appetite; enjoy your meal
bonjour: hello; good day
bon voyage: have a good trip
carte blanche: full power to act on one's own
cul de sac: end of a street or alley; dead end
double entendre: double meaning
enfant terrible: a horrible child
en masse: in a large group or mass
en route: on the route or on the way
faux pas: social error or mistake
hors d'oeuvre: appetizer
je ne sais quoi: I don't know what
laissez-faire: the attitude or practice that we shouldn't interfere in the affairs of others, especially concerning conduct
n'est-ce pas?: isn't that true?
nom de plume: pen name
objet d'art: an object of art
tout de suite: immediately; right away
tout le monde: everyone
vis-à-vis: face-to-face

List #146: **Common Foreign Words and Phrases Used in English** *(continued)*

Latin Phrases

ad hoc: for a particular purpose
ad infinitum: to infinity
ad nauseam: to a sickening degree
bona fide: in good faith
carpe diem: seize the day
caveat emptor: let the buyer beware
cogito ergo sum: I think, therefore I am
e pluribus unum: one from many
et cetera: and others, and so on
in memoriam: in memory of
in toto: totally
mea culpa: my fault
modus operandi: method of operating
non sequitur: it does not follow or is not related to the preceding
nota bene: note well or take notice
persona grata: a welcomed person
persona non grata: an unwelcome person
prima facie: clear and evident
pro rata: according to proportion
quid pro quo: something for something
sine qua non: indispensable
status quo: the way things are
tempus fugit: time flies
veni, vidi, vici: I came, I saw, I conquered
vice versa: conversely or in the reverse order
vox populi: the voice of the people

List #147 Greetings and Basic Phrases in Foreign Languages

	hello	good-bye	please	thank you	yes	no
German	hallo	auf Wiedersehen	bitte	danke	ja	nein
Dutch	hallo	tot ziens	alstublieft	dankjewel	ja	nee
French	bonjour	au revoir	s'il vous plaît	merci	oui	non
Spanish	hola	adios	por favor	gracias	si	no
Portuguese	ola	adeus	por favor	obrigado	sim	nao
Italian	ciao	arrivederci	per favore	grazie	si	no
Danish	hej	farvel	vaersgo	tak	ja	nej
Swedish	hej	hejda	tack	tack	ja	nej
Hebrew	shalom	lehitraot	bevakasha	toda	ken	lo
Irish	failte	slan	le do thoil	go raibh maith agat	sea	ni, ha
Swahili	jambo	kwa heri	tafadhali	asante	ndiyo	siyo
Japanese	konnichiwa	sayonara	kudasai	arigatou	hai	iie
Basque	kaixo	agur	mesedez	eskerrik asko	bai	ez
Esperanto	saluton	gis la revido	mi petas	dankon	jes	ne
Finnish	paivaa	nakemiin	ole hyva	kiitos	kylla	ei
Indonesian	selamat pagi	selamat tinggal	tolong	terima kasih	ya	tidak

List #148 Origin of English Language

Words and where they come from is an absolutely fascinating topic. Most children love to know "why," "where," and "how"—making the study of words a perfect activity for them!

English is a language that is made up of many other languages. Many people mistakenly call English a "Romance language," thinking it was derived from Latin (or the Romans' language, thus "Romance language"), but actually English has more in common with German. Just compare (with your child) some of the similarities between German and English in the "Similar Words in Seven Languages" and the "Greetings and Basic Phrases in Foreign Languages" lists (#145 and 147).

I would recommend that parents start any language study with a discussion of Genesis 11:1–9 (the story of Babel). It is important for children to know that it is God's decision that the languages of the world be diverse, but Jesus also tells us in the Great Commission to go into the world and share the good news. Therefore, I think it is important to respect that our languages all came from a common source and that the Lord also wants us to learn other languages so that we can share the Gospel with others.

After discussing the origin of language in general, you might want to explore how languages change and how English came to be such an important language. The following events are all very important in the development and expansion of the English language as we know it today. Explore the events in more detail with your child(ren):

- England's invasion by Julius Caesar in 55 B.C.*
- England's invasion by Emperor Claudius in 43 A.D.
- Christianity had come to England by the third century and Latin was the common language for the church
- England's invasion by Germanic tribes (Saxons, Jutes, Angles) in 449
- the Norman invasion of 1066
- the race to settle the New World by French, Spanish, English, and people of other countries

Now, consider the following questions with your child(ren):

- How much of a role does war play in the development of a language?
- Look at all the words we've "borrowed" from French. If the Norman invasion hadn't taken place, would we have these same words?
- Find a book of Old English, Middle English, and modern English and compare the words. Why do you think the words changed?
- Why have some languages contributed many words to the English language while others, like Czech, have contributed few?

List #148 **Origin of English Language** *(continued)*

- Sometimes new words are created practically, such as *dish/washer* or *base/ball* or *home/school*. Can you think of other words that you might create?
- Do you think languages will continue to change forever? Why or why not?
- Do you think languages have changed more or less since the invention of writing? What about since the invention of computers? Why or why not?

* By the way, the term "Englisc" was being used soon after the Germanic invasions. The term "Englaland" (which means "land of the Angles") didn't show up until about the year 1000, which means that the word for the English language was in use long before the country was called England! (Information from a great book called *A History of the English Language*, 3rd ed., Albert C. Baugh/Thomas Cable, Prentice-Hall, Inc., 1978. This was a textbook I used in college so you wouldn't be able to use it for your elementary age children, but certainly a linguistically gifted high school student might enjoy it!)

List #149 Major Languages Spoken Around the World

One thing I find quite interesting is how children view languages. If you ask the average child in the United States what is the most common language in the world, he will say "English." Of course he is answering based on what he sees, and this answer seems logical because English is spoken all around him, even in cities where Spanish is common.

It would be great if we had the linguistic diversity of Europe. Since we don't, I think every parent should at least present some basic language facts (words and basic grammar) to their children. This list shows the total number of speakers of various languages around the world. Notice that Chinese is actually number one and English comes in third, not first, as far as the total number of speakers.

Chinese, Mandarin	874 million
Hindi	366 million
English	341 million
Spanish	322–358 million
Bengali	207 million
Portuguese	176 million
Russian	167 million
Japanese	125 million
German, Standard	100 million
Korean	78 million
French	77 million
Chinese, Wu	77 million
Javanese	75 million
Chinese, Yue	71 million
Telugu	69 million

The data on this chart was taken from *The World Almanac and Book of Facts 2002* (New York: World Almanac Books). Another good book for students interested in the study of languages is *Dictionary of Languages*, by Andrew Dalby, revised edition published in 2004 (New York: Columbia University Press).

List #150 Interesting Language Facts

Number of living languages (still being spoken today): 6,912

Number of living languages that are nearly extinct: 516

Language spoken by the largest number of non-native speakers: English

Country with the most languages spoken: Papua New Guinea—820 living languages

Language with the most distinct words: English, with approximately 250,000 words

Language with the fewest words: Taki Taki, with 340 words (Taki Taki is an English-based Creole language spoken by 120,000 in the South American country of Suriname.)

Language with the longest alphabet: Khmer with 74 letters (This Austro-Asiatic language is the official language of Cambodia, where approximately 12 million people speak it.)

Language with the shortest alphabet: Rotokas, with 12 letters (This language is spoken by approximately 4,300 people in Papua New Guinea.)

Language with the fewest sounds (phonemes): Rotokas, with 11 phonemes

Language with the most sounds (phonemes): !Xóõ, with 112 phonemes (This language is spoken by approximately 4,200 people, most of whom live in the African country of Botswana.)

Language with the fewest consonant sounds: Rotokas, with six consonants

Language with the most consonant sounds: Ubyx, with 81 consonants (Before it became extinct in 1992, this language was once spoken in the Haci Osman village near Istanbul.)

Most widely published language: English

Longest word in the English language: pneumonoultramicroscopicsilicovolcanoconiosis (45 letters)

The information for this list has been obtained from *www.vistawide.com/languages*. It has a lot of other great language and culture information. Pay it a visit!

List #151 Meaning of -philia Words

In Greek, the word *philia* means "friendship" or "love," as in love for a friend like a brother. If you combine the suffix *–philia* with another root or prefix, you get *"the love of* something."

Word	Means "the love of . . ."
acustiophilia	noise/sounds
aerophilia	air, flight, being in the air
ailurophilia	cats
anglophilia	England, the English, English customs, etc. (or admiration for England, etc.)
anthophilous	flowers (referring to insects' love)
anthropophilia	people
astraphilia	lightning, thunder
astrophilia	stars
bibliophilia	books
brontophilia	thunderstorms
canophilia	dogs (from *canus,* Latin word for "dog")
chionophilia	snow
chromophilia	colors
dendrophilia	trees
ergophilia	work
graphophilia	writing
hippophilia	horses (ancient word *hippos* means "horse")
lacanophilia	vegetables
meterophilia	weather
metrophilia	poetry
ornithophilia	birds
retrophilia	things from the past
Scotophilia	things of Scotland or the Scots
soleciphilia	worms
toxophilia	archery
zoophilia	animals

List #152 Meaning of -phobia Words

Word	Means "the fear of . . ."
ablutophobia	taking bath
acarophobia	itching
acrophobia	heights or edges
aerophobia	flying
agoraphobia	crowds, crowded or public places
agrizoophobia	wild animals
apphobia	bees
bacteriophobia	bacteria
bibliophobia	books
blennophobia	slime
carnophobia	meat
chionophobia	snow
chronomentrophobia	clocks
cyberphobia	computers or working on computers
dentophobia	dentists
didaskaleinophobia	going to school
doraphobia	animals' skin or fur
epistemophobia	knowledge
equinophobia or hippophobia	horses
felinophobia (among others)	cats
gamophobia	marriage
gephyrophobia	bridges or crossing bridges
heliophobia	sun or sunlight
herpetophobia	creepy, crawly critters or reptiles
hydrophobia	water
ichthyophobia	fish
motorphobia	automobiles
neophobia	anything new
nosocomephobia	hospitals
ochophobia	a moving automobile
ornithophobia	birds
sociophobia	people—in general
technophobia	technology
traumatophobia	injuries

List #152 **Meaning of -phobia Words** *(continued)*

Word	Means "the fear of . . ."
xenophobia	strangers
zeusophobia	gods or God
zoophobia	animals

If you are interested in learning more *–phobia* words, there is a good Web site located at *www.phobialist.com*. I would caution parents, however, that this list contains many, many definitions not appropriate for children. Use it only for yourself if you're interested in finding the definition of a *–phobia* word not listed here. I've tried to list most of the words that homeschoolers might use for educational purposes.

List #153 Games to Learn Any Foreign Language

There are some things that you can do to make any of these games more fun for your students.

- Invite other students studying the same language to play the games with your child. Some of these games can be played one on one, but many of them require more children.
- Include younger siblings in language study and games. I had introduced languages to our daughter relatively early, but had not been making any effort to teach our younger son. One day I was teaching a group Latin class and he was sitting in because he wasn't feeling well. I was surprised at the number of words he knew, though he had received no formal training in Latin to that point.
- Keep a tally of winners and give out prizes at the end of a day or week of games.
- If students are studying more than one language, use words from the various languages in each of the games.
- Some of these games are easy and some are more difficult. Be sure to play games with varied difficulty and mix up the physical, action games with mental, thinking games so that students with differing abilities can have a measure of success.

Simon Says

Once a student knows commands, you can play Simon Says with him. Practice using positive (yes) commands and negative (no) commands so that the student hears both forms. Allow the student to be "Simon" sometimes so that he can practice giving the commands. You can change "Simon" to a name more common in the language that you're studying, such as "Jacques" (French), "Julius" (Latin), or "Juan" (Spanish).

Duck, Duck, Goose

This is a good outdoor game, and the more children that play, the better. Translate the animal names into the language you're studying, and you will have a fun, active language game. (Remember, you can change the animals so you play "Horse, horse, cow," "dog, dog, cat," etc.)

List #153 **Games to Learn Any Foreign Language** *(continued)*

King of the Hill

Put a chair at the front of the room. Ask questions (in the foreign language); whoever gets a correct answer takes over the chair. Set a timer, and at the end of thirty minutes (or however long you're playing) the "king" gets a reward or is allowed to choose the next game.

Buzz

This game is a great way to practice numbers in a foreign language. Pick a particular number (take four, for example). Start with your first student. (If there is only one student, it may be more fun if you play with him.) Count up from zero. Each time you come to a number that includes the selected number (four in this case) or that is divisible by that number, you say "buzz." So for fours, the student would count, "one, two, three, *buzz*, five, six, seven, *buzz*, nine, ten, eleven, *buzz*, thirteen, *buzz* (contains a four), fifteen, *buzz*," etc. Of course, the student should be counting in the language he is studying and in place of *buzz*, you can use an exclamation from the language.

Scavenger Hunt

Using the language being studied, write hints and place them around the house, yard, co-op building, etc. Give the students the first clue to translate and try to decide where they will find their next clue. One clue should lead to the next and so on. The last clue might lead to the freezer (where students can enjoy ice cream), to the teacher (who might give the students a treat), or to some other "treasure."

Scrabble and Other Common Word Games

My personal favorite for studying languages is to play a common game, such as Scrabble, and simply adjust the rules to allow foreign words. I think this not only helps the child with the foreign language but it also helps with English vocabulary and spelling. After introducing my daughter to Latin and changing the rules of Scrabble to include foreign words, she began consistently beating me at this game.

10

Great People

List #154 Famous People During Each Historical Era

You can use this list in many ways, but it can be a valuable resource to those who want to supplement their regular history curriculum with biographical studies. *The eras are basically arranged according to American history, but the individuals listed are not all Americans*. None of us lives in a vacuum, and studying biographies of people from around the world will enable children to see how our own history affects and is affected by others. Therefore, I encourage you to use the list for world history, American history, or simply as a resource in itself if you are looking for people to study from a particular era for other reasons. (The names in each era are in no particular order and sometimes are loosely placed in the era based on the time in the individuals' lives when they completed their greatest works or had the most influence.)

Ancient Times

- Aristotle
- Saint Athanaius
- Cleopatra
- Catherine the Great
- Theodora
- Socrates
- Julius Caesar
- Alexander the Great

Early Explorers (prior to 1600)

- Amerigo Vespucci
- Genghis Khan
- Marco Polo
- Queen Elizabeth
- Queen Isabella
- King Ferdinand II
- Leonardo da Vinci
- Johannes Gutenberg
- Edmund Campion
- Christopher Columbus
- Francisco de Orellana
- Leif Ericson
- Cabeza de Vaca
- Ambrose Paré
- Jacques Cartier
- Theo Paracelsus
- Ferdinand Magellan
- Henry Hudson
- William Shakespeare

Early Native Americans and Pilgrims (1600–1650)

- Pocohontas
- Squanto
- Anne Hutchinson
- Sequoyah
- Tecumsah
- Captain John Smith

Colonial America (1650–early 1700s)

- John Smith
- Myles Standish
- William Bradford
- Pontiac
- James Oglethorpe
- Benjamin Franklin
- Peter Stuyvesant
- St. John Baptist de La Salle
- Robert de La Salle
- Sir Isaac Newton
- Edmund Haley
- Peter the Great
- Sir Henry Morgan
- Father Junípero Serra
- Georg Friederich Händel
- William Penn
- Johann Sebastian Bach

List #154 **Famous People During Each Historical Era** *(continued)*

American Revolution (mid 1700s–1800)

- Abigail Adams
- Crispus Attucks
- Captain James Cook
- Benjamin Franklin
- Thomas Jefferson
- John Paul Jones
- Daniel Boone
- Paul Revere
- Alexander Hamilton
- Aaron Burr
- Franz Joseph Haydn
- Molly Pitcher
- Patrick Henry
- Marquis de La Fayette
- Dolly Madison
- Wolfgang Amadeus Mozart
- Francis Marion
- James Monroe
- Charles Cornwallis
- George Washington
- Martha Washington
- Daniel Webster
- John Wesley
- Anthony Wayne
- Israel Putnam
- John Hancock
- Nathan Hale

Westward Expansion (1780–late 1800s)

- Hans Christian Andersen
- Johnny Appleseed
- Robert Fulton
- Thomas Hopkins Gallaudet
- James Forten
- Henry Clay
- Michael Faraday
- Cochise
- Laurent Clerc
- Stephen Austin
- Geronimo
- Meriwether Lewis
- Simón Bolívar
- Fanny Crosby
- Charles Finney
- Jenny Lind
- David Livingstone
- Maria Mitchell
- Sitting Bull
- Louis Braille
- John James Audubon
- Sacagawea
- Zebulon Montgomery Pike
- Jim Bridger
- Ludwig van Beethoven
- Sarah Siddons
- Samuel Morse
- Chief Seattle
- Levi Strauss
- Queen Victoria
- Hudson Taylor
- Crazy Horse
- Stephen Decatur
- Zachary Taylor
- Henry David Thoreau
- Frédéric Chopin
- Kit Carson
- Franz Schubert
- Andrew Jackson
- Jim Beckwourth
- Jedediah Smith
- George Rogers Clark
- Washington Irving
- Buffalo Bill
- Sam Houston
- Ralph Waldo Emerson
- Charles Darwin
- Laura Ingalls Wilder
- Stephen Foster
- Francisco José de Goya
- Louis Pasteur
- Sam Patch
- Clara Schumann
- Patty Reed
- Brigham Young
- Charles Haddon Spurgeon

List #154 **Famous People During Each Historical Era** *(continued)*

Civil War Era (1860–1870)

- Abraham Lincoln
- Harriet Tubman
- Frederick Douglass
- Robert E. Lee
- Stonewall Jackson
- John Ericsson
- Ulysses S. Grant
- Chief Joseph
- Henry Brown
- Lucy Stone
- Robert Smalls
- Sojourner Truth
- J. E. B. Stuart
- George Mueller
- Florence Nightingale
- Father Damien of Molokai
- Jan Matzeliger
- Benito Pablo Juárez García
- Booker T. Washington

Progressive Era (1870–1900s)

- Jane Addams
- Helen Keller
- Thomas Nast
- George Eastman
- Emmeline Pankhurst
- Carl Sandburg
- George Washington Carver
- Albert Schweitzer
- Annie Oakley
- Frederick Olmstead
- Calamity Jane
- Marie Curie
- Pierre Curie
- John Muir
- Anne Sullivan
- Grandma Moses
- Alexander Graham Bell
- Henry Ford
- Margaret Mead
- Louisa May Alcott
- Amelia Earhart
- William and Charles Mayo
- Teddy Roosevelt
- Aldo Leopold
- Thomas Alva Edison
- Charles Lindbergh
- Billy Sunday
- Jacqueline Cochran
- Samuel Morris
- William Christopher Handy
- Ernest Hemingway
- Henry Ford
- Adolf Hitler
- P. T. Barnum
- Ernest Shackleton
- Neil Armstrong
- Alan Sheperd
- Mark Twain
- Oliver Wendell Holmes, Jr.
- Harry Houdini
- Gus Grissom
- A. P. Giannini
- Florence Sabin
- Lou Gehrig
- Robert Goddard
- Joseph Stalin
- Mikhail Gorbachev
- Mahatma Gandhi
- William Booth
- D. L. Moody
- Richard Wright
- Eleanor Roosevelt
- Franklin D. Roosevelt
- Theodore Roosevelt
- Wilbur and Orville Wright
- Samuel F. B. Morse
- Billy Graham
- Nellie Bly
- Dwight D. Eisenhower
- Johanne Brahms
- Rachel Carson
- Martin Luther King
- Elizabeth Blackwell
- Rosalynn Carter
- Thurgood Marshall
- Beatrix Potter
- Phillip Randolph Hearst
- Jacqueline Kennedy
- Gordon Parks
- César Chávez

List #155 Birthdays of Great People

Use this list to supplement regular curriculum work, create unit studies, or provide a reason for a weekly birthday celebration with an educational twist.

January 4 (1643)	Sir Isaac Newton	scientist
January 6 (1878)	Carl Sandburg	poet
January 14 (1886)	Hugh Lofting	author
January 19 (1736)	James Watt	inventor
January 19 (1807)	Robert E. Lee	commander of Confederate Army
January 21 (1824)	Thomas Jackson	soldier
January 26 (1880)	Douglas MacArthur	general
February 7 (1885)	Sinclair Lewis	novelist
February 8 (1828)	Jules Verne	author
February 13 (1891)	Grant Wood	artist
February 15 (1809)	Cyrus Hall McCormick	inventor
February 25 (1873)	Enrico Caruso	opera singer
February 26 (1845)	Buffalo Bill	cowboy, showman
February 27 (1897)	Marian Anderson	singer
March 2 (1793)	Sam Houston	frontiersman
March 5 (1853)	Howard Pyle	artist
March 7 (1849)	Luther Burbank	botanist
March 13 (1733)	Joseph Priestly	chemist
March 18 (1858)	Rudolf Diesel	German inventor
March 21 (1685)	Johann Sebastian Bach	composer
March 24 (1874)	Harry Houdini	magician
April 5 (1856)	Booker T. Washington	founder of Tuskegee Institute
April 10 (1829)	William Booth	founder of Salvation Army
April 16 (1889)	Charles Chaplin	actor, producer
April 21 (1926)	Queen Elizabeth II	princess, queen
April 26 (1564) (baptized)	William Shakespeare	author, poet, screenwriter
May 4 (1796)	Horace Mann	educational reformist, abolitionist
May 6 (1856)	Robert E. Peary	explorer
May 7 (1840)	Peter Tschaikovsky	composer
May 12 (1812)	Edward Lear	poet
May 25 (1803)	Ralph Waldo Emerson	philosopher

List #155 **Birthdays of Great People** *(continued)*

May 31 (1819)	Walt Whitman	poet
June 1 (1637)	Jacques Marquette	explorer
June 3 (1808)	Jefferson Davis	president of the Confederacy
June 8 (1778)	Robert Stevenson	lighthouse builder, grandfather of Robert Louis Stevenson
June 27 (1880)	Helen Keller	blind and deaf child who later came to live a wonderful life
June 29 (1858)	George Washington Goethals	engineer
July 4 (1753)	François Blanchard	French balloonist
July 5 (1810)	Phineas Taylor Barnum	showman
July 12 (1854)	George Eastman	founder of Eastman Kodak Company
July 12 (1730)	Josiah Wedgewood	English pottery maker, china designer
July 15 (1573)	Inigo Jones	architect
July 24 (1783)	Simon Bolívar	patriot
July 28 (1866)	Beatrix Potter	artist, author
July 31 (1803)	John Ericsson	inventor
August 1 (1818)	Maria Mitchell	astronomer
August 1 (1819)	Herman Melville	author
August 12 (1859)	Katherine Lee Bates	poet
August 13 (1818)	Lucy Stone	suffragette
August 15 (1771)	Sir Walter Scott	author
September 2 (1850)	Eugene Field	poet
September 7 (1860)	Grandma Moses (Anna Mary Robertson Moses)	artist
September 17 (1730)	Baron von Steuben	German leader who aided General George Washington at Valley Forge
September 18 (1709)	Samuel Johnson	dictionary writer
September 21 (1756)	John Loudon McAdam	road engineer
September 23 (1800)	William Holmes McGuffey	teacher, creator of McGuffey's Readers
September 26 (1898)	George Gershwin	jazz composer
September 26 (1774)	John Chapman	planter of apple trees
September 28 (1865)	Kate Douglas Wiggin	author

List #155 **Birthdays of Great People** *(continued)*

October 5 (1848)	Edward Trudeau	physician
October 12 (1451)	Christopher Columbus	explorer
October 20 (1859)	John Dewey	teacher, philosopher
October 22 (1843)	Stephen Babcock	farmer, chemist
October 31 (1860)	Juliette Lowe	founder of Girl Scouts of America
November 2 (1755)	Marie Antoinette	Queen of France
November 6 (1854)	John Philip Sousa	composer, band leader
November 7 (1867)	Marie Sklodovska Curie	scientist
November 9 (1801)	Gail Borden	father of modern dairy industry
November 11 (1872)	Maude Adams	actress
November 18 (1787)	Louis Daguerre	inventor
November 20 (1889)	Edwin Hubble	astronomer
November 25 (1835)	Andrew Carnegie	businessman, philanthropist
November 30 (1835)	Mark Twain (Samuel Clemens)	author
November 30 (1819)	Cyrus Field	businessman
December 2 (1761)	Nicholas-Louis Robert	inventor, balloonist
December 5 (1901)	Walt Disney	movie director
December 6 (1863)	Charles Martin Hall	scientist
December 8 (1765)	Eli Whitney	inventor
December 9 (1848)	Joel Chandler Harris	author
December 16 (1775)	Jane Austen	novelist
December 25 (1821)	Clara Barton	nurse, first president of American Red Cross
December 30 (1865)	Rudyard Kipling	author

List #156 Major Greek and Roman Gods

In Greek mythology, the Olympians overthrew the Titans to rule the world from the Greek Pantheon, which sat atop Mount Olympus.

Greek Name	Roman Name	Title
Aphrodite	Venus	goddess of love/beauty
Apollo	Phoebus Apollo	god of light
Ares	Mars	god of war; (Greek) son of Zeus and Hera
Artemis	Diana	goddess of the hunt; (Greek) Apollo's twin sister
Athena	Minerva	goddess of wisdom; (Greek) daughter of Zeus (with no mother)
*Demeter	Ceres	goddess of grain/crops
*Dionysus	Bacchus	god of wine
*Hades	Pluto	god of underworld
Hephaestus	Vulcan	god of fire
Hera	Juno	queen of the gods; (Greek) Zeus's wife and sister; protector of marriage
Hermes	Mercury	messenger of the gods; (Greek) son of Zeus and Maia
Poseidon	Neptune	god/ruler of the sea
Zeus	Jupiter	supreme ruler; king of gods

* Not every source considers the gods marked with an asterisk as major Olympian Greek gods.

List #157 Minor Greek Gods

Deity	Description
Asclepius	god of medicine
Chaos	the primeval state from which all the other gods appeared; Chaos was nothingness that had children, including Gaia (the Earth)
Charites	goddesses of grace, charm, beauty, fertility, and human creativity (Aglaea, Euphrosyne, Thalia, and sometimes others)
Dione	goddess without a specific purpose other than being the mother of Aphrodite (in Homer's *Iliad*)
Erebus	god of darkness
Erinyes (or Eumenides)	goddesses who personified vengeance
Eris	goddess of discord
Eros	god of love; in Roman mythology, Eros is known as Cupid
Ether or Aether	god of space and heaven
Fates or Moirae	goddesses (or one goddess, Moera) who determined men's destinies
Gaia	goddess of the Earth
Hebe	goddess of youth
Muses	goddesses of the arts and sciences; inspire those who excel in arts and sciences
Nemesis	goddess of divine justice and vengeance
Nymph	not actually gods or goddesses, the nymphs sometimes accompanied the gods and goddesses
Nyx	goddess of the night
Pan	god of shepherds, woods, pastures
Persephone	queen of the underworld
Tartarus	a place in the underworld below Hades
Thanatos	personification of death
Uranus or Ouranos	god of the sky, husband of Gaia

List #158 Minor Roman Gods

The Greeks and Romans were very creative when it came to thinking up fascinating stories about their gods. Here are some other gods with whom you can familiarize yourself. Activity idea: Try to guess which English words ultimately derived from these deities' names.

Deity	Description
Abeona	protector of children leaving the home
Abudantia	goddess of luck, abundance and prosperity; she distributed food and money from a cornucopia
Adeona	goddess who guides children back home
Aequitas	god of fair trade and honest merchants
Aera Cura	goddess associated with the underworld
Aeternitas	personification of eternity
Africus	god of the southwest wind
Alemonia	goddess who feeds unborn children
Angerona	goddess of secrecy and protector of Rome
Anna Perenna	goddess of the New Year; provider of food
Antevorte	goddess of the future
Aquilo	god of the north wind
Aurora	goddess of the dawn
Auster	god of the south wind
Bona Dea	goddess of fertility, healing, and women
Camenae (the)	goddesses of wells and springs
Candelifera	goddess of childbirth
Cardea	goddess of thresholds and door hinges
Carmenta	goddess of childbirth and prophecy
Carnea	goddess of the heart and other organs, and door handles
Cinxia	goddess of marriage
Clementia	goddess of mercy and clemency
Cloacina	goddess of the Cloaca Maxima, the system of sewers in Rome
Coelus	god of the sky
Concordia	goddess of agreement and understanding
Conditor	god of the harvest
Consus	god of grain storage
Convector	god of bringing in the crops from the fields
Copia	goddess of wealth and plenty

List #158 **Minor Roman Gods** *(continued)*

Deity	Description
Corus	god of the northwest wind
Cunina	goddess of infants
Dea Dia	goddess of growth
Dea Tacita	goddess of the dead
Decima	goddess of childbirth; with Nona and Morta she forms the Parcae (the three fates)
Devera	goddess of brooms used for purification
Deverra	goddess of women in labor and the patron of midwives
Dia Lucrii (the)	gods of profit
Disciplina	goddess of discipline
Discordia	goddess of discord and strife
Dius Fidus	god of oaths
Egestes	goddess of poverty
Empanda	goddess of openess, friendliness, and generosity
Eventus Bonus	god of success both in commerce and in agriculture
Fabulinus	god who taught children to speak
Fama	goddess of fame and rumor
Fauna (Bona Dea)	goddess of the Earth, mother goddess
Faunus	god of the wilds and fertility; he is the protector of cattle, also referred to as Lupercus
Faustitas	goddess protectress of herds of livestock
Favonius	god of the west wind
Febris	goddess who protected people against fevers
Felicitas	goddess of success
Feronia	goddess of freedom and good harvest; she was often worshiped by slaves to achieve their freedom
Fides	goddess of faithfulness and good faith
Flora	goddess of spring and the blooming flowers
Fontus	god of wells and springs
Fornax	goddess of bread-baking and ovens
Fortuna	goddess of fate
Fulgora	goddess of lightning
Furina	goddess of thieves
Honos	god of chivalry, honor, and military justice

List #158 **Minor Roman Gods** *(continued)*

Deity	Description
Indivia	goddess of jealousy
Juturna	goddess of lakes, wells, and springs
Juventas	goddess of youth
Lactans	god of agriculture
Lares (the)	guardian spirits of the house and fields
Liber	god of fertility and nature
Libera	fertility goddess
Liberalitas	god of generosity
Libertas	goddess of freedom
Libitina	goddess of funerals
Lima	goddess of thresholds
Lucifer	god of the morning star
Lucina	goddess of childbirth and midwifery
Luna	goddess of the moon
Maia	goddess of fertility and spring
Maiesta	goddess of honor and reverence
Matuta	goddess of the dawn, harbors and the sea; patron of newborn babies
Meditrina	goddess of wine and health
Mefitas	goddess of poisonous vapors from the Earth
Mellona	goddess and protector of bees
Mens	goddess of the mind and consciousness
Messor	god of agriculture and mowing
Moneta	goddess of prosperity
Mors	god of death
Morta	goddess of death and one of the three Parcae (the three fates)
Muta	goddess of silence
Mutinus Mutunus	god of fertility
Necessitas	goddess of destiny
Nemestrinus	god of the woods
Nona	goddess of pregnancy; one of the Parcae with the goddesses Morta and Decima (three fates)
Nox	personification of the night

List #158 **Minor Roman Gods** *(continued)*

Deity	Description
Nundina	goddess of the ninth day, on which the newborn child was given a name
Obarator	god of plowing
Occator	god of harrowing
Orbona	goddess of parents who lost their children
Orcus	god of death and the underworld; also a god of oaths and punisher of perjurers
Pales	goddess of shepherds and flocks
Parcae (the)	goddesses of fate; the goddesses Nona, Morta, and Decima make up the group; the three Parcae are also called Tria Fata
Pax	goddess of peace
Penates (the)	gods of the storeroom and the household
Picus	god of agriculture
Pietas	goddess of piety
Poena	goddess of punishment
Pomona	goddess of fruit trees and orchards
Portunes	god of ports and harbors; the guardian of storehouses and locked doors
Porus	god of plenty
Postverta	goddess of the past
Potina	goddess of children's drinks
Priapus	god of gardens, wine making, sailors, and fishermen
Prorsa Postverta	goddess of women in labor
Providentia	goddess of forethought
Pudicitia	goddess of modesty and chastity
Puta	goddess of the pruning of vines and trees
Quiritis	goddess of motherhood
Robigo	goddess of corn
Robigus	god who protected corn from diseases
Roma	personified goddess of the city of Rome
Rumina	goddess of nursing mothers
Sancus	god of oaths and good faith
Saritor	god of weeding and hoeing
Securitas	goddess of security and stability
Semonia	goddess of sowing

List #158 **Minor Roman Gods** *(continued)*

Deity	Description
Sors	god of luck
Spes	goddess of hope
Stata Mater	goddess who guards against fires
Strenua	goddess of strength and vigor
Suadela	goddess of persuasion, especially in matters of love
Subrincinator	god of weeding
Summanus	god of night thunder
Tempestes (the)	goddesses of storms
Terminus	god of boundaries
Terra Mater	(Mother Earth) goddess of fertility and growth
Trivia	goddess of the crossroads
Vacuna	goddess of agriculture
Veritas	goddess of truth
Vertumnus	god of the changing seasons and the ripening of fruits and grains
Viduus	god who separated the soul and the body after death
Virtus	god of courage and military prowess
Vitumnus	god who gave life to children in the womb
Volturnus	god of the waters
Volumna	goddess who protects the nursery
Vulturnus	god of the east wind

This table was reprinted in part with permission from the United Nations of Roma Victrix, which is dedicated to sharing and preserving Roman history. You can find more Roman history on the UNRV Web site at *www.unrv.com*.

List #159 Great Philosophers

Philosopher	Dates and Nationality	Important Works
Socrates	Greek	His written works no longer exist, so our knowledge of him is based on his students, including Plato
Plato	427–347 BC Greek	Apology of Socrates, Crito, Euthyphro, Laws, Phaedo, Phaedrus, Republic, Symposium, Timaeus
Aristotle	384–322 BC Greek	Dialogues, Metaphysics, On Monarchy, Nicomachean Ethics, Rhetoric, The Customs of Barbarians (and 158 Constitutions, including The Constitution of Athens)
Epicurus	342–270 BC Greek	About 300 books, all of which have been lost except a few fragments—letters, including To Herodotus, To Menoecus, To Pythocles
Ptolemy (Claudius Ptolemaeus)	90–170 Greek	Roman Almagest, Tetrabiblos, Geography
Marcus Aurelius	121–180 Roman	Meditations
Saint Thomas Aquinas	1225–1274 Italian	Disputed Questions, On Divine Names, Summa Contra Gentiles, Summa Theologica; Commentaries on Ethics, Metaphysics, Physics, Politics, etc.
Francis Bacon	1561–1626 English	Apothegms, Colors of Good and Evil, Confession of Faith, Essays, History of Life and Death, Maxims of Law, Natural History, New Atlantis, Silva Silvarum, The Advancement of Learning, The History of Henry VII
René Descartes	1596–1650 French	Discourse on the Method of Rightly Conducting the Reason, Geometry, Meditations on the First Philosophy, Principles of Philosophy, Rules for the Direction of the Mind, The Search After Truth, The World, Treatise on Man
Baruch Spinoza	1632–1677 Dutch	Essay on the Rainbow, Ethics, Metaphysical Thoughts, The Calculation of Chances, The Principles of the Cartesian Philosophy, Treatise on the Improvement of the Understanding, Treatise on Religion and Politics, Short Treatise on God, Man, and His Well-Being

List #159 **Great Philosophers** *(continued)*

Philosopher	Dates and Nationality	Important Works
John Locke	1632–1704 English	Essay Concerning the Human Understanding, Letters on Toleration, The Reasonableness of Christianity, Thoughts on Education, Two Treatises on Government
Voltaire (François Marie Arouet)	1694–1778 French	Artémire, Candide, Charles XII, Diatribe on Doctor Akakia, Mérope, Oedipe, Philosophic Dictionary, The Pupil of Nature, The World As It Goes, Zadig
David Hume	1711–1776 Scottish	Dialogues Concerning Natural Religion, History of England (five volumes), Inquiry Concerning the Principles of Mortals, Political Discourses, Treatise of Human Nature
Immanuel Kant	1724–1804 German	Metaphysic of Ethics, Metaphysic of Nature, Religion Within the Limits of Pure Reason, The Critique of Judgment, The Critique of Practical Reason, The Critique of Pure Reason
Goethe (Johann Wolfgang von)	1749–1832 German	Faust, Theory of Colours, Götz von Berlichingen, The Sorrows of Young Werther, Iphigenie auf Tauris
Georg Wilhelm Friedrich Hegel	1770–1831 German	Aesthetics, Encyclopedia of Philosophical Science, History of Philosophy, Life of Jesus, Phenomenology of Spirit, Philosophy of Art, Philosophy of History, Philosophy of Mind, Philosophy of Right, Science of Logic
Arthur Schopenhauer	1788–1860 German	Essays, On the Fourfold Root of Sufficient Reason, On the Will in Nature, The Art of Controversy, The Two Fundamental Problems of Ethics, The World as Will and Idea
Ralph Waldo Emerson	1803–1882 American	Beauty and Manners, Duty, English Traits, Essays, Journals, Letters and Social Aims, Literary Ethics, May Day and Other Pieces, Poems, Representative Man, Self-Reliance, The American Scholar, The Conduct of Life, The Oversoul, Truth
Søren Kierkegaard	1813–1855 Danish	On the Concept of Irony, The Present Age, Fear and Trembling, Repetition, Works of Love, Practice in Christianity

List #159 **Great Philosophers** *(continued)*

Philosopher	Dates and Nationality	Important Works
Herbert Spencer	1820–1903 English	Education: Intellectual, Moral, Physical; Autobiography, First Principles, Man Versus the State, Principles of Biology, Principles of Ethics, Principles of Psychology, Principles of Sociology, The Development Hypothesis, The Theory of Population, The Universal Postulate; Progress, Its Law and Cause
William James	1842–1910 American	A Pluralistic Universe, Essays in Radical Empiricism, Human Immortality, Letters (edited by his son Henry James), Talks to Teachers on Psychology and to Students on Some of Life's Ideals, The Meaning of Truth, The Principles of Psychology, The Varieties of Religious Experience, The Will to Believe and Other Essays in Popular Philosophy
Friedrich Wilhelm Nietzsche	1844–1900 German	Antichrist, Beyond Good and Evil, Ecce Homo (autobiography), Human All Too Human, Richard Wagner in Bayreuth, Schopenhauer as Educator, The Birth of Tragedy, The Dawn of Day, The Joyful Wisdom, The Genealogy of Morals, The Twilight of the Idols, The Will to Power
Henri Bergson	1859–1941 French	Creative Evolution, Laughter and Metaphysics, Matter and Memory, Mind-Energy, The Meaning of the War (of 1914), The Perception of Change, Time and Free Will
George Santayana	1863–1952 Spanish	Lucifer, a Theological Tragedy; Egotism in German Philosophy, Interpretations of Poetry and Religion, Persons and Places, Platonism and the Spiritual Life, Skepticism and Animal Faith, The Last Puritan, The Life of Reason (in five volumes), The Realm of Spirit, The Realm of Truth, The Sense of Beauty, Three Philosophical Poets (Lucretius, Dante and Goethe), Winds of Doctrine

List #160 Great Explorers

Dates	Name (and Nationality)	Area	Most Noted For
c. 2500 BC–1200 AD	Polynesians (brown-skinned people from Asia)	Hawaii and other islands in the Pacific Ocean	Discovered islands in the Pacific and established settlements
c. 960	Eric the Red (Viking)	Southwestern coast of Greenland	Founded the first settlement in Greenland
c. 1000	Vikings	Iceland, Greenland, North America	Explored in a time when others considered unknown waters forbidden territory. In 1961, a Viking settlement—thought to be the one Leif Ericson founded c. 1000—was discovered on the island of Newfoundland, Canada.
1254–1324	Marco Polo (Italian)	Persia, Indian Ocean, Sumatra, Java, China	Wrote thrilling details of his travels to China and back in *The Book of Marco Polo,* which became a guide for future exploration for men like Prince Henry of Portugal and Vasco da Gama
1394–1460	Prince Henry the Navigator (Portuguese)	Africa, Indian Ocean	Started the voyages that began the great "Age of Discovery" and eventually found the sea route around Africa to the Indies. (Though Prince Henry died before the route was discovered, his efforts made the discovery possible.)
1450–1498	John Cabot (English)	North America	Claimed North America for England
1451–1506	Christopher Columbus (Italian, exploring for Spain)	Atlantic Ocean, Central and South America	Wrongly credited with discovering North America, since he wasn't the first European to come across the Pacific; instead of landing in North America, he landed in Central and South America

List #160 **Great Explorers** *(continued)*

Dates	Name (and Nationality)	Area	Most Noted For
1451–1512	Amerigo Vespucci (Italian)	North and South America	Explored the continents of the New World and wrote numerous letters describing the inhabitants and his travels
c. 1469–1524	Vasco da Gama (Portuguese)	Eastern route to India from Portugal	Discovered an all-water route to India around the southern tip of Africa
1475–1519	Vasco Nuñez de Balboa (Spanish)	Panama to Pacific Ocean	Traveled through Panama to eastern shore of Pacific Ocean; explored and conquered South America for Spain
c. 1480–1521	Ferdinand Magellan (Portuguese, exploring for Spain)	Atlantic and Pacific Oceans	Proved that the world is round by traveling west from Spain around southern tip of South America and across Pacific Ocean (voyage was completed by his men after Magellan was killed on a Philippine Island); discovered Strait of Magellan
1485–1547	Hernando Cortés (Spanish)	Mexico	Led the expedition into Mexico that conquered Aztecs and opened up exploration of that part of the Americas
1491–1557	Jacques Cartier (French)	Newfoundland and Canada	Discovered and claimed St. Lawrence River (in what is now Canada) for France
c. 1500–1542	Hernando De Soto (Spanish)	southern area of North America	Explored southern area of North America; discovered Mississippi River, but enslaved Native Americans, destroying their towns along the way, seeking treasures
c. 1567–1635	Samuel de Champlain (French)	North America (Canada)	A navigator, map maker, and explorer who opened upper North America to French trade and settlement

List #160 **Great Explorers** *(continued)*

Dates	Name (and Nationality)	Area	Most Noted For
c. 1575–1611	Henry Hudson (English, exploring for Holland)	Atlantic Ocean, eastern shore and water routes of North America, Arctic Ocean	Failed to discover a new sea route to China through the Arctic Ocean, but did discover Hudson River, Hudson Strait, and Hudson Bay
1637–1675 (Marquette); 1645–1700 (Joliet)	Father Marquette and Louis Joliet (French)	Mississippi River	Found and explored the Mississippi River for the governor of New France
1643–1687	René Robert Cavelier, Sieur De La Salle (French)	Mississippi River	Claimed vast amounts of land for France along the Mississippi River Valley
1728–1779	Captain James Cook (English)	Pacific Ocean, Coast of New Zealand, Northern Coast of Australia, polar regions	Explored Pacific Ocean and polar regions of the Earth; discovered Hawaii
1768–1820	Alexander MacKenzie (Scottish)	Rocky Mountains, river flowing into Arctic Ocean (later named after him)	Was the first white man to cross the Rocky Mountains and reach the Pacific Ocean
1774–1809 (Lewis); 1770–1838 (Clark)	Meriwether Lewis and William Clark (American)	Western Territory	After the Louisiana Purchase, explored the Territory of Louisiana and then traveled all the way to the Pacific Ocean
1856–1920 (Peary); 1867–1955 (Henson)	Robert E. Peary and Matthew A. Henson (American)	Arctic regions and North Pole	Became the first humans to reach the North Pole
1879–1962	Vilhjalmur Stefansson (Canadian of Icelandic descent)	Arctic	Ethnologist and archaeologist noted for explorations of Arctic regions
1910–1997	Jacques-Yves Cousteau (French)	ocean	A pioneer in marine conservation
1930–	Neil A. Armstrong (American)	space	Was the first person to step on the surface of the moon

List #161 Native Americans to Know

Hiawatha

Though no actual documents have survived to give us firsthand accounts of Hiawatha, it is most likely that he lived in the early 1500s. We do know that he was an Iroquois Indian leader who helped establish peace among the five major Iroquois tribes: the Mohawk, Oneida, Onondaga, Seneca, and Cayuga. The five tribes formed an alliance called the Great Peace, or Iroquois League. These tribes lived in what is now upper New York State and their names live on as countries, cities, towns, or villages there today. Though American poet Henry Wadsworth Longfellow immortalized Hiawatha in his famous poem "The Song of Hiawatha," he had actually confused Hiawatha with Nanabozho, a mythological Indian hero of the Chippewa or Ojibwey tribe.

Powhatan

More commonly known as the father of Pocahontas, Powhatan (Wahunsunacock) lived during the latter half of the sixteenth century and the early part of the seventeenth century. According to the story, John Smith, who was a soldier, helped establish the first permanent English colony of North America. According to tradition, Powhatan captured John Smith and was going to kill him, but Pocahontas intervened, pleading for Smith's life. Since she was his favorite daughter, Powhatan allowed John Smith to live. Powhatan also established the Powhatan Confederacy of Virginia, which was actually like an empire with Powhatan as the leader of several united Algonquian tribes. He died in 1618 and the British destroyed his confederacy in 1644, but descendants of the confederacy tribes still live in Virginia today.

Pontiac

Pontiac, born around 1720, was a chief of the Ottawa tribe during the 1760s. He is recognized for trying to unite the Indian tribes of the Great Lakes area and the Ohio and Mississippi Valleys. Pontiac believed that Indians should abandon all trade with white men and that tribes should fight to keep the white men from taking more Indian lands. It is believed that Pontiac was killed by a Peoria Indian on April 20, 1769, in Cahokia, Illinois.

Little Turtle

Born around 1752 near the Eel River in what later became Indiana, Little Turtle became a chief of the Indiana and Ohio Miami Indians. During that

List #161 **Native Americans to Know** *(continued)*

time in history, one of the main goals of Native Americans was to protect their tribal lands, and Little Turtle fought for his lands like many other chiefs. In 1790, his forces defeated General Josiah Harmar's troops, and in 1791, Little Turtle defeated General Arthur St. Clair. Little Turtle and several other Indians signed a treaty in 1795 that opened up southern Ohio to settlement. He died in 1812 in Fort Wayne, Indiana.

Sequoyah

An Indian of mixed descent (a Cherokee mother and white father), Sequoyah was trained in the skills of hunting and fur trade. He was injured in a hunting accident and proceeded to devote all his time to devising a syllabary for the Cherokee language. A syllabary is a set of characters or symbols that represents syllables of a language and make it possible for the language to be in written form. Sequoyah lived from about 1776 to 1843.

Sacagawea

Sacagawea was a young Shoshone woman who accompanied Lewis and Clark on the Corps of Discovery to explore the United States to the Pacific coast and back. Sacagawea lived from about 1788 to December 20, 1812.

Sitting Bull

A Hunkpapa chief and medicine man, Sitting Bull is probably most famous for being at the Battle of Little Bighorn, in which Colonel George A. Custer and troops died. Sitting Bull lived during a time when the tensions between Native Americans and white men were at their greatest. The United States government and settlers were pushing Indians farther and farther west, taking away their lands along the way. When Sitting Bull was told to move to a reservation, he decided instead to take his band of followers to Canada, which is when Custer chased him and the famous Little Bighorn battle occurred. Sitting Bull returned to the United States in 1881, when he was confined to Fort Randall in South Dakota. When authorities went to arrest him in 1890, there was a fight and Sitting Bull was shot and killed. Sitting Bull lived from about 1831 to 1890.

Captain Jack

Captain Jack was born in 1837 with the Indian name Kintpuash. He was leader of a tribe of Modoc Indians that lived mainly in the Lost River Valley on the California-Oregon border near Tule Lake. When the U.S. government forced the tribe to move to the Klamath Reservation in Oregon in 1864, they had a difficult time supporting themselves on the land. Captain Jack led part of his tribe back to their homeland in 1872. He also led them against the United States Army during the ensuing war, known as the Modoc War of 1872–1873. When a peace meeting was held on April 11 and Brigadier General Edward Canby said he wouldn't remove his troops from the area, Captain Jack killed him. Captain Jack fled, but the United States Army captured and hanged him on October 3, 1873.

Crazy Horse

Crazy Horse, born around 1842, was only about thirty-two years old when he led the Sioux and Cheyenne Indians to defeat General George Crook in the Battle of the Rosebud in Montana. The fight began after the U.S. government ordered the Oglala Sioux, with Crazy Horse as their chief, to enter a reservation and they refused. Though many think of Sitting Bull as the leader at Little Bighorn, it was actually Crazy Horse who was chief at that battle where Colonel Custer and his command were killed. In 1877, Crazy Horse voluntarily surrendered to United States troops, and that same year he was killed by a soldier trying to force him into a jail cell.

Quanah Parker

Quanah Parker was born in 1845, near what is now Lubbock, Texas. His father, Nokoni, was a Comanche chief and his mother, Cynthia Ann Parker, was a white captive. Quanah adopted ways of his Indian father and his white mother. When he became chief, Quanah's mission was to stop the slaughter of the buffalo in his homeland of Texas. Quanah led his warriors against white settlers, but he was forced to surrender to the United States Army in 1875. Shortly thereafter Quanah and his tribe moved to a reservation near Fort Sill, in what is now southwestern Oklahoma. At that time, it appears that he decided to accept the fate of the white man's ways as he tried to encourage his people to obtain an education and learn to farm. He also encouraged them to work with the white man and even make money from them by leasing lands. Finally, many years before other Indians thought to do so, Quanah obtained full United States citizenship for his tribe members. He was the last free Commanche chief and he died in 1911.

List #162 Influential People of the American Revolution

Adams, Abigail	wife of John Adams; mother of John Quincy Adams
Adams, John	Founding Father and politician; served as the country's first vice-president and second president
Adams, John Quincy	lawyer, politician, and diplomat; served as U.S. president 1825–1829
Adams, Samuel	a main leader of Patriot cause; led protests such as the Boston Tea Party
Allen, Ethan	revolutionary; fought in Revolutionary War
Arnold, Benedict	general in Continental Army; betrayed Americans by plotting to surrender West Point to British
Attucks, Crispus	a man of mixed race (African with Native American or white ancestry) thought to be the first casualty in the American Revolution when he was killed in the Boston Massacre
Bassett, Richard	veteran of American Revolution; delegate to 1787 Constitutional Convention
Broom, Jacob	Founding Father; signed U.S. Constitution
Chase, Samuel	signer of U.S. Constitution; associate justice of the U.S. Supreme Court
Clinton, George	soldier, politician, and governor of New York State; served as vice-president
Dawes, William	though Paul Revere gets most of the credit, Dawes also rode to tell the minutemen that the British were approaching
Deane, Silas	not much is known about this Patriot, but he was a congressman for a time (A good Web site about Deane is at *www.silasdeaneonline.com.*)
Franklin, Benjamin	author, politician, and Founding Father; printer, scientist, inventor, and much more
de Galvez, Bernardo	Spanish governor of Louisiana
Gates, Horatio	American general
Gorham, Nathaniel	Founding Father; signer of U.S. Constitution
Green, Nathaniel	served as a general in the Continental Army
Hale, Nathan	captain in Continental Army; best remembered for his "I only regret that I have but one life to lose for my country" speech
Hamilton, Alexander	politician, military officer, and leading statesman; founder of Federalist Party

List #162 Influential People of the American Revolution *(continued)*

Hancock, John	president of Second Continental Congress; first person to sign Declaration of Independence (which led to the expression "Put your John Hancock here," meaning signature)
Henry, Patrick	Patriot; his famous "Give me liberty or give me death" speech appears in list #184
Jay, John	Founding Father, politician, and statesman; revolutionary, writer, jurist, and diplomat
Jefferson, Thomas	main author of Declaration of Independence; third president of U.S. (1801–1809)
Jones, John Paul	most known for his "I have not yet begun to fight" statement while captain of the *BONHOMME RICHARD* and subsequent capture of British ship *SERAPIS*
King, Rufus	delegate to the Continental Congress (not to be confused with a Civil War general by the same name)
Knox, Henry	bookseller who became the chief artillery officer in Continental Army; first secretary of war for United States
de Lafayette, Marquis	French aristocrat who agreed to help Patriots fight in American Revolution without pay; in 2002, was given honorary citizenship of the U.S. (only 6 people have this honor; others are: Winston Churchill, Mother Teresa, Raoul Wallenberg, William Penn, and Hannah Callowhill Penn—wife of William Penn)
Lee, Charles	major general in Continental Army; previously a Bristish soldier who settled in Virginia
Lee, Henry	cavalry officer in Continental Army; U.S. congressman, governor of Virginia, and father to Robert E. Lee
Lincoln, Benjamin	major general in Continental Army
Madison, James	fourth president of U.S. (1809–1817)
Marion, Francis	lieutenant colonel in Continental Army; known as "Swamp Fox" due to his ability to elude the British
McHenry, James	statesman; signed U.S. Constitution
Morgan, Daniel	pioneer and soldier; U.S. representative from Virginia
Paine, Thomas	English revolutionary, scholar, writer; helped inspire American Revolution
Penn, William	founded colony of Pennsylvania that became state of same name; believed in a utopian society
Pitcher, Molly	carried pitcher after pitcher of cool water to men at the Battle of Monmouth; after her husband fell in battle, she took his place at the cannon

List #162 **Influential People of the American Revolution** *(continued)*

Poor, Salem	a slave who bought his freedom in 1769 and then fought for Patriots at Bunker Hill, Saratoga, and Monmouth
Prescott, Samuel	completed Paul Revere's ride to deliver warning to Concord of the arrival of British troops
Prescott, William	colonel in Continental Army; commanded American forces at Battle of Bunker Hill
Revere, Paul	silversmith and Patriot who made the famous ride to warn Patriots that the British were coming
Rochambeau, Jean Baptiste	commanded the French troops that aided Patriots during American Revolution
Salomon, Haym	a Jewish believer in the Patriot cause, he provided much financial support for the American Revolution
Schuyler, Philip	homeschooled; leader in oppostition against British
Sherman, Roger	one of only two people (Robert Morris was other) to have signed all three major American documents: Declaration of Independence, Articles of Confederation, and U.S. Constitution
Spaight, Richard Dobbs, Sr.	anti-Federalist governor of North Carolina who attended Constitutional Convention
Warren, Joseph	physician and soldier; killed during American Revolution
Washington, George	led Continental Army; served as first president of the United States (1789–1797)
Washington, Martha	wife of George Washington
Wayne, Anthony	general and statesman
Wilkinson, James	statesman who fought as a soldier in the Continental Army
Williams, William	signed Declaration of Independence; political leader
Wolcott, Oliver	signed Declaration of Independence; fought in French and Indian War

List #163 Other American Revolution–Era Names to Know

Richard Allen
Jeffrey Amherst
Sarah Bache
Benjamin Banneker
Joshua Barney
Josiah Bartlett
Sir William Blackstone
James Bowdoin
Joseph Brant
Mary Brant
Carter Braxton
John Burgoyne
Edmund Burke
Thomas Burke
Aaron Burr
John Campbell
Sir Guy Carleton
Charles Carroll
Abraham Clark
George Roger Clark
Sir Henry Clinton
George Clymer
Charles Cornwallis
Michel Crevecouer
Jean Claude De Reyneval
John Dickinson
Gerry Elbridge
William Ellery
Francis Fauquier
William Floyd
Elizabeth Freeman
Christopher Gadsen
Thomas Gage
Horatio Gates
King George III
Mary Goddard
François Grasse-Rouville
Nathanael Greene
George Grenville
Button Guinett
Lyman Hall
Prince Hall
Benjamin Harrison
John Hazelwood
Joseph Hewes
Thomas Heyward
William Hooper
Stephen Hopkins
Francis Hopkinson
John Eager Howard
Richard Howe
William Howe
David Hume
Samuel Huntington
Thomas Hutchison
Jared Ingersoll
William Johnson
Johann Kalb
Thaddeus Kosciuszko
Henry Laurens
Rowlins Lawndes
Ann Lee
Arthur Lee
Francis Lee
Richard Lee
Francis Lewis
Morris Lewis
Philip Livingston

List #163 **Other American Revolution–Era Names to Know** *(continued)*

Robert Livingston
William Livingston
John Locke
Thomas Lynch, Jr.
Lachlan MacIntosh
Jane McCrea
Alexander McDougall
Timothy McGillivary
Sarah McGinn
Thomas McKean
Arthur Middleton
Richard Montgomery
Gouverneur Morris
Mary White Morris
Robert Morris
John Morton
Judith Murray
Thomas Nelson
Frederick North
James Otis
William Paca
Robert Pain
John Penn
William Pitt
Pontiac
Charles Pratt
Casimir Pulaski
Israel Putnam
Rufus Putnam
Edmund Randolph
Peyton Randolph
George Read
Ceasar Rodney
Betsy Ross
Benjamin Rush
Edward Rutledge
Peter Salem
Isaac Sears
William Shippen
William Smallwood
Adam Smith
James Smith
Jonathan Smith
Samuel Smith
Arthur St. Clair
Friederich Steuben
Richard Stockton
Thomas Stone
John Sullivan
Thomas Sumter
Sir Banastre Tarleton
George Taylor
Matthew Thornton
Charles Townshend
James Varnum
Jean Baptiste Vimeur
George Walton
Artemas Ward
Seth Warner
Mercy Otis Warren
William Washington
Phillis Wheatley
William Whipple
Otho Williams
James Wilson
John Witherspoon
George Wythe

List #164 Founding Fathers

The following men were delegates to the Constitutional Convention of 1787. There were fifty-five delegates in attendance. Of those, thirty-nine signed the Constitution. The ones who did not are noted below with an asterisk (*).

Connecticut
- William Samuel Johnson
- Roger Sherman
- Oliver Ellsworth*

Delaware
- George Read
- Gunning Bedford, Jr.
- John Dickinson
- Richard Bassett
- Jacob Broom

Georgia
- William Few
- Abraham Baldwin
- William Houston
- William Leigh Pierce*

Maryland
- James McHenry
- Daniel of St. Thomas Jenifer
- Daniel Carroll
- Luther Martin*
- John Francis Mercer*

Massachusetts
- Nathaniel Gorham
- Rufus King
- Elbridge Gerry*
- Caleb Strong*

New Hampshire
- John Langdon
- Nicholas Gilman

New Jersey
- William Livingston
- David Brearly
- William Paterson
- Jonathan Dayton
- William C. Houston*

New York
- Alexander Hamilton
- John Lansing, Jr.*
- Robert Yates*

North Carolina
- William Blount
- Richard Dobbs Spaight, Sr.
- Hugh Williamson
- William Richardson Davie*
- Alexander Martin*

Pennsylvania
- Benjamin Franklin
- Thomas Mifflin
- Robert Morris
- George Clymer
- Thomas Fitzsimons
- Jared Ingersoll
- James Wilson
- Gouverneur Morris

South Carolina
- John Rutledge
- Charles Cotesworth Pinckney
- Charles Pinckney
- Pierce Butler

Rhode Island
- No delegates attended on behalf of Rhode Island.

Virginia
- John Blair
- James Madison
- George Washington
- George Mason*
- James McClurg*
- Edmund Randolph*
- George Wythe*

List #165 Presidents of the United States

Name	Birth/Death	Dates of Presidency	Vice President
George Washington	2-22-1732/12-14-1799	1789–1797	John Adams
John Adams	10-30-1735/7-4-1826	1797–1801	Thomas Jefferson
Thomas Jefferson	4-13-1743/7-4-1826	1801–1809	Aaron Burr George Clinton
James Madison	3-16-1751/6-28-1836	1809–1817	George Clinton Elbridge Gerry
James Monroe	4-28-1758/7-4-1831	1817–1825	Daniel D. Tompkins
John Quincy Adams	7-11-1767/2-23-1848	1825–1829	John C. Calhoun
Andrew Jackson	3-15-1767/6-8-1845	1829–1837	John C. Calhoun Martin Van Buren
Martin Van Buren	12-5-1782/7-24-1862	1837–1841	Richard M. Johnson
William Henry Harrison	2-9-1773/4-4-1841	1841	John Tyler
John Tyler	3-29-1790/1-18-1862	1841–1845	none
James Knox Polk	11-2-1795/6-15-1849	1845–1849	George M. Dallas
Zachary Taylor	11-24-1784/7-9-1850	1849–1850	Millard Fillmore
Millard Fillmore	1-7-1800/3-8-1874	1850–1853	none
Franklin Pierce	11-23-1804/10-8-1869	1853–1857	William R. King
James Buchanan	4-23-1791/6-1-1868	1857–1861	John C. Breckinridge
Abraham Lincoln	2-12-1809/4-15-1865	1861–1865	Hannibel Hamlin Andrew Johnson
Andrew Johnson	12-29-1808/7-31-1875	1865–1869	none
Ulysses Simpson Grant	4-27-1822/7-23-1885	1869–1877	Schuyler Colfax Henry Wilson
Rutherford Birchard Hayes	10-4-1822/1-17-1893	1877–1881	William A. Wheeler
James Abram Garfield	11-19-1831/9-19-1881	1881	Chester Alan Arthur
Chester Alan Arthur	10-5-1829/11-18-1886	1881–1885	none
Grover Cleveland	3-18-1837/6-24-1908	1885–1889	Thomas Hendricks
Benjamin Harrison	8-20-1833/3-13-1901	1889–1893	Levi P. Morton
Grover Cleveland	3-18-1837/6-24-1908	1893–1897	Adlai E. Stevenson
William McKinley	1-29-1843/9-14-1901	1897–1901	Garret A. Hobart Theodore Roosevelt
Theodore Roosevelt	10-27-1858/1-6-1919	1901–1909	Charles W. Fairbanks
William Howard Taft	9-15-1857/3-8-1930	1909–1913	James S. Sherman

List #165 **Presidents of the United States** *(continued)*

Name	Birth/Death	Dates of Presidency	Vice President
Woodrow Wilson	12-18-1856/2-3-1924	1913–1921	Thomas R. Marshall
Warren Gamaliel Harding	11-2-1865/8-2-1923	1921–1923	Calvin Coolidge
Calvin Coolidge	7-4-1872/1-5-1933	1923–1929	Charles G. Dawes
Herbert Hoover	8-10-1874/10-20-1964	1929–1933	Charles Curtis
Franklin Delano Roosevelt	1-30-1882/4-12-1945	1933–1945	John Nance Garner Henry A. Wallace Harry S. Truman
Harry S. Truman	5-8-1884/12-26-1972	1945–1953	Alben W. Barkley
Dwight David Eisenhower	10-14-1890/3-28-1969	1953–1961	Richard Milhous Nixon
John Fitzgerald Kennedy	5-19-1917/11-22-1963	1961–1963	Lyndon Baines Johnson
Lyndon Baines Johnson	8-27-1908/1-22-1973	1963–1969	Hubert Horatio Humphrey
Richard Milhous Nixon	1-9-1913/4-22-1994	1969–1974	Spiro T. Agnew Gerald Rudolph Ford
Gerald Rudolph Ford	7-14-1913/12-26-2006	1974–1977	Nelson Rockefeller
James Earl (Jimmy) Carter	10-1-1924	1977–1981	Walter Mondale
Ronald Wilson Reagan	2-6-1911/6-5-2004	1981–1989	George Herbert Walker Bush
George H. W. Bush	6-12-1924	1989–1993	J. Danforth Quayle
William Jefferson (Bill) Clinton	8-19-1946	1993–2001	Albert Gore, Jr.
George Walker Bush	7-6-1946	2001–	Richard Cheney

List #166 First Ladies of the United States

Name	Birth and Death Dates (and Locations)	President, Date of Marriage (and Location if Known)	Children
Martha Dandridge Custis Washington	June 2, 1731 (New Kent County, Va.); May 22, 1802 (Mount Vernon, Va.)	George Washington; January 6, 1759 (Kent County, Va.)	John Parke Custis and Martha Parke Custis (both from her former marriage)
Abigail Smith Adams	November 23, 1744 (Weymouth, Mass.); October 28, 1818 (Quincy, Mass.)	John Adams; October 25, 1764 (Weymouth, Mass.)	Abigail Amelia, John Quincy (future U.S. president), Susanna, Charles, Thomas Boylston
Martha Wayles Skelton Jefferson	October 30, 1748 (Charles City County, Va.); September 6, 1782 (Charlottesville, Va.)	Thomas Jefferson; January 1, 1772 (Charles City County, Va.)	Martha, Maria, Lucy Elizabeth, and 2 girls and 1 boy who died in infancy
Dolley Payne Todd Madison	May 20, 1768 (Guilford County, N.C.); July 12, 1849 (Washington, D.C.)	James Madison; September 15, 1794 (Harewood, Va.)	Payne Todd (from former marriage)
Elizabeth Kortright Monroe	June 30, 1768 (New York, N.Y.); September 23, 1830 (Oak Hill, Va.)	James Monroe; February 16, 1786 (New York, N.Y.)	Eliza, Maria Hester
Louisa Catherine Johnson Adams	February 12, 1775 (London, England); May 15, 1852 (Washington, D.C.)	John Quincy Adams; July 26, 1797 (London, England)	George Washington, John, Charles Francis, Louisa Catherine
Rachel Donelson Robards Jackson (died before her husband took office)	June 15, 1767 (Halifax County, Va.); December 22, 1828 (Nashville, Tenn.)	Andrew Jackson; August 1, 1791 (Natchez, Miss.)—second ceremony: January 17, 1794 (Nashville, Tenn.)	Andrew (adopted)

List #166 **First Ladies of the United States** *(continued)*

Name	Birth and Death Dates (and Locations)	President, Date of Marriage (and Location if Known)	Children
Hannah Hoes Van Buren (died before her husband was elected president)	March 8, 1783 (Kinderhook, N.Y.); February 5, 1819 (Albany, N.Y.)	Martin Van Buren; February 21, 1807 (Catskill, N.Y.)	Abraham, John, Martin Jr., Smith Thompson
Anna Symmes Harrison	July 25, 1775 (Morristown, N.J.); February 25, 1864 (North Bend, Ohio)	William Harrison; November 25, 1795	Elizabeth Bassett, John Cleves Symmes, Lucy Singleton, William Henry, Jr., John Scott, Benjamin, Mary Symmes, Carter Bassett, Anna Tuthill, James Findlay
Letitia Christian Tyler	November 12, 1790 (New Kent County, Va.); September 10, 1842 (Washington, D.C.)	John Tyler; March 29, 1813	Mary, Robert, John, Letitia, Elizabeth, Anne, Alice, Tazewell
Julia Gardiner Tyler	May 4, 1820 (Gardiner's Island, N.Y.); July 10, 1889 (Richmond, Va.)	John Tyler; June 26, 1844	David Gardiner, John Alexander, Julia Gardiner, Lachlan, Lyon Gardiner, Robert Fitzwalter, Pearl
Sarah Childress Polk	September 4, 1803 (Murfreesboro, Tenn.); August 14, 1891 (Nashville, Tenn.)	James Polk; January 1, 1824 (Murfreesboro, Tenn.)	none
Margaret Smith Taylor	September 21, 1788 (Calvert County, Md.); August 18, 1852 (Pascagoula, Miss.)	Zachary Taylor; June 21, 1810	Ann Mackall, Sarah Knox, Octavia Pannill, Margaret Smith, Mary Elizabeth, Richard

List #166 **First Ladies of the United States** *(continued)*

Name	Birth and Death Dates (and Locations)	President, Date of Marriage (and Location if Known)	Children
Abigail Powers Filmore	March 13, 1798 (Stillwater, N.Y.); March 30, 1853 (Washington, D.C.)	Millard Fillmore; February 5, 1826	Mary, Millard
Jane Means Appleton Pierce	March 12, 1806 (Hampton, N.H.); December 2, 1863 (Andover, Mass.)	Franklin Pierce; November 19, 1834	Franklin, Frank Robert, Benjamin
Harriet Lane (served as official hostess to her uncle James Buchanan)	May 9, 1830 (Mercersburg, Penn.); July 3, 1903 (R.I.)	James Buchanan	none (he never married)
Mary Todd Lincoln	December 13, 1818 (Lexington, Ky.); July 16, 1882 (Springfield, Ill.)	Abraham Lincoln; November 4, 1842 (Springfield, Ill.)	Robert Todd, Edward Baker, William Wallace, Thomas
Eliza McCardle Johnson	October 4, 1810 (Leesburg, Tenn.); January 15, 1876 (Greene County, Tenn.)	Andrew Johnson; December 17, 1827 (Greeneville, Tenn.)	Martha, Charles, Mary, Robert, Andrew
Julia Dent Grant	January 26, 1826 (St. Louis, Mo.); December 14, 1902 (Washington, D.C.)	Ulysses Grant; August 22, 1848 (St. Louis, Mo.)	Frederick Dent, Ulysses Simpson, Ellen Wrenshall, Jesse Root
Lucy Webb Hayes	August 28, 1831 (Chillicothe, Ohio); June 25, 1889 (Freemont, Ohio)	Rutherford Hayes; December 30, 1852 (Cincinnati, Ohio)	Birchard Austin, Webb Cook, Rutherford Platt, Joseph Thompson, George Crook, Fanny, Scott Russell, Manning Force
Lucretia Rudolph Garfield	April 19, 1832 (Hiram, Ohio); March 14, 1918 (Pasadena, Calif.)	James Garfield; November 11, 1858 (Hiram, Ohio)	Eliza Arabella, Harry Augustus, James Rudolph, Mary, Irvin McDowell, Abram, Edward

List #166 **First Ladies of the United States** *(continued)*

Name	Birth and Death Dates (and Locations)	President, Date of Marriage (and Location if Known)	Children
Ellen Herndon Arthur (died before her husband took office, and his sister Mary Arthur McElroy served as his official hostess)	August 30, 1837 (Fredericksburg, Va.); January 12, 1880 (New York, N.Y.)	Chester Alan Arthur; October 25, 1859 (New York, N.Y.)	William Lewis Herndon, Chester Alan, Ellen
Frances Folsom Cleveland	July 21, 1864 (Buffalo, N.Y.); October 29, 1947 (Baltimore, Md.)	Grover Cleveland; June 2, 1886 (White House, Washington, D.C.)	Ruth, Esther, Marion, Richard Folsom, Francis Grover
Caroline Scott Harrison	October 1, 1832 (Oxford, Ohio); October 25, 1892 (Washington, D.C.)	Benjamin Harrison; October 20, 1853 (Oxford, Ohio)	Russell Benjamin, Mary Scott
Ida Saxton McKinley	June 8, 1847 (Canton, Ohio); May 26, 1907 (Canton, Ohio)	William McKinley; January 25, 1871 (Canton, Ohio)	Katherine, Ida
Edith Kermit Carow Roosevelt	August 6, 1861 (Norwich, Conn.); September 30, 1948 (Oyster Bay, N.Y.)	Theodore Roosevelt; December 2, 1886 (London, England)	Alice Lee (stepdaughter from Theodore's previous marriage), Theodore, Kermit, Ethel Carow, Archibald Bulloch, Quentin
Helen Herron Taft	June 2, 1861 (Cincinnati, Ohio); May 22, 1943 (Washington, D.C.)	William Taft; June 19, 1886 (Cincinnati, Ohio)	Robert Alphonso, Helen, Charles Phelps II
Ellen Axon Wilson	May 15, 1860 (Savannah, Ga.); August 6, 1914 (Washington, D.C.)	Woodrow Wilson; June 24, 1885 (Savannah, Ga.)	Margaret Woodrow, Jessie Woodrow, Eleanor Randolph

List #166 **First Ladies of the United States** *(continued)*

Name	Birth and Death Dates (and Locations)	President, Date of Marriage (and Location if Known)	Children
Edith Bolling Galt Wilson	October 15, 1872 (Wytheville, Va.); December 28, 1961 (Washington, D.C.)	Woodrow Wilson; December 18, 1915 (Washington, D.C.)	Margaret, Jessie, Eleanor
Florence Kling Harding	August 15, 1860 (Marion, Ohio); November 21, 1924 (Marion, Ohio)	Warren Gamaliel Harding; July 8, 1891 (Marion, Ohio)	Marshall deWolfe (from her former marriage)
Grace Goodhue Coolidge	January 3, 1879 (Burlington, Vt.); July 8, 1957 (Northhampton, Mass.)	Calvin Coolidge; October 4, 1905 (Burlington, Vt.)	John, Calvin
Lou Henry Hoover	March 29, 1874 (Waterloo, Iowa); January 7, 1944 (New York, N.Y.)	Herbert Hoover; February 10, 1899 (Monterey, Calif.)	Herbert Clark Jr., Allan Henry
Anna Eleanor Roosevelt Roosevelt (Her maiden and married surname were both Roosevelt.)	October 11, 1884 (New York, N.Y.); November 7, 1962 (New York, N.Y.)	Franklin Delano Roosevelt; March 17, 1905 (New York, N.Y.)	Anna Eleanor, James, Elliott, Franklin Delano, John Aspinwall, 1 boy who died in infancy
Elizabeth Wallace Truman	February 13, 1885 (Independence, Mo.); October 18, 1982 (Independence, Mo.)	Harry S. Truman; June 28, 1919 (Independence, Mo.)	Margaret
Mamie Doud Eisenhower	November 14, 1896 (Boone, Ia.); November 11, 1979 (Gettysburg, Penn.)	Dwight David Eisenhower; July 1, 1916 (Denver, Colo.)	Doud Dwight, John Sheldon

List #166 **First Ladies of the United States** *(continued)*

Name	Birth and Death Dates (and Locations)	President, Date of Marriage (and Location if Known)	Children
Jacqueline Bouvier Kennedy	July 28, 1929 (Southhampton, N.Y.); May 19, 1994 (New York, N.Y.)	John Fitzgerald Kennedy; September 12, 1953 (Newport, R.I.)	Caroline Bouvier, John Fitzgerald, Patrick Bouvier
Claudia Taylor (Lady Bird) Johnson	December 12, 1912 (Karnack, Tex.); July 11, 2007 (Austin, Tex.)	Lyndon Baines Johnson; November 17, 1934 (San Antonio, Tex.)	Lynda Bird, Luci Baines
Thelma Catherine Ryan (Pat) Nixon	March 16, 1912 (Ely, Nev.); June 22, 1993 (Park Ridge, N.J.)	Richard Milhous Nixon; June 21, 1940 (Riverside, Calif.)	Patricia, Julie
Elizabeth (Betty) Bloomer Ford	April 8, 1918 (Chicago, Ill.) —	Gerald Rudolph Ford; October 15, 1948 (Grand Rapids, Mich.)	Michael Gerald, John Gardner, Steven Meigs, Susan Elizabeth
Rosalynn Smith Carter	August 18, 1927 (Plains, Ga.) —	James Earl (Jimmy) Carter; July 7, 1946 (Plains, Ga.)	John William, James Earl III, Jeffrey, Amy Lynn
Nancy Davis Reagan	July 6, 1921 (New York, N.Y.) —	Ronald Wilson Reagan; March 4, 1952 (San Fernando Valley, Calif.)	Patti Davis, Ronald Prescott
Barbara Pierce Bush	June 8, 1925 (Bronx, N.Y.) —	George H. W. Bush; January 6, 1945 (Rye, N.Y.)	George Walker (future U.S. President), Robin, John Ellis, Neil Mallon, Marvin Pierce, Dorothy
Hillary Rodham Clinton	October 26, 1947 (Park Ridge, Ill.) —	William Jefferson (Bill) Clinton; October 11, 1975 (Fayetteville, Ark.)	Chelsea
Laura Welch Bush	November 4, 1946 (Midland, Tex.) —	George Walker Bush; November 5, 1977 (Midland, Tex.)	Barbara, Jenna

List #167 Supreme Court Justices

Judge	From	Appointed by	Active	Reason for Termination
James Wilson	Penn.	Washington	October 5, 1789 – August 21, 1798	death
John Jay	N.Y.	Washington	October 19, 1789 – June 29, 1795	resignation
William Cushing	Mass.	Washington	February 2, 1790 – September 13, 1810	death
John Blair	Va.	Washington	February 2, 1790 – October 25, 1795	resignation
John Rutledge	S.C.	Washington	February 15, 1790 – March 5, 1791	resignation
James Iredell	N.C.	Washington	May 12, 1790 – October 20, 1799	death
Thomas Johnson	Md.	Washington	August 6, 1792 – January 16, 1793	resignation
William Paterson	N.J.	Washington	March 11, 1793 – September 9, 1806	death
John Rutledge	S.C.	Washington	August 12, 1795 – December 15, 1795	Served during Senate recess, but rejected for appointment
Samuel Chase	Md.	Washington	February 4, 1796 – June 19, 1811	death
Oliver Ellsworth	Conn.	Washington	March 8, 1796 – December 15, 1800	resignation
Bushrod Washington	Va.	J. Adams	February 4, 1799 – November 26, 1829	death
Alfred Moore	N.C.	J. Adams	April 21, 1800 – January 26, 1804	resignation
John Marshall	Va.	J. Adams	February 4, 1801 – July 6, 1835	death
William Johnson	S.C.	Jefferson	May 7, 1804 – August 4, 1834	death
Henry Brockholst Livingston	N.Y.	Jefferson	January 20, 1807 – March 18, 1823	death
Thomas Todd	Ky.	Jefferson	May 4, 1807 – February 7, 1826	death
Gabriel Duvall	Md.	Madison	November 23, 1811 – January 14, 1835	resignation

List #167 **Supreme Court Justices** *(continued)*

Judge	From	Appointed by	Active	Reason for Termination
Joseph Story	Mass.	Madison	February 3, 1812 – September 10, 1845	death
Smith Thompson	N.Y.	Monroe	September 1, 1823 – December 18, 1843	death
Robert Trimble	Ky.	J. Q. Adams	June 16, 1826 – August 25, 1828	death
John McLean	Ohio	Jackson	January 11, 1830 – April 4, 1861	death
Henry Baldwin	Penn.	Jackson	January 18, 1830 – April 21, 1844	death
James Moore Wayne	Ga.	Jackson	January 14, 1835 – July 5, 1867	death
Roger B. Taney	Md.	Jackson	March 28, 1836 – October 12, 1864	death
Philip Pendleton Barbour	Va.	Jackson	May 12, 1836 – February 25, 1841	death
John Catron	Tenn.	Van Buren	May 1, 1837 – May 30, 1865	death
John McKinley	Ala.	Van Buren	January 9, 1838 – July 19, 1852	death
Peter Vivian Daniel	Va.	Van Buren	January 10, 1842 – May 31, 1860	death
Samuel Nelson	N.Y.	Tyler	February 27, 1845 – November 28, 1872	retirement
Levi Woodbury	N.H.	Polk	September 23, 1845 – September 4, 1851	death
Robert Cooper Grier	Penn.	Polk	August 10, 1846 – January 31, 1870	retirement
Benjamin Robbins Curtis	Mass.	Fillmore	October 10, 1851 – September 30, 1857	resignation
John Archibald Campbell	Ala.	Pierce	April 11, 1853 – April 30, 1861	resignation
Nathan Clifford	Maine	Buchanan	January 21, 1858 – July 25, 1881	death

List #167 **Supreme Court Justices** *(continued)*

Judge	From	Appointed by	Active	Reason for Termination
Noah Haynes Swayne	Ohio	Lincoln	January 27, 1862 – January 24, 1881	retirement
Samuel Freeman Miller	Iowa	Lincoln	July 21, 1862 – October 13, 1890	death
David Davis	Ill.	Lincoln	December 10, 1862 – March 4, 1877	resignation
Stephen Johnson Field	Calif.	Lincoln	May 20, 1863 – December 1, 1897	retirement
Salmon P. Chase	Ohio	Lincoln	December 15, 1864 – May 7, 1873	death
William Strong	Penn.	Grant	March 14, 1870 – December 14, 1880	retirement
Joseph Philo Bradley	N.J.	Grant	March 23, 1870 – January 22, 1892	death
Ward Hunt	N.Y.	Grant	January 9, 1873 – January 27, 1882	retirement
Morrison Waite	Ohio	Grant	March 4, 1874 – March 23, 1888	death
John Marshall Harlan	Ky.	Hayes	December 10, 1877 – October 14, 1911	death
William Burnham Woods	Ga.	Hayes	January 5, 1881 – May 14, 1887	death
Thomas Stanley Matthews	Ohio	Garfield	May 17, 1881 – March 22, 1889	death
Horace Gray	Mass.	Arthur	January 9, 1882 – September 15, 1902	death
Samuel Blatchford	N.Y.	Arthur	April 3, 1882 – July 7, 1893	death
Lucius Quintus Cincinnatus Lamar	Miss.	Cleveland	January 18, 1888 – January 23, 1893	death
Melville Fuller	Ill.	Cleveland	October 8, 1888 – July 4, 1910	death

List #167 **Supreme Court Justices** *(continued)*

Judge	From	Appointed by	Active	Reason for Termination
David Josiah Brewer	Kans.	B. Harrison	January 6, 1890 – March 28, 1910	death
Henry Billings Brown	Mich.	B. Harrison	January 5, 1891 – May 28, 1906	retirement
George Shiras, Jr.	Penn.	B. Harrison	October 10, 1892 – February 23, 1903	retirement
Howell Edmunds Jackson	Tenn.	B. Harrison	March 4, 1893 – August 8, 1895	death
Edward Douglass White	La.	Cleveland (associate appointment); Taft (chief appointment)	March 12, 1894 – May 19, 1921	death
Rufus Wheeler Peckham	N.Y.	Cleveland	January 6, 1896 – October 24, 1909	death
Joseph McKenna	Calif.	McKinley	January 26, 1898 – January 5, 1925	retirement
Oliver Wendell Holmes, Jr.	Mass.	T. Roosevelt	December 8, 1902 – January 12, 1932	retirement
William R. Day	Ohio	T. Roosevelt	March 2, 1903 – November 13, 1922	retirement
William Henry Moody	Mass.	T. Roosevelt	December 17, 1906 – November 20, 1910	retirement
Horace Harmon Lurton	Tenn.	Taft	January 3, 1910 – July 12, 1914	death
Charles Evans Hughes	N.Y.	Taft	October 10, 1910 – June 10, 1916	resignation
Willis Van Devanter	Wyo.	Taft	January 3, 1911 – June 2, 1937	death
Joseph Rucker Lamar	Ga.	Taft	January 3, 1911 – January 2, 1916	death
Mahlon Pitney	N.J.	Taft	March 18, 1912 – December 31, 1922	resignation

List #167 **Supreme Court Justices** *(continued)*

Judge	From	Appointed by	Active	Reason for Termination
James Clark McReynolds	Tenn.	Wilson	October 12, 1914 – January 31, 1941	death
Louis Brandeis	Mass.	Wilson	June 5, 1916 – February 13, 1939	death
John Hessin Clarke	Ohio	Wilson	October 9, 1916 – September 18, 1922	resignation
William Howard Taft	Conn.	Harding	July 11, 1921 – February 3, 1930	resignation
George Sutherland	Utah	Harding	October 2, 1922 – January 17, 1938	death
Pierce Butler	Minn.	Harding	January 2, 1923 – November 16, 1939	death
Edward Terry Sanford	Tenn.	Harding	February 19, 1923 – March 8, 1930	death
Harlan Fiske Stone	N.Y.	Coolidge (associate appointment); F. Roosevelt (chief appointment)	March 2, 1925 – April 22, 1946	death
Charles Evans Hughes	N.Y.	Hoover	February 24, 1930 – June 30, 1941	retirement
Owen Josephus Roberts	Penn.	Hoover	June 2, 1930 – July 31, 1945	resignation
Benjamin N. Cardozo	N.Y.	Hoover	March 14, 1932 – July 9, 1938	death
Hugo Black	Ala.	F. Roosevelt	August 19, 1937 – September 17, 1971	death
Stanley Forman Reed	Ky.	F. Roosevelt	January 31, 1938 – February 25, 1957	death
Felix Frankfurter	Mass.	F. Roosevelt	January 30, 1939 – August 28, 1962	death
William O. Douglas	Conn.	F. Roosevelt	April 17, 1939 – November 12, 1975	death

List #167 **Supreme Court Justices** *(continued)*

Judge	From	Appointed by	Active	Reason for Termination
Frank Murphy	Mich.	F. Roosevelt	February 5, 1940 – July 19, 1949	death
James F. Byrnes	S.C.	F. Roosevelt	July 8, 1941 – October 3, 1942	resignation
Robert H. Jackson	N.Y.	F. Roosevelt	July 11, 1941 – October 9, 1954	death
Wiley Blount Rutledge	Iowa	F. Roosevelt	February 15, 1943 – September 10, 1949	death
Harold Hitz Burton	Ohio	Truman	October 1, 1945 – October 13, 1958	death
Fred M. Vinson	Ky.	Truman	June 24, 1946 – September 8, 1953	death
Tom C. Clark	Tex.	Truman	August 24, 1949 – June 12, 1967	death
Sherman Minton	Ind.	Truman	October 12, 1949 – October 15, 1956	death
Earl Warren	Calif.	Eisenhower	October 5, 1953 – June 23, 1969	death
John Marshall Harlan II	N.Y.	Eisenhower	March 28, 1955 – September 23, 1971	death
William J. Brennan	N.J.	Eisenhower	October 16, 1956 – July 20, 1990	death
Charles Evans Whittaker	Mo.	Eisenhower	March 25, 1957 – March 31, 1962	resignation
Potter Stewart	Ohio	Eisenhower	October 14, 1958 – July 3, 1981	retirement
Byron White	Colo.	Kennedy	April 16, 1962 – June 28, 1993	death
Arthur Goldberg	Ill.	Kennedy	October 1, 1962 – July 25, 1965	resignation
Abe Fortas	Tenn.	L. Johnson	October 4, 1965 – May 14, 1969	resignation
Thurgood Marshall	N.Y.	L. Johnson	October 2, 1967 – October 1, 1991	retirement
Warren E. Burger	Va.	Nixon	June 23, 1969 – September 26, 1986	death

List #167 **Supreme Court Justices** *(continued)*

Judge	From	Appointed by	Active	Reason for Termination
Harry Blackmun	Minn.	Nixon	June 9, 1970 – August 3, 1994	death
Lewis Franklin Powell, Jr.	Va.	Nixon	January 7, 1972 – June 26, 1987	death
William Rehnquist	Ariz.	Nixon (associate appointment); Reagan (chief appointment)	January 7, 1972 – September 3, 2005	death
John Paul Stevens	Ill.	Ford	December 19, 1975 – present	—
Sandra Day O'Connor	Ariz.	Reagan	September 25, 1981 – January 31, 2006	resignation
Antonin Scalia	Va.	Reagan	September 26, 1986 – present	—
Anthony Kennedy	Calif.	Reagan	February 18, 1988 – present	—
David Souter	N.H.	G. H. W. Bush	October 9, 1990 – present	—
Clarence Thomas	Ga.	G. H. W. Bush	October 23, 1991 – present	—
Ruth Bader Ginsburg	N.Y.	Clinton	August 10, 1993 – present	—
Stephen Breyer	Mass.	Clinton	August 3, 1994 – present	—
John Roberts	Md.	G. W. Bush	September 29, 2005 – present	—
Samuel Alito	N.J.	G. W. Bush	January 31, 2006 – present	—

List #168 Leaders of the Abolitionist Movement

William Allen
Anthony Benezet
Thomas Binney
Jacques Pierre Brissot
John Brown
Aaron Burr
Joseph Cinquez
Thomas Clarkson
Alexander Cummell
Frederick Douglass
Charles Finney
Benjamin Franklin
Amos Noë Freeman
Elizabeth Fry
Henry Highland Garnet
William Lloyd Garrison
Samuel Gurney
Alexander Hamilton
John Jay
William Knibb
Anne Knight
Toussaint L'Ouverture
Theobold Mayhew
Daniel O'Connell
Elizabeth Pease
Thomas Pringle
James Ramsay
Charles Lenox Remond
Benjamin Rush
Granville Sharp
Gerrit Smith
James Somersett
Lysander Spooner
John Gabriel Stedman
George Stephen
Joseph Sturge
Harriet Tubman
Samuel Ringgold Ward
William Wilberforce

List #169 Pioneers of Flight

9th century	Muslim Moor Abbas Qasim Ibn Firnas built and flew a glider.
c. 1010	Eilmer of Malmesbury builds and flies gliders.
13th century	Marco Polo returns from China with reports of human-carrying kites.
15th century	Leonardo da Vinci designs a glider that was never built, but could have flown.
17th century	Lagari Hasan Çelebi, a Turkish scientist, launches himself in a rocket about 300 meters into the air.
1638	Hezarfen Ahmet Çelebi (Lagari's brother) uses wings to fly off a 5-meter-high tower.
1716	Emanuel Swedenborg publishes the first paper on aviation in "Sketch of a Machine for Flying in the Air."
1783	Jean-François Pilâtre de Rozier and François d'Arlandes take what is generally recognized as the first human flight. In Paris in 1783, they travel 5 miles in a hot air balloon.
1799	At the end of the 18th century, Sir George Cayley begins the first meticulous study of the physics of flight.
1848	John Stringfellow conducts a successful unmanned test flight of a steam-powered flying machine.
1852	In France, Henri Giffard flies 15 miles in a craft with a steam engine.
1856	Frenchman Jean-Marie Le Bris conducts the first flight above his level of takeoff, pulled by a horse.
1874	Félix du Temple builds a large plane, called the "Monoplane," in Brest, France. The plane reportedly gains liftoff on its own power, glides for a short time, and lands safely. Though only for a short distance, this is the first successful powered flight in history.
1877	Wilhelm Kress constructs a delta hang glider near Vienna.
1883	John J. Montgomery flies a modern glider in a controlled manner on August 28.
1884	Charles Renard and Arthur Krebs build *LA FRANCE,* a fully controllable free-flight airship.
1889	German Otto Lilienthal publishes the research he had been conducting on fliers for a number of years.
1890s	Percy Pilcher, of the United Kingdom, builds several working gliders and a prototype powered aircraft. Pilcher died in a glider accident before he could build and fly his prototype, but recent studies show that it could have flown.

List #169 **Pioneers of Flight** *(continued)*

1890	France's Clément Ader successfully flies his steam-powered Eole flying machine for 50 meters. This is considered the first self-propelled "long distance" flight in history.
1891	Otto Lilienthal conducts several flights of 25 meters or more and is considered one of the first men to travel in a heavier-than-air machine.
1891	Samuel Pierpont Langley publishes *Experiments in Aerodynamics*.
1894	Sir Hiram Maxim builds a huge flying machine that flies about 600 feet.
1896	Otto Lilienthal dies when a wind gust breaks the wing of his glider and he falls 56 feet, fracturing his spine.
1896	Octave Chanute funds the design and testing of several gliders in Indiana.
1899	German Ferdinand von Zeppelin advances the design of the airship.
1900	The first Zeppelin flight occurs on July 2.
1901	Brazilian Alberto Santos-Dumont flies an airship (later called a blimp) *NUMBER 6* over Paris.
1901	Samuel Langley flies his Aerodrome twice on June 18.
1903	Samuel Langley's attempts to launch his aircrafts result in crashes into the water.
1903	On December 17, Orville Wright flies 120 feet in 12 seconds at Kitty Hawk, North Carolina, in the power-controlled aircraft created by Orville and his brother Wilbur. Later that day, Wilbur flies 852 feet in 59 seconds.
1906	Alberto Santos-Dumont makes a public flight on September 13 in Europe. He travels nearly 200 feet in 6 seconds. This is considered by many Europeans to be more significant than the Wright brothers' flight (even though it occurred nearly 3 years later) because the plane did not need catapults.
1907	Paul Cornu, a Frenchman, designs and builds the first helicopter known to successfully get off the ground. He takes off in Cornu, France.
1908	One of the Wright brothers takes Charlie Furnas as a passenger on what is considered the first 2-person aircraft flight on May 14.
1908	On September 17, Orville Wright crashes his 2-passenger aircraft and passenger Thomas Selfridge dies, making him the first person killed in a powered aircraft.

List #169 **Pioneers of Flight** *(continued)*

1909	Frenchman Louis Bleroit makes the first crossing of the English Channel by airplane. He travels 25 miles in 37 minutes in the Bleriot XI, which he designed.
1910	On May 28, Glenn H. Curtiss flies his Hudson Flyer in a record flight from Albany to New York, 135.4 miles, in 2 hours, 32 minutes.
1910	Eugene Ely takes off from the deck of the U.S. cruiser *BIRMINGHAM* at Hampton Roads, Va., making this November 14 flight the first one from the deck of a ship.
1911	Calbraith P. Rodgers travels from Sheepshead Bay, Long Island, New York, to Long Beach, California. The trip, which took place from September 17 to December 10, was the first transcontinental flight.
1912–13	Bulgaria is the first country to use planes for a military use in the First Balkan War.
1919	Captain John Alcock and Lieutenant Arthur Brown co-pilot a plane nonstop from St. John's Newfoundland to Clifden, Ireland, winning the Northcliffe prize for the first nonstop crossing of the Atlantic.
1927	On May 20, Charles Lindbergh takes off from Long Island, New York, on what becomes the first successful solo nonstop flight across the Atlantic. He arrives 33 and one-half hours later in Paris.
1937	The airship *HINDENBURG* bursts into flames during its landing on May 6, killing 35 of the 97 people on board, essentially bringing an end to travel by airships, or blimps.
1939	The first functional jet ship, a Heinkel He-178, is flown by Erich Warsitz at Rostock, Germany, on August 27.
1947	Major Chuck Yeager of the U.S. Air Force takes a rocket-powered Bell X-1 past the speed of sound.
1948	The first jet crossing of the Atlantic occurs.
1952	The first nonstop flight from England to Australia occurs.
1957	The Soviet Union launches *SPUTNIK 1*.
1961	Yuri Gagarin orbits Earth once in 108 minutes.
1969	Neil Armstrong and Buzz Aldrin step on the moon.
1969	Boeing develops the Boeing 747, which revolutionizes commercial air travel.

List #170 Christian Missionaries

Gladys Aylward	missionary to China; *The Inn of the Sixth Happiness* is a movie based on her story
Andrew van der Bijl (Brother Andrew)	Dutch missionary who carried the gospel behind the Iron Curtain
Rowland Bingham	helped found Sudan Interior Mission (SIM) and began taking the gospel into Africa
David Brainerd	one of the first to take the gospel to North American Indians
Mildred Cable	missionary to China; spread the gospel in the Gobi Desert
William Carey	missionary to India
Amy Carmichel	missionary to India
Loren Cunningham	founder of Youth With A Mission (YWAM), a Christian organization that takes the Word of God around the world through training and evangelism
Jim Elliot	missionary and martyr; his death prompted many others to begin seeing the need for missionaries
Jonathan Goforth	missionary to China
Betty Greene	female pilot who helped missionary efforts around the world
George Grenfell	missionary to Africa
Sir Wilfred Thomason Grenfell	medical missionary to Newfoundland and Labrador
Clarence Jones	helped spread the Word of God through radio broadcasts
Adoniram Judson	missionary to Burma
Eric Liddell	British athlete, born in China, who later became a missionary; raced in Olympic Games, but refused to run on Sunday and won the next race; *Chariots of Fire* is based on his story
David Livingstone	Scottish missionary doctor to Africa; the recipient of the famous question, "Dr. Livingstone, I presume?"
D. L. Moody	Bible teacher
Lottie Moon	missionary to China
George Müller	provided a home for orphaned children in England
Nate Saint	pilot and missionary who was martyred
Rachel Saint	missionary to Ecuador's murderous Waorani Indians, also known as the Aucas

List #170 **Christian Missionaries** *(continued)*

Ida Scudder	missionary to Indian women
Sundar Singh	missionary in Himalayan mountains to Hindus, Buddhists, Sikhs, and thieves
Mary Slessor	Scottish missionary to Africa
John and Betty Stam	missionaries to China who were executed during a Communist uprising, but remained true to their faith
C. T. Studd	English missionary to China, India, and Africa
James Hudson Taylor	the first missionary to take the gospel to inland China
Robert Jermain Thomas	a Protestant missionary to Korea who was martyred
William Cameron Townsend	started Wycliffe Bible Translators, which continues today to carry the Word of God into the world
Lillian Trasher	missionary in Egypt
John Williams	missionary to inhabitants of islands of Pacific Ocean
Florence Young	missionary to people in Solomon Islands and also in China during the Boxer Rebellion

If you would like more information about these Christian missionaries or other great Christians, I would highly recommend the biographical books from YWAM (Youth With A Mission). You can visit their Web site at *www.ywampublishing.com* or call them at (800) 922–2143. These books are good for children or adults and make wonderful additions to any home library!

List #171 More Christians to Know

Wellesley Bailey	founder of the Leprosy Mission
William and Catherine Booth	founders of the Salvation Army
F. F. Bosworth	author of the bestselling book *Christ the Healer* and one of the first healing evangelists
John Bunyan	author of *Pilgrim's Progress*
John Calvin	Christian reformer
Thomas Cranmer	archbishop to Henry VIII; made a major impact on the reformation and split from Church of England
Oliver Cromwell	a constitutional reformer who brought political stability after England's civil war
Fanny Crosby	a blind hymn writer who gave us such beautiful songs as "Blessed Assurance," "Sweet Hour of Prayer," and "To God Be the Glory"
Jonathan Edwards	a revival preacher
Desiderius Erasmus	printed the first Greek version of the New Testament
John Foxe	wrote *Foxe's Book of Martyrs*
Elizabeth Fry	prison visitor and social reformer
Billy Graham	the people's evangelist; led crusades around the world
Patrick Hamilton	a Scottish martyr who influenced the Scottish and English church with his preaching
William Hunter	boy martyr
John Huss	opposed the Roman Church; preached the gospel and was martyred
Helen Keller	became blind and deaf after an infection at age 2; changed people's thinking about the blind and deaf after she gracefully accomplished in life more than an average person
John Knox	participated in reformation in Scotland
C. S. Lewis	Christian author
Martin Luther	A German priest and professor who started the Protestant Reformation when he wrote 95 theses that detailed the abuses he saw in the Roman Church
Samuel Morris	a tribal prince in Africa who gave his life to God and came to America to preach against slavery and discrimination
John Newton	strongly and widely opposed the slave trade

List #171 **More Christians to Know** *(continued)*

Jerome Savonarola	a pioneer of the Reformation
Charles Haddon Spurgeon	the "Great Orator"
Billy Sunday	an evangelist who became a preacher
Corrie ten Boom	helped hide Jewish refugees during World War II; became an evangelist in a concentration camp after she was imprisoned by German authorities
William Tyndale	translated the New Testament into English; was martyred
Charles Wesley	one of the best and most prolific hymn writers ever; his songs helped spread Methodist movement
John Wesley	founder of Methodist church
George Whitfield	a revival preacher
William Wilberforce	Christian politician who brought an end to the slave trade in England
John Wycliffe	gave us the first English translation of the Bible
Count Zinzendorf	a Christian education reformer

List #172 Foreign Heroes

Joan of Arc

This young maid from Domrémy, France, was born in 1412. According to Joan, voices she heard told her that she would help the King of France and lead the country to victory over the English. She eventually dressed as a boy, left her home, and began to lead the soldiers of France in their fight against the English. Joan helped the Dauphin attain his title of King of France, but when the English captured Joan, the Dauphin made no attempt to pay the ransom to retrieve the young maid. Because she had heard voices (and probably because of jealousy over her successes), Joan was tried for witchcraft and burned at the stake in 1431. Pope Benedict XV made Joan a saint in 1920.

Simon Bolivar

Bolivar was born in Caracas, Venezuela, in 1783. He was a soldier, statesman, and Revolutionary War leader who led the revolts in the early nineteenth century that ultimately freed Venezuela and Colombia from Spanish rule. Bolivar served as president of Colombia, then Venezuela, and when he freed Peru from Spain in 1824, he was made president of that country as well. When Bolivar organized a new country north of Peru, it was named Bolivia in his honor. Simon Bolivar died in 1830.

Giuseppe Garibaldi

Though he was born in Nice, France, in 1807, Garibaldi was an Italian whose parents were living in France to escape the tyranny in Italy during the late eighteenth and early nineteenth centuries. He fought in the Revolution for Italian freedom, but when his side lost, he fled to the United States in 1849. He returned to Italy in 1854 and fought for Italy's freedom once more. This time the patriots, as they were called, won. Garibaldi died in 1882.

Sun Yat-Sen

Sun Yat-Sen, born in 1866, was a Chinese statesman and revolutionary leader. In 1894, he was the first graduate of the new College of Medicine in Hong Kong. He was forced to leave China the next year, however, because he advocated democracy. After he returned from exile in 1911, Yat-Sen established a republic. He died in 1925.

List #172 **Foreign Heroes** *(continued)*

Mohandas Gandhi

Gandhi, known as Mahatma ("great soul"), was born in western India in 1869. As a Hindu nationalist and spiritual leader, Gandhi not only preached passive resistance against aggression, he practiced it as well. He was assassinated in India on January 30, 1948.

Winston Churchill

Sir Winston Leonard Spencer Churchill was a British statesman, writer, and military leader. He was born in 1874, fought in World War I, and was elected to Parliament in 1900. Churchill was prime minister of England throughout World War II. He died in 1965.

List #173 Nobel Prize Winners—Peace

1901 Henri Dunant, Frédéric Passy
1902 Élie Ducommun, Albert Gobat
1903 Randal Cremer
1904 Institute of International Law
1905 Bertha von Suttner
1906 Theodore Roosevelt
1907 Ernesto Teodoro Moneta, Louis Renault
1908 Klas Pontus Arnoldson, Fredrik Bajer
1909 Auguste Beernaert, Paul Henri d'Estournelles de Constant
1910 International Peace Bureau
1911 Tobias Asser, Alfred Fried
1912 Elihu Root
1913 Henri La Fontaine
1914 Prize not awarded
1915 Prize not awarded
1916 Prize not awarded
1917 International Committee of the Red Cross
1918 Prize not awarded
1919 Woodrow Wilson
1920 Léon Bourgeois
1921 Hjalmar Branting, Christian Lange
1922 Fridtjof Nansen
1923 Prize not awarded
1924 Prize not awarded
1925 Sir Austen Chamberlain, Charles G. Dawes
1926 Aristide Briand, Gustav Stresemann
1927 Ferdinand Buisson, Ludwig Quidde
1928 Prize not awarded
1929 Frank B. Kellogg
1930 Nathan Söderblom
1931 Jane Addams, Nicholas Murray Butler
1932 Prize not awarded
1933 Sir Norman Angell
1934 Arthur Henderson
1935 Carl von Ossietzky
1936 Carlos Saavedra Lamas
1937 Robert Cecil
1938 Nansen International Office for Refugees
1939 Prize not awarded
1940 Prize not awarded
1941 Prize not awarded
1942 Prize not awarded
1943 Prize not awarded
1944 International Committee of the Red Cross
1945 Cordell Hull
1946 Emily Greene Balch, John R. Mott
1947 American Friends Service Committee, Friends Service Council (FSC)
1948 Prize not awarded
1949 Lord Boyd Orr
1950 Ralph Bunche
1951 Léon Jouhaux
1952 Albert Schweitzer
1953 George C. Marshall
1954 Office of the United Nations High Commissioner for Refugees
1955 Prize not awarded
1956 Prize not awarded
1957 Lester B. Pearson
1958 Georges Pire
1959 Philip Noel-Baker
1960 Albert Lutuli
1961 Dag Hammarskjöld
1962 Linus Pauling
1963 International Committee of the Red Cross, League of Red Cross Societies
1964 Martin Luther King, Jr.
1965 United Nations Children's Fund
1966 Prize not awarded
1967 Prize not awarded
1968 René Cassin
1969 International Labor Organization (ILO)
1970 Norman Borlaug
1971 Willy Brandt
1972 Prize not awarded
1973 Henry Kissinger, Le Duc Tho (declined the prize)
1974 Seán MacBride, Eisaku Sato

List #173 Nobel Prize Winners—Peace *(continued)*

1975 Andrei Sakharov
1976 Mairéad Corrigan, Betty Williams
1977 Amnesty International
1978 Menachem Begin, Anwar al-Sadat
1979 Mother Teresa
1980 Adolfo Pérez Esquivel
1981 Office of the United Nations High Commissioner for Refugees
1982 Alfonso García Robles, Alva Myrdal
1983 Lech Walesa
1984 Desmond Tutu
1985 International Physicians for the Prevention of Nuclear War
1986 Elie Wiesel
1987 Oscar Arias Sánchez
1988 United Nations Peacekeeping Forces
1989 The 14th Dalai Lama
1990 Mikhail Gorbachev
1991 Aung San Suu Kyi
1992 Rigoberta Menchú Tum
1993 F. W. de Klerk, Nelson Mandela
1994 Yasir Arafat, Shimon Peres, Yitzhak Rabin
1995 Pugwash Conferences, Joseph Rotblat
1996 Carlos Filipe Ximenes Belo, José Ramos-Horta
1997 International Campaign to Ban Landmines, Jody Williams
1998 John Hume, David Trimble
1999 Medecins Sans Frontieres
2000 Kim Dae-jung
2001 United Nations, Kofi Annan
2002 Jimmy Carter
2003 Shirin Ebadi
2004 Wangari Maathai
2005 International Atomic Energy Agency (IAEA), Mohamed El Baradei
2006 Muhammad Yunus, Grameen Bank

List #174 Nobel Prize Winners—Physics

1901 Wilhelm Conrad Röentgen
1902 Hendrik A. Lorentz, Pieter Zeeman
1903 Henri Becquerel, Pierre Curie, Marie Curie
1904 Lord Rayleigh
1905 Philipp Lenard
1906 Joseph John Thomson
1907 Albert A. Michelson
1908 Gabriel Lippmann
1909 Guglielmo Marconi, Karl Ferdinand Braun
1910 Johannes Diderik van der Waals
1911 Wilhelm Wien
1912 Gustaf Dalén
1913 Heike Kamerlingh Onnes
1914 Max von Laue
1915 William Bragg, Lawrence Bragg
1916 Prize not awarded
1917 Charles Glover Barkla
1918 Max Planck
1919 Johannes Stark
1920 Charles Edouard Guillaume
1921 Albert Einstein
1922 Niels Bohr
1923 Robert A. Millikan
1924 Manne Siegbahn
1925 James Franck, Gustav Herz
1926 Jean Baptiste Perrin
1927 Arthur H. Compton, Charles T. R. Wilson
1928 Owen Willans Richardson
1929 Louis de Broglie
1930 Venkata Raman
1931 Prize not awarded
1932 Werner Heisenberg
1933 Erwin Schrödinger, Paul A. M. Dirac
1934 Prize not awarded
1935 James Chadwick
1936 Victor F. Hess, Carl D. Anderson
1937 Clinton Davisson, George Paget Thomson
1938 Enrico Fermi
1939 Ernest Lawrence
1940 Prize not awarded
1941 Prize not awarded
1942 Prize not awarded
1943 Otto Stern
1944 Isidor Isaac Rabi
1945 Wolfgang Pauli
1946 Percy W. Bridgman
1947 Edward V. Appleton
1948 Patrick M. S. Blackett
1949 Hideki Yukawa
1950 Cecil F. Powell
1951 John D. Cockcroft, Ernest T. S. Walton
1952 Felix Bloch, E. M. Purcell
1953 Frits Zernike
1954 Max Born, Walther Bothe
1955 Willis Lamb, Polykarp Kusch
1956 William Shockley, John Bardeen, Walter Houser Brattain
1957 Chen Ning Yang, Tsung-Dao Lee
1958 Pavel A. Cherenkov, Ilya M. Frank, Igor Y. Tamm
1959 Emilio Segre, Owen Chamberlain
1960 Donald A. Glaser
1961 Robert Hofstadter, Rudolf L. Moessbauer
1962 Lev Davidovich Landau
1963 Eugene P. Wigner, Maria Goeppert-Mayer, Johannes Hans D. Jensen
1964 Charles H. Townes, Nikolai G. Basov, Aleksandr M. Prokhorov
1965 Sin-Itiro Tomonaga, Julian S. Schwinger, Richard P. Feynman
1966 Alfred Kastler
1967 Hans Bethe
1968 Luis W. Alvarez
1969 Murray Gell-Mann
1970 Hannes Alfvén, Louis Neel
1971 Dennis Gabor
1972 John Bardeen, Leon N. Cooper, Robert J. Schrieffer
1973 Leo Esaki, Ivar Giaever, Brian D. Josephson
1974 Martin Ryle, Antony Hewish
1975 Aage N. Bohr, Benjamin R. Mottelson, James Rainwater
1976 Burton Richter, Samuel C. C. Ting

List #174 **Nobel Prize Winners—Physics** *(continued)*

1977 Philip W. Anderson, Sir Nevill Francis Mott, John H. van Vleck
1978 Pyotr Kapitsa, Arno Penzias, Robert W. Wilson
1979 Sheldon Glashow, Abdus Salam, Steven Weinberg
1980 James Cronin, Val Fitch
1981 Nicolaas Bloembergen, Arthur L. Schawlow, Kai M. Siegbahn
1982 Kenneth G. Wilson
1983 Subrahmanyan Chandrasekhar, William A. Fowler
1984 Carlo Rubbia, Simon van der Meer
1985 Klaus von Klitzing
1986 Ernst Ruska, Gerd Binning, Heinrich Rohrer
1987 J. Georg Bednorz, K. Alexander Müller
1988 Leon M. Lederman, Melvin Schwartz, Jack Steinberger
1989 Norman F. Ramsey, Hans G. Dehmelt, Wolfgang Paul
1990 Jerome I. Friedman, Henry W. Kendall, Richard E. Taylor
1991 Pierre-Gilles de Gennes
1992 Georges Charpak
1993 Russell A. Hulse, Joseph H. Taylor, Jr.
1994 Bertram N. Brockhouse, Clifford G. Shull
1995 Martin L. Perl, Frederick Reines
1996 David M. Lee. Douglas D. Osheroff, Robert C. Richardson
1997 Steven Chu, Claude Cohen-Tannoudji, William D. Phillips
1998 Robert B. Laughlin, Horst L. Stormer, Daniel C. Tsui
1999 Gerardus't Hooft, Martinus J. G. Veltman
2000 Zhores I. Alferov, Herbert Kroemer, Jack S. Kilby
2001 Eric A. Cornell, Wolfgang Ketterle, Carl E. Wieman
2002 Raymond Davis, Jr., Masatoshi Koshiba, Riccardo Giacconi
2003 Alexei A. Abrikosov, Vitaly L. Ginzburg, Anthony J. Leggett
2004 David J. Gross, H. David Politzer, Frank Wilczek
2005 Roy J. Glauber, John L. Hall, Theodor W. Hänsch
2006 John C. Mather, George F. Smoot

List #175 Nobel Prize Winners—Chemistry

1901 Jacobus H. van't Hoff
1902 Emil Fischer
1903 Svante August Arrhenius
1904 Sir William Ramsay
1905 Adolf von Baeyer
1906 Henri Moissan
1907 Eduard Buchner
1908 Ernest Rutherford
1909 Wilhelm Ostwald
1910 Otto Wallach
1911 Marie Curie
1912 Victor Grignard, Paul Sabatier
1913 Alfred Werner
1914 Theodore W. Richards
1915 Richard M. Willstätter
1916 Prize not awarded
1917 Prize not awarded
1918 Fritz Haber
1919 Prize not awarded
1920 Walther Nernst
1921 Frederick Soddy
1922 Francis W. Aston
1923 Fritz Pregl
1924 Prize not awarded
1925 Richard Zsigmondy
1926 The (Theodor) Svedberg
1927 Heinrich Wieland
1928 Adolf Windaus
1929 Arthur Harden, Hans von Euler-Chelpin
1930 Hans Fischer
1931 Carl Bosch, Friedrich Bergius
1932 Irving Langmuir
1933 Prize not awarded
1934 Harold C. Urey
1935 Frederic Joliot, Irene Joliot-Curie
1936 Peter Debye
1937 Norman Haworth, Paul Karrer
1938 Richard Kuhn
1939 Adolf Butenandt, Leopold Ruzicka
1940 Prize not awarded
1941 Prize not awarded
1942 Prize not awarded
1943 George de Hevesy
1944 Otto Hahn
1945 Artturi I. Virtanen
1946 James B. Sumner, John H. Northrop, Wendell M. Stanley
1947 Sir Robert Robinson
1948 Arne Tiselius
1949 William F. Giauque
1950 Otto Diels, Kurt Alder
1951 Edwin M. McMillan, Glenn T. Seaborg
1952 Archer J. P. Martin, Richard L. M. Synge
1953 Hermann Staudinger
1954 Linus Pauling
1955 Vincent du Vigneaud
1956 Sir Cyril Hinshelwood, Nikolay Semenov
1957 Lord Alexander R. Todd
1958 Frederick Sanger
1959 Jaroslav Heyrovsky
1960 Willard F. Libby
1961 Melvin Calvin
1962 Max F. Perutz, John C. Kendrew
1963 Karl Ziegler, Giulio Natta
1964 Dorothy Crowfoot Hodgkin
1965 Robert Burns Woodward
1966 Robert S. Mulliken
1967 Manfred Eigen, Ronald G. W. Norrish, George Porter
1968 Lars Onsager
1969 Derek H. R. Barton, Odd Hassel
1970 Luis F. Leloir
1971 Gerhard Herzberg
1972 Christian B. Anfinsen, Stanford Moore, William H. Stein
1973 Ernst Otto Fischer, Geoffrey Wilkinson
1974 Paul J. Flory
1975 John Warcup Cornforth, Vladimir Prelog
1976 William Nunn Lipscomb, Jr.
1977 Ilya Prigogine
1978 Peter D. Mitchell
1979 Herbert C. Brown, Georg Wittig
1980 Paul Berg, Walter Gilbert, Frederick Sanger
1981 Kenichi Fukui, Roald Hoffmann
1982 Aaron Klug
1983 Henry Taube

List #175 **Nobel Prize Winners—Chemistry** *(continued)*

1984 Bruce Merrifield
1985 Herbert A. Hauptman, Jerome Karle
1986 Dudley R. Herschbach, Yuan T. Lee, John C. Polanyi
1987 Donald J. Cram, Jean-Marie Lehn, Charles J. Pedersen
1988 Johann Deisenhofer, Robert Huber, Hartmut Michel
1989 Sidney Altman, Thomas R. Cech
1990 Elias James Corey
1991 Richard R. Ernst
1992 Rudolph A. Marcus
1993 Kary B. Mullis, Michael Smith
1994 George A. Olah
1995 Paul J. Crutzen, Mario J. Molina, F. Sherwood Rowland
1996 Robert Curl, Sir Harold Kroto, Richard Smalley
1997 Paul D. Boyer, John E. Walker, Jens C. Skou
1998 Walter Kohn, John A. Pople
1999 Ahmed H. Zewail
2000 Alan J. Heeger, Alan G. MacDiarmid, Hideki Shirakawa
2001 William S. Knowles, Ryoji Noyori, K. Barry Sharpless
2002 Kurt Wuthrich, John B. Fenn, Koichi Tanaka
2003 Peter Agre, Roderick MacKinnon
2004 Aaron Ciechanover, Avram Hershko, Irwin Rose
2005 Yves Chauvin, Robert H. Grubbs, Richard R. Schrock
2006 Roger D. Kornberg

List #176 Nobel Prize Winners—Medicine

1901 Emil von Behring
1902 Ronald Ross
1903 Niels Ryberg Finsen
1904 Ivan Pavlov
1905 Robert Koch
1906 Camillo Golgi, Santiago Ramon y Cajal
1907 Alphonse Laveran
1908 Ilya Mechnikov, Paul Ehrlich
1909 Theodor Kocher
1910 Albrecht Kossel
1911 Allvar Gullstrand
1912 Alexis Carrel
1913 Charles Richet
1914 Robert Barany
1915 Prize not awarded
1916 Prize not awarded
1917 Prize not awarded
1918 Prize not awarded
1919 Jules Bordet
1920 August Krogh
1921 Prize not awarded
1922 Archibald V. Hill, Otto Meyerhof
1923 Frederick G. Banting, John Macleod
1924 Willem Einthoven
1925 Prize not awarded
1926 Johannes Fibiger
1927 Julius Wagner-Jauregg
1928 Charles Nicolle
1929 Christiaan Eijkman, Sir Frederick Hopkins
1930 Karl Landsteiner
1931 Otto Warburg
1932 Sir Charles Sherrington, Edgar Adrian
1933 Thomas H. Morgan
1934 George H. Whipple, George R. Minot, William P. Murphy
1935 Hans Spemann
1936 Sir Henry Dale, Otto Loewi
1937 Albert Szent-Gyorgyi
1938 Corneille Heymans
1939 Gerhard Domagk
1940 Prize not awarded
1941 Prize not awarded
1942 Prize not awarded
1943 Henrik Dam, Edward A. Doisy
1944 Joseph Erlanger, Herbert S. Gasser
1945 Sir Alexander Fleming, Ernst B. Chain, Sir Howard Florey
1946 Hermann Muller
1947 Carl Cori, Gerty Theresa Cori, Bernardo Houssay
1948 Paul Müller
1949 Walter Hess, Egas Moniz
1950 Edward C. Kendall, Tadeus Reichstein, Philip S. Hench
1951 Max Theiler
1952 Selman A. Waksman
1953 Hans Krebs, Fritz Lipmann
1954 John F. Enders, Thomas H. Weller, Frederick C. Robbins
1955 Hugo Theorell
1956 Andre F. Cournand, Werner Forssmann, Dickinson W. Richards
1957 Daniel Bovet
1958 George Beadle, Edward Tatum, Joshua Lederberg
1959 Severo Ochoa, Arthur Kornberg
1960 Sir Frank Macfarlane Burnet, Peter Medawar
1961 Georg von Békésy
1962 Francis Crick, James Watson, Maurice Wilkins
1963 Sir John Eccles, Alan L. Hodgkin, Andrew F. Huxley
1964 Konrad Bloch, Feodor Lynen
1965 Francois Jacob, Andre Lwoff, Jacques Monod
1966 Peyton Rous, Charles B. Huggins
1967 Ragnar Granit, Haldan K. Hartline, George Wald
1968 Robert W. Holley, Gobind Khorana, Marshall W. Nirenberg
1969 Max Delbruck, Alfred D. Hershey, Salvador E. Luria
1970 Sir Bernard Katz, Ulf von Euler, Julius Axelrod
1971 Earl W. Sutherland, Jr.

List #176 **Nobel Prize Winners—Medicine** *(continued)*

1972 Gerald M. Edelman, Rodney R. Porter
1973 Karl von Frisch, Konrad Lorenz, Nikolaas Tinbergen
1974 Albert Claude, Christian de Duve, George E. Palade
1975 David Baltimore, Renato Dulbecco, Howard M. Temin
1976 Baruch S. Blumberg, D. Carleton Gajdusek
1977 Roger Guillemin, Andrew V. Schally, Rosalyn Yalow
1978 Werner Arber, Daniel Nathans, Hamilton O. Smith
1979 Allan M. Cormack, Godfrey N. Hounsfield
1980 Baruj Benacerraf, Jean Dausset, George D. Snell
1981 Roger W. Sperry, David H. Hubel, Torsten N. Wiesel
1982 Sune K. Bergstrom, Bengt I. Samuelsson, John R. Vane
1983 Barbara McClintock
1984 Niels K. Jerne, Georges J. F. Kohler, Cesar Milstein
1985 Michael S. Brown, Joseph L. Goldstein
1986 Stanley Cohen, Rita Levi-Montalcini
1987 Susumu Tonegawa
1988 Sir James W. Black, Gertrude B. Elion, George H. Hitchings
1989 J. Michael Bishop, Harold E. Varmus
1990 Joseph E. Murray, E. Donnall Thomas
1991 Erwin Neher, Bert Sakmann
1992 Edmond H. Fischer, Edwin G. Krebs
1993 Richard J. Roberts, Phillip A. Sharp
1994 Alfred G. Gilman, Martin Rodbell
1995 Edward B. Lewis, Christiane Nusslein-Volhard, Eric F. Wieschaus
1996 Peter C. Doherty, Rolf M. Zinkernagel
1997 Stanley B. Prusiner
1998 Robert F. Furchgott, Louis J. Ignarro, Ferid Murad
1999 Gunter Blobel
2000 Arvid Carlsson, Paul Greengard, Eric R. Kandel
2001 Leland H. Hartwell, R. Timothy Hunt, Paul M. Nurse
2002 Sydney Brenner, H. Robert Horvitz, John E. Sulston
2003 Paul C. Lauterbur, Sir Peter Mansfield
2004 Richard Axel, Linda B. Buck
2005 Barry J. Marshall, J. Robin Warren
2006 Andrew Z. Fire, Craig C. Mello

List #177 Nobel Prize Winners—Literature

1901 Sully Prudhomme
1902 Theodor Mommsen
1903 Bjørnstjerne Bjørnson
1904 Frédéric Mistral, Jóse Echegaray
1905 Henryk Sienkiewicz
1906 Giosue Carducci
1907 Rudyard Kipling
1908 Rudolf Eucken
1909 Selma Lagerlof
1910 Paul Heyse
1911 Maurice Maeterlinck
1912 Gerhart Hauptmann
1913 Rabindranath Tagore
1914 Prize not awarded
1915 Romain Rolland
1916 Verner von Heidenstam
1917 Karl Gjellerup, Henrik Pontoppidan
1918 Prize not awarded
1919 Carl Friedrich Georg Spitteler
1920 Knut Hamsun
1921 Anatole France
1922 Jacinto Benavente
1923 William Butler Yeats
1924 Wladyslaw Reymont
1925 George Bernard Shaw
1926 Grazia Deledda
1927 Henri Bergson
1928 Sigrid Undset
1929 Thomas Mann
1930 Sinclair Lewis
1931 Erik Axel Karlfeldt
1932 John Galsworthy
1933 Ivan Bunin
1934 Luigi Pirandello
1935 Prize not awarded
1936 Eugene O'Neill
1937 Roger Martin du Gard
1938 Pearl S. Buck
1939 Frans Eemil Sillanpää
1940 Prize not awarded
1941 Prize not awarded
1942 Prize not awarded
1943 Prize not awarded
1944 Johannes Jensen
1945 Gabriela Mistral
1946 Hermann Hesse
1947 André Gide
1948 T. S. Eliot
1949 William Faulkner
1950 Bertrand Russell
1951 Pär Lagerkvist
1952 Francois Mauriac
1953 Sir Winston Churchill
1954 Ernest Hemingway
1955 Halldor Laxness
1956 Juan Ramón Jiménez
1957 Albert Camus
1958 Boris Pasternak
1959 Salvatore Quasimodo
1960 Saint-John Perse
1961 Ivo Andric
1962 John Steinbeck
1963 Giorgos Seferis
1964 Jean-Paul Sartre (declined the prize)
1965 Mikail Sholokhov
1966 Shmuel Yosef Agnon, Nelly Sachs
1967 Miguel Angel Asturias
1968 Yasunari Kawabata
1969 Samuel Beckett
1970 Alexandr Solzhenitsyn
1971 Pablo Neruda
1972 Heinrich Boll
1973 Patrick White
1974 Eyvind Johnson, Harry Martinson
1975 Eugenio Montale
1976 Saul Bellow
1977 Vicente Aleixandre
1978 Isaac Bashevis Singer
1979 Odysseas Elytis
1980 Czeslaw Milosz
1981 Elias Canetti
1982 Gabriel Garcia Márquez
1983 William Golding
1984 Jaroslav Seifert
1985 Claude Simon
1986 Wole Soyinka
1987 Joseph Brodsky
1988 Naguib Mahfouz
1989 Camilo Jose Cela
1990 Octavio Paz

List #177 Nobel Prize Winners—Literature *(continued)*

1991 Nadine Gordimer
1992 Derek Walcott
1993 Toni Morrison
1994 Kenzaburo Oe
1995 Seamus Heaney
1996 Wislawa Szymborska
1997 Dario Fo
1998 Jose Saramago
1999 Günter Grass
2000 Gao Xingjian
2001 Vidiadhar Surajprasad Naipaul
2002 Imre Kertesz
2003 J. M. Coetzee
2004 Elfriede Jelinek
2005 Harold Pinter
2006 Orhan Pamuk

List #178 Nobel Prize Winners—Economics

1969 Ragnar Frisch, Jan Tinbergen
1970 Paul Samuelson
1971 Simon Kuznets
1972 Kenneth J. Arrow, John R. R. Hicks
1973 Wassily Leontief
1974 Gunnar Myrdal, Friedrich A. von Hayek
1975 Leonid Kantorovich, Tjalling C. Koopmans
1976 Milton Friedman
1977 Bertil Ohlin, James Meade
1978 Herbert Simon
1979 Sir Arthur Lewis, Theodore W. Schultz
1980 Lawrence R. Klein
1981 James Tobin
1982 George J. Stigler
1983 Gerard Debreu
1984 Richard Stone
1985 Franco Modigliani
1986 James Buchanan
1987 Robert Solow
1988 Maurice Allais
1989 Trygve Haavelmo
1990 Merton Miller, William Sharpe, Harry Markowitz
1991 Ronald Coase
1992 Gary Becker
1993 Robert Fogel, Douglas North
1994 John Nash, John Harsanyi, Reinhart Selton
1995 Robert Lucas
1996 James Mirrlees, William Vickrey
1997 Robert Merton, Myron Scholes
1998 Amartya Sen
1999 Robert Mundell
2000 James Heckman, Daniel McFadden
2001 George Akerlof, Michael Spence, Joseph Stiglitz
2002 Daniel Kahneman, Vernon Smith
2003 Robert F. Engle, Clive W. J. Granger
2004 Finn E. Kydland, Edward C. Prescott
2005 Robert J. Aumann, Thomas C. Schelling
2006 Edmund S. Phelps

11

Quotations, Speeches, and Other Documents

List #179 Fairy Tales

Fairy tales are as old as any other ancient literature with which we are familiar. They have been passed down in the oral tradition for thousands of years. The following guide lists fairy tales with which your child should be familiar. For younger children, simply read the fairy tales and introduce them to the great stories. Then as children progress in age, require that they also memorize the authors of these enduring stories and perhaps short quotes from the stories. For additional enrichment, read biographies of the authors and learn about the lives of the men and women who wrote these tales that relate our most basic problems in terms even a child can understand.

Title	Author
Beauty and the Beast	Madame LePrince de Beaumont
Cinderella	Charles Perrault
The Elves and the Shoemaker	The Brothers Grimm
The Emperor's New Clothes	Hans Christian Andersen
The Frog Prince	The Brothers Grimm
Hansel and Gretel	The Brothers Grimm
Jack and the Beanstalk	Old English fairy tale, author unknown
Puss in Boots	Charles Perrault
Rapunzel	The Brothers Grimm
The Real Princess	Hans Christian Andersen
Red Riding Hood	The Brothers Grimm
Rumpelstiltskin	The Brothers Grimm
The Sleeping Beauty in the Wood	Charles Perrault
The Snow Queen	Hans Christian Andersen
Snow White	The Brothers Grimm
The Steadfast Tin Soldier	Hans Christian Andersen
Thumbelina	Hans Christian Andersen
The Twelve Dancing Princesses	The Brothers Grimm
The Valiant Little Tailor	The Brothers Grimm

List #180 Proverbs From Other Countries

This is a fun list that can be used in many ways. Supplement geography, history, or missionary studies with it. Try to decide why particular proverbs developed in certain countries. Compare similar proverbs. Read the proverbs with your child and try to determine the meaning of each saying.

Proverb	Country of Origin
Don't show me the palm tree; show me the dates.	Afghanistan
No one says his own buttermilk is sour.	Afghanistan
A little water is a sea to an ant.	Afghanistan
Before shooting, one must aim.	Africa
Only a fool tests the depth of the water with both feet.	Africa
The sun at home warms better than the sun elsewhere.	Albania
Don't put gold buttons on a torn coat.	Albania
Don't call the alligator a big-mouth until you have crossed the river.	Belize
A wise man learns at the fool's expense.	Brazil
You can only take out of a bag what is already in it.	Brazil
If you let everyone walk over you, you become a carpet.	Bulgaria
A clever person turns great troubles into little ones and little ones into none at all.	China
Life is short, but a smile takes barely a second.	Cuba
Listen to what they say of others and you will know what they say about you.	Cuba
Do not protect yourself with a fence, but rather by your friends.	Czech Republic
A lazy boy and a warm bed are difficult to part.	Denmark
Learn politeness from the impolite.	Egypt
What one hopes for is always better than what one has.	Ethiopia
The frog wanted to be as big as the elephant and he burst.	Ethiopia
Wait until it is night before saying it has been a fine day.	France
There is no pillow so soft as a clear conscience.	France
God gives the nuts, but he does not crack them.	Germany
Begin to weave and God will provide the thread.	Germany
A lean agreement is better than a fat lawsuit.	Germany
Hunger is felt by a slave and hunger is felt by a king.	Ghana
Milk the cow, but do not pull off the udder.	Greece
The pencil of God has no eraser.	Haiti
Don't insult the alligator until you've crossed the river.	Haiti

List #180 **Proverbs From Other Countries** *(continued)*

Proverb	Country of Origin
He who lives without discipline dies without honor.	Iceland
Don't judge a man until you've walked two moons in his moccasins.	India
Don't bargain for fish that are still in the water.	India
A blind man who sees is better than a sighted man who is blind.	Iran
Every tear has a smile behind it.	Iran
When you go to a donkey's house, don't talk about ears.	Jamaica
Fall seven times, stand up eight.	Japan
He who does not know one thing knows another.	Kenya
Words have no wings, but they can fly many thousands of miles.	Korea (South)
Distracted by what is far away, he does not see his nose.	Madagascar
Words are like eggs—when they are hatched, they have wings.	Madagascar
The turtle lays thousands of eggs without anyone knowing, but when the hen lays an egg, the whole country is informed.	Malaysia
He who goes to bed hungry dreams of pancakes.	Malta
It is not enough to know how to ride—you must also know how to fall.	Mexico
Envious persons never compliment—they only swallow.	Mexico
Instruction in youth is like engraving in stone.	Morocco
The more you ask how much longer it will take, the longer it will seem.	New Zealand
If you make a habit of buying things you do not need, you will soon be selling things you do.	Philippines
There are a thousand paths to every wrong.	Poland
Even a clock that is not going is right twice a day.	Poland
God grant me a good sword and no use for it.	Poland
There is no shame in not knowing; the shame lies in not finding out.	Russia
Success and rest don't sleep together.	Russia
If you are building a house and a nail breaks, do you stop building or do you change the nail?	Rwanda
A book is a garden carried in the pocket.	Saudi Arabia
God gives every bird his worm, but he does not throw it into the nest.	Sweden
At high tide the fish eat ants; at low tide the ants eat fish.	Thailand

List #181 Famous Shakespearean Quotes

William Shakespeare

"Good night, good night! parting is such sweet sorrow. . . ."—spoken by Juliet (from *Romeo and Juliet,* Act II, Scene II)

"Et tu, Brute!"—spoken by Julius Caesar (from *Julius Caesar,* Act III, Scene I)

"Friends, Romans, countrymen, lend me your ears; I come to bury Caesar, not to praise him."—spoken by Mark Antony (from *Julius Caesar,* Act III, Scene II)

"To be, or not to be: that is the question."—spoken by Hamlet (from *Hamlet,* Act III, Scene I)

"Neither a borrower nor a lender be; For loan oft loses both itself and friend, and borrowing dulls the edge of husbandry."—spoken by Hamlet (from *Hamlet,* Act I, Scene III)

"This above all: to thine own self be true."—spoken by Hamlet (from *Hamlet,* Act I, Scene III)

"So sweet, ne'er so fatal."—spoken by Othello (from *Othello,* Act IV, Scene II)

"If you can look into the seed of time, and say which grain will grow and which will not, speak then to me."—spoken by Banquo (from *Macbeth,* Act I, Scene III)

List #182 The Code of Hammurabi

Hammurabi, King of Babylonia—18th Century BC

The following are excerpts from one of the earliest codes of law, The Code of Hammurabi, which was created by the King of Babylonia, Hammurabi, in the eighteenth century BC. The laws were carved on an eight-foot-high stone found in 1901. Only a few of the hundreds of laws are listed here.

> If a judge has given a verdict, rendered a decision, granted a written judgment, and afterward has altered his judgment, that judge shall be prosecuted for altering the judgment he gave and shall pay twelvefold the penalty laid down in that judgment. Further, he shall be publicly expelled from his judgment-seat and shall not return nor take his seat with the judges at a trial. (rule #5)
>
> If a man has stolen a child, he shall be put to death. (rule #14)
>
> If a man has induced a male or female slave from the house of a patrician, or plebian, outside the city gates [to escape], he shall be put to death. (rule #15)
>
> If a man has harbored in his house a male or female slave from a patrician's or plebian's house, and has not caused the fugitive to leave on the demand of the officer over the slaves condemned to public forced labor, that householder shall be put to death. (rule #16)
>
> If a man has committed highway robbery and has been caught, that man shall be put to death. (rule #22)
>
> If any one be too lazy to keep his dam in proper condition, and does not so keep it; if then the dam breaks and all the fields be flooded, then shall he in whose dam the break occurred be sold for money, and the money shall replace the [grain] which he has caused to be ruined. (rule #53)
>
> If he be not able to replace the [grain], then he and his possessions shall be divided among the farmers whose corn he has flooded. (rule #54)
>
> If a "sister of a god" [nun] open a tavern, or enter a tavern to drink, then shall this woman be burned to death. (rule #110)
>
> If a man wishes to separate from his wife who has borne him no children, he shall give her the amount of her purchase money and the

List #182 **The Code of Hammurabi** *(continued)*

dowry which she brought from her father's house, and let her go. (rule #138)

From the time that the woman entered into the man's house they together shall be liable for all debts subsequently incurred. (rule #152)

If a son strikes his father, his hands shall be [cut] off. (rule #195)

If a patrician puts out the eye of another patrician, his eye shall be put out. (rule #196)

If a man has broken the limb of a patrician, his limb shall be broken. (rule #197)

If a man puts out the eye of a commoner or breaks the bone of a commoner, he shall pay one mina. (rule #198)

If a surgeon has operated with the bronze lancet on a patrician for a serious injury, and has cured him, or has removed with a bronze lancet a cataract for a patrician, and has cured his eye, he shall take ten shekels of silver. (rule #215)

If a surgeon has operated with the bronze lancet on a patrician for a serious injury, and has caused his death, or has removed a cataract for a patrician, with the bronze lancet, and has made him lose his eye, his hands shall be cut off. (rule #218)

List #183 Revolutionary War Documents

Declaration of Independence: document in which the 13 Colonies declared their independence from the Kingdom of Great Britain.

The U.S. Constitution: the "law" of the United States.

The U.S. Bill of Rights: the first 13 amendments to the Constitution, most of which define some basic human rights.

First Inaugural Address of President George Washington: April 30, 1789, his inauguration speech.

The Virginia Declaration of Rights: claimed that individuals are born with inherent natural rights.

Sugar and Stamp Acts: levies (taxes) that Parliament of Britain placed on these goods being used in the Colonies.

Letter of Transmittal of the U.S. Constitution: the letter that the delegates of the Constitutional Convention wrote to the Congress recommending that they ratify the Constitution.

Mecklenburg Declaration: a written declaration of independence from Great Britain signed by over 25 prominent members of Mecklenburg County in North Carolina on May 20, 1775, over a year before the Declaration of Independence.

The New York Petition to the House of Commons: October 18, 1764, letter from New York to the House of Commons basically protesting taxation without representation.

In Opposition to Writs of Assistance by James Otis: James Otis represented Boston merchants in 1761 in opposition of the writs of assistance, which gave customs officers not only the right to search shops but private homes as well.

Resolutions of Congress on Lord North's Conciliatory Proposal in Congress: In 1775, Thomas Jefferson wrote resolutions in response to Lord North's proposals for reconciliation between Britain and the Colonies.

Locke's Second Treatise: Philosopher John Locke's ideas of the structure, aim, and origin of civil government.

The Declaratory Act: an act that declared Britain and King's rule over Colonies and anything they did outside Parliament's approval was null and void

The Navigation Act: This act of 1651 banned foreign ships from transporting to England any goods that were not from Europe. The main goal was to exclude the Dutch from shipping.

Proclamation of 1763, The Royal Proclamation: an attempt to organize Britain's empire in North America and soothe relationships with the Native Americans.

List #183 **Revolutionary War Documents** *(continued)*

A Bill for Proportioning Crimes and Punishments: In 1777, Thomas Jefferson tried to pass a bill that would change Virginia's death penalty laws so that only murder and treason cases were punishable by death, but the bill was defeated by one vote.

The Articles of Confederation (the precursor to the U.S. Constitution): the first governing document that united the brand-new United States.

Treaty of Paris: a peace treaty signed by Great Britain, France, Spain, and Portugal ending the French/Indian War in 1763.

John Jay's Treaty: After the War of Independence ended, English ships continued to capture American ships and press the sailors into service for English war against France. Jay's Treaty negotiated an agreement between England and the U.S., averting another potential war.

Thomas Paine's Common Sense: a document challenging the authority of the British government and monarchy.

List #184 ". . . give me liberty or give me death."

Patrick Henry

Speech delivered March 23, 1775, at St. John's Episcopal Church in Richmond, Virginia, at the Second Virginia Convention.

No man thinks more highly than I do of the patriotism, as well as abilities, of the very worthy gentlemen who have just addressed the House. But different men often see the same subject in different lights; and, therefore, I hope it will not be thought disrespectful to those gentlemen if, entertaining as I do opinions of a character very opposite to theirs, I shall speak forth my sentiments freely and without reserve. This is no time for ceremony. The question before the House is one of awful moment to this country. For my own part, I consider it as nothing less than a question of freedom or slavery; and in proportion to the magnitude of the subject ought to be the freedom of the debate. It is only in this way that we can hope to arrive at the truth, and fulfill the great responsibility which we hold to God and our country. Should I keep back my opinions at such a time, through fear of giving offense, I should consider myself as guilty of treason toward my country and of an act of disloyalty toward the Majesty of Heaven, which I revere above all earthly kings.

Mr. President, it is natural to man to indulge in the illusions of hope. We are apt to shut our eyes against a painful truth, and listen to the song of that siren till she transforms us into beasts. Is this the part of wise men, engaged in a great and arduous struggle for liberty? Are we disposed to be of the numbers of those who, having eyes, see not, and, having ears, hear not, the things which so nearly concern their temporal salvation? For my part, whatever anguish of spirit it may cost, I am willing to know the whole truth, to know the worst, and to provide for it.

I have but one lamp by which my feet are guided, and that is the lamp of experience. I know of no way of judging the future but by the past. And judging by the past, I wish to know what there has been in the conduct of the British ministry for the last ten years to justify those hopes with which gentlemen have been pleased to solace themselves and the House. Is it that insidious smile with which our petition has been lately received?

Trust it not, sir; it will prove a snare to your feet. Suffer not yourselves to be betrayed with a kiss. Ask yourselves how this gracious reception of our petition comports with those warlike preparations which cover our waters and darken our land. Are fleets and armies necessary to a work of love and reconciliation? Have we shown ourselves so unwilling to be reconciled that force must be called in to win back our love? Let us not deceive ourselves, sir. These are the implements of war and subjugation; the last arguments to which kings resort. I ask, gentlemen, sir, what means this martial array, if its purpose be not to force us to submission? Can gentlemen assign any other possible motive for it? Has Great Britain any enemy, in this quarter of the world, to call for all this accumulation of navies and armies? No, sir, she has none. They are meant for us: they can be meant for no other. They are sent over to bind and rivet upon us those chains which the British ministry have been so long forging. And what have we to oppose them? Shall we try argument? Sir, we have been trying that for the last ten years. Have we anything new to offer upon the subject? Nothing. We have held the subject up in every light of which it is capable; but it has been all in vain. Shall we resort to entreaty and humble supplication? What terms shall we find which have not been already exhausted? Let us not, I beseech you, sir, deceive ourselves. Sir, we have done everything that could be done to avert the storm which is now coming on. We have petitioned; we have remonstrated; we have supplicated; we have prostrated ourselves before the throne, and have implored its interposition to arrest the tyrannical hands of the ministry and Parliament. Our petitions have been slighted; our remonstrances have produced additional violence and insult; our supplications have been disregarded; and we have been spurned, with contempt, from the foot of the throne! In vain, after these things, may we indulge the fond hope of peace and reconciliation.

There is no longer any room for hope. If we wish to be free—if we mean to preserve inviolate those inestimable privileges for which we have been so long contending—if we mean not basely to abandon the noble struggle in which we have been so long engaged, and which we have pledged ourselves never to abandon until the glorious object of our contest shall be obtained—we must fight! I repeat it, sir, we must fight! An appeal to arms and to the God of hosts is all that is left us! They tell us, sir, that we are weak, unable to cope with so formidable an adversary. But when shall we be stronger? Will it be the next week, or the next year? Will it be when we are totally disarmed, and when a British guard shall be stationed in every house? Shall we gather strength but irresolution and inaction? Shall we acquire the means of effectual resistance by lying supinely on our backs and hugging the delusive phantom of hope, until our enemies shall have bound us hand and foot? Sir, we are not weak if we make a proper use of those means which the God of nature hath placed in our power. The millions of people, armed in the holy cause of liberty, and in such a country as that which we possess, are invincible by any force which our enemy can send against us. Besides, sir, we shall not fight our battles alone. There is a just God who presides over the destinies of nations, and who will raise up friends to fight our battles for us. The battle, sir, is not to the strong alone; it is to the vigilant, the active, the brave. Besides, sir, we have no election. If we were base enough to desire it, it is now too late to retire from the contest. There is no retreat but in submission and slavery!

List #184 ". . . give me liberty or give me death." *(continued)*

Our chains are forged! Their clanking may be heard on the plains of Boston! The war is inevitable—and let it come! I repeat it, sir, let it come.

It is in vain, sir, to extentuate the matter. Gentlemen may cry, Peace, Peace—but there is no peace. The war is actually begun! The next gale that sweeps from the north will bring to our ears the clash of resounding arms! Our brethren are already in the field! Why stand we here idle? What is it that gentlemen wish? What would they have? Is life so dear, or peace so sweet, as to be purchased at the price of chains and slavery? Forbid it, Almighty God! I know not what course others may take; but as for me, give me liberty or give me death!

List #185 ". . . the whites of their eyes"

William Prescott

At the Battle of Bunker Hill, June 17, 1775, the men were low on ammunition. Colonel William Prescott led the rebel forces that day and commanded his soldiers:

> "Do not fire until you see the whites of their eyes."

This became a famous quote of the American Revolution and a wise piece of advice since it saved valuable ammunition for a more likely shot.

List #186 Preamble to the Constitution

We the People of the United States, in Order to form a more perfect Union, establish Justice, insure domestic Tranquility, provide for the common defence, promote the general Welfare, and secure the Blessings of Liberty to ourselves and our Posterity, do ordain and establish this Constitution for the United States of America.

List #187 The Bill of Rights

The first ten amendments of the Constitution are called the Bill of Rights.

First Amendment*—freedom of religion, speech, press, peaceable assembly, and to petition the government*

"Congress shall make no law respecting an establishment of religion, or prohibiting the free exercise thereof; or abridging the freedom of speech, or of the press; or the right of the people peaceably to assemble, and to petition the Government for a redress of grievances."

Second Amendment*—right of the people to keep and bear arms*

"A well regulated Militia, being necessary to the security of a free State, the right of the people to keep and bear Arms shall not be infringed."

Third Amendment*—protection from quartering of troops without consent*

"No Soldier shall, in time of peace be quartered in any house, without the consent of the Owner, nor in time of war, but in a manner to be prescribed by law."

Fourth Amendment*—protection from unreasonable search and seizure*

"The right of the people to be secure in their persons, houses, papers, and effects, against unreasonable searches and seizures, shall not be violated, and no Warrants shall issue, but upon probable cause, supported by Oath or affirmation, and particularly describing the place to be searched, and the persons or things to be seized."

Fifth Amendment*—due process, double jeopardy, self-incrimination, seizure of private property*

"No person shall be held to answer for any capital, or otherwise infamous crime, unless on a presentment or indictment of a Grand Jury, except in cases arising in the land or naval forces, or in the Militia, when in actual service in time of War or public danger; nor shall any person be subject for the same offence to be twice put in jeopardy of life or limb; nor shall be compelled in any criminal case to be a witness against himself, nor be deprived of life, liberty, or property, without due process of law; nor shall private property be taken for public use, without just compensation."

List #187 **The Bill of Rights** *(continued)*

Sixth Amendment*—trial by jury and other rights of the accused*

"In all criminal prosecutions, the accused shall enjoy the right to a speedy and public trial, by an impartial jury of the State and district wherein the crime shall have been committed, which district shall have been previously ascertained by law, and to be informed of the nature and cause of the accusation; to be confronted with the witnesses against him; to have compulsory process for obtaining witnesses in his favor, and to have the Assistance of Counsel for his defense."

Seventh Amendment*—civil trial by jury*

"In suits at common law, where the value in controversy shall exceed twenty dollars, the right of trial by jury shall be preserved, and no fact tried by a jury, shall be otherwise reexamined in any court of the United States, than according to the rules of the common law."

Eighth Amendment*—prohibition of excessive bail or fines; prohibition of cruel and unusual punishment*

"Excessive bail shall not be required, nor excessive fines imposed, nor cruel and unusual punishments inflicted."

Ninth Amendment*—protection of rights not specifically enumerated in the Bill of Rights*

"The enumeration in the Constitution, of certain rights, shall not be construed to deny or disparage others retained by the people."

Tenth Amendment*—powers of states and people*

"The powers not delegated to the United States by the Constitution, nor prohibited by it to the states, are reserved to the states respectively, or to the people."

List #188 Constitutional Amendments

Amendment	Concerns	Date Proposed	Date Ratified
1st	freedoms of religion, speech, press, peaceable assembly, and to petition the government	September 25, 1789	December 15, 1791
2nd	right of people to keep and bear arms	September 25, 1789	December 15, 1791
3rd	protection from quartering of troops without consent	September 25, 1789	December 15, 1791
4th	protection from unreasonable search and seizure; warrants	September 25, 1789	December 15, 1791
5th	due process, double jeopardy, self-incrimination, seizure of private property	September 25, 1789	December 15, 1791
6th	trial by jury and other rights of the accused	September 25, 1789	December 15, 1791
7th	right to trial by jury in civil cases	September 25, 1789	December 15, 1791
8th	prohibition of excessive bail and fines; prohibition of cruel and unusual punishment	September 25, 1789	December 15, 1791
9th	rights not specifically enumerated in Bill of Rights	September 25, 1789	December 15, 1791
10th	powers reserved to states or people	September 25, 1789	December 15, 1791
11th	immunity of states to foreign suits	March 4, 1794	February 7, 1795
12th	revision of presidential election procedures	December 9, 1803	June 15, 1804
13th	abolition of slavery	January 31, 1865	December 6, 1865
14th	citizenship, state due process, state equal protection	June 13, 1866	July 9, 1868
15th	racial suffrage (the right to vote, regardless of race)	February 26, 1869	February 3, 1870
16th	federal income tax	July 12, 1909	February 3, 1913
17th	direct election to the United States Senate	May 13, 1912	April 8, 1913
18th	prohibition of alcohol (repealed by the 21st amendment)	December 18, 1917	January 16, 1919

List #188 **Constitutional Amendments** *(continued)*

Amendment	Concerns	Date Proposed	Date Ratified
19th	women's suffrage (the right to vote, regardless of gender)	June 4, 1919	August 18, 1920
20th	term commencement for Congress and president	March 2, 1932	January 23, 1933
21st	repeal of 18th amendment; state and local governments can prohibit alcohol	February 20, 1933	December 5, 1933
22nd	limits the president to two terms of service	March 24, 1947	February 27, 1951
23rd	representation of Washington, D.C., in electoral college	June 16, 1960	March 29, 1961
24th	suffrage and prohibition of poll taxes	September 14, 1962	January 23, 1964
25th	presidential disabilities	July 6, 1965	February 10, 1967
26th	age suffrage (voting age lowered to 18)	March 23, 1971	July 1, 1971
27th	variance of congressional compensation	September 25, 1789	May 7, 1992

List #189 The Gettysburg Address

Abraham Lincoln

Delivered November 19, 1863, in Gettysburg, Pennsylvania

There are a few different written records of President Abraham Lincoln's speech at Gettysburg. The versions contain minor variations of wording, punctuation, and structure. The following text is the so-called Bliss version, to which Lincoln affixed his signature.

> Four score and seven years ago our fathers brought forth on this continent a new nation, conceived in Liberty, and dedicated to the proposition that all men are created equal.
>
> Now we are engaged in a great civil war, testing whether that nation, or any nation, so conceived and so dedicated, can long endure. We are met on a great battle-field of that war. We have come to dedicate a portion of that field, as a final resting place for those who here gave their lives that that nation might live. It is altogether fitting and proper that we should do this.
>
> But, in a larger sense, we can not dedicate—we can not consecrate—we can not hallow—this ground. The brave men, living and dead, who struggled here, have consecrated it, far above our poor power to add or detract. The world will little note, nor long remember what we say here, but it can never forget what they did here. It is for us the living, rather, to be dedicated here to the unfinished work which they who fought here have thus far so nobly advanced. It is rather for us to be here dedicated to the great task remaining before us—that from these honored dead we take increased devotion to that cause for which they gave the last full measure of devotion—that we here highly resolve that these dead shall not have died in vain—that this nation, under God, shall have a new birth of freedom—and that government of the people, by the people, for the people, shall not perish from the earth.

List #190 ". . . a date which will live in infamy"

Franklin Delano Roosevelt

Delivered December 8, 1941, to a joint session of Congress

Yesterday, December 7th, 1941—a date which will live in infamy—the United States of America was suddenly and deliberately attacked by naval and air forces of the Empire of Japan.

The United States was at peace with that nation and, at the solicitation of Japan, was still in conversation with its government and its emperor looking toward the maintenance of peace in the Pacific.

Indeed, one hour after Japanese air squadrons had commenced bombing in the American island of Oahu, the Japanese ambassador to the United States and his colleagues delivered to our Secretary of State a formal reply to a recent American message. While this reply stated that it seemed useless to continue the existing diplomatic negotiations, it contained no threat or hint of war or of armed attack.

It will be recorded that the distance of Hawaii from Japan makes it obvious that the attack was deliberately planned many days or even weeks ago. During the intervening time, the Japanese government has deliberately sought to deceive the United States by false statements and expressions of hope for continued peace.

The attack yesterday on the Hawaiian Islands has caused severe damage to American naval and military forces. I regret to tell you that very many American lives have been lost. In addition, American ships have been reported torpedoed on the high seas between San Francisco and Honolulu.

Yesterday, the Japanese government also launched an attack against Malaya.

Last night, Japanese forces attacked Hong Kong.

Last night, Japanese forces attacked Guam.

Last night, Japanese forces attacked the Philippine Islands.

Last night, the Japanese attacked Wake Island.

This morning, the Japanese attacked Midway Island.

Japan has, therefore, undertaken a surprise offensive extending throughout the Pacific area. The facts of yesterday and today speak for themselves. The people of the United States have already formed their opinions and well understand the implications to the very life and safety of our nation. As commander in chief of the Army and Navy, I have directed that all measures be taken for our defense. But always will our whole nation remember the character of the onslaught against us.

No matter how long it may take us to overcome this premeditated invasion, the American people in their righteous might will win through to absolute victory.

List #190 **". . . a date which will live in infamy"** *(continued)*

I believe that I interpret the will of the Congress and of the people when I assert that we will not only defend ourselves to the uttermost, but will make it very certain that this form of treachery shall never again endanger us.

Hostilities exist. There is no blinking at the fact that our people, our territory, and our interests are in grave danger.

With confidence in our armed forces, with the unbounding determination of our people, we will gain the inevitable triumph—so help us God.

I ask that the Congress declare that since the unprovoked and dastardly attack by Japan on Sunday, December 7th, 1941, a state of war has existed between the United States and the Japanese empire.

List #191 ". . . one small step for man"

Neil Armstrong

Delivered on the moon, July 20, 1969

"That's one small step for man, one giant leap for mankind."

(Note: Armstrong has since commented that he actually said—or intended to say: "That's one small step for a man, one giant leap for mankind.")

12

Computers

List #192 Computer Terminology

boot	to start up an operating system; if the computer is already running, it is called a "reboot"
browser	a program used to search or browse the Web
bug	a mistake or error in the design of computer software
click	to press a mouse button; if you do this twice in rapid succession, it is called a "double-click"
cursor	usually a line or block that indicates where you are on the computer screen
desktop	a computer that is designed to sit on a desk
directory	also known as a "folder," this is a collection of files
disk	an object that is used to store data; some disks can be taken out of the computer and some must stay in the computer; all disks must have disk drives
drive	a device that is used to store or retrieve data
e-book	an electronic book
e-mail	electronic mail; messages that are sent from one computer to another via a network or the Internet
graphics	displays on the computer that are not text
hardware	the physical parts of the computer
hypertext	text that contains a pointer to link the text to another portion of the (or a completely different) document
Internet	the worldwide network of computers
laptop	a computer that is smaller than a desktop computer and meant to run a short time on batteries and thus can be carried around
modem	allows two computers to communicate via phone lines
monitor	the screen used to view computer information
mouse	the object used to move the pointer around the computer screen
network	a group of computers that work on the same system and communicate together
notebook	a small laptop computer
operating system (OS)	the program that manages a computer's resources; akin to the computer's brain
organizer	a very small hand-held computer that is used much like a datebook for names, addresses, memos, etc.
PC	"personal computer"

List #192 **Computer Terminology** *(continued)*

PDA	personal digital assistant; a small battery-powered computer much like the organizer
processor	also known as the CPU (central processing unit); the part of the computer that actually runs the programs
program	a set of instructions for the computer
software	the opposite of hardware, the software is the non-physical part of the computer; programs of a computer
spreadsheets	these programs enable the user to perform various calculations on the computer
Trojan	a computer program that is sent as an attachment, but it contains harmful computer coding like a virus
user	the person using or operating the computer
virus	a computer code that attaches itself to files and can be transferred from one computer to another, damaging software, hardware, and files along the way
worm	similar to a virus, a worm "infects" a computer, but the big difference is that a worm can actually send copies of itself to everyone in your address book, thus infecting far more computers in the long run than a virus if it is not caught quickly
www	Worldwide Web; basically this includes all the public-access portions of the Internet

List #193 How to Keep Your Computer Safe

- Use an Internet firewall.
- Keep your anti-virus software up to date and check it often to make sure it is working properly.
- Never open an attachment from an unknown source.
- Never download software from an unreliable source.
- Never open anything attached to an e-mail message unless you were expecting the file and are aware of its contents.
- Do not use disks copied from someone else's computer. Not only is this risking a virus, but also it could be a copyright infringement, depending on the disk's contents.
- Instead of clicking directly on links in an e-mail, type the address into your browser.
- Give out your e-mail address selectively.

List #194 Computer Maintenance Tips

- Create specific folders for your files and organize them by topic.
- Choose how you want your folders and files viewed. Some people may prefer to view only file names. On our computer, however, we prefer the preview mode. This saves time as we are working on various files.
- Delete programs, files, and folders you no longer need.
- Make and keep your computer secure.
- Perform regular computer maintenance (or hire someone to do this for you).
- Back up your files regularly.
- Copy important files to writable CDs. These are slim and easy to store.

List #195 How to Know If Your Computer Has a Virus

- Your computer is functioning slower than normal.
- It may be unresponsive.
- It may repeatedly crash.
- If it is very bad, you may see a blank screen when you boot up.

List #196 How to Be Safe From Scams

- Remember that the Internet makes it easy to spread fraudulent material, whether that is a scam, a hoax, an urban legend, or whatever.
- Criminals can obtain portions of your personal information and then send you an e-mail from a source that you believe to be legitimate, asking for additional information. Too frequently, people have provided this additional personal information, which then enables the criminals to steal your identity, your money, your credit, and more.
- If it sounds too good to be true, it most likely is. It's very unlikely that you're going to inherit money from a long-lost relative whom you don't remember. Don't succumb to the "get-rich-quick" schemes that come through e-mail or the "free vacation" type offers that pop up on the Internet. Many of these are scams.
- Never give your personal information to anyone via the computer unless you know who it is, why they need it, and that it is being sent via a secure site.
- Report suspicious e-mails to your Internet provider.
- Check the security certificate when you are sending personal information via web sites.
- Never send money for an "investment," for "up-front fees," or for other such charges.

List #197 If You Become a Victim of Fraud

- File a report with the local authorities. This is necessary so that you can file the police report with your bank and creditors so that they are aware of the situation.
- Notify your bank, credit card companies, and other creditors of the fraud.
- Contact one of the three credit bureaus in the United States and place a fraud alert on your credit reports. Request that no new credit charges or changes to your credit information be allowed. The three credit bureaus are:

  Equifax (800) 525-6285

  Experian (888) 397-3742

  TransUnion (800) 680-7289
- Review your credit card statements and a copy of your credit report carefully to make sure that no unauthorized charges have been made and no new accounts have been opened.
- Close any fraudulent accounts that have been opened in your name. Close any accounts that have been accessed by someone else without your authorization.
- If you have been a victim of fraud because you thought a genuine company contacted you and needed information and you gave it to them, contact that company yourself and tell them that someone is using their name for fraud.
- Change your passwords for any online accounts.
- File a complaint with the Federal Trade Commission (FTC). Their Identity Theft Hotline number is (877) 438-4338.
- Keep all records of your attempts to rectify the situation. You may need these records later.

List #198 Game Ratings

The Entertainment Software Rating Board (ESRB) was created to assign ratings to the content of video and computer games. The board is a nonprofit corporation. Below are the ratings they use and with which parents should be familiar. This list is especially useful if you have teenagers. (*Note to parents:* While you should familiarize yourself with these ratings and preferably educate your child about ratings that are appropriate for them, the content of this list, especially the content descriptors, is not appropriate for children.) For additional information about the ratings or the ESRB, visit their Web site at *www.esrb.org.*

Early Childhood
Titles rated EC (Early Childhood) have content that may be suitable for ages three and older. Contains no material that parents would find inappropriate.

Everyone
Titles rated E (Everyone) have content that may be suitable for ages six and older. Titles in this category may contain minimal cartoon, fantasy or mild violence, and/or infrequent use of mild language.

Everyone 10+
Titles rated E10+ (Everyone ten and older) have content that may be suitable for ages ten and older. Titles in this category may contain more cartoon, fantasy or mild violence, mild language, and/or minimal suggestive themes.

Teen
Titles rated T (Teen) have content that may be suitable for ages thirteen and older. Titles in this category may contain violence, suggestive themes, crude humor, minimal blood, simulated gambling, and/or infrequent use of strong language.

Mature
Titles rated M (Mature) have content that may be suitable for persons ages seventeen and older. Titles in this category may contain intense violence, blood and gore, sexual content, and/or strong language.

List #198 **Game Ratings** *(continued)*

Adults Only

Titles rated AO (Adults Only) have content that should only be played by persons eighteen years and older. Titles in this category may include prolonged scenes of intense violence and/or graphic sexual content and nudity.

Rating Pending

Titles listed as RP (Rating Pending) have been submitted to the ESRB and are awaiting final rating. (The symbol appears only in advertising prior to a game's release.)

ESRB Content Descriptors

Alcohol Reference	reference to and/or images of alcoholic beverages
Animated Blood	discolored and/or unrealistic depictions of blood
Blood	depictions of blood
Blood and Gore	depictions of blood or the mutilation of body parts
Cartoon Violence	violent actions involving cartoon-like situations and characters; may include violence where a character is unharmed after the action has been inflicted
Comic Mischief	depictions or dialogue involving slapstick or suggestive humor
Crude Humor	depictions or dialogue involving vulgar antics, including "bathroom" humor
Drug Reference	reference to and/or images of illegal drugs
Edutainment	content of product provides user with specific skills development or reinforcement learning within an entertainment setting; skill development is an integral part of product
Fantasy Violence	violent actions of a fantasy nature, involving human or non-human characters in situations easily distinguishable from real life
Informational	overall content of product contains data, facts, resource information, reference materials or instructional text
Intense Violence	graphic and realistic-looking depictions of physical conflict; may involve extreme and/or realistic blood, gore, weapons, and depictions of human injury and death
Language	mild to moderate use of profanity
Lyrics	mild references to profanity, sexuality, violence, alcohol, or drug use in music

List #198 **Game Ratings** *(continued)*

Mature Humor	depictions or dialogue involving "adult" humor, including sexual references
Mild Violence	mild scenes depicting characters in unsafe and/or violent situations
Nudity	graphic or prolonged depictions of nudity
Partial Nudity	brief and/or mild depictions of nudity
Real Gambling	player can gamble, including betting or wagering real cash or currency
Sexual Themes	mild to moderate sexual references and/or depictions; may include partial nudity
Sexual Violence	depictions of rape or other violent sexual acts
Simulated Gambling	player can gamble without betting or wagering real cash or currency
Some Adult Assistance May Be Needed	intended for very young ages
Strong Language	explicit and/or frequent use of profanity
Strong Lyrics	explicit and/or frequent references to profanity, sex, violence, alcohol, or drug use in music
Strong Sexual Content	graphic references to and/or depictions of sexual behavior, possibly including nudity
Suggestive Themes	mild provocative references or materials
Tobacco Reference	reference to and/or images of tobacco products
Use of Drugs	the consumption or use of illegal drugs
Use of Alcohol	the consumption of alcoholic beverages
Use of Tobacco	the consumption of tobacco products
Violence	scenes involving aggressive conflict

Online Rating Notice

Online games that include user-generated content (e.g., chat, maps, skins) carry the notice "Game Experience May Change During Online Play" to warn consumers that content created by players of the game has not been rated by the ESRB.

13

Art and Music

List #199 Types of Greek Columns

The use of architectural columns began in ancient Greece. The Greeks were expert builders and the design of their columns changed over time as their skills steadily improved. The three main Greek column types were Doric, Ionic, and Corinthian.

Doric: The Dorians were one of two Greek races who lived in the Greek homeland. Doric columns (to the right) were the preferred style in southern Italy. These columns were developed in 600 BC and were used to construct the Parthenon at Athens, Greece.

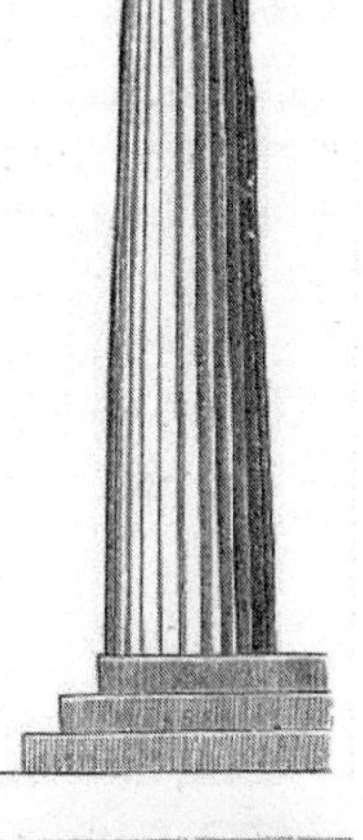

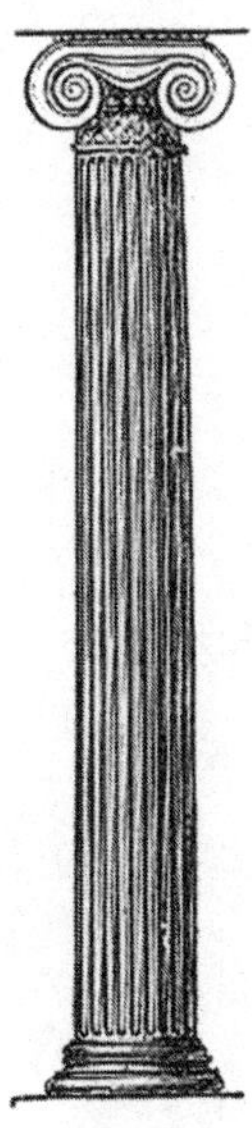

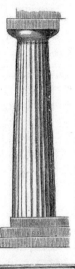

Ionic columns were more slender and had deeper shafts than the Doric columns. They were also more elaborate and ornate. An example appears to the left. Ionic columns can be seen on the Theater of Marcellus in Rome, Italy.

The most ornate, and most common, of the Greek columns were without a doubt the Corinthian style columns. These columns were more slender than their predecessors and had a more ornate base as well as a capital, or top, shown to the right. Corinthian columns can be found on the Temple of Mars Ultar.

The column drawings on this page were taken from A. Rosengarten's book *A Handbook of Architectural Styles,* printed in 1898. I would highly recommend this book for budding architects. Copies are difficult to come by because the book is out of print, but I found several online.

List #200 Types of Roman Columns

The Romans came up with their own version of columns, but basically they adapted Greek columns to suit their own needs and decorative desires. The three Greek styles and the two Roman styles form the ancient orders or styles of column architecture. These styles have been passed down through the centuries and still influence our architecture and design choices today.

The Roman Tuscan column was simpler than the Doric column. You can see on the Tuscan columns to the left that the design is very simple and there is basically no decoration at the base or the capital (top). This illustration comes from Andrea Palladio's *Quattro Libri di Architettura*, published in 1570.

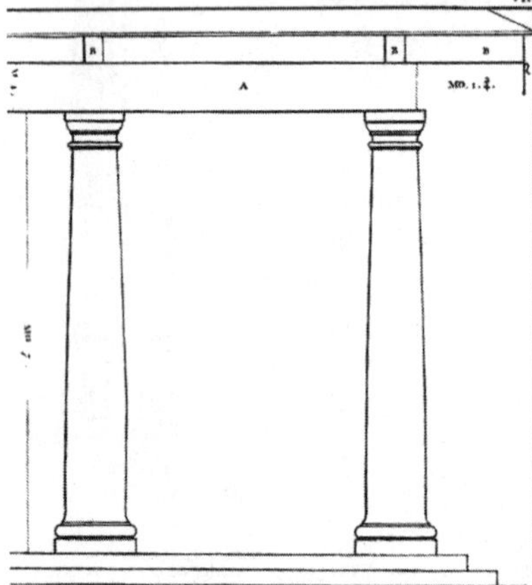

The Roman Composite, shown below, was more ornate than the Doric, which the Romans used to form the basic design of the Composite. This type of column used to be considered a Roman Corinthian column, but when the unique aspects, such as larger spirals at the top, were considered, they were branded a separate order during the Renaissance. The Arch of Titus in Rome has Composite order columns.

List #201 Art Supplies

If your child especially loves art, you may want to invest in more art supplies than the average household. Of course, supplies will vary depending on the type of art your child wants to pursue, so be creative and add to this list if you need to. Here are some supplies to consider:

acrylic paint
apron
blending stump
brushes (various sizes)
canvas (for oil painting)
clay
clay slicer
compressed charcoal
cotton rags (for cleanup)
dipping tongs (for pottery)
drawing pads
drawing pencils (high quality)
easel
graphite sticks
kiln
kneaded eraser
masking tape
modeling paste
oil paint
paddles (for pottery)
palette
palette knife
pencil sharpener
pot lifters (for pottery)
pottery wheel
sponge brushes
sponges (various types)
spray bottle (for water)
tempera paint
watercolor paint
watercolor paper
white drawing paper

List #202 Art Styles and Periods

Style	Description	Primary Artists or Major Works of Art From the Period
Classical Art	Greek and Roman art are included in this time period. Artistic endeavors included such work as architecture, sculpture, vase painting, art objects, and wall painting. The artists of this period focused on simple art with attention to detail, harmony, and proportion.	Greek—Lydos, Epiktetos, Pamphaios, Douris, Epimenes, Euphronios, Andokides, Euxitheos, Exekias, Oltos, Xenophantos, Myron, Phidias, and others
Romanesque Art (11th century; developed in France)	Many major works of architecture, including buildings with beautiful columns and arches, were completed during this period. Since these resemble ancient Roman buildings, the period was named "Romanesque."	Abbey of Pomposa, Durham Cathedral, Leaning Tower of Pisa, Cathedral of Salvador (Romanesque/Gothic), Fontenay Abbey
Gothic Art (1200s)	Also called the Age of the Cathedral, many magnificent cathedrals were built during this period. Other works of this period began to have a more graceful manner than had previously existed.	Chartres Cathedral and Cathedral of Notre Dame in Paris, Seville Cathedral, Cathedral of Milan
Renaissance Art (1400–1600)	The Rennaissance began in Italy. Classical forms were stressed, with an emphasis on scientific accuracy. The High Renaissance was from c. 1495–1520, during which such masters as Michelangelo, da Vinci, and Raphael created their great works of art.	Michelangelo, Leonardo da Vinci, Raphael; also German artists Hans Holbein, Albrecht Dürer
Baroque Art (1600–1790)	Perhaps opulence and grandeur best describe Baroque art. The art is characterized by strong emotions, vivid lighting and coloring, and sharp movement.	Holland—Rembrandt, Frans Hals, Johannes Vermeer; Flanders—Peter Paul Rubens, Anthony van Dyck, Jacob Jordaens; France—Nicolas Poussin, Claude Lorrain; Italy—Gianlorenzo Bernini, Caravaggio; Spain—Diego Velázquez

List #202 **Art Styles and Periods** *(continued)*

Style	Description	Primary Artists or Major Works of Art From the Period
Rococo Art (1700s; originated in France)	Strongly influenced by Baroque precedents, but the artists were trying to create something different by paying attention to elegance and creating decorative art rather than showing off with grandeur and elegance.	François Boucher, Jean-Honoré Fragonard, Antoine Watteau
Neoclassicism (late 1700s–early 1800s)	Influenced by Classical Art	Jacques-Louis David
Romanticism (late 1700s–mid-1800s)	The art of this period is known for richness in color, passionate subject matter, and bold portrayals. Focused on romantic subject matter and emotion over reason.	Eugène Delacroix, Théodore Géricault, J. M. W. Turner, William Blake
Realism (1800s)	This movement was particularly popular in France and included art that reflected artists' desire to depict the real world.	Gustave Courbet, Honoré Daumier, Jean- François Millet
Pre-Raphaelite Art (mid to late 1800s)	Art created by a group of English painters who rejected materialism of the Victorian era and were influenced by Reniassance painters prior to Raphael, who lived from 1483–1520.	Dante Gabriel Rossetti, William Morris, Edward Bume-Jones
Impressionism (1860–1900; originated in France)	Artist left viewer with a distinct impression of the scene and paintings were frequently scenes taken directly from nature.	Claude Monet, Auguste Renoir, Camille Pissarro
Post-Impressionism (1880–1905)	This style is referred to by some as art that was created by artists who didn't like the limits of Impressionism.	Paul Gauguin, Vincent van Gogh, Pierre Bonnard, Paul Cézanne
Symbolism (1880s–1890s)	While it drew on literature and poetry for inspiration, the artists of this period relied heavily on symbolism, with subject matter frequently suggested rather than actually presented.	Odilon Redon, Gustave Moreau

List #202 **Art Styles and Periods** *(continued)*

Style	Description	Primary Artists or Major Works of Art From the Period
Art Nouveau (late 1800s)	Artists in various fields (architecture, painting, pottery, etc.) used plants, flowing forms, and decorative patterns.	Alphonse Mucha, Hector Germain Guimard, Arthur Lasenby Liberty
Expressionism (early 1900s; particularly 1905–1925)	Artists used emphasis, distorted subject matter to communicate the emotion(s) they wished to convey.	Edvard Munch, Emil Nolde, Paul Klee, Wassily Kandinsky, Georges Rouault, Oskar Kokoschka, Egon Schiele
Cubism (early 1900s)	Artists of the Cubism movement believed that they should invent art, not copy it. The works from this period are certainly like no other.	Pablo Picasso, Georges Braque, Juan Gris, Fernand Leger
Dada (c. 1915–23)	This art form developed as a form of social and political protest.	Jean Arp, Marcel Duchamp
Surrealism (1920s–1930s; began in France)	The Surrealism movement is called such because it encouraged artists to explore the subconscious, often obtaining subject matter from images in dreams.	Salvador Dali, René Magritte, Joan Miró, Max Ernst
Art Deco (1920s–1930s)	Art was characterized by straight lines and slender forms rather than choppy edges.	René Lalique, Romain de Tirtoff, Adolphe Mouron Cassandre, Paul Manship; New York's Chrysler Building and Empire State Building

Note: There is a really neat Web site that has architectural examples of art styles and other interesting information at *www.greatbuildings.com*. Check it out.

List #203 Additional Art Styles

If your child is really into art, have her do a unit study on some of the art styles listed below. The most commonly referenced art styles are listed in the previous chart, but this list contains additional art styles that may interest your child. (*A note to parents:* I would recommend that any parent closely supervise the study of any art topics taken on by students. Many contain quite liberal concepts, controversial subject matter, and even offensive artwork. The study of art is worthy but should be undertaken with caution for your child's sake.)

- Abstract
- Baroque
- Constructivism
- Fauvism
- Graffiti
- Hard-Edge
- Mannerism
- Modernism
- Naïve Art
- Op-Art
- Orientalism
- Pointillism
- Pop-Art
- Postmodernism
- Socialist Realism

List #204 Old Masters

The great European painters who lived in the sixteenth through nineteenth centuries are known as Old Masters. In addition, a painting by one of these painters can be referred to as an Old Master. This is a sampling of Old Master painters, their nationality, and the dates they lived. This list will be especially useful if you would like to incorporate art study into a unit study about another topic or into any other study you are completing, such as historical studies.

Name	Nationality	Lived
Pieter Bruegel the Elder	Flemish	c. 1525–1569
Caravaggio	Italian	1573–1610
Leonardo da Vinci	Italian	1452–1519
Albrecht Dürer	German	1471–1528
El Greco	Greek	1541–1614
Frans Hals	Dutch	1580–1666
Michelangelo	Italian	1475–1564
Nicolas Poussin	French	1594–1665
Raphael	Italian	1480–1520
Peter Paul Rubens	Flemish	1577–1640
Giovanni Battista Tiepolo	Italian	1691–1770
Jacopo Tintoretto	Italian	1518–1594
Titian	Italian	c. 1477–1576
Diego Velázquez	Spanish	1599–1660
Johannes Vermeer	Dutch	1632–1675
Paolo Veronese	Italian	c. 1528–1588

List #205 Renowned Artists of Various Periods

Name	Dates	Nationality	Names of Major Works
Bierstadt, Albert	1830–1902	American	Rocky Mountains; Landers' Peak; Mountains in the Mist
Bouguereau, Adolphe-William	1825–1905	French	First Kiss; Birth of Venus
Bruegel, Pieter, the Elder	c. 1525–1569	Flemish	Tower of Babel
Buonarotti, Michelangelo	1475–1564	Italian	Sistine Chapel; David
Caravaggio	1573–1610	Italian	Calling of Saint Matthew; Supper at Emmaus
Cézanne, Paul	1839–1906	French	Cardplayers; Great Bathers
Chagall, Marc	1887–1932	Russian	Over Vitebsk; The Violinist; The Praying Jew; I and the Village
Dali, Salvador	1904–1989	Spanish	The Persistence of Memory; Crucifixion; The Sacrament of the Last Supper
David, Jacques Louis	1748–1825	French	Death of Socrates; Death of Morat
da Vinci, Leonardo	1452–1519	Italian	Mona Lisa; The Last Supper; Madonna and Child; The Virgin of the Rocks
Degas, Edgar	1834–1917	French	Dance Class
Escher, M. C.	1898–1972	Dutch	Relativity; Reptiles
Gainsborough, Thomas	1727–1788	English	Blue Boy
Gauguin, Paul	1848–1903	French	Riders on the Beach
Geddes, Anne	1956–	Australian	baby photographs
Goya, Francisco	1746–1828	Spanish	Third of May 1808
Homer, Winslow	1836–1910	American	Snap-the-Whip
Kandinsky, Wassily	1866–1944	Russian	Upwards
Klee, Paul	1887–1940	Swiss	Fish Magic; Around the Fish; Landscape with Yellow Birds
Manet, Edouard	1832–1883	French	Luncheon on the Grass; Olympia
Matisse, Henri	1869–1954	French	Chapel of the Rosary in Venice; The Snail; Beasts of the Sea; Creole Dancer; La Fougère Noire
Monet, Claude	1840–1926	French	Morning Haze; Marine Near Etretat; Lily Pond

List #205 **Renowned Artists of Various Periods** *(continued)*

Name	Dates	Nationality	Names of Major Works
Munch, Edvard	1863–1944	Norwegian	The Sick Child; Love and Pain; The Scream
Picasso, Pablo	1881–1973	Spanish	Guernica; Three Musicians; The Three Dancers; Self-Portrait: Yo Picasso
Pollock, Jackson	1912–1956	American	No. 5, 1948
Raphael	1483–1520	Italian	Madonna dell Granduca; School of Athens; The Nymph Galatea
Rembrandt	1606–1669	Dutch	Passion of Christ; Angel Appearing to the Shepherds
Renoir, Pierre-Auguste	1841–1919	French	Le Bal au Moulin de la Galette; Jeanne Samary; Bathers; The Swing
Rockwell, Norman	1894–1978	American	*Saturday Evening Post* covers; Sunset; Four Freedoms; Bottom of the Sixth
Rousseau, Henri	1844–1910	French	The Sleeping Gypsy; The Happy Quartet; Jungle With a Lion
Rubens, Peter Paul	1577–1640	Belgian	Portrait of a Young Man
Seurat, Georges	1859–1891	French	Sunday Afternoon on the Island of La Grande Jatte
de Toulouse-Lautrec, Henri	1864–1901	French	Portrait of Vincent Van Gogh; Moulin-Rouge; At the Moulin-Rouge; The Jockey
Titian (Tiziano Vecelli)	1488–1576	Italian	Assumption; Worship of Venus; Resurrection of Christ
Van Gogh, Vincent	1853–1890	Dutch	The Starry Night; Wheatfield With Crows
Vermeer, Johannes	1632–1675	Dutch	Girl With a Pearl Earring
Warhol, Andy	1928–1987	American	Andy Warhol is famous for painting the Campbell's soup can label paintings.

List #206 Instruments in an Orchestra

Strings

Violin, Viola, Cello, Bass

Winds

Piccolo, Flute, Oboe, Clarinet, Bassoon, Trumpet, Horn, Trombone, Tuba

Percussion

Timpani, Snare Drum, Bass Drum, Cymbals, Bells, Piano, various other percussion/rhythm instruments, such as Triangle, Maracas, Wood block, etc.

List #207 Instruments in a Band

Woodwinds

Piccolo, Flute, Oboe, Clarinet, Saxophone (Alto, Tenor, Baritone), Bassoon

Brass

Trumpet, Horn, Trombone, Baritone, Tuba

Percussion

Timpani, Snare Drum, Bass Drum, Cymbals, Bells, various other percussion/rhythm instruments, such as Triangle, Maracas, Wood block, etc.

List #208 Types of Smaller Musical Ensembles

Solo	one musician
Duet	two musicians
Trio	three musicians
Quartet	four musicians
Quintet	five musicians
Sextet	six musicians
Wind Quintet (or Woodwind Quintet)	Flute, Oboe, Clarinet, Horn, Bassoon
Chamber Orchestra	smaller than a regular orchestra, and often members play Baroque-style period instruments and/or Baroque pieces of music

List #209 Vocal Parts

Soprano Mezzo-Soprano Alto Contralto Tenor Baritone Bass

List #210 How to Remember Treble Clef Notes

Line notes E (*Every*), G (*Good*), B (*Boy*), D (*Does*), F (*Fine*)
Space notes F, A, C, E (spells the word *face*)

List #211 How to Remember Bass Clef Notes

Line notes G (*Good*), B (*Boys*), D (*Do*), F (*Fine*), A (*Always*)
Space notes A, C, E, G

List #212 Order of Flats

B-flat, E-flat, A-flat, D-flat, G-flat, C-flat, F-flat

List #213 Order of Sharps

F-sharp, C-sharp, G-sharp, D-sharp, A-sharp, E-sharp, B-sharp

List #214 Musical Terms

Word or Phrase	Definition	Borrowed From What Language
A tempo	return to the original tempo	Italian
Ad libitum	at the performer's pleasure	Latin
Adagio	slow	Italian
Allegretto	slower than *allegro*	Italian
Allegro	quick or lively	Italian
Andante	a moderate tempo or walking pace	Italian
Andantino	a quicker tempo than *andante*	Italian
Animato	animated	Italian
Ben marcato	well marked	Italian
Con anima	with animation	Italian
Con brio	with spirit or force	Italian
Con espressione	with expression	Italian
Con grazia	with grace	Italian
Con moto	with movement	Italian
Con spirito	with spirit or energy	Italian
Crescendo	gradually growing louder	Italian
Decrescendo	gradually growing softer	Italian
Diminuendo	gradually growing softer	Italian
Dolce	softly or sweetly	Italian
Energico	energetic	Italian
Forte (*f*)	loudly	Italian
Fortissimo (*ff*)	very loudly	Italian
Grazioso	gracefully, elegantly	Italian
Largo	slowly, broadly	Italian
Legato	continuous or smooth flowing	Italian
Lento	slowly	Italian
Maestoso	with dignity or majesty	Italian
Marcato	distinct or emphasized; literally "marked"	Italian
Meno mosso	with less speed	Italian
Mesto	mournfully or sadly	Italian
Meter	pattern of rhythm	Italian
Mezza voce	half voice (medium volume)	Italian

List #214 **Musical Terms** *(continued)*

Word or Phrase	Definition	Borrowed From What Language
Mezzo forte (*mf*)	half loudly (moderately loud)	Italian
Mezzo piano (*mp*)	half softly (moderately soft)	Italian
Peu à peu	little by little	French
Piano (*p*)	softly	Italian
Pianissimo (*pp*)	very softly	Italian
Più	more	Italian
Rallentando (*rall.*)	becoming progressively slower	Italian
Rapido	quickly	Italian
Repente	suddenly	Italian
Restez	stay on a note or string	French
Semplice	simply	Italian
Sforzando	with particular emphasis	Italian
Sostenuto	sustained	Italian
Tempo	the pace or speed of a piece of music	Italian
Tranquillamente	calmly or quietly	Italian
Vivace	very lively	Italian
Vivo	lively	Italian

List #215 Music in Nature

Whether you study music regularly or just started lessons, music can actually be found all around you every day in nature. God was the first great composer. Listed below are some of the musical sounds of nature that you can hear with your children. (In today's industrial society, you might have to make a concerted effort to take your child into the country or to a national park to hear some of this beautiful "music.") Discuss with your children the differences in the sounds and how God's music differs from our own. Music-related activities can be particularly fun and intriguing for children who have special needs.

water rushing through creeks or rivers
a waterfall
ocean waves crashing against the shore
rain (on a metal roof, falling through trees, sprinkling into a pond, etc.)
frogs croaking in a pond
birds chirping in the trees
ducks quacking by a lake
geese honking as they fly overhead
cicadas mating
male grasshoppers looking for a female
the musical katydids
crickets calling on a summer night
elephants trumpeting
thunder booming
fire crackling
wolves howling
owls hooting
whale sounds
mosquitos humming
chipmunks chattering
horses neighing
bees buzzing
cows mooing
water dripping from wet leaves
autumn leaves crunching underfoot

Can your child hear other sounds that aren't listed above? Can you help him identify the source? Are the sounds of nature peaceful? Why?

List #216 Patriotic Songs

Children who attend public or private schools are usually exposed to the traditional patriotic songs of our country through some sort of music class. For children taught at home, it is a good idea for parents to make a concerted effort to see that children are not only exposed to these songs, but that they recognize the tunes and memorize the lyrics for the sake of patriotism. I would also recommend studying biographies of the songwriters.

Song	Songwriter	When Song Was Written
America (This was written to the music of the most popular tune in history, even though author Samuel Francis Smith did not know it at the time.)	Samuel Francis Smith	February 1831
America the Beautiful (Writer was inspired with words of this song during a visit to Pike's Peak.)	Katherine Lee Bates	summer 1893
Battle Hymn of the Republic (Lyrics are from a poem that appeared in *Atlantic Monthly* in 1861.)	Julia Ward Howe	1861
Dixie (Written a day prior to a New York City minstrel show in which it was to debut.)	Daniel Emmett	April 3, 1859
God Bless America (Originally written in 1918, but Berlin changed wording slightly to be a patriotic song for America as it prepared to join World War II.)	Irving Berlin	1918 and in 1938 (slight changes)
The Star-Spangled Banner (On March 3, 1931, President Herbert Hoover signed a law making this song our national anthem.)	Francis Scott Key (to a popular tune of that day that had probably been written by John Stafford Smith)	September 1814 (during War of 1812 after British bombed Fort McHenry)
Yankee Doodle (Reportedly written by an Englishman for American troops during the French and Indian War, the Americans turned around to claim this song during the Revolutionary War.)	Dr. Richard Shuckburg	1755

List #216 **Patriotic Songs** *(continued)*

Song	Songwriter	When Song Was Written
When Johnny Comes Marching Home (Patrick Gilmore, bandmaster of the Union Army, is usually given credit for writing the words to this song, although there was another version entitled *Johnny, I Hardly Knew Ye,* and no one knows for certain which came first.)	Patrick S. Gilmore	1863

The information for this list has been obtained from several sources, but the best by far is *America the Beautiful: Stories of Patriotic Songs* by Robert Kraske. This book was published in 1972 by Garrard Publishing. It goes into detail on only a few songs, but the stories are worth reading. There are also several Internet sites that feature stories of songs, the best of those being *www.contemplator.com*.

List #217 Musical Periods and Major Composers

Middle Ages	450 AD–1450	Gregorian Chants
Renaissance	1400–1600	Palestrina, Marenzio, des Prez
Baroque Era	1580–1750	Bach, Handel, Vivaldi
Classical Era	1750–1830	Mozart, Haydn, Beethoven
Romantic Era	1830–1900	Beethoven, Chopin, Wagner
Twentieth Century	1900–2000	Copland, Stravinsky, Debussy

List #218 Renowned Composers

The compositions listed have been chosen because they are the better known ones from these particular composers. You can teach your child to recognize the names of composers, the time period in which they lived, and the compositions they created. One good way to do this is to obtain music by that composer and play it every day as background music while the child plays, in the car as you run errands, and as he goes to sleep at night, over a period of a week or two. Each time you play the music, casually ask the child to tell you again who the composer is. Gradually add more composers (one at a time) and occasionally throw in a work by one of the composers you've already studied to help your child learn the music of the master musicians. Additional well-known composers are found in list #219.

Birth/Death Dates	Composer	Samples of Famous Compositions
1685–1750	Johann Sebastian Bach	Mass in B Minor, St. Matthew Passion, St. John Passion, The Art of the Fugue
1685–1759	Georg Friedrich Handel	Organ Concertos (1–12), Messiah, The Passion of Christ, Water Music (suite for a full orchestra)
1732–1809	Franz Joseph Haydn	Arianna a Naxos, Children's Symphony, The Creation, The Seasons, Surprise Symphony, The Ten Commandments
1756–1791	Wolfgang Amadeus Mozart	Don Giovanni, Eine Kleine Nachtmusik, Prague Symphony, Requiem, Symphony in G Minor, The Magic Flute, The Marriage of Figaro
1770–1827	Ludwig van Beethoven	Christ on the Mount of Olives, Mass in C, Mass in D (Missa Solemnis), Ninth Symphony, Pastoral
1797–1828	Franz Schubert	Der Wanderer, Die schöne Müllerin, Die Winterreise, Erlkönig, Gretchen am Spinnrade, Heidenröslein, Moments Musicales, Schwannengesang, Unfinished Symphony
1809–1847	Felix Mendelssohn	Elijah, Lobgesang, Overture to A Midsummer Night's Dream, Songs without Words, Symphonies in C minor, A minor, A major, and D major
1809–1849	Frederic François Chopin	Etudes for Piano (Series I and II), Sonata, other songs, ballads, waltzes, etc.
1810–1856	Robert Schumann	Carnaval, Concerto in A minor, Faust, Genoveva, Papillons, Paradise and the Peri, Requiem for Mignon

List #218 **Renowned Composers** *(continued)*

Birth/Death Dates	Composer	Samples of Famous Compositions
1811–1885	Franz Liszt	Dante, Faust, Hamlet, Orpheus, Piano Concerto No. 1, Piano Concerto No. 2, Prometheus, St. Frances Walking on the Water, Todtentanz (Dance of Death)
1813–1883	Wilhelm Richard Wagner	Der fliegende Holländer, Der Ring das Nibelungen (Das Rheingold, Die Valkyrie, Siegfried, Götterdämmerung), Parsifal
1813–1901	Giuseppe Verdi	Ave Maria, Ernani, Falstaff, Giovanna d'Arco (Joan of Arc), I Lombardi, Il Trovatore, Jerusalem, La Traviata, Macbeth, Othello, Pater Noster, Requiem, Songs in Praise of the Virgin, String Quartet
1818–1893	Charles François Gounod	Faust, Funeral March of a Marionette, La Nonne Sanglante, Mass in G, Meditation, Nazareth, Philemon and Baucis, Romeo and Juliet, Sappho, Ulysse
1833–1897	Johannes Brahms	Academic Festival Overture, German Requiem, Rinaldo, Rhapsody, Tragic Overture, Triumphlied
1840–1893	Peter Ilich Tchaikovsky	Coronation Cantata, Francesca da Rimini, Hamlet, Italian Caprice, Manfred, Romeo and Juliet, Sleeping Beauty, Snow Maiden, Symphonie Pathétique, The Lake of the Swans, The Nutcracker Suite, The Tempest
1844–1908	Nikolay Rimsky-Korsakov	Christmas Eve, Easter Overture, Kashtchei, Sadko, Serbian Fantasy, Snyegoorotchka (Snow Maiden), Spanish Caprice, The Czar's Bride
1858–1924	Giacomo Puccini	Edgar, Gianni Schicchi, Hymn to Rome, La Bohème, Le Villi, Sinfonia Capriccio, The Girl of the Golden West, The Swallow, Turandot
1862–1918	Claude-Achille Debussy	Arabesques, Clair de Lune, Hommage à Rameau, Jardins Sous la Pluie, La Mer, Le Martyre de Saint-Sébastien, L'Enfant Prodigue
1865–1957	Jean Sibelius	Belshazzar's Feast, En Saag, Finlandia, Kullervo, Scènes Historiques, Tapiola, Valse Triste
1882–1971	Igor Stravinsky	Apollon Musagète, Japanese Lyrics, Les Noces, L'Historie d'un Soldat, Mavra, Octet for Winds, Oedipus, Petrushka, Symphony of Psalms

List #219 Additional Composers

After your child has mastered the Renowned Composers list (#218), choose additional composers to study from the following list:

Isaac Albeniz
John Barry
Georges Bizet
Luigi Boccherini
William Byrd
Antonin Dvorak
Edvard Grieg
Scott Joplin
György Ligeti
Gustav Mahler
Ennio Morricone
Johann Pachelbel
Sergei Prokofiev
Henry Purcell
Erik Satie
Franz Schubert
Dmitri Shostakovich
Fernando Sor
Richard Strauss
Thomas Tallis
Yann Tiersen
Dimitri Tiomkin
Andrew Lloyd Webber
John Williams
Hans Zimmer

List #220 Poetry

This list includes introductory lyrics of some of the most well-known poems ever written, as well as two entire poems (by Sappho and by Sir Walter Raleigh). Although they are now in the public domain, our goal is not to take advantage of the poets' work but to expose these wonderful pieces so that you can further investigate their writing.

Blow, Blow, Thou Winter Wind

Shakespeare

Blow, blow, thou winter wind,
Thou art not so unkind
As man's ingratitude;
Thy tooth is not so keen. . . .

How Do I Love Thee?

Elizabeth Barrett Browning

How do I love thee? Let me count the ways.
I love thee to the depth and breadth and height
My soul can reach, when feeling out of sight
For the ends of Being and ideal Grace. . . .

Lochinvar

Sir Walter Scott

Oh! young Lochinvar is come out of the west,
Through all the wide Border his steed was the best;
And save his good broadsword he weapons had none.
He rode all unarmed and he rode all alone. . . .

My Native Land

Sir Walter Scott

Breathes there the man, with soul so dead,
Who never to himself hath said,
This is my own, my native land!
Whose heart hath ne'er within him burn'd. . . .

Without Warning

Sappho

Without warning
as a whirlwind
swoops on an oak
Love shakes my heart

List #220 **Poetry** *(continued)*

Seven Ages of Man

William Shakespeare

All the world's a stage,
And all the men and women merely players,
They have their exits and entrances,
And one man in his time plays many parts. . . .

Dust of Snow

Robert Frost

The way a crow
Shook down on me
The dust of snow
From a hemlock tree. . . .

A Vision Upon the Fairy Queen

Sir Walter Raleigh

Methought I saw the grave where Laura lay,
Within that temple where the vestal flame
Was wont to burn; and, passing by that way,
To see that buried dust of living fame,
Whose tomb fair Love, and fairer Virtue kept:
All suddenly I saw the Fairy Queen;
At whose approach the soul of Petrarch wept,
And, from thenceforth, those Graces were not seen:
For they this queen attended; in whose stead
Oblivion laid him down on Laura's hearse:
Hereat the hardest stones were seen to bleed,
And groans of buried ghosts the heavens did pierce:
Where Homer's spright did tremble all for grief,
And cursed the access of that celestial thief!

Because I Could Not Stop for Death

Emily Dickinson

Because I could not stop for Death—
He kindly stopped for me—
The Carriage held but just Ourselves—
And Immortality. . . .

List #220 **Poetry** *(continued)*

Believe Me, If All Those Endearing Young Charms

Thomas Moore

Believe me, if all those endearing young charms,
Which I gaze on so fondly today,
Were to change by tomorrow, and fleet in my arms,
Like fairy-gifts fading away,
Thou wouldst still be adored, as this moment thou art,
Let thy loveliness fade as it will,
And around the dear ruin each wish of my heart
Would entwine itself verdantly still. . . .

List #221 Poets

If your child likes poetry, or if you want to supplement your regular studies with poetry, consider one of the following poets or a collection that contains poetry by several of these well-known poets.

Hilaire Belloc
William Blake
Elizabeth Barrett Browning
Robert Browning
Robert Burns
Lord Byron
Lewis Carroll
Samuel Taylor Coleridge
Emily Dickinson
John Donne
Robert Frost
Thomas Hardy
Robert Herrick
John Keats
Rudyard Kipling
Henry Wadsworth Longfellow
Edgar Allan Poe
Robert Louis Stevenson
Sarah Teasdale
Lord Alfred Tennyson
Walt Whitman
William Wordsworth
William Butler Yeats

14

Curriculum and Homeschool Methodologies

List #222 Various School Settings

Primary school and secondary school divisions will vary depending on the area of the country. For the purpose of this list, the definitions cover kindergarten through twelfth grade.

Type of School	Definition
Boarding	In this setting students receive meals and lodging as well as educational instruction.
Catholic	a school founded with Catholic principles and beliefs
Charter	Charter schools that receive public funding, but are privately run by parents, teachers, and companies who support the mission of the school.
Christian	a school founded with Christian principles
Church	a school sponsored by a particular church
Co-op	Short for “cooperative education,” this is a school setting in which one or more families come together to share the responsibilities and work together with the common goal of educating the children in the co-op. This type of educational setting is becoming common among homeschoolers in order to provide training in areas where other parents have more expertise, to allow the children to participate in group activities such as sports, and to encourage fellowship.
Finishing	a school in which the fine graces of young womanhood, social skills, academics, and the arts are taught to girls, usually those approaching college age
Home: through church-related school	Parents educate their own children while being registered with a church-related school (sometimes called an “umbrella school”).
Home: through local school system	Parents educate their own children while being registered with the local superintendent’s office or local office of education.
Magnet	These schools are basically like public schools with one big difference: they specialize in particular subjects or subject areas (such as fine arts or foreign languages).
Military	a school run by the military, which is particularly good for students who plan for a commission into the armed forces
Montessori	Based on the teachings of Italian educator Maria Montessori, this educational setting is patterned after the “Montessori method,” which includes a lot of hands-on activities and independent learning.
Parochial	founded and maintained by a religious organization such as a church
Private	founded and maintained by a private organization
Public	a school that is funded by public expense, usually through property taxes and taxes to the state and federal governments

List #222 **Various School Settings** *(continued)*

Type of School	Definition
Reformatory	This is somewhat like a detention program, but in general is a school for boys or girls who have been in some kind of trouble. In this school setting they not only learn academics but also "reform" by learning positive skills related to work, behavior, social interaction, and anger management.
Satellite	In this school setting, students learn via satellite from teachers whose lessons are broadcast to classrooms or homes. This is a popular option for many homeschoolers, particularly those families with several children to teach or with students in more advanced high school courses.

List #223 Popular Homeschool Methods

Method	Philosophy / Methodology
Charlotte Mason Method	Charlotte Mason, a Christian educator in Britain in the late 1800s, was a hands-on educator who believed in giving children the tools that would guide them throughout life. She did this by encouraging "living books," whole books, and firsthand sources for children rather than reading secondhand material from textbooks. The Charlotte Mason Method encourages the reading of entire books, particularly the classics and other great books, either by or to the children. Also encouraged is narration—allowing a child to relate back what he or she has read or heard from a book. There is no homework and there is lots of free time for children to run, climb, play, and enjoy leisure hours in the various activities of childhood. **How to use *The Homeschooler's Book of Lists* with the Charlotte Mason Method:** Since whole books and life experiences are encouraged, use the charts and lists in this book for reference, such as the recommended reading lists. If you are reading Greek myths and your child wants to know more about the gods, post in your home the lists of Greek and Roman gods while you are enjoying the myths connected to each of them. Though Charlotte Mason didn't advocate memorization, she did encourage copy work. Any of the lists in the book can be used for copy work. Also, some people combine education methods. You may want to use *The Homeschooler's Book of Lists* as reference material for the parent-teacher only or use the lists to supplement the Charlotte Mason Method with some required memorization—such as Bible verses—or a quick-reference guide for the student.
Classical Education	Focus is placed on guiding the child through the three stages of the Trivium: grammar, dialectic or logic, and rhetoric. The content in each stage of learning is suited to the child's mental abilities at particular ages. During the grammar period (early childhood), for example, the child memorizes large amounts of material, including multiplication facts, dates, classification, etc., even though he may not understand the significance of this material. During the dialectic period (ages 12–14), the child actually begins to understand what he or she has learned and then uses reason to ask questions about the topics. From ages 14 to 16, the child begins to develop the ability to form persuasive arguments. **How to use *The Homeschooler's Book of Lists* in a Classical Education:** The teacher who desires to provide a classical education to his or her pupils can benefit greatly from this book. Throughout the elementary and middle school journey, lists can be used to provide the foundation of a classical education. Copy or print out lists for your student for the current topic(s) of concentration and have the student memorize portions of each list based on age level and ability. As the student progresses through the stages, use the lists as a starting point for further research.

List #223 **Popular Homeschool Methods** *(continued)*

Method	Philosophy / Methodology
DVD/Video School	There is a growing trend of students, particularly high-schoolers, who use DVD or video courses as their primary source of learning. This is particularly helpful to parents who want to teach their children at home but they can't devote the necessary time each day or the subject matter is over their heads. It is important to know that these parents are still available for their child's questions, but the DVD or video courses provide a good foundation of knowledge for that child. **How to use *The Homeschooler's Book of Lists* if your child does DVD/Video School:** Allow the child to have access to the book, especially if he is an independent learner. He may enjoy looking up much of the resource information for himself.
Eclectic Method	Most homeschoolers fall into the category of using a variety of curriculum, books, and methods. This in itself is a method: the "eclectic method" of homeschooling. Basically, eclectic homeschoolers use a little of everything. This might include workbooks for math, copy work or memorization for studying the Bible, living books for read-alouds, and plenty of freedom to make changes. Eclectic homeschoolers frequently participate in outside classes, field trips, and clubs to round out their child's education. This method allows parents to choose the best of everything. The only real disadvantage is that some parents become overwhelmed with all the choices and the lack of structure. This can be corrected with some effort. **How to use *The Homeschooler's Book of Lists* with the Eclectic Method:** Use the lists to answer questions or as a starting point to decide what to study next. Homeschoolers who prefer the eclectic method also frequently choose a certain amount of memorization, for which the lists are extremely helpful.
Internet / Computer Courses	Many homeschoolers use Internet- or computer-based courses for their education. These can be particularly helpful if you have a child who learns best in a multisensory manner—eyes to see the screen, ears to listen to audio input, and hands to operate the mouse and keyboard. Internet and computer courses aren't necessarily ideal for all your child's educational work, since sitting in front of a computer screen for hours at a time can be hard on the eyes, but these courses can be beneficial sometimes. **How to use *The Homeschooler's Book of Lists* if your child does mostly Internet or Computer Courses:** You can answer your child's questions with this book, use the checklists, and also allow your child to browse through the topics to find subjects he is interested in studying. There are also notes throughout the book of great Web sites that you will find useful.

List #223 **Popular Homeschool Methods** *(continued)*

Method	Philosophy / Methodology
Montessori Method	Maria Montessori wanted children to be children. She allowed them to explore, play, and pretend, and discouraged traditional "schooling" techniques of testing and competition. This Montessori Method works especially well for preschool or elementary-level children. The method encourages independence and freedom with responsibility. This means that parents are to provide children with a learning environment and guide them through their educational journey. For more details, you might consider borrowing or buying a copy of the guidebook for the Montessori method: *The Montessori Way* by Tim Seldin and Paul Epstein (available through the Montessori Foundation Web site at *www.montessori-foundation-books.org*). **How to use *The Homeschooler's Book of Lists* with the Montessori Method:** Given the right tools, children can learn a good amount of material. While you may not want to "require" memorization of the lists with the Montessori method, this certainly doesn't mean you can't provide children with copies of lists to study at their own leisure, particularly if they are interested in a specific topic (space flights, animals at risk of extinction, etc.).
School-at-Home	Some families choose to recreate the traditional school environment at home. This might include desks, textbooks, grades, a strict schedule, and record keeping. You can purchase a complete prepackaged curriculum, make up your own lesson plans, or use several different types of curriculum. Either way, the school-at-home method may cause more stress for some families who do not realize that one advantage of homeschooling is the flexibility to do it your own way. For some families, though, the extra scheduling may be just what they need to achieve their homeschool goals. **How to use *The Homeschooler's Book of Lists* if you recreate traditional school at home:** Supplement any curriculum with the lists in this book or use the lists to help you design your own curriculum. Either way, print out each list that pertains to the subject you are studying and provide handouts to your students. Later, test them on the material.
Unit Studies	With unit studies, all the subjects are taught with a given theme for a period of time. Unit study topics might include animals; a virtue, such as patience; a show, such as *Little House on the Prairie;* or even a book, such as *Little Women*. For a unit study on ancient Rome, for example, the student would study biographies of people such as Julius Caesar (biographical studies), the history of ancient Rome (history), Roman numerals (mathematics), the politics of ancient Romans (government), and Latin (language). There are numerous ways to incorporate various subjects into each unit study. **How to use *The Homeschooler's Book of Lists* for Unit Studies:** Ideas for unit studies are found throughout this book. Also find lists in each chapter to go with your unit study topics. This will save you a lot of time and energy and will enable you to plan your own unit studies at home.
Unschooling	This method of homeschooling is child-directed. The child follows his or her own academic and extracurricular interests. **How Unschoolers can use *The Homeschooler's Book of Lists*:** Just give the child this book, and he will find plenty to interest him!

List #223 **Popular Homeschool Methods** *(continued)*

Method	Philosophy / Methodology
Waldorf Education	Rudolf Steiner, an Austrian philosopher, scientist, and artist, gave a series of lectures at the Waldorf-Astoria cigarette factory in Stuttgart, Germany, in 1919. The factory's owner asked Steiner to establish and lead a school for the factory employees' children. The Free Waldorf School opened in September of that same year. While the Waldorf schools have classroom settings like traditional schools, they are different in that they emphasize the arts, music, creativity, storytelling, and freethinking. For homeschool parents, a Waldorf education is still obtainable. Pre-academics with music, art, and creative play are encouraged in the early years and academic study begins after grade one. Students are encouraged to seek answers for themselves. Waldorf curriculum is available online and there are also Waldorf education support groups. **How to use *The Homeschooler's Book of Lists* with a Waldorf Education:** Use the lists to help you find good-quality stories to read aloud to your child. Pick a list to read out loud and allow students to make associations or write journal entries about the subject matter. The Foreign Language chapter (chapter 9) is very useful for introducing languages to young children, which is a fundamental aspect of the Waldorf methodology. Of course, parents can use the book to look up answers to their students' questions.

For additional information about the methods of teaching your children at home, I would recommend Paul and Gena Suarez's book *Homeschooling Methods*, published by Broadman & Holman Publishers in 2006.

Curriculum Overview

With literally hundreds of curriculum options available to students who learn at home, it would be difficult in any book to list them all. Lists #224–230 focus on the top curricula for each subject area. These lists are based on many years of personal experience plus the recommendations of other veteran home educators. Because there are so many other books available on the topic of curricula specifically, I list only those with which I have had the most success. If you would like more in-depth information on specific curricula, talk with others who have used the products or check out a curriculum-review book such as Cathy Duffy's *100 Top Picks for Homeschool Curriculum* (B&H Publishing).

List #224 Comprehensive Curricula

While the other lists in this Curriculum section are divided by subject, the companies listed here provide packages for children of various grade levels with multiple subject options. If you're looking for supplemental material for a particular subject, try one of the other curriculum lists for a recommendation, but if you would like to purchase curriculum from one supplier, you can do that with the companies in this list. One of the great things to keep in mind about most of the companies that sell homeschool curriculum is that their founders started out just like you and me—teaching their children in their own home. Usually the parents saw a need and created a way to meet that need.

Sonlight Curriculum, 8042 South Grant Way, Littleton, CO 80122-2705, (303) 730-6292, *www.sonlight.com*

Sonlight provides literature-based curricula with an international focus, which is especially terrific if you want to expose your children to a larger Christian worldview with a focus on missions. They have materials for ages four through eighteen in all the major subjects, plus many elective subjects. I especially love Sonlight's emphasis on history and missions.

Veritas Press, 1829 William Penn Way, Lancaster, PA 17601, (800) 922-5082, *www.veritaspress.com*

The mission of Veritas Press is to provide top-quality materials for classical Christian education. They have many original educational materials, such as a program to teach children how to learn 160 history events and 160 biblical events in five years.

Calvert Education Services, 10713 Gilroy Road, Suite B, Hunt Valley, MD 21031, (888) 487-4652

Calvert offers complete curricula for preschool through eighth grade. Though I've never had the pleasure of using Calvert myself, I have friends that have. I've looked through their materials and Calvert seems to have a good mix of reading and workbooks rather than just one or the other. Another wonderful feature is that in addition to all the necessary subjects, they also integrate frequently overlooked subjects, such as art and poetry, in their curriculum packages. Although the materials can be a little costly, the academic program is comparable to a private school program and it's certainly much more economical.

List #225 For Younger Children

I hesitate to list anything here because one of the best things about homeschooling is the fact that younger children are allowed to play and not be stuck in front of a desk or table with worksheets half the day. With that said, and considering the fact that our youngest two children begged to "do schoolwork" long before we were ready for them to begin, I am including this short list of curriculum ideas for children ages five and under. Allow your younger child to be the initiator of "school" sessions that directly involve him, but if he wants to listen in while older children have their lessons, that's great! Our three-year-old learned to read just by listening in (by his own choice) on the lessons I was doing with our five-year-old.

Kumon workbooks, Kumon Publishing North America, Inc., Glenpointe Centre East, 5th Floor, 300 Frank Burr Blvd., Teaneck, NJ 07666, (877) 586-6673, *www.kumon.com*

These colorful workbooks are geared toward very young children—beginning at age two—but they do have materials available for children through age eight. While the subject matter of some of the workbooks is expected, such as addition, subtraction, and telling time, one of the great things about these workbooks is that they offer subject matter not typically offered—cutting, pasting, folding, tracing, and mazes, to name a few. If you can invest in a few, these make great workbooks for preschoolers or for other children who need the enrichment activities. Children with special needs or motor skill difficulties would also benefit from the basic skills offered in these workbooks.

Dover coloring books, Dover Publications, Inc., 32 East 2nd Street, Mineola, NY 11501, (800) 223-3130, *www.doverpublications.com*

This company offers a full line of paper dolls, sticker albums, and other products, but homeschoolers are especially fond of their fabulous coloring books. They offer coloring books on almost every topic you can imagine with accurate illustrations and identifying captions.

Bob Jones University Press, Greenville, South Carolina, (800) 845-5731, *www.bjupress.com*

If your preschooler is especially precocious or if you would like to establish a habit of "doing" school early, Bob Jones makes some great workbooks tailored perfectly to the preschool child.

List #225 **For Younger Children** *(continued)*

Miscellaneous

Offer your preschooler time with good quality puzzles, educational toys, games, and pretend play materials (such as dress-up clothes, dolls, a miniature kitchen); Ravensburger puzzles (*www.ravensburger.com*); and almost any of the products from the Melissa & Doug line of educational toys, puzzles, and games. Providing plenty of these types of educational toys and activities while a child is young will allow her imagination to soar and her mind to grasp new concepts each day.

List #226 Phonics and Reading Curricula

Sing, Spell, Read, and Write, Pearson Education, P.O. Box 2500, Lebanon, IN 46052, (800) 526-9907, *www.pearsonlearning.com*

This phonics-based language arts program is one of the more costly (around $275), but it is worth it when you consider the benefits. Depending on how long it takes your child to go through all the raceway levels, it can serve as the phonics curriculum for a child for one to two years. It is very easy to use this program with more than one child at a time or in different years. *Sing, Spell, Read, and Write* is especially appealing to boys with its raceway theme and interesting stories.

Bob Books, 784 Main Street, Erie, CO 80516, (303) 828-1255, *www.bobbooks.com*

These phonics-based readers are particularly appealing for beginning readers. As long as a child can already recognize the most common letters, he or she should be able to read a book at the first sitting. This is a great boost to confidence. If your child has the basic phonics sounds mastered, you may want to start with one of the later sets in the series. The later books are longer and focus on more complex sounds.

Basic phonics readers and graded readers, A Beka Book, P.O. Box 18000, Pensacola, FL 32532, (877) 223-5226, *www.abeka.org*

A Beka Book has phonics-based readers for each grade level. Many homeschool parents use A Beka material because the books are well written, have colorful illustrations that children enjoy, and have corresponding teacher manuals. The early readers may be a bit too difficult for children without a good phonics background, so if you're just starting out, test your child with a particular level book before you invest in a complete set for that grade.

Jumpstart, Knowledge Adventure, *www.knowledgeadventure.com*
Reader Rabbit, The Learning Company, *www.learningcompany.com*

Both of these are computer software programs for children that are highly effective. All of our children and the children in several other families I know have used Jumpstart and/or Reader Rabbit and have been very satisfied. If your child is anxious to have "computer time," you might want to allow thirty minutes per day, but I believe it should

List #226 **Phonics and Reading Curricula** *(continued)*

consist of educational software, such as these programs. They are available in several different levels and in various subjects as well.

Teach Your Child to Read in 100 Easy Lessons, by Siegfried Engelmann, Phyllis Haddox, and Elaine Bruner (New York: Simon and Schuster, 1983)

For children who don't like to sit still, this book can be trying, since you are supposed to spend twenty minutes per day on each lesson. There are a lot of repetitive drills, which don't work for some kids. With that said, this is a great book for those who don't mind the drills and who like to see their progress. Children progressively learn more and more sounds that will enable them to read. We've never finished the whole book, but I've used parts of this book with all our children and I intend to use it with our youngest.

Reading aloud isn't a "curriculum," but I feel compelled to mention as part of this section that one of the best ways to teach your child phonics is to read to him or her frequently. Pick age-appropriate books (see lists #232 and #233 for some great ideas) and then try to read aloud to your child daily. Occasionally run your finger along the words as you read or ask the child to "read" to you a book that she has memorized. Have your young child point out items on the page as you read. Ask your child to point out letters he might recognize, like those in his name. Each of these activities involves pre-reading skills. Remember, though, the goal is to instill in your child a love for books and reading, so forget the activities if he doesn't enjoy them.

List #227 Language Arts Curricula

Spelling Workout (Levels A–G), Modern Curriculum Press/Pearson Learning Group, P.O. Box 2500, Lebanon, IN 46052, (800) 526-9907, *www.pearsonlearning.com*

These consumable workbooks present lessons in more of a traditional-school approach, with a spelling list for each lesson, crossword puzzles, and activities to go with each lesson. Some children enjoy these extra activities, while others simply want to memorize the spelling words. Either way, these workbooks are beneficial in helping children learn to spell. Modern Curriculum Press also offers workbooks in other subjects. Their math workbooks are particularly helpful if students are struggling with a particular area, such as multiplication, by doing numerous drills on the same subject matter.

Bob Jones University Press, Greenville, South Carolina, (800) 845-5731, *www.bjupress.com*

While Bob Jones Press offers many wonderful workbooks, they are listed here because they are one of the few publishers creating language arts curricula that can hold the interest of a child. Their workbooks feature lively, colorful pages that are appealing, but not distracting. They present the material within a multi-disciplinary approach—using biography, history, sports, and interesting tidbits of information from other areas to interest the reader in grammar without sacrificing content. Children using the Bob Jones curriculum for any subject at any grade level should be well prepared for standardized tests and still have a love for learning.

List #228 Math Curricula

Saxon, Harcourt Achieve, Attn: Customer Service, 5th Floor, 6277 Sea Harbor Drive, Orlando, FL, 32887, (800) 284-7019, *www.saxonpublishers.harcourtachieve.com*

If you want repetition and drill, Saxon could be the perfect math curriculum for your child. Saxon is listed here among the most highly recommended math curricula for the simple reason that it works. Parents will occasionally need to explain concepts to children, but for the most part, the Saxon math workbooks designed for homeschoolers are created for independent work. They present a concept, such as adding fractions, then subsequent chapters will present new concepts, but also will drill students on old material. At times the precocious student may want to skip a few chapters at a time, because the student wants to proceed at a faster pace, and this is fine as long as they know the material.

Spectrum, School Specialty Publishing, 3195 Wilson Drive, NW, Grand Rapids, MI 49534, (800) 417-3261, *www.FrankSchaffer.com*

The *Spectrum* workbooks by Frank Schaffer are hard to top for no-fluff presentation of the subject matter. The books are divided by grade level and subject matter, and each book does a thorough job of presenting the material and then providing drills for the student. In the fifth grade *Spectrum Math*, for example, the book covers two- through six-digit addition and subtraction, multiplication and division, geometry, and fractions. In addition, each of these workbooks includes an answer key. One of the things I like about these workbooks is that they are affordable and children can write directly in them. *Spectrum* workbooks are available for spelling, test preparation and practice, word study and phonics, vocabulary, and more.

Skill Builders, Carson-Dellosa Publishing, PO Box 35665, Greensboro, NC 27425, (800) 321-0943, *www.summerbridgeactivities.com*

These small yet sturdy little workbooks are great for individual or group drill of a particular subject. The books are divided by subject and grade level and cover all the skills necessary for each subject and grade level, providing various types of problems by which the child can review those skills. In addition to math, this company produces *Skill Builders* workbooks in U.S. Geography, Phonics, Spelling, Vocabulary, Grammar, and several other subjects. You could use the books to teach a subject, determine where your student needs extra work in a subject, supplement other curriculum on a particular subject, or review a given subject matter before testing. Reproduction for classroom use is allowed, and each workbook includes an answer key.

List #229 History Curricula

Sonlight Curriculum, 8042 South Grant Way, Littleton, CO 80122-2705, (303) 730-6292, *www.sonlight.com*

Though Sonlight is listed as a comprehensive curriculum, I would recommend it in itself as a history curriculum. If you start in early elementary grades, your child will proceed through history in a chronological manner and then repeat the material in later grades so that they learn it thoroughly before high school.

The Story of the World books, by Susan Wise Bauer, available through Peace Hill Press, 18021 The Glebe Lane, Charles City, VA 23030, (877) 322-3445, *www.peacehillpress.com*

These delightful history books are written in a manner that children find interesting and can understand. You can use them as read-alouds for elementary-age children, or older children can read them on their own.

List #230 Science Curriculum

Apologia Science, 1106 Meridian Plaza, Suite 220, Anderson, IN 46016, (888) 524-4724, *www.apologiaonline.com*

Though there are many good science programs and science kits, the best science curriculum I've used is Apologia Science. The books keep the children interested, and they are written in a kid-friendly manner with lots of diagrams, illustrations, and colored pictures.

List #231 Recommended Authors

Most of the following authors write historical nonfiction for juveniles. There are some fiction authors listed as well, and though the Newbery list (#262) contains tons of fiction books, this will give you a balance. The authors listed here were selected for their historically accurate writing, their attention to detail, and the fact that they have each written numerous appropriate books for young readers. I would recommend any of their books.

Around age ten, children become particularly interested in reading books in a series. If your child likes reading series books, you might suggest that he also try reading all the books by a particular author. Of course, check out the lists that contain series books as well.

Louisa May Alcott
Janet and Geoff Benge
Clyde Robert Bulla
Frances Cavannah
Alice Dalgliesh
James Daugherty
Ingri and Edgar Parin D'Aulaire
Margaret Davidson
Sid Fleischman
Russell Freedman
Jean Fritz
Lois Lenski
Ann McGovern
Enid L. Meadowcroft
Jim Murphy
Margaret Pumphrey
Howare Pyle
Arleta Richardson
Augusta Stevenson
Ronald Syme
Gertrude Chandler Warner
Laura Ingalls Wilder

List #232 Recommended Reading for Toddlers and Preschoolers

Bearhide and Crow by Paul Brett Johnson
Dr. Seuss books
Drummer Hoff by Barbara Emberly
Fireflies for Nathan by Shulamith Levey Oppenheim
Goodnight Moon by Margaret Wise Brown
The House that Jack Built by Jeanette Winter
Little Bear books by Martin Waddell
Millions of Cats by Wanda Gag
The Mitten by Alvin Tresselt
The Napping House by Audrey Wood
Sandra Boynton board books
Sweet Clara and the Freedom Quilt by Deborah Hopkinson
There's a Duck in My Closet! by John Trent
The Very Hungry Caterpillar by Eric Carle

Beyond these books, I recommend that parents take their children to the library and let them pick some out themselves. To ensure that they also get plenty of good quality books in the mix, read the Caldecott Medal winners on a regular basis as well. You might also mix in some of the books from the next list (for early elementary students) as read-alouds for your littler ones.

Note: The recommended books and award winners listed in *The Homeschooler's Book of Lists* have been selected with conservative Christian families in mind. However, parent-teachers are always encouraged to choose and monitor reading materials based on their own preferences.

List #233 Recommended Reading for Early Elementary Students (ages 5–8)

Since reading levels vary greatly, some children will be able to read these books on their own by first or second grade. However, many of these books are meant to be read aloud by parents. Almost all children enjoy listening to Mom or Dad read aloud, and establishing this routine while they are young will not only make your homeschooling journey go a little smoother but it will also instill in your child a love for reading.

The Aesop for Children by Mio Winter
Amelia Bedelia books by Peggy Parish
And the Word Came with Power by Joanne Shetler
The Apple & the Arrow by Conrad Buff
The Berenstain Bears books by Stan and Jan Berenstain
The Big Balloon Race by Eleanor Coerr
The Borrowers by Mary Norton
Capyboppy by Bill Peet
Catching Their Talk in a Box by Betty M. Hockett
A Child's Garden of Verses by Robert Louis Stevenson
A Child's History of the World by V. M. Hillyer
The Complete Tales of Beatrix Potter by Beatrix Potter
The Cricket in Times Square by George Selden
Daniel's Duck by Clyde Robert Bulla
Detectives in Togas by Henry Winterfeld
Dolphin books by Wayne Grover
The Door in the Wall by Marguerite De Angeli
Dr. Seuss books
The Family Under the Bridge by Natalie Savage Carlson
The Fire Cat by Esther Averill
Five True Dog Stories by Margaret Davidson
Frog and Toad books by Arnold Lobel
Gladys Aylward by Janet and Geoff Benge
A Grain of Rice by Helena Clare Pittman
The Great Dinosaur Mystery and the Bible by Paul S. Taylor
Greg's Microscope by Millicent E. Selsam
Hero Tales (four volumes) by Dave and Neta Jackson
Hill of Fire by Thomas P. Lewis
Homer Price by Robert McCloskey

List #233 **Recommended Reading for Early Elementary Students (ages 5–8)** *(continued)*

The Hundred Dresses by Eleanor Estes
IN GRANDMA'S ATTIC books by Arleta Richardson
In the Year of the Boar and Jackie Robinson by Bette Bao Lord
THE INDIAN IN THE CUPBOARD books by Lynne Reid Banks
James and the Giant Peach by Roald Dahl
James Herriot's Treasury for Children by James Herriot
Johnny Appleseed by Aliki
The Light at Tern Rock by Julia L. Sauer
A Lion to Guard Us by Clyde Robert Bulla
LITTLE BEAR books by Else Holmelund Minarik
Little Pear by Eleanor Frances Lattimore
The Little Riders by Margaretha Shemin
THE LITTLES books by John Peterson
MAGIC SCHOOL BUS books by Joanna Cole
MAGIC TREE HOUSE books by Mary Pope Osborne
Marie Curie's Search for Radium by Beverly Birch
MCBROOM books by Sid Fleischman
Mother Goose
Mouse Tales by Arnold Lobel
MY FATHER'S DRAGON books by Ruth S. Gannett
The Napping House by Audrey Wood
NATE THE GREAT books by Marjorie W. Sharmat
Owl at Home by Arnold Lobel
Peter the Great by Diane Stanley
Pompeii . . . Buried Alive! by Edith Kunhardt Davis
Red Sails to Capri by Ann Weil
Rikki-Tikki-Tavi by Rudyard Kipling
The Story About Ping by Marjorie Flack
The Story of Dr. Dolittle by Hugh Lofting
Strawberry Girl by Lois Lenski
Surprises by Lee Bennett Hopkins
The Sword in the Tree by Clyde Robert Bulla
Tikki Tikki Tembo by Arlene Mosel
The Titanic: Lost and Found by Judy Donnelly
Tolliver's Secret by Esther Wood Brady

List #233 **Recommended Reading for Early Elementary Students (ages 5–8)** *(continued)*

The True Story of the Three Little Pigs by John Scieszka
Twenty and Ten by Claire Huchet Bishop and Janet Joly
The Twenty-One Balloons by William Pene du Bois
Wagon Wheels by Barbara Brenner
We're Going on a Bear Hunt by Michael Rosen
Where the Wild Things Are by Maurice Sendak
White Stallion of Lipizza by Marguerite Henry
Window on the World by Daphne Spraggett
WINNIE-THE-POOH books by A. A. Milne
The Wonderful Wizard of Oz by L. Frank Baum

List #234 Recommended Reading for Older Elementary Students (ages 9–11)

Older elementary and middle school students (grades 4–8) should be familiar with the following books (whether by reading the books themselves or through read-aloud time with a parent reading the books).

Across Five Aprils by Irene Hunt
An American Adventure books by Lee Roddy
And Then What Happened, Paul Revere? by Jean Fritz
Betsy books by Dorothy Canfield Fisher
Boxcar Children books by Gertrude Chandler Warner
By the Great Horn Spoon by Sid Fleischman
The Cabin Faced West by Jean Fritz
Caddie Woodlawn by Carol Ryrie Brink
Carry On, Mr. Bowditch by Jean Lee Latham
Cheaper by the Dozen by Frank B. Gilbreth and Ernestine Gilbreth
Freedom Train by Dorothy Sterling
The Great Turkey Walk by Kathleen Karr
If You books published by Scholastic
In Search of the Source by Neil Anderson
In the Year of the Boar and Jackie Robinson by Bette Bao Lord
Johnny Tremain by Esther Forbes
Landmark books published by Random House (see list #259)
A Letter to Mrs. Roosevelt by C. Coco De Young
Little Britches by Ralph Moody
The Matchlock Gun by Walter D. Edmonds
Miracles on Maple Hill by Virginia Sorensen
Moccasin Trail by Eloise Jarvis McGraw
Old Yeller by Fred Gipson
Om-kas-toe by Kenneth Thomasma
Otto of the Silver Hand by Howard Pyle
Pedro's Journal by Pam Conrad
Phoebe the Spy by Judith Berry Griffin
Plain Girl by Virginia Sorensen Waugh
Pocahontas and the Strangers by Clyde Robert Bulla
Roll of Thunder, Hear My Cry by Mildred D. Taylor

List #234 **Recommended Reading for Older Elementary Students (ages 9–11)** *(continued)*

Sarah, Plain and Tall by Patricia MacLachlan
The Seventeenth Swap by Eloise Jarvis McGraw
Shades of Gray by Carolyn Reeder
The Sign of the Beaver by Elizabeth George Speare
THE STORY OF THE USA books by Franklin Escher, Jr.
Thimble Summer by Elizabeth Enright
Turn Homeward, Hannalee by Patricia Beatty
The Twenty-One Balloons by William Pène Du Bois
Walk the World's Rim by Betty Baker
The Witch of Blackbird Pond by Elizabeth George Speare

List #235 Recommended Reading for Middle School Students (ages 11–13)

Adam of the Road by Elizabeth Janet Gray
The Adventures of Huckleberry Finn by Mark Twain
The Adventures of Tom Sawyer by Mark Twain
After the Dancing Days by Margaret I. Rostkowski
Amos Fortune, Free Man by Elizabeth Yates
Anna and the King by Margaret Landon
Archimedes and the Door of Science by Jeanne Bendick
Augustus Caesar's World by Genevieve Foster
Banner in the Sky by James Ramsey Ullman
The Beduins' Gazelle by Frances Temple
Beverly Cleary books
Beyond the Desert Gate by Mary Ray
Black Horses for the King by Anne McCaffrey
Bound for Oregon by Jean Van Leeuwen
The Bronze Bow by Elizabeth George Speare
Call of the Wild by Jack London
Catherine Called Birdy by Karen Cushman
Charlotte's Web by E. B. White
THE CHRONICLES OF NARNIA by C. S. Lewis
The Dark Frigate by Charles Boardman Hawes
D'Aulaire's Book of Greek Myths by Ingri D'Aulaire and Edgar Parin D'Aulaire
Eagle of the Ninth by Rosemary Sutcliff
Enchantress From the Stars by Sylvia Engdahl
Encyclopedia Brown by Donald J. Sobol
The Endless Steppe by Esther Hautzig
Escape from Warsaw by Ian Serraillier
Flame Over Tara by Madeleine A. Polland
The Flames of Rome by Paul L. Maier
From the Mixed-Up Files of Mrs. Basil E. Frankweiler by E. L. Konigsberg
The Gammage Cup by Carol Kendall
A Gathering of Days by Joan Blas
George Washington's World by Genevieve Foster (and her other "World" books)
Ginger Pye by Eleanor Estes
God King: A Story in the Days of King Hezekiah by Joanne Williamson
God's Smuggler by Brother Andrew

List #235 **Recommended Reading for Middle School Students (ages 11–13)** *(continued)*

Going Solo by Roald Dahl
The Golden Goblet by Eloise Jarvis McGraw
The Great and Terrible Quest by Margaret Lovett
The Great Brain by John D. Fitzgerald
Great Expectations by Charles Dickens
HARDY BOYS series by Franklin W. Dixon
A HISTORY OF U.S. series by Joe Hakim
Hittite Warrior by Joanne Williamson
Holes by Louis Sachar
I, Juan de Pareja by Elizabeth Borton De Trevino
I Am David by Anne Holm
The Ides of April by Mary Ray
ILLUSTRATED CLASSICS books published by Baronet Books
In Search of Honor by Donna L. Hess
Indian Captive: The Story of Mary Jemison by Lois Lenski
It's a Jungle Out There! by Ron Snell
Jane Eyre by Charlotte Brontë
Kidnapped by Robert Louis Stevenson
The Kingdom Strikes Back: The Secret Missions by Roberta H. Winter
LEFT BEHIND books by Frank Peretti
Luther: Biography of a Reformer by Frederick Nohl
Madeleine L'Engle books
Maniac Magee by Jerry Spinelli
Mara, Daughter of the Nile by Eloise Jarvis McGraw
Mary, Bloody Mary by Carolyn Meyer
Master Cornhill by Eloise Jarvis McGraw
Moonshiner's Son by Carolyn Reeder
Mrs. Frisby and the Rats of NIMH by Robert C. O'Brien
My Side of the Mountain by Jean Craighead George
The Mystery of the Roman Ransom by Henry Winterfeld
NANCY DREW books by Carolyn Keene
Number the Stars by Lois Lowry
Oliver Twist by Charles Dickens
Otto of the Silver Hand by Howard Pyle
Out of the Dust by Karen Hesse
A Parcel of Patterns by Jill Paton Walsh
Peace Child by Don Richardson

List #235 **Recommended Reading for Middle School Students (ages 11–13)** *(continued)*

The Phantom Tollbooth by Norton Juster
Pictures of Hollis Woods by Patricia Reilly Giff
Pilgrim's Progress in Today's English retold by James Thomas
A Proud Taste for Scarlet and Miniver by E. L. Konigsburg
The Ramsay Scallop by Frances Temple
The Random House Book of Poetry for Children by Jack Prelutsky
The Red Badge of Courage by Stephen Crane
REDWALL books by Brian Jacques
"Rip Van Winkle" (a short story) by Washington Irving
Robinson Crusoe by Daniel Defoe
The Samurai's Tale by Erik C. Haugaard
The Second Mrs. Giaconda by E. L. Konigsburg
A Separate Peace by John Knowles
Shadow of a Bull by Maia Wojciechowska
Shakespeare Stealer by Gary Blackwood
The Singing Tree by Kate Seredy
A Single Shard by Linda Sue Park
The Slopes of War by Norah Perez
Snow Treasure by Marie McSwigan
Sounder by William H. Armstrong
Strange Case of Dr. Jekyll and Mr. Hyde—and Other Tales by Robert Louis Stevenson
Streams to the River, River to the Sea by Scott O'Dell
Stuart Little by E. B. White
Theras and His Town by Caroline Dale Snedeker
Till We Have Faces by C. S. Lewis
To Kill a Mockingbird by Harper Lee
Traitor: The Case of Benedict Arnold by Jean Fritz
Treasure Island by Robert Louis Stevenson
The Trojan War by Olivia E. Coolidge
The Trumpet of the Swan by E. B. White
The Trumpeter of Krakow by Eric P. Kelly
The Westing Game by Ellen Raskin
The Wheel on the School by Meindert DeJong
The Wind in the Willows by Kenneth Graham
The World of Columbus and Sons by Genevieve Foster
A Year Down Yonder by Richard Peck

List #236 Recommended Reading for High School Students (ages 13–18)

I have a lot of interaction with teenagers through church, the community, foster care, homeschooling, etc. I enjoy talking with them about what they are learning or have learned. All too frequently, high school students today are not being properly prepared for college, and many are not reading the basic texts that will give them historical, social, and political background to make decisions or study a subject in context with a certain time period. Home educators sometimes ask me what their high school students should read before graduating. The books listed here are the ones I think every homeschool student (every high school student!) should read before completing his or her pre-college work.

The Adventures and the Memoirs of Sherlock Holmes (and other works, including *The Hound of the Baskervilles*) by Arthur Conan Doyle

The Adventures of Huckleberry Finn (and other works) by Mark Twain

The Aeneid of Virgil by Elizabeth Vandiver

Alas, Babylon by Pat Frank

Alice's Adventures in Wonderland (and *Through the Looking-Glass*) by Louis Carroll

All Quiet on the Western Front by Erich Maria Remarque

All the King's Men by Robert Penn Warren

Anna Karenina and *War and Peace* by Leo Tolstoy

Anne Frank: Diary of a Young Girl by Anne Frank

Anne of Green Gables (and other works) by Lucy Maud Montgomery

Around the World in 80 Days by Jules Verne

Belle Prater's Boy by Ruth White

Beowulf (author unknown)

Best Short Stories of 0. Henry by O. Henry

Billy Budd (and other works, including *Moby Dick*) by Herman Melville

Black Like Me by John Howard Griffin

Brave New World by Aldous Huxley

Bud, Not Buddy by Christopher Paul Curtis

Canterbury Tales (and *Canterbury Quintet*) by Geoffrey Chaucer

"The Charge of the Light Brigade" by Alfred Lord Tennyson

Children of the River by Linda Crew

China's Long March by Jean Fritz

Christy by Catherine Marshall

The Confessions of St. Augustine by St. Augustine

List #236 **Recommended Reading for High School Students (ages 13–18)** *(continued)*

The Contender by Robert Lipsyte
The Crucible by Arthur Miller
Cry, the Beloved Country by Alan Paton
Darkness at Noon by Arthur Koestler
David Copperfield (and other works, including *Great Expectations* and *A Tale of Two Cities*) by Charles Dickens
The Day They Came to Arrest the Book by Nat Hentoff
"The Devil and Daniel Webster" by Stephen Vincent Benet
The Divine Comedy by Dante
Don Quixote by Miguel de Cervantes
Dr. Jekyll and Mr. Hyde by Robert Louis Stevenson
The Dry Divide by Ralph Moody
Dubliners (a collection of short stories) by James Joyce
Emancipating Slaves, Enslaving Free Men by Jeffrey Rogers
Emma (and other works) by Jane Austen
A Farewell to Arms (and *For Whom the Bell Tolls* and *The Old Man and the Sea*) by Ernest Hemingway
Frankenstein by Mary Shelley
The Giver by Lois Lowry
The Godless Constitution: The Case Against Religious Correctness by Isaac Kramnick and R. Laurence Moore
The Grapes of Wrath (and other works, including *Of Mice and Men, The Pearl,* and *The Red Pony*) by John Steinbeck
The Great Brain by John D. Fitzgerald
The Great Gatsby by F. Scott Fitzgerald
The Great Gilly Hopkins by Katherine Paterson
Gulliver's Travels (and other works) by Jonathan Swift
Hamlet (and other works, including *MacBeth, A Midsummer Night's Dream,* the Sonnets, and *Romeo and Juliet*) by William Shakespeare
Heart of Darkness by Joseph Conrad
The Hiding Place by Corrie ten Boom
The Iliad (and *The Odyssey*) by Homer
The Importance of Being Earnest by Oscar Wilde
The Invisible Man by Ralph Ellison
Jacob Have I Loved by Katherine Paterson
Jane Eyre by Charlotte Brontë

List #236 **Recommended Reading for High School Students (ages 13–18)** *(continued)*

Julie of the Wolves by Jean Craighead George
Kon-Tiki by Thor Heyerdahl
Labor's Untold Story by Richard O. Boyer and Herbert M. Morais
The Last of the Mohicans (and other works) by James Fenimore Cooper
"The Legend of Sleepy Hollow" by Washington Irving
Les Miserables by Victor Hugo
Lies My Teacher Told Me by James W. Loewen
The Life and Times of Frederick Douglass by Frederick Douglass
Life: Our Century in Pictures for Young People by Richard Stolley
Little Women by Louisa May Alcott
Living on the Devil's Doorstep by Floyd McClung
Lord of the Flies by William Golding
The Lord of the Rings Trilogy by J. R. R. Tolkien
Mere Christianity (and other works, including *The Great Divorce, The Screwtape Letters,* and *Perelandra*) by C. S. Lewis
The Moves Make the Man by Bruce Brooks
Murder on the Orient Express by Agatha Christie
My Antonia by Willa Cather
Oedipus Rex (and other works, including *Antigone*) by Sophocles
Our Town by Thornton Wilder
The Outsiders by S. E. Hinton
Paradise Lost by John Milton
A Passage to India by E. M. Forster
Persuasion by Jane Austen
Peter Pan by J. M. Barrie
Pilgrim's Progress by John Bunyan
The Portable Poe by Edgar Allen Poe
"A Portrait of the Artist as a Young Man" by James Joyce
Pride and Prejudice by Jane Austen (I would also highly recommend the TV mini-series adaptation. We don't usually watch movies, but this is one worth watching with your teenagers.)
Pygmalion by George Bernard Shaw
Red Scarf Girl by Ji-li Jiang
The Republic (and other works) by Plato
Right Ho, Jeeves by P. G. Wodehouse

List #236 **Recommended Reading for High School Students (ages 13–18)** *(continued)*

The Rime of the Ancient Mariner by Samuel Taylor Coleridge
Robert Frost: Selected Poems by Robert Frost
Robinson Crusoe by Daniel Defoe
The Scarlet Letter (and *The House of Seven Gables*) by Nathaniel Hawthorne
The Secret Sharer and Other Stories by Joseph Conrad
A Severe Mercy by Sheldon Vanauken
Shadow of the Almighty by Elisabeth Elliot
Silas Marner by George Eliot
Sir Gawain and the Green Knight (author unknown)
The Snow Goose by Paul Gallico
Three Men in a Boat by Jerome K. Jerome
"Tiger, Tiger" (and other poems) by William Blake
The Time Machine by H. G. Wells
To Kill a Mockingbird by Harper Lee
A Tree Grows in Brooklyn by Betty Smith
20,000 Leagues Under the Sea by Jules Verne
Uncle Tom's Cabin by Harriet Beecher Stowe
Up From Slavery by Booker T. Washington
The View from Saturday by E. L. Konigsburg
"Walden and Civil Disobedience" by Henry David Thoreau
Walk Two Moons by Sharon Creech
When Hitler Stole Pink Rabbit by Judith Kerr
Winston Churchill by John Severance
Wuthering Heights by Emily Brontë
The Yearling (and other works, including *Cross Creek*) by Marjorie K. Rawlings
You Want Women to Vote, Lizzie Stanton? by Jean Fritz

List #237 Unit Study Topics

Several education-related distributors and private entrepreneurs offer unit study kits via the Internet or mail order. You can do a unit study on just about any subject that interests your child. I've listed some unit study topics below, but there are others who know a lot more about unit studies than I do. I recommend Jennifer Steward's *Everything You Need to Know About Homeschool Unit Studies* (available at *www.unitstudies.com*) or Amanda Bennett's unit study books (available at *www.unitstudy.com*).

Aerodynamics
Airplanes
Ancient civilizations (Mayan, Incan, Mesopotamian, Sumerian, etc.)
Animals (cats, dogs, horses, sea creatures, jungle animals, desert animals, or any other individual animals or groups of animals)
Art
Author (a unit study based on a particular author)
Auto racing
Automobiles
Baseball (or any sport)
Birthday
Boats
Christmas (or any holiday)
Computer games
Computers
Craft (pick any craft—chair-making, painting—and do a focused unit study)
Culture of a particular people
Dolls
Electronics
Food
Foreign language (pick any one or more)
Furniture
Gardens
Geographical area (pick any city, state, region, country, or continent)
Geographical phenomenon (volcanoes, earthquakes, tsunamis, etc.)
History of clothing
Horse racing
Kings and queens
Knights
Lighthouses
Movies
Music
Ocean (pick any ocean or do a unit study on all the oceans)
Police (or other public service jobs such as fire fighters)
Religion
Scrapbooking
Space (planets, moons, comets, or other space objects)
Space program (NASA)
Trains
World War II (or any other war)

List #238 Creating a Portfolio

Whether your state requires you to keep samples of your child's work or not, creating a yearly portfolio for each student is a great idea. You can compare what your child achieves from year to year, show off samples of his best work to Grandma, and maintain a record of accomplishments.

Creating a portfolio is simple and you should do what works best for your family. If you like using file drawers, you could keep portfolio material in a file folder. Other options for portfolios are expandable plastic file folders, two-gallon Ziploc bags, small plastic containers, manila envelopes, three-ring binders, or an expandable zipper file. The expandable zipper files and plastic file folders are great because you can keep loose items such as photographs, as well as papers and odd-sized items. If you're especially creative, you could put all your child's portfolio items into a scrapbook (or during a scrapbook unit study at the end of the year!). Either way, here are some suggestions for what to keep in a portfolio:

- a cover page listing what is in the portfolio
- a list of books the child has read (This list and others in the portfolio pertain to that particular year.)
- a list of books you have read aloud to the child
- a list of field trips taken and photographs from field trips
- a list of unit studies and what you did for the studies
- loose photos or a photo collage of the student's activities throughout the year
- an assessment of the student in each subject area
- any testing results the student may have
- samples of the student's best work in each subject (a writing sample, results of a speed drill, graphs and charts, etc.)
- a collection of cute or funny sayings your child has said that you want to remember
- awards, achievements, lists of activities, or recognitions from scouting programs, clubs, academic programs, co-op classes, or other activities your child has participated in
- fliers or brochures from places you've visited, particularly other cities and states
- anything else you want in your child's portfolio

List #239 Good Study Habits for Homeschoolers

(This list is for Rachel and all the other homeschoolers who wanted a good study habits list just for them!)

Take responsibility for your studies. Whether you want to become an artist, doctor, physical therapist, farmer, or a stay-at-home mom, you will have responsibilities in your life. Right now your "job" in life is to honor and obey your parents, love others, and give glory to the Lord in what you do. Decide today that you are going to glorify the Lord by taking responsibility for your actions and your academic assignments.

Create an environment that promotes learning. Ask your parents if you can decorate your desk, wall, or notebooks. Make your study area and your materials special to you. If you are having difficulty studying at the kitchen table with your siblings, ask your parents if you can have your own desk or other private study area.

Sometimes a little distraction can be a good thing. While I don't advocate having the television on while studying, I have found that my children do seem to be able to concentrate better with a tape or CD playing quietly in the background. Ask your parents if you can try this, but make sure you actually do your work—the goal is to show how it will *help* you get your schoolwork done.

If you're especially frustrated, stop studying and pray. Spend some time with the Lord and ask Him to help you process the material.

If something isn't working, try something different. If writing your spelling words ten times each isn't helping you learn to spell them correctly, try making index cards, which work great for almost any subject. If writing out math problems is a bore, ask your mom if she can call math problems out to you while you do chores together.

Take care of yourself. If you are not getting enough sleep, if you are not eating well, or if you are stressed out about other obligations, your studies are likely to suffer. Following good health habits will help your study skills by making you more alert, more energetic, and less distracted.

Above all, don't give up!! The Lord will not give you more than you can handle, though it may take a lot of work to understand certain things. Remember, though, if you are reading this, you have accomplished one of the most amazing feats—mastering a written language. When you were a baby, you had no idea how to read, but now you are kind of having a conversation with me and we haven't even met. That's pretty cool!

List #240 Standardized Tests

Here are the five most commonly used achievement tests. If testing is required in your area or if you decide to test your child, I would recommend that you use the same test each time so that you can compare scores from one time to the next. Each of these tests provides a composite score and a sub score for each area.

Iowa Test of Basic Skills (ITBS)

This test is considered among the more difficult achievement tests and is a top-rated nationally recognized standardized achievement test. The test consists of subsections such as vocabulary, reading comprehension, language usage and expression, word analysis, mathematics concepts, social studies, science, and reference materials. This test is available for grades K–8 and takes less time than the Stanford Achievement Test. It is never made available to individual parents or teachers. The test administrator must have a four-year baccalaureate degree in any subject. This test is available through Bob Jones University Press at *www.bjup.com* or by calling (800) 845-5731. You can read more about the ITBS at *www.education.uiowa.edu/itp/itbs.*

Stanford Achievement Test (SAT)

The Stanford Achievement Test is also a top-rated, nationally recognized test for K–12. The test includes study skills, listening skills, social science, reading comprehension, math, science, and much more. The test administrator must have a baccalaureate degree in any field. This test can also be ordered through Bob Jones at *www.bjup.com* or by calling (800) 845-5731.

California Achievement Test (CAT)

This test covers the typical subjects (math, science, spelling, social studies, language mechanics, vocabulary, etc.) but from a more traditional viewpoint, which is appealing to many homeschool parents. An administrator is necessary to give general directions and provide a time limit, but otherwise there is little parental involvement necessary. Children in grades 4–12 can take the test together since the timing and directions are identical. Children in grades K–3 will need a parent to read sections from the examiner's manual. This test is available from the Family Learning Organization at *www.familylearning.org* and available only to home educators. You also certify that you will give the test and return the materials within two weeks of receipt if you order through them.

List #240 **Standardized Tests** *(continued)*

Comprehensive Test of Basic Skills (CTBS)

The **CTBS** tests all academic areas (reading, spelling, language arts, science, math, and social studies) and reference skills. The test is available for grades K–12. With the CTBS scores, your child receives a critique of his or her performance. You can order this test through Bayside School Service at *www.BaysideSchoolServices.com* or by calling (800) 723-3057.

Personalized Achievement Summary System (PASS)

This test was developed with homeschoolers in mind. It is available only for grades 3–8 in the subjects of reading, language, and math. You should check with your school system to see if they will recognize it for any required testing. You can order the test through Hewitt Research Foundation at (800) 348-1750 or find out more information at *www.hewitthomeschooling.com*.

List #241 What to Do When You Are Having a Bad Day

- Pray.
- Light some candles in your bathroom and take a hot bath.
- Have the children sit on their beds and look at books while you relax for a few moments.
- Put the children down for a nap.
- Do something different.
- Go to the park, zoo, a pet store, or someplace else that you find serene and relaxing. (I personally love aquariums! Buy a family pass to save money.)
- Skip the regular schoolwork and housework, gather the children on your couch, and read books aloud.
- If it's warm enough, send the children outside to play while you regroup your thoughts.
- Pop some popcorn, forget about schoolwork and chores for the day, and watch a fun movie with your kids.
- Go to bed early.
- Look through photo albums of your children when they were younger and remember that this time, too, will pass.
- Write in a journal or diary.
- Call a homeschool friend to share your frustrations, but make sure you don't complain about the children or their dad (or mom) while they are nearby.
- Go online and read the news. When I read aloud all the horrible things going on in the world (and in some schools), I find myself much more motivated to continue homeschooling.
- Remember that every homeschooling mother sometimes wants to put her children on the yellow bus. You're not alone. You're just having a bad day.
- If you're having more bad days than good, or if you're so depressed that you would consider hurting yourself or someone else, call a friend or relative to take your children, and seek professional help immediately. If you have no one to help you with the children, take them with you and find help.

List #242 Support for Home Educators

There are times when everyone can use a little support, so I believe that each homeschool family should consider joining a support group, whether local, regional, or national. With all the wonderful teaching resources in this book, we do not have the space to list every local or state support group. However, there are a couple of really great Web sites that will link you to support groups and also provide resources such as articles about homeschooling.

The Web sites I recommend are listed below for your convenience. Check out the sites, and if you like them, bookmark them so that you can find them easier next time. Refer your family or friends to these Web sites if they want to know more about homeschooling (or buy them a copy of this book to see all the great things your children are learning!).

www.hslda.org This nonprofit advocacy organization is designed to promote and defend our constitutional right to teach our children at home. I would definitely recommend joining the Home School Legal Defense Association (HSLDA). They send out newsletters and announcements to keep you abreast of the latest legal developments related to homeschooling, but you get so much more through their advice and resources. You do not have to be a member to cruise their Web site, where you can also find some state and local support groups.

www.nathhan.com The National Challenged Homeschoolers Associated Network (NATHHAN) has resources for families homeschooling children with special needs. This is the largest support group of its type in the United States, and I would highly recommend that families with special needs children visit this site and consider becoming members.

www.homeschool.com This is a great Web site with lots of articles, advice, links, and message boards.

www.home-school.com The official Web site of *Practical Homeschooling Magazine* offers a lot of timely information that I couldn't include in this book, such as news articles, upcoming events, and updated information on support groups.

www.homeschoolfoundation.org The Home School Foundation was established by Home School Legal Defense Association as a charitable organization to help promote homeschooling and help homeschooling families in need through a "Widow's Fund," a "Special Needs Children's Fund," etc.

www.tnhomeed.com Although this Web site is geared toward Tennessee homeschoolers, it has a lot of good resources, legislative information, and details about curriculum sales all across Tennessee.

15

Organizational and Reference Lists for Teachers, Parents, and Students

List #243 Supply Checklist for Public, Private, and Homeschool Classrooms

Of course when you teach your children at home, the whole house (and sometimes far beyond the walls of a house) becomes your classroom! If you're a new home educator, however, it's nice to have a minimal amount of materials on hand. If you are a veteran home educator, you have already figured out that there are many things you can get by without, but there are items that make it much easier to teach your children at home. These are the things that will be included in this list. They aren't necessarily essential, but they will make your homeschool journey much smoother. If you're new, start with what you can. If you've already been teaching for some time, use the list as a sort of "wish list" and obtain the remaining items gradually (through purchases, in trade with others, or as gifts from friends or relatives who desire to support your homeschooling endeavor).

- ☐ pencils
- ☐ glue
- ☐ lined paper
- ☐ unlined, plain white paper—If you have young children, unlined paper is great for expressing creativity, drawing, painting, coloring, and even writing.
- ☐ construction paper
- ☐ scissors
- ☐ tissues
- ☐ dry erase board—Though not essential, dry erase boards are quite useful in the classroom during instruction. Students in small classrooms or homeschool students usually enjoy practicing math problems on dry erase boards.
- ☐ dry erase markers
- ☐ a very large world map (It is best if this is placed on a north wall, though it's not a big deal if you can't do that.)
- ☐ three-ring binders—Students can use these to organize their work and Mom can use them to organize homeschool notes.
- ☐ three-hole punch
- ☐ stapler
- ☐ pencil sharpener
- ☐ pens
- ☐ red pens for grading
- ☐ crayons
- ☐ colored pencils

List #243 **Supply Checklist for Public, Private, and Homeschool Classrooms** *(continued)*

- ☐ markers
- ☐ coloring books—You can purchase educational coloring books that teach/supplement history material that you may be teaching your student(s). These coloring books can be put to use while you are reading aloud sections from living history books.
- ☐ modeling clay or dough—Many families make this themselves at home, but we always prefer to buy ours. Also, though with most things we bargain shop, with modeling clay or dough, we usually purchase the more expensive brand, such as Play-Doh, because it is more pliable and is less likely to stain.
- ☐ globe
- ☐ chalk
- ☐ chalkboard—This is not essential for the homeschool classroom, but there are families who use them.
- ☐ easel with chalkboard on one side and dry erase or painting area on other side
- ☐ musical instruments—These don't have to be expensive. Of course you can have nicer ones, but to start out, buy a harmonica, castanets, a small drum, a flute; others you can purchase inexpensively at yard sales, on discount tables, or even in the toy section.
- ☐ calendar—Pick one with big squares on it. You can write birthdays, conferences, doctor appointments, and community events. For homeschoolers, you could even mark each school day with an "S." This is especially helpful for those who have to complete daily attendance forms at some point during the year.
- ☐ puzzles—Puzzles are great for students of all ages. Keep a variety of puzzles on hand for children who are at different levels of capability.
- ☐ books of all sorts (See the Book Buying Bargains list, #244, for ideas on where to buy books below retail price.)
- ☐ permanent markers
- ☐ resealable plastic bags like Ziploc bags (to hold collections of rocks, crayons, etc.)

List #244 Book Buying Bargains

- *Used book stores*—You can frequently find exceptional bargains at used book stores. Some even provide discounts for teachers with proper identification. (For homeschoolers, identification to show teacher status can usually include an ID card from your church-related school, a letter from the superintendent's office if you're registered through the county, or a membership card from a homeschool support group.)
- *Used curriculum sales*—Most larger cities or areas have at least one used curriculum sale yearly and some have several. This is where many homeschoolers, like me, purchase the bulk of our supplies. I've found readers for fifty cents, new workbooks for a dollar, a complete math curriculum (loose pages, but unused) for three dollars, and a whole box of science supplies for ten dollars. Some curriculum sales provide a place for free items as well, and you can frequently find older books, damaged books, or partially used workbooks. Picking up some of these free, partially used materials is a good way to sample a curriculum before you actually purchase it.
- *Yard sales*—We have come across some of our best bargains at yard sales. You might get lucky and find a yard sale of a fellow teacher or homeschooler. We have found books for ten cents apiece or a whole box for five dollars at yard sales.
- *Thrift magazines/newsletters*—There are bargain-type magazines in most communities. These don't usually list miscellaneous books, but most thrift publications are great places to find discounted sets of encyclopedias, which are a must for the homeschool environment (yes, even if you have Internet access). Sometimes you can find encyclopedias for as little as twenty dollars per set through thrift magazines.
- *Public library book sales*—If you purchase a large quantity of books for your students throughout the year, as most educators do, you might consider joining a Friends of the Library or other similar local program. These groups typically hold book sales once or twice per year, and "Friends" usually are allowed to shop before the general public. Even if you don't join a Friends-type program, attending the book sales would be a good investment of your time to find great deals. I have purchased encyclopedias, Newbery books, out-of-print history books, and much more for as little as a dime apiece.
- *Civic organization sales*—Many civic organizations hold book sales to raise money for charities, scholarships, or other causes.
- *Church book sales*—Churches will sometimes join in the summer sales frenzy by offering their own versions of yard sales. These sometimes include out-of-print and other older books from the church's collection. The authors have found many out-of-print or hard-to-find books at these sorts of book sales.

List #245 Having a Successful Field Trip

When a new Food City grocery store was built in our town, I took my children shopping. They enjoyed going there so much that it was like a field trip each time. A few months later, we planned a vacation. Bags were packed, snacks were in the cooler, everyone was loaded into the van, and we started to pull out of the driveway. When we told the children we were finally leaving for vacation, the younger ones shouted, "Yeah, we're going to Food City!"

I share that story to remind teachers and parents that any outing can be an educational experience, especially for younger students. There are endless possibilities for field trips. Exposure to various people, places, and events is beneficial for students of any age. Young students in particular absorb much more from their surroundings than we often realize. Take your children to as many cultural, educational, social, religious, and athletic events as possible. Focus on providing positive experiences when you take field trips and learning will occur.

Here are some suggestions to help your field trips or outings be a positive experience for everyone.

- Depending on the type of field trip, if it involves any sort of "business" (fire departments, airports, museums, etc.), call ahead and make a reservation for the field trip, especially if you have a large group. This is also a good idea in general since it may not be convenient to have visitors if the location isn't prepared in advance for your visit.
- Have children write out questions they would like to have answered. Consider having them write their questions on index cards—they are small and easy to keep track of; students can easily keep an index card in a pocket or small purse; index cards are sturdy and not as likely to get torn as regular paper; students can continue to take notes on the back of the index card for follow-up after the field trip.
- Go over a list of vocabulary terms that the students might hear while on the field trip. Explain the meaning of each word before the trip.
- Give the children a list of vocabulary words to define after the field trip.
- Have children bring notebooks to jot questions and make notes.
- Have children bring sketch books on some outings to document nature, draw animals or people, or make diagrams.
- Keep track of who you spoke with when arranging a field trip.
- Keep a record for yourself of the places you've visited and when. You might also want to make notes about what you liked (or didn't) about a particular outing. Index cards, with a simple filing system, are a good way to keep track of this.
- Remember that many professionals would enjoy the opportunity to encourage a student in whatever field he or she might be considering. If

you homeschool, setting up meetings with professionals is a great way to encourage your student to find out more about a particular area of interest.

- Check out the weather forecast a few days before your field trip and plan accordingly. Send home a note with students reminding parents that you will be on an outing and students should be dressed in pants, jacket, gloves, raincoats, or whatever is appropriate.
- Each child could keep a "Field Trip Journal," documenting places they've visited, the dates, and what they learned on the trip.
- Tailor field trips to suit what you are studying in the classroom.
- If you are a public school teacher, encourage your students to take field trips outside of those you can offer. If they go on field trips or special outings with their family, give them extra credit for writing reports about their excursions.
- Browse your local Yellow Pages for ideas for low cost or free field trips.
- Make sure you have enough chaperones. Regardless of your school setting, taking a group of children into an unfamiliar environment always has challenges. Enlist the help of mothers, teachers aides, or (if homeschooling) teenagers. I once went halfway across the United States and visited seven states with my five young children and the help of another homeschooled teenager. It was a very positive educational experience for all!
- Either take it with you or mail it later, but always follow each field trip with a thank-you note.

List #246 Free/Inexpensive Field Trip Options

Note: We have done many of these, but since 9/11 many places have become very strict about and may even prohibit field trips/tours. Call ahead.

- *Library*—Check to see what services your library offers. Many have a "story time" program for different age groups. Use the time on a field trip to teach your student(s) about the card catalog system (if they still have one), how to use library computers, where to locate audio-visual materials, and about appropriate library behavior.
- *Fire department*—Most fire departments will let the children explore the trucks, see how the emergency system works, help spray the hoses, and see other on-site equipment. They are usually eager to answer the children's questions.
- *Police department*—Some cities may allow you to tour the facilities. If not, you might still be able to inspect a police cruiser and have the officer give the children a job description.
- *Local transit system*—Ride the local transit system with your children. This usually costs a small fee but is often less than one dollar per person. Of course, this type of field trip is more beneficial for children who live in rural settings and thus rarely have the need to ride a "city bus." Use the time to see how the transit system works, take a ride from a central location to another point for lunch or a museum, and then return to your original location. Point out sites and areas you might not have noticed before and discuss with the children safety precautions or lack of them on the buses. You can even discuss the origin of words like "bus" and "automobile" or have older students read schedules and fares to determine how much it would cost to go from one location to another. (One word of caution for this field trip: Buses rarely have seat belts so keep this in mind. Also, do not leave your children in a stroller beside you. Put them on a seat with a belt or hold them tightly in your lap. We were taking a field trip one time with a toddler in the stroller, which is allowed, but when the bus turned a corner quickly, the stroller fell over with her in it!)
- *Local air rescue*—Most hospitals will allow you to view the rescue helicopter, and the staff can give the children a guided tour of their facility. Since most of the tour guides are rescue workers who welcome questions, it's a good idea to have students try to think of a few questions in preparation for the visit.
- *Dairy farm*—See how a real dairy system works. Ask if you can help feed calves or milk a cow. There are also some good children's books on this topic that would make a nice introduction for the students before your visit.

List #246 **Free/Inexpensive Field Trip Options** *(continued)*

- *Post office*—See how mail is received, sorted, and delivered. Find out about the different classes of mail. Have students each write a letter before the field trip and mail it while you're at the post office. They could even mail a postcard to themselves and see how long it takes to reach their home.
- *Beehive keeper*—Visiting someone who raises bees is a great opportunity to get firsthand information about bees and how they make honey. You might want to find out about the allergies of your students. If anyone is severely allergic to bee stings, it might be best to stay away from this particular field trip. A member of a local beekeeping association might be willing to do a presentation at your location and this may be a safer alternative than going to a beekeeping location.
- *Courthouse*—Many court cases are open to the public, but use good judgment regarding the cases you allow your children to hear. If used correctly, this is a great chance to learn how the court system works. This is an especially beneficial field trip for older students and one we think would be prudent to require of high-school–age students so that they would better understand the justice system and how it works. You might suggest that the students take detailed notes and in a later class debate whether or not they would have decided the cases the same way.
- *Airport*—Students can learn about the different types of planes and jets, baggage control, and safety measures. Help them gain knowledge of how air traffic control works. Perhaps you could arrange an interview with a pilot or flight attendant.
- *College campus*—This would be a good field trip for the older student to see how college campuses are set up. Visit the admissions office to procure a map for use in challenging your older students to find the various buildings. This would also be an excellent opportunity for younger students to challenge their mapping skills.
- *College library*—Take this opportunity to show older students the differences and similarities between a public library and a college library.
- *Old cemetery*—Old cemeteries are fine places to do etchings. The older the cemetery the better the trip, as you will probably be able to find headstones that may correlate with the time period you are studying. Note the dates of birth and death. Students can try to guess the cause of death based on epidemics (did many people in that cemetery die in the same year, etc.) or they can make up stories about how the families lived. Older students can take the investigation even further by doing research on the deceased individuals through census records.
- *Farm*—A good opportunity for younger children to see various live animals and gain firsthand knowledge of the workings of a farm. There may be an

List #246 **Free/Inexpensive Field Trip Options** *(continued)*

opportunity to volunteer to do certain chores (help feed animals, brush animals, clean up stalls, etc.) in exchange for the field trip.

- *Veterinary clinic*—Depending on the veterinarian, children may be allowed to tour the facility and see how the practice works. Some veterinarians only see large animals in the animal's home environment, and may allow you to meet him/her there and see how the practice works.
- *Fish hatchery*—A good trip to understand fish life cycles. (There are several good books on fish life cycles that could supplement research for this field trip and there are even puzzles that display the fish life cycle. Check your preferred homeschool distributor or the Internet for these supplies.)
- *Wildlife resource agency*—See how animals are protected by these services and learn about the endangered animals in your area.
- *Trucking company*—Let your children experience firsthand how products are shipped and received. This could be a very instructive geography field trip.
- *Horse ranch*—Most children at some time or another want a pony. Let your children see how much care is required in keeping these magnificent animals. As with a farm, offer to do chores in exchange for the field trip.
- *Pond, river, lake, stream, etc.*—These would be good field trips to plan during each of the four seasons. Have your students document and discuss the differences they find depending on the time of year.
- *Rescue squad*—This is another opportunity to gain knowledge about the emergency medical services in your area.
- *Museum*—Visit an art museum, science museum, car museum, museum of flight, or whatever you have in your area. Find out ahead of time what you will see in the museum you have chosen, and then gear your studies toward that particular area (great for unit studies!). If you anticipate visiting a local museum frequently, as many homeschool families do, you might consider purchasing a membership. Many museums have reciprocal agreements so that if you do join, you can also visit other museums across the United States for no additional fee or for a reduced admission fee. This is a great deal and you're still supporting the museum!
- *Aquarium*—Aquariams make great field trips for any age. Let children learn the difference between freshwater and saltwater species. Again, you might consider a membership to a local aquarium so that you can visit at any time.
- *Radio station*—This is a chance to learn how the broadcasting system works. Depending on the station and the age of the children, DJs might allow children the opportunity to read an announcement or make a comment on the air.

List #246 **Free/Inexpensive Field Trip Options** *(continued)*

- *Television station*—Visiting a TV station is another good opportunity to learn about how broadcasting works, especially "live" television. This would also serve as a wonderful opportunity to learn about weather. Arrange your trip so that you can meet some of the staff (meteorologist, sportscaster, reporter, etc.).
- *Zoo*—A wonderful field trip for any age. Be creative when thinking about how to make the trip fit your current studies. Let your children take a notebook and classify the animals they see. Take a sketch pad and some colored pencils and have them draw the animals and their habitats. Discuss the reproduction cycles of various animals. This is the type of trip that can be tailored to challenge any age child. Some cities have wonderful free zoos. For those that charge a fee, you might consider a zoo membership.
- *Co-op*—Help your children understand how co-ops work. Any kind of co-op would be suitable. You could try a local farmer's co-op, a food co-op, etc. Ask if your children may help unload boxes, sort produce, etc.
- *Farmers' market*—Expose your children to the various produce grown in your area. Let them talk to the vendors and learn how much labor is put into raising productive crops. Encourage students to practice using their foreign language skills to talk with migrant workers.
- *Plant farm*—Learn about the different plant species, what grows well in your area, what is your zone. Let the children purchase inexpensive flowers and have their own small flower garden or container.
- *911 communication center*—Many 911 systems allow tours to let your child see how vital this system is to the community. In the classroom, discuss what constitutes an emergency, when to use 911, and basic first aid techniques. This is an especially important lesson for younger students.
- *Community theater*—See the plays, but also try to make arrangements to let your children get a behind-the-scenes glimpse of the work that goes into the productions. If your child is into drama, allow him to audition for a play.
- *Local symphony orchestra*—Most orchestras play a variety of music. This trip could be expensive, so call and check if your local symphony has a free concert. Many do one or two per year for school groups.
- *RV center*—Younger children enjoy seeing these homes on wheels. Go during an off-season. Most centers have campers/travel trailers or the like set up so you can tour them. For those that allow rentals, rent an RV and take your children camping for a week or travel to an out-of-state relative's home in a rented RV.
- *Boating center*—Similar to the RV center, but what young child doesn't love boats?

List #246 **Free/Inexpensive Field Trip Options** *(continued)*

- *Sanitation department*—Another great opportunity to learn about your community and how employees work to keep streets and water clean. Expand discussions to include topics such as the effect of trash on animal life or the average amount of water used by a household each day.
- *Water treatment station*—If you are doing a unit study on the water cycle, waste water treatment, or other topics related to city water usage, a trip to your local water treatment station could prove beneficial.
- *Auto repair garage*—Many children may enjoy the opportunity to see how engines work. Let them talk to a mechanic and watch any repairs that might interest them. Let the older pupil learn some valuable car maintenance.
- *Recycling center*—Raise awareness in your children of how wasteful our country is. Challenge your child to do his/her part to reduce waste.
- *Foreign cuisine restaurants*—Raise cultural awareness in children. Let them sample a variety of cuisines. Learn a few phrases in the language of restaurant owners from foreign countries and practice using these. This field trip could be the reward at the end of geography lessons where the child has learned of places like India, Mexico, Japan, Italy. Go with what you have in your area. *(Do not take a bag of fast food into another restaurant! Not only is this disrespectful to the restaurant, it is allowing your children to be picky eaters, and does not teach them to be thankful and eat what is provided for them.)*
- *Nonprofit organization*—Visit an agency like the American Heart Association or American Lung Association. These agencies have many educational brochures. This type of field trip could be incorporated into a health and nutrition class or even a science class. In most communities there are a variety of these agencies. Another great one would be the American Red Cross. Older students should be encouraged to volunteer time at a nonprofit organization.
- *Bank*—A trip to the bank can be adapted to any age child. Let the younger child get some beginning knowledge about money and simple financial terms. Challenge the older student to find out about loans, interest, and the various types of accounts offered. Students can find out the differences between credit unions and banks.
- *Local state representative's or senator's office*—What is his/her job description? How does he/she work with other lawmakers? This would be an excellent outing for a middle school or high school student studying government.
- *City hall*—Take your students to meet their mayor and commissioners. Challenge them to find out how local government works.

List #246 **Free/Inexpensive Field Trip Options** *(continued)*

- *Dam*—If you have a dam in your area, let children learn what type it is. Let them learn what purposes dams serve and how they affect the waterways. Follow up this field trip with another one. Find a shallow creek and have students try to build an effective dam. Just make certain to tear it down before you leave!
- *Medical clinic*—If possible, visit a clinic to learn about the services they provide. There are several types of clinics. Observe whichever interest your pupils. Learn from doctors and nurses about preventable illnesses and diseases. Learn what normal vital signs are such as a resting heart rate or respirations. Find out what these terms mean. Perhaps your students could learn to take a blood pressure reading.
- *Newspaper*—Students will enjoy learning about the various aspects of newspaper production. Writing is such a vital part of speaking, and so many occupations rely on people who have the ability to write well. Make the most of this field trip. Talk to the editors and journalists. See how the paper is put together and printed. Find out how newspapers sell advertising and determine where it goes in the paper. Have them write sample articles or create their own newspaper.
- *Publishing house*—If you have the advantage of living in a large city, there may be a larger publisher near you. If you live in a rural area, you might find a small or local publishing house nearby. Either way, schedule a visit and allow your children to see the process of how a book is made. If possible, interview an author before you visit the publisher and have the author explain the process of how he obtained a book contract, how long he worked on the book, the process of writing and submitting the text, the editing process, etc. Then, at the publishing house, follow the process of making a book after the author has turned in the text.

List #247 Suggested Items for Bartering

Bartering is an ancient practice. It is simply the practice of trading goods or services for other goods or services. Bartering is a great way to put your own talents and gifts to use. Since most homeschooling families are also one-income families, bartering is also a good way to save money, yet still obtain something you need or want.

Services

This is just a partial list and you may be the giver or receiver here, depending on your own abilities and talents, of course!

- haircutting
- scanning family photos
- pet sitting
- running errands
- providing financial advice
- teaching someone to cook
- baby-sitting
- caring for lawn (mowing, etc.)
- pet grooming
- automotive repair
- providing family or individual counseling
- tutoring
- typing
- computer repair
- house-sitting
- cooking meals
- teaching a class

Items

This is definitely a partial list since the items you can barter would be only as limited as the things you have to barter. We've bartered everything from books and kids' toys to a car—in exchange for baby-sitting.

- books
- toys
- gift certificates
- leftover wallpaper, paint, etc. (You usually can't return these items, but someone else might be able to use them in a smaller room.)
- baby supplies/equipment
- pots, pans, dishes, china
- clothing
- household items
- postcards (from various locations)
- kids' collector cards (like American Girl trading cards)
- food
- movies, CDs, etc.
- homeschool supplies
- vehicles (trade for a different vehicle)
- night(s) in your guest room or whole house if there is a special event where you live (of course, you wouldn't want to barter this with just anyone! Choose your guests carefully.)
- plants (trade one variety for another)
- garden supplies ("Use my rake and I'll borrow your spade.")

List #248 Chore Ideas for Toddlers

Since children vary greatly in their abilities, remember that these are just suggestions. While most toddlers would be able to set the table and most ten-year-olds should be able to sweep and mop the kitchen floor thoroughly, use this as a guide rather than a set of rules. Above all, do chores with your children until you are certain that they know how to do them and then encourage them as they take on these tasks alone. With the chore lists, each older age group should also be able to do the chores for the younger age group(s), so if necessary, assign chores with this in mind. Depending on your own family dynamics, each child should also be doing age appropriate chores in any family business or farm, helping with elderly parents, etc.

- Set table (plates and silverware—not sharp knives)
- Take dirty laundry (in small piles) to laundry room
- Dust (particularly handy to have an "ostrich feather" or other similar hand duster and avoid sprays)
- Help unload dishwasher
- Take small bags of trash to trash can
- Help wash kitchen floor (with small rag)
- Wash front of cabinets, dishwasher, stove (make sure it's not hot!), refrigerator
- Put their own clothes away (not including folding)
- Fold washcloths
- Pick up toys
- Feed chickens
- Check mail (with a parent)

List #249 Chore Ideas for Ages 3–5

- All of the chores for younger ages (see previous list), plus:
- Bring in groceries after a shopping trip
- Help prepare meals
- Help set table (including food dishes that aren't hot)
- Wash bathroom, sink, floor, bathtub and toilet (with supervision)
- Feed pets (like fish, rabbits, other easy to feed animals)
- Help take folded laundry to correct rooms
- Help get out ingredients to cook
- Take items to other parts of the house
- Run a message to neighbor (with adult supervision and not across a road)
- Take mail to box and put up flag (with supervision)
- weed garden (with supervision)
- water plants
- help make beds

List #250 Chore Ideas for Ages 6–9

- All of the chores for younger ages (see previous lists), plus:
- Take out the kitchen trash and replace trash bag
- Mop kitchen floor (with mop or with rags)
- Vacuum (depending on size and ability to use vacuum, of course)
- Dust (with feather duster or with cloth and spray)
- Clean windows and mirrors with glass cleaner
- Wash dishes with help
- Help younger siblings fix bowls of cereal, bagels, other non-cooking type foods
- Play with or keep an eye on younger siblings for short periods of time while mom cleans or does school
- Feed *and* water pets and smaller outside farm animals
- Change litter boxes (may need help to clean the whole litter box)
- Empty dishwasher (put away silverware—not sharp knives—and stack plates and cups on counter for mom or older sibling to put away)
- Watch timer for items in oven and call Mom or Dad when they are ready (teaches responsibility and beginning cooking, but the child is not old or big enough to take items out of the oven yet without help)
- Weed garden, flower area, etc. (some younger children could help with this, but they should know the difference between a weed and a plant or flower)

List #251 Chore Ideas for Ages 10–12

- All of the chores for younger ages (see previous lists), plus:
- Help mom or dad cook
- Begin to cook some items alone with adult supervision
- Empty all trash in house and replace trash bags
- Help sort laundry to be washed
- Load washer, add detergent, and start load
- Put clothes from washer to dryer and start
- Unload dryer and sort clean laundry
- Help fold clothes
- Mow yard (could start a little younger, but either way make sure the child has constant supervision, as mowers are dangerous machines)
- Wash dishes without help
- Clean up kitchen after meals
- Help groom animals (brush cats, dogs, horses; clip nails; etc.)

List #252 Chore Ideas for Ages 13–15

- All of the chores for younger ages (see previous lists), plus:
- Watch younger siblings at home alone for short periods of time
- Cook meals without supervision (an adult should be in the house, however, in case of emergency)
- Do laundry alone (from washing it to putting it in rooms to be put away)
- Take trash and recycle boxes to roadside
- Be fully responsible for care of animals (feeding, cleaning, grooming, etc.)
- Help with paperwork (depending on family preferences for allowing this sort of work, child may be able to complete forms, pay bills, etc.)
- Take care of household chores and take on neighborhood jobs if desired
- Mow lawn
- Use grass trimmer (with supervision)

List #253 Chore Ideas for Ages 16 and Up

We believe that a child who has been taught properly up to this point should essentially be able to do all household and yard chores. A century ago, a young person age sixteen or older frequently began his or her own life through marriage, having children, obtaining a job, and living with his or her own new family. As home educators, many of us believe that teenagers should be treated more as adults and less as children. For this reason, the responsibility of chores and household tasks increases gradually until age fifteen. At that point, the "child" should essentially be able to care for him or herself and the household in which he or she lives. The older teenager should be able not only to help with household and yard chores, but also should have started obtaining experience and learning skills that will serve the young person in the career of his or her choice (even if the choice is to become a homemaker and raise a family; encourage that young adult to practice skills such as sewing, gardening, and even teaching).

List #254 Tasks to Do in Five Minutes or Less

When you don't have a lot of time for cleaning, but you do have a few minutes, just take a quick look at this list for ideas about how you can make the most of that five minutes you DO have. If you have a large family, make a copy of this chart and assign these five-minute tasks to various family members on a monthly basis. Laminate the list and it will be easy for you to change the person responsible by using a dry erase marker. You can even have daily "five-minute clean-up alerts" at various times throughout the day.

Tasks to do in 5 minutes or less	Person responsible for this 5-minute activity this month is...
Empty the dishwasher	
Fill the dishwasher	
Sweep the kitchen	
Take out the trash	
Gather all library books and put them in designated location so that they can be returned to library	
Empty litter box	
Feed pets	
Wipe kitchen table and chairs	
Wipe all doorknobs in house (especially useful during the winter months to prevent spread of germs; this is one that younger children can do)	
Write a thank-you note to someone	
Pick up toys	
Do a "quick, de-clutter clean-up" (Just push all items on a table or in a certain room into a laundry basket and sort it all out later. This is especially helpful if you have unexpected company show up.)	
Take old food out of fridge.	
Bag up all the trash from your vehicle and throw it away.	
Put all the videos or DVDs by the television back in their cases and where they are stored	

List #255 Baby-Sitter's Checklist

If you have a young person in your family who baby-sits for others, share this list with him or her: Make or print copies of this list and use the copies to create a "Baby-sitter's Binder." Keep a Baby-sitter's Checklist for each family you serve and then take your binder with you each time you baby-sit. On (or before) your first job with a particular family, make sure you complete the checklist before the parents leave the house.

Parents' names: ______________________________

Parents' cell phones: ______________________________

Children's names: ______________________________

Address and home phone number: ______________________________

____

Emergency number (for police and fire, if not 9-1-1): ______________

Childrens' allergies: ______________________________

Bedtime: __________ Bedtime routine: ______________

____

Instructions for handling phone calls: ______________

____

What television shows the children are allowed to watch or games they are allowed to play: ______________________________

Friendly neighbors who can assist in an emergency: ______________

____

Special instructions for today (write in pencil): ______________

____

Where parents can be reached (write in pencil, as this will change each time you baby-sit): ______________________________

When parents will return (write in pencil): ______________

List #256 Boy Scout Merit Badges

Boy Scouts learn about science, sports, mathematics, careers, and all sorts of other amazing subjects while they have fun earning merit badges. More information about earning merit badges can be found at *www.meritbadges.com*.

- American Business
- American Culture
- American Heritage
- American Labor
- Animal Science
- Archaeology
- Archery
- Architecture
- Art
- Astronomy
- Athletics
- Auto Mechanics
- Aviation
- Backpacking
- Basketry
- Bird Study
- Bugling
- Camping
- Canoeing
- Chemistry
- Cinematography
- Citizenship in the Community
- Citizenship in the Nation
- Citizenship in the World
- Climbing
- Coin Collecting
- Collections
- Communications
- Composite Materials
- Computers
- Cooking
- Crime Prevention
- Cycling
- Dentistry
- Disabilities Awareness
- Dog Care
- Drafting
- Electricity
- Electronics
- Emergency Preparedness
- Energy
- Engineering
- Entrepreneurship
- Environmental Science
- Family Life
- Farm Mechanics
- Fingerprinting
- Fire Safety
- First Aid
- Fish and Wildlife Management
- Fishing
- Fly-Fishing
- Forestry
- Gardening
- Genealogy
- Geology
- Golf
- Graphic Arts
- Hiking
- Home Repairs
- Horsemanship
- Indian Lore
- Insect Study
- Journalism
- Landscape Architecture
- Law
- Leatherwork
- Lifesaving
- Mammal Study
- Medicine
- Metalwork
- Model Design and Building
- Motorboating
- Music
- Nature
- Nuclear Science
- Oceanography
- Orienteering
- Painting
- Personal Fitness
- Personal Management
- Pets
- Photography
- Pioneering
- Plant Science
- Plumbing
- Pottery
- Public Health
- Public Speaking
- Pulp and Paper
- Radio
- Railroading
- Reading
- Reptile and Amphibian Study
- Rifle Shooting
- Rowing
- Safety
- Salesmanship
- Scholarship
- Sculpture
- Shotgun Shooting
- Skating
- Small-Boat Sailing
- Snow Sports
- Soil and Water Conservation
- Space Exploration
- Sports
- Stamp Collecting
- Surveying
- Swimming
- Textile
- Theater
- Traffic Safety
- Truck Transportation
- Veterinary Medicine
- Water Skiing
- Weather
- Whitewater
- Wilderness Survival
- Wood Carving
- Woodwork

List #257 Five in a Row Books

Jane Claire Lambert created Five in a Row (FIAR) books as a result of the homeschooling journey with her own children. The Five in a Row volumes contain wonderful unit studies—each one based on a particular book read aloud to the child for five days. The lesson plans in each unit study are geared toward children age four to eight and include social studies, language, art, science, and applied math. In addition to the four main volumes of Five in a Row, there are also FIAR volumes for use with younger or older children.

The purpose of the following list is simply to familiarize the parent educator with Five in a Row books and to provide a checklist that you can use when collecting FIAR books for use with FIAR materials. To benefit from the lesson plans and unit studies compiled during years of research, purchase Five in a Row materials appropriate to your child's age level from the Lamberts' Web site at *www.fiveinarow.com*.

Do we have this book?	Have we read it?	Have we completed FIAR activities?	Title and Author
			Volume 1
☐	☐	☐	*The Story About Ping* by Marjorie Flack and Kurt Wiese
☐	☐	☐	*Lentil* by Robert McCloskey
☐	☐	☐	*Madeline* by Ludwig Bemelmans
☐	☐	☐	*A Pair of Red Clogs* by Masako Matsuno
☐	☐	☐	*The Rag Coat* by Lauren Mills
☐	☐	☐	*Who Owns the Sun?* by Stacy Chbosky
☐	☐	☐	*Mike Mulligan and His Steam Shovel* by Virginia Lee Burton
☐	☐	☐	*The Glorious Flight* by Alice and Martin Provensen
☐	☐	☐	*How to Make an Apple Pie and See the World* by Marjorie Priceman
☐	☐	☐	*Grandfather's Journey* by Allen Say
☐	☐	☐	*Cranberry Thanksgiving* by Wende and Harry Devlin
☐	☐	☐	*Another Celebrated Dancing Bear* by Gladys Scheffrin-Falk
☐	☐	☐	*Papa Piccolo* by Carol Talley
☐	☐	☐	*Very Last First Time* by Jan Andrews
☐	☐	☐	*The Clown of God* by Tomie DePaola
☐	☐	☐	*Storm in the Night* by Mary Stoltz
☐	☐	☐	*Katy and the Big Snow* by Virginia Lee Burton
☐	☐	☐	*Night of the Moonjellies* by Mark Shasha
☐	☐	☐	*Stopping by Woods on a Snowy Evening* by Robert Frost, ill. by Susan Jeffers

List #257 FIVE IN A ROW Books *(continued)*

Do we have this book?	Have we read it?	Have we completed FIAR activities?	Title and Author
			Volume 2
☐	☐	☐	*The Giraffe That Walked to Paris* by Nancy Milton
☐	☐	☐	*Three Names* by Patricia MacLachlan
☐	☐	☐	*Wee Gillis* by Munro Leaf
☐	☐	☐	*Owl Moon* by Jane Yolen
☐	☐	☐	*A New Coat for Anna* by Harriet Ziefert
☐	☐	☐	*Mrs. Katz and Tush* by Patricia Polacco
☐	☐	☐	*Mirette on the High Wire* by Emily Arnold McCully
☐	☐	☐	*They Were Strong and Good* by Alice and Robert Lawson
☐	☐	☐	*Babar, To Duet or Not to Duet* based on characters by DeBrunhoff
☐	☐	☐	*The Story of Ferdinand* by Munro Leaf
☐	☐	☐	*Down, Down the Mountain* by Ellis Credle
☐	☐	☐	*Make Way for Ducklings* by Robert McCloskey
☐	☐	☐	*The Tale of Peter Rabbit* written and ill. by Beatrix Potter
☐	☐	☐	*Mr. Gumpy's Motor Car* by John Burningham
☐	☐	☐	*All Those Secrets of the World* by Jane Yolen
☐	☐	☐	*Miss Rumphius* by Barbara Cooney
☐	☐	☐	*The Little Red Lighthouse and the Great Gray Bridge* by Hildegarde Swift
☐	☐	☐	*Follow the Drinking Gourd* by Jeanette Winter
☐	☐	☐	*Harold and the Purple Crayon* by Crockett Johnson
☐	☐	☐	*When I Was Young in the Mountains* by Cynthia Rylant
☐	☐	☐	*Gramma's Walk* by Anna Grossnickle Hines
			Volume 3
☐	☐	☐	*The Bee Tree* by Patricia Polacco
☐	☐	☐	*Andy and the Circus* by Ellis Credle
☐	☐	☐	*The Wild Horses of Sweetbriar* by Natalie Kinsey-Warnock
☐	☐	☐	*Paul Revere's Ride* by Henry Wadsworth Longfellow, ill. by Ted Rand
☐	☐	☐	*Henry the Castaway* by Mark Taylor
☐	☐	☐	*The Finest Horse in Town* by Jacqueline Briggs Martin
☐	☐	☐	*Truman's Aunt Farm* by Jama Kim Rattigan
☐	☐	☐	*The Duchess Bakes a Cake* by Virginia Kahl
☐	☐	☐	*Andy and the Lion* by James Daugherty

List #257 Five in a Row Books *(continued)*

Do we have this book?	Have we read it?	Have we completed FIAR activities?	Title and Author
☐	☐	☐	*Daniel's Duck* by Clyde Robert Bulla
☐	☐	☐	*Warm as Wool* by Scott Russell Sanders
☐	☐	☐	*The Salamander Room* by Anne Mazer
☐	☐	☐	*Climbing Kansas Mountains* by George Shannon
☐	☐	☐	*Amber on the Mountain* by Tony Johnston
☐	☐	☐	*Little Nino's Pizzeria* by Karen Barbour
			Volume 4
☐	☐	☐	*Roxaboxen* by Alice McLerran
☐	☐	☐	*The Raft* by Jim LaMarche
☐	☐	☐	*Mailing May* by Michael O. Tunnell
☐	☐	☐	*Snowflake Bentley* by Jacqueline Briggs Martin
☐	☐	☐	*The Gullywasher* by Joyce Rossi
☐	☐	☐	*Arabella* by Wendy Orr
☐	☐	☐	*Higgins Bend Song and Dance* by Jacqueline Briggs Martin
☐	☐	☐	*Cowboy Charlie* by Jeanette Winter
☐	☐	☐	*Grass Sandals* by Dawnine Spivak
☐	☐	☐	*Albert* by Donna Jo Napoli
☐	☐	☐	*The Hickory Chair* by Lisa Rose Fraustino
☐	☐	☐	*Hanna's Cold Winter* by Trish Marx
☐	☐	☐	*The Hatmaker's Sign* Retold by Candace Fleming
☐	☐	☐	*The Pumpkin Runner* by Marsha Diane Arnold
☐	☐	☐	*Angelo* by David Macaulay

List #258 | Cornerstones of Freedom Books

The Cornerstones of Freedom series is a lively, well-researched series of history books for children ages eight to twelve. The books cover a wide variety of historical subjects and average thirty-two pages.

Do we have this title?	Have we read it?	Title
☐	☐	*The Story of D-Day*
☐	☐	*The Story of Fort Sumter*
☐	☐	*The Story of Gold at Sutter's Mill*
☐	☐	*The Story of Jamestown*
☐	☐	*The Story of Marquette and Jolliet*
☐	☐	*The Story of Monticello*
☐	☐	*The Story of Mount Rushmore*
☐	☐	*The Story of Mount Vernon*
☐	☐	*The Story of Old Glory*
☐	☐	*The Story of Old Ironsides*
☐	☐	*The Story of the Alamo*
☐	☐	*The Story of the Arlington National Cemetery*
☐	☐	*The Story of the Barbary Pirates*
☐	☐	*The Story of the Battle for Iwo Jima*
☐	☐	*The Story of the Battle of the Bulge*
☐	☐	*The Story of the Bonhomme Richard*
☐	☐	*The Story of the Capitol*
☐	☐	*The Story of the Chicago Fire*
☐	☐	*The Story of the Clipper Ships*
☐	☐	*The Story of the Conestoga Wagon*
☐	☐	*The Story of the Constitution*
☐	☐	*The Story of the Declaration of Independence*
☐	☐	*The Story of the Flight at Kitty Hawk*
☐	☐	*The Story of the Gettysburg Address*
☐	☐	*The Story of the Golden Spike*
☐	☐	*The Story of the Homestead Act*
☐	☐	*The Story of the Liberty Bell*
☐	☐	*The Story of the Lincoln Memorial*
☐	☐	*The Story of the Mayflower Compact*
☐	☐	*The Story of the New England Whalers*
☐	☐	*The Story of the Nineteenth Amendment*

List #258 **Cornerstones of Freedom Books** *(continued)*

Do we have this title?	Have we read it?	Title
☐	☐	*The Story of the Panama Canal*
☐	☐	*The Story of the Pony Express*
☐	☐	*The Story of the Pullman Strike*
☐	☐	*The Story of the Smithsonian Institution*
☐	☐	*The Story of the Star-Spangled Banner*
☐	☐	*The Story of the Statue of Liberty*
☐	☐	*The Story of the Supreme Court*
☐	☐	*The Story of the Underground Railroad*
☐	☐	*The Story of the U.S.S. Arizona*
☐	☐	*The Story of the White House*

List #259 LANDMARK Books

Random House began publishing LANDMARK books (about American History) and WORLD LANDMARK books (about World History) in the 1950s. The books are extremely accurate, thorough histories for young people. The reading levels vary from book to book, but basically they were written for children ages nine to fifteen. The stories are so interesting and well written that they also make nice reading material for older students, adults, or as read-alouds for younger children. A few of the books contain material that might be best suited for young adults. These books are highly collectible.

Do we have this book?	Have we read it?	Title	Author
☐	☐	*Abe Lincoln: Log Cabin to White House*	Sterling North
☐	☐	*The Adventures and Discoveries of Marco Polo*	Richard J. Walsh
☐	☐	*The Adventures of Ulysses*	Gerald Gottlieb
☐	☐	*The Alaska Gold Rush*	May McNeer
☐	☐	*Alexander Hamilton & Aaron Burr*	Anna and Russell Crouse
☐	☐	*Alexander the Great*	John Gunther
☐	☐	*The American Revolution*	Bruce Bliven, Jr.
☐	☐	*Americans Into Orbit: The Story of Project Mercury*	Gene Gurney
☐	☐	*America's First World War: General Pershing*	Henry Castor
☐	☐	*Andrew Carnegie and the Age of Steel*	Katherine B. Shippen
☐	☐	*Balboa: Swordsman & Conquistador*	Felix Riesenberg
☐	☐	*The Barbary Pirates*	C. S. Forester
☐	☐	*The Battle for Iwo Jima*	Robert Leckie
☐	☐	*The Battle for the Atlantic*	Jay Williams
☐	☐	*The Battle of Britain*	Quentin Reynolds
☐	☐	*The Battle of the Bulge*	John Toland
☐	☐	*Ben Franklin of Old Philadelphia*	Margaret Cousins
☐	☐	*Ben-Gurion and the Birth of Israel*	Joan Comay
☐	☐	*Betsy Ross and the Flag*	Jane Mayer
☐	☐	*Buffalo Bill's Great Wild West Show*	Walter Havighurst
☐	☐	*The Building of the First Transcontinental Railroad*	Adele Nathan
☐	☐	*The California Gold Rush*	May McNeer
☐	☐	*Captain Cook Explores the South Seas*	Armstrong Sperry
☐	☐	*Captain Cortes Conquers Mexico*	William Johnson

List #259 LANDMARK **Books** *(continued)*

Do we have this book?	Have we read it?	Title	Author
☐	☐	*Catherine the Great*	Katherine Scherman
☐	☐	*Chief of the Cossacks*	Harold Lamb
☐	☐	*Clara Barton, Founder of the American Red Cross*	Helen Boylston
☐	☐	*Cleopatra of Egypt*	Leonora Hornblow
☐	☐	*Clipper Ship Days*	John Jennings
☐	☐	*Combat Nurses of World War II*	Wyatt Blassingame
☐	☐	*The Coming of the Mormons*	Jim Kjelgaard
☐	☐	*The Commandos of World War II*	Hodding Carter
☐	☐	*Commodore Perry and the Opening of Japan*	Ferdinand Kuhn
☐	☐	*The Conquest of the North and South Poles*	Russell Owen
☐	☐	*The Copper Kings of Montana*	Marian T. Place
☐	☐	*The Crusades*	Anthony West
☐	☐	*Custer's Last Stand*	Quentin Reynolds
☐	☐	*Daniel Boone and the Opening of the Wilderness Road*	John Mason Brown
☐	☐	*Davy Crockett*	Stewart H. Holbrook
☐	☐	*Disaster at Johnstown: The Great Flood*	Hildegarde Dolson
☐	☐	*The Doctors Who Conquered Yellow Fever*	Ralph Nading Hill
☐	☐	*Dolley Madison*	Jane Mayer
☐	☐	*Dwight D. Eisenhower*	Malcom Moos
☐	☐	*The Early Days of Automobiles in America*	Elizabeth Janeway
☐	☐	*The Erie Canal*	Samuel Hopkins Adams
☐	☐	*Ethan Allen and the Green Mountain Boys*	Slater Brown
☐	☐	*Evangeline and the Acadians*	Robert Tallant
☐	☐	*The Exploits of Xenophon*	Geoffrey Household
☐	☐	*The Explorations of Pere Marquette*	Jim Kjelgaard
☐	☐	*Exploring the Himalayas*	William O. Douglas
☐	☐	*The Fall of Constantinople*	Bernadine Kielty
☐	☐	*Famous Pirates of the New World*	A. B. C. Whipple
☐	☐	*The F.B.I.*	Quentin Reynolds
☐	☐	*Ferdinand Magellan: Master Mariner*	Seymour Gates Pond
☐	☐	*The First Men in the World*	Anne Terry White
☐	☐	*The First Overland Mail*	Robert Pinkerton
☐	☐	*The First Transatlantic Cable*	Adele Gutman Nathan

List #259 **Landmark Books** *(continued)*

Do we have this book?	Have we read it?	Title	Author
☐	☐	*Flat Tops*	Edmund Castillo
☐	☐	*The Flight and Adventures of Charles II*	Charles Norman
☐	☐	*Florence Nightingale*	Ruth Fox Hume
☐	☐	*The Flying Aces of World War I*	Gene Gurney
☐	☐	*The Flying Tigers*	John Toland
☐	☐	*The French Foreign Legion*	Wyatt Blassingame
☐	☐	*From Casablanca to Berlin*	Bruce Bliven, Jr.
☐	☐	*From Pearl Harbor to Okinawa*	Bruce Bliven, Jr.
☐	☐	*Garibaldi: Father of Modern Italy*	Marcia Davenport
☐	☐	*General Brock and Niagara Falls*	Samuel Hopkins Adams
☐	☐	*Genghis Kahn and the Mongol Horde*	Harold Lamb
☐	☐	*George Washington Carver*	Anne Terry White
☐	☐	*George Washington: Frontier Colonel*	Sterling North
☐	☐	*Geronimo: Wolf of the Warpath*	Ralph Moody
☐	☐	*Gettysburg*	MacKinlay Kantor
☐	☐	*The Golden Age of Railroads*	Stewart H. Holbrook
☐	☐	*Great American Fighter Pilots of World War II*	Robert D. Loomis
☐	☐	*Great Men of Medicine*	Ruth Fox Hume
☐	☐	*Guadalcanal Diary*	Richard Tregaskis
☐	☐	*Hawaii, Gem of the Pacific*	Oscar Lewis
☐	☐	*Hero of Trafalgar*	A. B. C. Whipple
☐	☐	*Heroines of the Early West*	Nancy Wilson Ross
☐	☐	*Hudson's Bay Company*	Richard Morenus
☐	☐	*Jesus of Nazareth*	Harry Emerson Fosdick
☐	☐	*Joan of Arc*	Nancy Wilson Ross
☐	☐	*John F. Kennedy and PT 109*	Richard Tregaskis
☐	☐	*John James Audubon*	Margaret and John Kieran
☐	☐	*John Paul Jones, Fighting Sailor*	Armstrong Sperry
☐	☐	*Julius Caesar*	John Gunther
☐	☐	*King Arthur and His Knights*	Mabel Louise Robinson
☐	☐	*Kit Carson and the Wild Frontier*	Ralph Moody
☐	☐	*The Landing of the Pilgrims*	James Daugherty
☐	☐	*Lawrence of Arabia*	Alistair MacLean

List #259 LANDMARK **Books** *(continued)*

Do we have this book?	Have we read it?	Title	Author
☐	☐	*Lee and Grant at Appomattox*	MacKinlay Kantor
☐	☐	*Leonardo da Vinci*	Emily Hahn
☐	☐	*The Lewis and Clark Expedition*	Richard L. Neuberger
☐	☐	*The Life of Saint Patrick*	Quentin Reynolds
☐	☐	*The Life of Saint Paul*	Harry Emerson Fosdick
☐	☐	*Lincoln and Douglas: The Years of Decision*	Regina Z. Kelly
☐	☐	*The Louisiana Purchase*	Robert Tallant
☐	☐	*The Magna Charta*	James Daugherty
☐	☐	*The Man Who Changed China: The Story of Sun Yat-sen*	Pearl S. Buck
☐	☐	*Marie Antoinette*	Bernadine Kielty
☐	☐	*Marquis de Lafayette: Bright Sword of Freedom*	Hodding Carter
☐	☐	*Martin Luther*	Harry Emerson Fosdick
☐	☐	*Mary, Queen of Scots*	Emily Hahn
☐	☐	*Medal of Honor Heroes*	Colonel Red Reeder
☐	☐	*Medical Corps Heros of World War II*	Wyatt Blassingame
☐	☐	*Midway, Battle for the Pacific*	Edmund L. Castillo
☐	☐	*The Mississippi Bubble*	Thomas B. Costain
☐	☐	*The Moniter and the Merrimac*	Fletcher Pratt
☐	☐	*Mr. Bell Invents the Telephone*	Katherine B. Shippen
☐	☐	*The Mysterious Voyage of Captain Kidd*	A. B. C. Whipple
☐	☐	*Napoleon and the Battle of Waterloo*	Frances Winwar
☐	☐	*Old Ironsides, the Fighting Constitution*	Harry Hansen
☐	☐	*Our Independence and the Constitution*	Dorothy Canfield Fisher
☐	☐	*The Panama Canal*	Bob Considine
☐	☐	*Paul Revere and the Minute Men*	Dorothy Canfield Fisher
☐	☐	*Peter Stuyvesant of Old New York*	Anna and Russell Crouse
☐	☐	*The Pharoahs of Ancient Egypt*	Elizabeth Payne
☐	☐	*The Pirate Lafitte and the Battle of New Orleans*	Robert Tallant
☐	☐	*Pocahontas and Captain John Smith*	Marie Lawson
☐	☐	*The Pony Express*	Samuel Hopkins Adams
☐	☐	*Prehistoric America*	Anne Terry White
☐	☐	*Queen Elizabeth and the Spanish Armada*	Frances Winwar

List #259 Landmark **Books** *(continued)*

Do we have this book?	Have we read it?	Title	Author
☐	☐	*Queen Victoria*	Noel Streatfeild
☐	☐	*Remember the Alamo!*	Robert Penn Warren
☐	☐	*The Rise and Fall of Adolf Hitler*	William L. Shirer
☐	☐	*Robert E. Lee and the Road of Honor*	Hodding Carter
☐	☐	*Robert Fulton and the Steamboat*	Ralph Nading Hill
☐	☐	*Rogers' Rangers and the French & Indian War*	Bradford Smith
☐	☐	*The Royal Canadian Mounted Police*	Richard L. Neuberger
☐	☐	*Sam Houston, the Tallest Texan*	William Johnson
☐	☐	*The Santa Fe Trail*	Samuel Hopkins Adams
☐	☐	*The Seabees of World War II*	Edmund Castillo
☐	☐	*Sequoyah: Leader of the Cherokees*	Alice Marriott
☐	☐	*Simon Bolivar, the Great Liberator*	Arnold Whitridge
☐	☐	*The Sinking of the Bismarck*	William L. Shirer
☐	☐	*The Slave Who Freed Haiti: The Story of Toussaint Louverture*	Katherine Scherman
☐	☐	*Stonewall Jackson*	Jonathan Daniels
☐	☐	*The Story of Albert Schweitzer*	Anita Daniel
☐	☐	*The Story of Atomic Energy*	Laura Fermi
☐	☐	*The Story of Australia*	A. Grove Day
☐	☐	*The Story of D-Day: June 6, 1944*	Bruce Bliven, Jr.
☐	☐	*The Story of Oklahoma*	Lon Tinkle
☐	☐	*The Story of San Francisco*	Charlotte Jackson
☐	☐	*The Story of Scotland Yard*	Laurence Thompson
☐	☐	*The Story of Submarines*	George Weller
☐	☐	*The Story of the Air Force*	Robert Loomis
☐	☐	*The Story of the Naval Academy*	Felix Riesenberg, Jr.
☐	☐	*The Story of the Paratroops*	George Weller
☐	☐	*The Story of the Secret Service*	Ferdinand Kuhn
☐	☐	*The Story of the Thirteen Colonies*	Clifford Lindsey Alderman
☐	☐	*The Story of the U.S. Coast Guard*	Eugene Rachlis
☐	☐	*The Story of the U.S. Marines*	George Hunt
☐	☐	*The Story of Thomas Alva Edison*	Margaret Cousins
☐	☐	*The Swamp Fox of the Revolution*	Stewart H. Holbrook

List #259 **Landmark Books** *(continued)*

Do we have this book?	Have we read it?	Title	Author
☐	☐	*Teddy Roosevelt and the Rough Riders*	Henry Castor
☐	☐	*The Texas Rangers*	Will Henry
☐	☐	*Thirty Seconds Over Tokyo*	Ted Lawson and Bob Considine
☐	☐	*Thomas Jefferson, Father of Democracy*	Vincent Sheean
☐	☐	*Tippecanoe and Tyler, Too!*	Stanley Young
☐	☐	*To California by Covered Wagon*	George R. Stewart
☐	☐	*Trappers and Traders of the Far West*	James Daugherty
☐	☐	*The United Nations in War and Peace*	T. R. Fehrenback
☐	☐	*Up the Trail From Texas*	J. Frank Dobie
☐	☐	*The U.S. Border Patrol*	Clement Hellyer
☐	☐	*The U.S. Frogmen of World War II*	Wyatt Blassingame
☐	☐	*The Vikings*	Elizabeth Janeway
☐	☐	*The Voyages of Christopher Columbus*	Armstrong Sperry
☐	☐	*The Voyages of Henry Hudson*	Eugene Rachlis
☐	☐	*Walk in Space: the Story of Project Gemini*	Gene Gurney
☐	☐	*Walter Raleigh*	Henrietta Buckmaster
☐	☐	*The War Chief of the Seminoles*	May McNeer
☐	☐	*The War in Korea: 1950–1953*	Robert Leckie
☐	☐	*The West Point Story*	Col. Red Reeder and Nardi Reeder Campion
☐	☐	*Wild Bill Hickok Tames the West*	Stewart H. Holbrook
☐	☐	*Will Shakespeare and the Globe Theater*	Anne Terry White
☐	☐	*William Penn: Quaker Hero*	Hildegarde Dolson
☐	☐	*William the Conqueror*	Thomas B. Costain
☐	☐	*Winston Churchill*	Quentin Reynolds
☐	☐	*The Winter at Valley Forge*	Van Wyck Mason
☐	☐	*The Witchcraft of Salem Village*	Shirley Jackson
☐	☐	*Women of Courage*	Dorothy Nathan
☐	☐	*The World's Greatest Showman: P. T. Barnum*	J. Bryan III
☐	☐	*The Wright Brothers*	Quentin Reynolds
☐	☐	*Wyatt Earp: U.S. Marshall*	Stewart H. Holbrook
☐	☐	*Young Mark Twain and the Mississippi*	Harnett T. Kane

List #260 CHILDHOOD OF FAMOUS AMERICANS BOOKS

The CHILDHOOD OF FAMOUS AMERICANS books provide fabulous, historically accurate portrayals of famous Americans in their youth and they end by telling the individuals' achievements. The column with the boxes is provided to indicate if you have the book. These books, geared toward children ages nine to twelve, are meant to be read over and over, enjoyed, memorized, and relished so that children can become more acquainted with these significant individuals. The books are published by Aladdin (an imprint of Simon & Schuster) and are widely available.

	Title	Author
☐	*A. P. Giannini: Boy of San Francisco*	Marie Hammontree
☐	*Abe Lincoln: Frontier Boy*	Augusta Stevenson
☐	*Abigail Adams: Girl of Colonial Days*	Jean Brown Wagoner
☐	*Abraham Lincoln: The Great Emancipator*	Augusta Stevenson
☐	*Adlai Stevenson: Young Ambassador*	Martha Eads Ward
☐	*Albert Einstein: Young Thinker*	Marie Hammontree
☐	*Alec Hamilton: The Little Lion*	Helen Boyd Higgins
☐	*Aleck Bell: Ingenious Boy*	Mabel C. Widdemer
☐	*Althea Gibson: Young Tennis Player*	Beatrice Gromley
☐	*Amelia Erhart: Young Aviator*	Beatrice Gromley
☐	*Andrew Carnegie: Young Steelmaker*	Joanne Landers Henry
☐	*Andrew Jackson: Young Patriot*	George E. Stanley
☐	*Annie Oakley: Young Markswoman*	Ellen Wilson
☐	*Anthony Wayne: Daring Boy*	Augusta Stevenson
☐	*Arthur Ashe: Young Tennis Champion*	Paul Mantell
☐	*Babe Didrikson: Girl Athlete*	Lena and Lynn de Grummond
☐	*Babe Ruth: Baseball Boy*	Guernsey Van Riper
☐	*Bedford Forrest: Horseback Boy*	Aileen Wells Parks
☐	*Benjamin Franklin: Young Printer*	Augusta Stevenson
☐	*Betsy Ross: Designer of Our Flag*	Ann Weil
☐	*Booker T. Washington: Ambitious Boy*	Augusta Stevenson
☐	*Buffalo Bill: Boy of the Plains*	Augusta Stevenson
☐	*Carl Ben Eielson: Young Alaskan Pilot*	H. Myers, Ruth Burnett
☐	*Cecil B. DeMille: Young Dramatist*	H. Myers, Ruth Burnett
☐	*Christopher Reeve: Young Actor*	Kathleen Kudlinski
☐	*Clara Barton: Girl Nurse*	Augusta Stevenson

List #260 **CHILDHOOD OF FAMOUS AMERICANS Books** *(continued)*

Title	Author
☐ *Crazy Horse: Young War Chief*	George E. Stanley
☐ *Crispus Attucks: Boy of Valor*	Dharathula Millender
☐ *Cyrus McCormick: Farm Boy*	Lavinia Dobler
☐ *Dale Earnhardt: Young Race Car Driver*	Paul Mantell
☐ *Dan Webster: Union Boy*	Bradford Smith
☐ *Daniel Boone: Boy Hunter*	Augusta Stevenson
☐ *David Farragut: Boy Midshipman*	Laura Long
☐ *Davy Crockett: Young Rifleman*	Aileen W. Parks
☐ *DeWitt Clinton: Boy Builder*	Mabel Cleland Widdemer
☐ *Dolley Madison: Quaker Girl*	Helen Albee Monsell
☐ *Dorothea Dix: Girl Reformer*	Grace Hathaway Melin
☐ *Douglas MacArthur: Young Protector*	Laura Long
☐ *Dr. Seuss: Young Author and Artist*	Kathleen Kudlinski
☐ *Dwight D. Eisenhower: Young Military Leader*	George E. Stanley
☐ *Eddie Rickenbacker: Young Racer and Flyer*	Cathrine Cleven
☐ *Eleanor Roosevelt: Courageous Girl*	Ann Weil
☐ *Eli Whitney: Boy Mechanic*	Dorothea J. Snow
☐ *Elias Howe: Inventive Boy*	Jean Corcoran
☐ *Elizabeth Blackwell: Girl Doctor*	Joanne Landers Henry
☐ *Ernie Pyle: Boy From Back Home*	Ellen Wilson
☐ *Ethel Barrymore: Girl Actress*	Shirlee P. Newman
☐ *Eugene Field: Young Poet*	K. Borland, Helen Speicher
☐ *F. W. Woolworth: Five and Ten Boy*	H. Myers, P. Elisabeth
☐ *Frances Willard: Girl Crusader*	Miriam Mason
☐ *Francis Marion: Young Swamp Fox*	William O. Steele
☐ *Franklin Delano Roosevelt: Champion of Freedom*	Kathleen Kudlinski
☐ *Franklin Roosevelt: Boy of the Four Freedoms*	Ann Weil
☐ *Gail Borden: Resourceful Boy*	Adrian Paradis
☐ *George Carver: Boy Scientist*	Augusta Stevenson
☐ *George Dewey: Vermont Boy*	Laura Long
☐ *George Eastman: Young Photographer*	Joanne Landers Henry
☐ *George Gershwin: Young Composer*	Bernice Bryant
☐ *George S. Patton: War Hero*	George E. Stanley
☐ *George Pullman: Young Sleeping-Car Builder*	Elisabeth P. Myers

List #260 | Childhood of Famous Americans Books *(continued)*

☐	*George Rogers Clark: Boy of the Old Northwest*	Katharine E. Wilkie
☐	*George Washington: Boy Leader*	Augusta Stevenson
☐	*George Westinghouse: Young Inventor*	Montrew Dunham
☐	*Geronimo: Young Warrior*	George Edward Stanley
☐	*Glenn L. Martin: Boy Conqueror of the Air*	Ruth W. Harley
☐	*Harriet Tubman: Freedom's Trailblazer*	Kathleen Kudlinski
☐	*Harry Houdini: Young Magician*	K. Borland, H. Speicher
☐	*Harry S. Truman: Missouri Farm Boy*	Wilma J. Hudson
☐	*Harry S. Truman: Thirty-Third President of the United States*	George E. Stanley
☐	*Helen Keller: From Tragedy to Triumph*	Katharine E. Wilkie
☐	*Henry Clay: Mill Boy of the Slashes*	Helen A. Monsell
☐	*Henry Ford: Young Man With Ideas*	Hazel Aird, C. Ruddiman
☐	*Her Own Way: The Story of Lottie Moon*	Helen A. Monsell
☐	*Herbert Hoover: Boy Engineer*	Mildred H. Comfort
☐	*Israel Putnam: Fearless Boy*	Augusta Stevenson
☐	*J. Sterling Morton: Arbor Day Boy*	Clyde B. Moore
☐	*Jackie Robinson: Young Sports Trailblazer*	Herb Dunn
☐	*Jacqueline Kennedy Onassis: Friend of the Arts*	Beatrice Gormley
☐	*James Fenimore Cooper: Leatherstocking Boy*	Gertrude Hecker Winders
☐	*James Monroe: Good Neighbor Boy*	Mabel Cleland Widdemer
☐	*James Oglethorpe: Young Defender*	Aileen Wells Parks
☐	*James Whitcomb Riley: Hoosier Boy*	Minnie Belle Mitchell
☐	*Jeb Stuart: Boy in the Saddle*	Gertrude Hecker Winders
☐	*Jesse Owens: Young Record Breaker*	M. M. Eboch
☐	*Jessie Fremont: Girl on Capitol Hill*	Jean Brown Wagoner
☐	*Jim Bridger: Mountain Boy*	Gertrude Hecker Winders
☐	*Jim Thorpe: Indian Athlete*	Guernsey Van Riper
☐	*Joe DiMaggio: Young Sports Hero*	Herb Dunn
☐	*John Alden: Young Puritan*	Olive W. Burt
☐	*John F. Kennedy: America's Youngest President*	Lucy Post Frisbee
☐	*John Glenn: Young Astronaut*	Michael Burgan
☐	*John Hancock: New England Boy*	Catherine Seward Cleven
☐	*John Jacob Astor: Boy Trader*	Dorothy S. Anderson
☐	*John L. Lewis: Young Militant Labor Leader*	George Korson

List #260 **Childhood of Famous Americans Books** *(continued)*

☐	*John Marshall: Boy of Young America*	Helen A. Monsell
☐	*John Muir: Young Naturalist*	Montrew Dunham
☐	*John Peter Zenger: Young Defender of Free Press*	Laura Long
☐	*John Philip Sousa: Marching Boy*	Ann Weil
☐	*John Quincy Adams: Boy Patriot*	Ann Weil
☐	*John Wanamaker: Boy Merchant*	Olive W. Burt
☐	*Juliette Low: Girl Scout*	Helen Boyd Higgins
☐	*Kit Carson: Boy Trapper*	Augusta Stevenson
☐	*Knute Rockne: Young Athlete*	Guernsey Van Riper
☐	*Laura Ingalls Wilder: Young Pioneer*	Beatrice Gormley
☐	*Lee DeForest: Electronics Boy*	Lavinia Dobler
☐	*Lew Wallace: Boy Writer*	Martha E. Schaaf
☐	*Liliuokalani: Young Hawaiian Queen*	Shirlee Petkin Newman
☐	*Lotta Crabtree: Girl of the Gold Rush*	Marian T. Place
☐	*Lou Gehrig: One of Baseball's Greatest*	Guernsey Van Riper
☐	*Louisa Alcott: Girl of Old Boston*	Jean Brown Wagoner
☐	*Louisa May Alcott: Young Novelist*	Beatrice Gormley
☐	*Luther Burbank: Boy Wizard*	Olive W. Burt
☐	*Lyndon B. Johnson: Young Texan*	Thomas Frank Barton
☐	*Mahalia Jackson: Young Gospel Singer*	Montrew Dunham
☐	*Maria Mitchell: Girl Astronomer*	Grace Hathaway Melin
☐	*Mark Twain: Boy of Old Missouri*	Miriam E. Mason
☐	*Martha Washington: Girl of Old Virginia*	Jean Brown Wagoner
☐	*Martin Luther King, Jr.: Young Man With a Dream*	Dharathula Millender
☐	*Mary Mapes Dodge: Jolly Girl*	Miriam E. Mason
☐	*Mary Todd Lincoln: Girl of the Bluegrass*	Katharine E. Wilkie
☐	*Matthew Calbraith Perry: Boy Sailor*	Alexander Scharbach
☐	*Meriwether Lewis: Boy Explorer*	Carlotta M. Bebenroth
☐	*Molly Pitcher: Young Patriot*	Augusta Stevenson
☐	*Mr. Rogers: Young Friend and Neighbor*	George E. Stanley
☐	*Myles Standish: Adventurous Boy*	Augusta Stevenson
☐	*Narcissa Whitman: Pioneer Girl*	Ann Spence Warner
☐	*Nathan Hale: Puritan Boy*	Augusta Stevenson
☐	*Nathanael Greene: Independent Boy*	Howard Peckham

List #260 | Childhood of Famous Americans Books *(continued)*

Title	Author
☐ *Neil Armstrong: Young Flyer*	Montrew Dunham
☐ *Noah Webster: Boy of Words*	Helen Boyd Higgins
☐ *Oliver Hazard Perry: Boy of the Sea*	Laura Long
☐ *Oliver Wendell Holmes, Jr: Boy of Justice*	Montrew Dunham
☐ *Patrick Henry: Boy Spokesman*	Thomas Frank Barton
☐ *Paul Revere: Boston Patriot*	Augusta Stevenson
☐ *Peter Stuyvesant: Boy with Wooden Shoes*	Mabel C. Widdemer
☐ *Pocahontas: Brave Girl*	Flora Warren Seymour
☐ *Pontiac: Young Ottawa Leader*	Howard Peckham
☐ *Raphael Semmes: Tidewater Boy*	Dorothea J. Snow
☐ *Ray Charles: Young Musician*	Susan Sloate
☐ *Richard Byrd: Boy Who Braved the Unknown*	Guernsey Van Riper
☐ *Robert E. Lee: Boy of Old Virginia*	Helen A. Monsell
☐ *Robert Frost: Boy with Promises to Keep*	Ellen Wilson
☐ *Robert Fulton: Boy Craftsman*	Marguerite Henry
☐ *Robert Goddard: Pioneer Rocket Boy*	Clyde B. Moore
☐ *Robert Peary: Boy of the North Pole*	Electa Clark
☐ *Roberto Clemente: Young Ball Player*	Montrew Dunham
☐ *Ronald Reagan: Young Leader*	Montrew Dunham
☐ *Rosa Parks: Young Rebel*	Kathleen Kudlinski
☐ *Sacagawea: Bird Girl*	Flora Warren Seymour
☐ *Samuel Morse: Inquisitive Boy*	Dorothea J. Snow
☐ *Sequoyah: Young Cherokee Guide*	Dorothea J. Snow
☐ *Sitting Bull: Dakota Boy*	Augusta Stevenson
☐ *Sojourner Truth: Voice of Freedom*	Kathleen Kudlinski
☐ *Squanto: Young Indian Hunter*	Augusta Stevenson
☐ *Stephen Decatur: Gallant Boy*	Bradford Smith
☐ *Stephen Foster: Boy Minstrel*	Helen Boyd Higgins
☐ *Susan B. Anthony: Champion of Women's Rights*	Montrew Dunham
☐ *Teddy Roosevelt: All-Round Boy*	Edd Winfield Parks
☐ *The Telegraph Boy*	Augusta Stevenson
☐ *Thomas Edison: Boy Inventor*	Sue Guthridge
☐ *Thurgood Marshall: Young Justice*	Montrew Dunham
☐ *Tom Jefferson: Boy in Colonial Days*	Helen A. Monsell
☐ *Vilhjalmur Stefansson: Young Arctic Explorer*	H. Myers, Ruth Burnett

List #260 CHILDHOOD OF FAMOUS AMERICANS **Books** *(continued)*

	Title	Author
☐	*Virgil I. Grissom: Boy Astronaut*	Carl L. Chappell
☐	*Virginia Dare: Mystery Girl*	Augusta Stevenson
☐	*Walt Disney: Young Movie Maker*	Marie Hammontree
☐	*Walter Chrysler: Boy Mechanist*	Ethel Weddle
☐	*Walter Reed: Boy Who Wanted to Know*	Helen Boyd Higgins
☐	*Washington Irving: Boy of Old New York*	Mabel C. Widdemer
☐	*Wilbur and Orville Wright: Boys With Wings*	Augusta Stevenson
☐	*Will and Charlie Mayo: Boy Doctors*	Marie Hammontree
☐	*Will Rogers: Young Cowboy*	Guernsey Van Riper
☐	*William Fargo: Boy Mail Carrier*	Katharine E. Wilkie
☐	*Wilma Rudolph: Olympic Runner*	Jo Harper
☐	*Woodrow Wilson: Boy President*	Helen A. Monsell
☐	*Young Audubon: Boy Naturalist*	Miriam E. Mason
☐	*Zack Taylor: Young Rough and Ready*	Katharine E. Wilkie
☐	*Zeb Pike: Boy Traveler*	Augusta Stevenson

If your children like the CHILDHOOD OF FAMOUS AMERICANS series, there are also CHILDHOOD OF WORLD FIGURES books (published by Simon & Schuster) available now as well. These tell about the childhoods of such people as Anne Frank, Christopher Columbus, Princess Diana, Gandhi, Julius Caesar, Leonardo da Vinci, Mother Teresa, and Marie Curie.

List #261 Caldecott Medal Winners and Honor Books

The Caldecott Medal was named in honor of nineteenth-century English illustrator Randolph Caldecott. It is awarded annually to the artist of the "most distinguished American picture book for children" by the Association for Library Service to Children, a division of the American Library Association.

Do we have this book?	Have we read it?		Study Ideas / Notes
☐	☐	**2007 Medal Winner:** *Flotsam* by David Wiesner (Clarion)	
		2007 Honor Books:	
☐	☐	*Gone Wild: An Endangered Animal Alphabet* by David McLimans (Walker)	
☐	☐	*Moses: When Harriet Tubman Led Her People to Freedom* by Kadir Nelson and Carole Boston Weatherford (Hyperion/Jump at the Sun)	
☐	☐	**2006 Medal Winner:** *The Hello, Goodbye Window* by Chris Raschka and Norton Juster (Michael di Capua Books)	
		2006 Honor Books:	
☐	☐	*Rosa* by Bryan Collier and Nikki Giovanni (Henry Holt)	
☐	☐	*Zen Shorts* by Jon J. Muth (Scholastic)	
☐	☐	*Hot Air: The (Mostly) True Story of the First Hot-Air Balloon Ride* by Marjorie Priceman (Simon & Schuster)	
☐	☐	*Song of the Water Boatman and Other Pond Poems* by Beckie Prange and Joyce Sidman (Houghton Mifflin)	
☐	☐	**2005 Medal Winner:** *Kitten's First Full Moon* by Kevin Henkes (Green Willow Books/HarperCollins)	
		2005 Honor Books:	
☐	☐	*The Red Book* by Barbara Lehman (Houghton Mifflin)	
☐	☐	*Coming on Home Soon* by E. B. Lewis and Jacqueline Woodson (G. P. Putnam's Sons)	
☐	☐	*Knuffle Bunny* by Mo Willems (Hyperion)	
☐	☐	**2004 Medal Winner:** *The Man Who Walked Between the Towers* by Mordicai Gerstein (Roaring Brook Press/Millbrook Press)	
		2004 Honor Books:	
☐	☐	*Ella Sarah Gets Dressed* by Margaret Chodos-Irvine (Harcourt, Inc.)	

List #261 **Caldecott Medal Winners and Honor Books** *(continued)*

Do we have this book?	Have we read it?		Study Ideas / Notes
☐	☐	*What Do You Do With a Tail Like This?* by Steve Jenkins and Robin Page (Houghton-Mifflin)	
☐	☐	*Don't Let the Pigeon Drive the Bus* by Mo Willems (Hyperion)	
☐	☐	**2003 Medal Winner:** *My Friend Rabbit* by Eric Rohmann (Roaring Brook Press/Millbrook Press)	
		2003 Honor Books:	
☐	☐	*The Spider and the Fly* illustrated by Tony DiTerlizzi, written by Mary Howitt (Simon & Schuster Books for Young Readers)	
☐	☐	*Hondo & Fabian* by Peter McCarty (Henry Holt)	
☐	☐	*Noah's Ark* by Jerry Pinkney (SeaStar Books)	
☐	☐	**2002 Medal Winner:** *The Three Pigs* by David Wiesner (Clarion/Houghton Mifflin)	
		2002 Honor Books:	
☐	☐	*The Dinosaurs of Waterhouse Hawkins* by Brian Selznick and Barbara Kerley (Scholastic)	
☐	☐	*Martin's Big Words: The Life of Dr. Martin Luther King, Jr.* by Bryan Collier and Doreen Rappaport (Jump at the Sun/Hyperion)	
☐	☐	*The Stray Dog* by Marc Simont (HarperCollins)	
☐	☐	**2001 Medal Winner:** *So You Want to Be President?* by David Small and Judith St. George (Philomel)	
		2001 Honor Books:	
☐	☐	*Casey at the Bat* illustrated by Christopher Bing and Ernest Thayer (Handprint)	
☐	☐	*Click, Clack, Moo: Cows That Type* by Betsy Lewin and Doreen Cronin (Simon & Schuster)	
☐	☐	*Olivia* by Ian Falconer (Atheneum)	
☐	☐	**2000 Medal Winner**: *Joseph Had a Little Overcoat* by Simms Taback (Viking)	
		2000 Honor Books:	
☐	☐	*A Child's Calendar* illustrated by Trina Schart Hyman and John Updike (Holiday House)	
☐	☐	*Sector 7* by David Wiesner (Clarion Books)	

List #261 Caldecott Medal Winners and Honor Books *(continued)*

Do we have this book?	Have we read it?		Study Ideas / Notes
☐	☐	*When Sophie Gets Angry—Really, Really Angry* by Molly Bang (Scholastic)	
☐	☐	*The Ugly Duckling* by Jerry Pinkney; text by Hans Christian Andersen, adapted by Jerry Pinkney (Morrow)	
☐	☐	**1999 Medal Winner:** *Snowflake Bentley* by Mary Azarian and Jacqueline Briggs Martin (Houghton)	
		1999 Honor Books:	
☐	☐	*Duke Ellington: The Piano Prince and the Orchestra* by Brian Pinkney and Andrea Davis Pinkney (Hyperion)	
☐	☐	*No, David!* by David Shannon (Scholastic)	
☐	☐	*Snow* by Uri Shulevitz (Farrar)	
☐	☐	*Tibet Through the Red Box* by Peter Sis (Frances Foster)	
☐	☐	**1998 Medal Winner**: *Rapunzel* by Paul O. Zelinsky (Dutton)	
		1998 Honor Books:	
☐	☐	*The Gardener* by David Small and Sarah Stewart (Farrar)	
☐	☐	*Harlem* by Christopher Myers and Walter Dean Myers (Scholastic)	
☐	☐	*There Was an Old Lady Who Swallowed a Fly* by Simms Taback (Viking)	
☐	☐	**1997 Medal Winner:** *Golem* by David Wisniewski (Clarion)	
		1997 Honor Books:	
☐	☐	*Hush! A Thai Lullaby* by Holly Meade and Minfong Ho (Melanie Kroupa/Orchard Books)	
☐	☐	*The Graphic Alphabet* by David Pelletier (Orchard Books)	
☐	☐	*The Paperboy* by Dav Pilkey (Richard Jackson/Orchard Books)	
☐	☐	*Starry Messenger* by Peter Sís (Frances Foster Books/Farrar Straus Giroux)	
☐	☐	**1996 Medal Winner:** *Officer Buckle and Gloria* by Peggy Rathmann (Putnam)	

List #261 **Caldecott Medal Winners and Honor Books** *(continued)*

Do we have this book?	Have we read it?		Study Ideas / Notes
		1996 Honor Books:	
☐	☐	*Alphabet City* by Stephen T. Johnson (Viking)	
☐	☐	*Zin! Zin! Zin! a Violin* by Marjorie Priceman and Lloyd Moss (Simon & Schuster)	
☐	☐	*Faithful Friend* by Brian Pinkney and Robert D. San Souci (Simon & Schuster)	
☐	☐	*Tops & Bottoms,* adapted and illustrated by Janet Stevens (Harcourt)	
☐	☐	**1995 Medal Winner:** *Smoky Night* by David Diaz and Eve Bunting (Harcourt)	
		1995 Honor Books:	
☐	☐	*John Henry* by Jerry Pinkney and Julius Lester (Dial)	
☐	☐	*Swamp Angel* by Paul O. Zelinsky and Anne Isaacs (Dutton)	
☐	☐	*Time Flies* by Eric Rohmann (Crown)	
☐	☐	**1994 Medal Winner:** *Grandfather's Journe*y by Allen Say and Walter Lorraine (Houghton)	
		1994 Honor Books:	
☐	☐	*Peppe the Lamplighte*r by Ted Lewin and Elisa Bartone (Lothrop)	
☐	☐	*In the Small, Small Pond* by Denise Fleming (Holt)	
☐	☐	*Raven: A Trickster Tale From the Pacific Northwest* by Gerald McDermott (Harcourt)	
☐	☐	*Owen* by Kevin Henkes (Greenwillow)	
☐	☐	*Yo! Yes?* by Chris Raschka and Richard Jackson (Orchard)	
☐	☐	**1993 Medal Winner:** *Mirette on the High Wire* by Emily Arnold McCully (Putnam)	
		1993 Honor Books:	
☐	☐	*The Stinky Cheese Man and Other Fairly Stupid Tales* by Lane Smith and Jon Scieszka (Viking)	
☐	☐	*Seven Blind Mice* by Ed Young (Philomel Books)	
☐	☐	*Working Cotton* by Carole Byard and Sherley Anne Williams (Harcourt)	
☐	☐	**1992 Medal Winner**: *Tuesday* by David Wiesner (Clarion Books)	

List #261 Caldecott Medal Winners and Honor Books *(continued)*

Do we have this book?	Have we read it?		Study Ideas / Notes
		1992 Honor Book:	
☐	☐	*Tar Beach* by Faith Ringgold (Crown Publishers)	
☐	☐	**1991 Medal Winner:** *Black and White* by David Macaulay (Houghton)	
		1991 Honor Books:	
☐	☐	*Puss in Boots* by Fred Marcellino; text: Charles Perrault, trans. by Malcolm Arthur (Di Capua/Farrar)	
☐	☐	*"More More More," Said the Baby: Three Love Stories* by Vera B. Williams (Greenwillow)	
☐	☐	**1990 Medal Winner:** *Lon Po Po: A Red-Riding Hood Story From China* by Ed Young (Philomel)	
		1990 Honor Books:	
☐	☐	*Bill Peet: An Autobiography* by Bill Peet (Houghton)	
☐	☐	*Color Zoo* by Lois Ehlert (Lippincott)	
☐	☐	*The Talking Eggs: A Folktale From the American South* by Jerry Pinkney and Robert D. San Souci (Dial)	
☐	☐	*Hershel and the Hanukkah Goblins* by Trina Schart Hyman and Eric Kimmel (Holiday House)	
☐	☐	**1989 Medal Winner:** *Song and Dance Man* by Stephen Gammell and Karen Ackerman (Knopf)	
		1989 Honor Books:	
☐	☐	*The Boy of the Three-Year Nap* by Allen Say and Diane Snyder (Houghton)	
☐	☐	*Free Fall* by David Wiesner (Lothrop)	
☐	☐	*Goldilocks and the Three Bears* by James Marshall (Dial)	
☐	☐	*Mirandy and Brother Wind* by Jerry Pinkney and Patricia C. McKissack (Knopf)	
☐	☐	**1988 Medal Winner:** *Owl Moon* by John Schoenherr and Jane Yolen (Philomel)	
		1988 Honor Book:	
☐	☐	*Mufaro's Beautiful Daughters: An African Tale* by John Steptoe (Lothrop)	
☐	☐	**1987 Medal Winner:** *Hey, Al* by Richard Egielski and Arthur Yorinks (Farrar)	

List #261 **Caldecott Medal Winners and Honor Books** *(continued)*

Do we have this book?	Have we read it?		Study Ideas / Notes
		1987 Honor Books:	
☐	☐	*The Village of Round and Square Houses* by Ann Grifalconi (Little, Brown)	
☐	☐	*Alphabatics* by Suse MacDonald (Bradbury)	
☐	☐	*Rumpelstiltskin* by Paul O. Zelinsky (Dutton)	
☐	☐	**1986 Medal Winner:** *The Polar Express* by Chris Van Allsburg (Houghton)	
		1986 Honor Books:	
☐	☐	*The Relatives Came* by Stephen Gammell and Cynthia Rylant (Bradbury)	
☐	☐	*King Bidgood's in the Bathtub* by Don Wood and Audrey Wood (Harcourt)	
☐	☐	**1985 Medal Winner:** *Saint George and the Dragon* by Trina Schart Hyman and Margaret Hodges (Little, Brown)	
		1985 Honor Books:	
☐	☐	*Hansel and Gretel* by Paul O. Zelinsky and Rika Lesser (Dodd)	
☐	☐	*Have You Seen My Duckling?* by Nancy Tafuri (Greenwillow)	
☐	☐	*The Story of Jumping Mouse: A Native American Legend* by John Steptoe (Lothrop)	
☐	☐	**1984 Medal Winner:** *The Glorious Flight: Across the Channel With Louis Bleriot* by Alice and Martin Provensen (Viking)	
		1984 Honor Books:	
☐	☐	*Little Red Riding Hood* by Trina Schart Hyman (Holiday)	
☐	☐	*Ten, Nine, Eight* by Molly Bang (Greenwillow)	
☐	☐	**1983 Medal Winner:** *Shadow* by Marcia Brown; original text in French: Blaise Cendrars (Scribner)	
		1983 Honor Books:	
☐	☐	*A Chair for My Mother* by Vera B. Williams (Greenwillow)	
☐	☐	*When I Was Young in the Mountains* by Diane Goode and Cynthia Rylant (Dutton)	

List #261 **Caldecott Medal Winners and Honor Books** *(continued)*

Do we have this book?	Have we read it?		Study Ideas / Notes
☐	☐	**1982 Medal Winner:** *Jumanji* by Chris Van Allsburg (Houghton)	
		1982 Honor Books:	
☐	☐	*Where the Buffaloes Begin* by Stephen Gammell and Olaf Baker (Warne)	
☐	☐	*On Market Street* by Anita and Arnold Lobel (Greenwillow)	
☐	☐	*Outside Over There* by Maurice Sendak (Harper)	
☐	☐	*A Visit to William Blake's Inn: Poems for Innocent and Experienced Travelers* by Alice and Martin Provensen; Nancy Willard (Harcourt)	
☐	☐	**1981 Medal Winner:** *Fables* by Arnold Lobel (Harper)	
		1981 Honor Books:	
☐	☐	*The Bremen-Town Musicians* by Ilse Plume (Doubleday)	
☐	☐	*The Grey Lady and the Strawberry Snatcher* by Molly Bang (Four Winds)	
☐	☐	*Mice Twice* by Joseph Low (McElderry/Atheneum)	
☐	☐	*Truck* by Donald Crews (Greenwillow)	
☐	☐	**1980 Medal Winner:** *Ox-Cart Man* by Barbara Cooney and Donald Hall (Viking)	
		1980 Honor Books:	
☐	☐	*Ben's Trumpet* by Rachel Isadora (Greenwillow)	
☐	☐	*The Garden of Abdul Gasazi* by Chris Van Allsburg (Houghton)	
☐	☐	*The Treasure* by Uri Shulevitz (Farrar)	
☐	☐	**1979 Medal Winner:** *The Girl Who Loved Wild Horses* by Paul Goble (Bradbury)	
		1979 Honor Books:	
☐	☐	*Freight Train* by Donald Crews (Greenwillow)	
☐	☐	*The Way to Start a Day* by Peter Parnall and Byrd Baylor (Scribner)	
☐	☐	**1978 Medal Winner:** *Noah's Ark* by Peter Spier (Doubleday)	
		1978 Honor Books:	
☐	☐	*Castle* by David Macaulay (Houghton)	

List #261 Caldecott Medal Winners and Honor Books *(continued)*

Do we have this book?	Have we read it?		Study Ideas / Notes
☐	☐	*It Could Always Be Worse* by Margot Zemach (Farrar)	
☐	☐	**1977 Medal Winner:** *Ashanti to Zulu: African Traditions* by Leo and Diane Dillon; Margaret Musgrove (Dial)	
		1977 Honor Books:	
☐	☐	*The Amazing Bone* by William Steig (Farrar)	
☐	☐	*The Contest*, retold and illustrated by Nonny Hogrogian (Greenwillow)	
☐	☐	*Fish for Supper* by M. B. Goffstein (Dial)	
☐	☐	*The Golem: A Jewish Legend* by Beverly Brodsky McDermott (Lippincott)	
☐	☐	*Hawk, I'm Your Brother* by Peter Parnall and Byrd Baylor (Scribner)	
☐	☐	**1976 Medal Winner:** *Why Mosquitoes Buzz in People's Ears* by Leo and Diane Dillon; Verna Aardema (Dial)	
		1976 Honor Books:	
☐	☐	*The Desert Is Theirs* by Peter Parnall and Byrd Baylor (Scribner)	
☐	☐	*Strega Nona* by Tomie de Paola (Prentice-Hall)	
☐	☐	**1975 Medal Winner:** *Arrow to the Sun* by Gerald McDermott (Viking)	
		1975 Honor Book:	
☐	☐	*Jambo Means Hello: A Swahili Alphabet Book* by Tom Feelings and Muriel Feelings (Dial)	
☐	☐	**1974 Medal Winner:** *Duffy and the Devil* by Margot Zemach and Harve Zemach (Farrar)	
		1974 Honor Books:	
☐	☐	*Three Jovial Huntsmen* by Susan Jeffers (Bradbury)	
☐	☐	*Cathedral* by David Macaulay (Houghton)	
☐	☐	**1973 Medal Winner:** *The Funny Little Woman* by Blair Lent and Arlene Mosel (Dutton)	
		1973 Honor Books:	
☐	☐	*Anansi the Spider: A Tale from the Ashanti* by Gerald McDermott (Holt)	

List #261 **Caldecott Medal Winners and Honor Books** *(continued)*

Do we have this book?	Have we read it?		Study Ideas / Notes
☐	☐	*Hosie's Alphabet* by Leonard Baskin and Hosea, Tobias, and Lisa Baskin (Viking)	
☐	☐	*Snow-White and the Seven Dwarfs* by Nancy Ekholm Burkert and Randall Jarrell; retold from the Brothers Grimm (Farrar)	
☐	☐	*When Clay Sings* by Tom Bahti and Byrd Baylor (Scribner)	
☐	☐	**1972 Medal Winner:** *One Fine Day* by Nonny Hogrogian (Macmillan)	
		1972 Honor Books:	
☐	☐	*Hildilid's Night* by Arnold Lobel and Cheli Durán Ryan (Macmillan)	
☐	☐	*If All the Seas Were One Sea* by Janina Domanska (Macmillan)	
☐	☐	*Moja Means One: Swahili Counting Book* by Tom and Muriel Feelings (Dial)	
☐	☐	**1971 Medal Winner:** *A Story, A Story* by Gail E. Haley (Atheneum)	
		1971 Honor Books:	
☐	☐	*The Angry Moon* by Blair Lent and William Sleator (Atlantic)	
☐	☐	*Frog and Toad Are Friends* by Arnold Lobel (Harper)	
☐	☐	*In the Night Kitchen* by Maurice Sendak (Harper)	
☐	☐	**1970 Medal Winner:** *Sylvester and the Magic Pebble* by William Steig (Windmill Books)	
		1970 Honor Books:	
☐	☐	*Goggles!* by Ezra Jack Keats (Macmillan)	
☐	☐	*Alexander and the Wind-Up Mouse* by Leo Lionni (Pantheon)	
☐	☐	*Pop Corn & Ma Goodness* by Robert Andrew Parker and Edna Mitchell Preston (Viking)	
☐	☐	*Thy Friend, Obadiah* by Brinton Turkle (Viking)	
☐	☐	*The Judge: An Untrue Tale* by Margot Zemach and Harve Zemach (Farrar)	

List #261 **Caldecott Medal Winners and Honor Books** *(continued)*

Do we have this book?	Have we read it?		Study Ideas / Notes
☐	☐	**1969 Medal Winner:** *The Fool of the World and the Flying Ship* by Uri Shulevitz and Arthur Ransome (Farrar)	
		1969 Honor Book:	
☐	☐	*Why the Sun and the Moon Live in the Sky* by Blair Lent and Elphinstone Dayrell (Houghton)	
☐	☐	**1968 Medal Winner:** *Drummer Hoff* by Ed Emberley and Barbara Emberley (Prentice-Hall)	
		1968 Honor Books:	
☐	☐	*Frederick* by Leo Lionni (Pantheon)	
☐	☐	*Seashore Story* by Taro Yashima (Viking)	
☐	☐	*The Emperor and the Kite* by Ed Young and Jane Yolen (World)	
☐	☐	**1967 Medal Winner:** *Sam, Bangs & Moonshine* by Evaline Ness (Holt)	
		1967 Honor Book:	
☐	☐	*One Wide River to Cross* by Ed Emberley and Barbara Emberley (Prentice-Hall)	
☐	☐	**1966 Medal Winner:** *Always Room for One More* by Nonny Hogrogian and Sorche Nic Leodhas, pseud. [Leclair Alger] (Holt)	
		1966 Honor Books:	
☐	☐	*Hide and Seek Fog* by Roger Duvoisin and Alvin Tresselt (Lothrop)	
☐	☐	*Just Me* by Marie Hall Ets (Viking)	
☐	☐	*Tom Tit Tot* by Evaline Ness (Scribner)	
☐	☐	**1965 Medal Winner:** *May I Bring a Friend?* by Beni Montresor and Beatrice Schenk de Regniers (Atheneum)	
		1965 Honor Books:	
☐	☐	*Rain Makes Applesauce* by Marvin Bileck and Julian Scheer (Holiday)	
☐	☐	*The Wave* by Blair Lent and Margaret Hodges (Houghton)	
☐	☐	*A Pocketful of Cricket* by Evaline Ness and Rebecca Caudill (Holt)	

List #261 **Caldecott Medal Winners and Honor Books** *(continued)*

Do we have this book?	Have we read it?		Study Ideas / Notes
☐	☐	**1964 Medal Winner:** *Where the Wild Things Are* by Maurice Sendak (Harper)	
		1964 Honor Books:	
☐	☐	*Swimmy* by Leo Lionni (Pantheon)	
☐	☐	*All in the Morning Early* by Evaline Ness and Sorche Nic Leodhas, pseud. [Leclaire Alger] (Holt)	
☐	☐	*Mother Goose and Nursery Rhymes* by Philip Reed (Atheneum)	
☐	☐	**1963 Medal Winner:** *The Snowy Day* by Ezra Jack Keats (Viking)	
		1963 Honor Books:	
☐	☐	*The Sun Is a Golden Earring* by Bernarda Bryson and Natalia M. Belting (Holt)	
☐	☐	*Mr. Rabbit and the Lovely Present* by Maurice Sendak and Charlotte Zolotow (Harper)	
☐	☐	**1962 Medal Winner:** *Once a Mouse* by Marcia Brown (Scribner)	
		1962 Honor Books:	
☐	☐	*Fox Went Out on a Chilly Night: An Old Song* by Peter Spier (Doubleday)	
☐	☐	*Little Bear's Visit* by Maurice Sendak and Else H. Minarik (Harper)	
☐	☐	*The Day We Saw the Sun Come Up* by Adrienne Adams and Alice E. Goudey (Scribner)	
☐	☐	**1961 Medal Winner:** *Baboushka and the Three Kings* by Nicolas Sidjakov and Ruth Robbins (Parnassus)	
		1961 Honor Book:	
☐	☐	*Inch by Inch* by Leo Lionni (Obolensky)	
☐	☐	**1960 Medal Winner:** *Nine Days to Christmas* by Marie Hall Ets and Aurora Labastida (Viking)	
		1960 Honor Books:	
☐	☐	*Houses From the Sea* by Adrienne Adams and Alice E. Goudey (Scribner)	
☐	☐	*The Moon Jumpers* by Maurice Sendak and Janice May Udry (Harper)	

List #261 **Caldecott Medal Winners and Honor Books** *(continued)*

Do we have this book?	Have we read it?		Study Ideas / Notes
☐	☐	**1959 Medal Winner:** *Chanticleer and the Fox* by Barbara Cooney; adapted from Chaucer's *Canterbury Tales* (Crowell)	
		1959 Honor Books:	
☐	☐	*The House That Jack Built: La Maison Que Jacques A Batie* by Antonio Frasconi (Harcourt)	
☐	☐	*What Do You Say, Dear?* by Maurice Sendak and Sesyle Joslin (W. R. Scott)	
☐	☐	*Umbrella* by Taro Yashima (Viking)	
☐	☐	**1958 Medal Winner:** *Time of Wonder* by Robert McCloskey (Viking)	
		1958 Honor Books:	
☐	☐	*Fly High, Fly Low* by Don Freeman (Viking)	
☐	☐	*Anatole and the Cat* by Paul Galdone and Eve Titus (McGraw-Hill)	
☐	☐	**1957 Medal Winner:** *A Tree Is Nice* by Marc Simont and Janice Udry (Harper)	
		1957 Honor Books:	
☐	☐	*Mr. Penny's Race Horse* by Marie Hall Ets (Viking)	
☐	☐	*1 Is One* by Tasha Tudor (Walck)	
☐	☐	*Anatole* by Paul Galdone and Eve Titus (McGraw-Hill)	
☐	☐	*Gillespie and the Guards* by James Daugherty and Benjamin Elkin (Viking)	
☐	☐	*Lion* by William Pène du Bois (Viking)	
☐	☐	**1956 Medal Winner:** *Frog Went A-Courtin'* by Feodor Rojankovsky and John Langstaff (Harcourt)	
		1956 Honor Books:	
☐	☐	*Play With Me* by Marie Hall Ets (Viking)	
☐	☐	*Crow Boy* by Taro Yashima (Viking)	
☐	☐	**1955 Medal Winner:** *Cinderella, or The Little Glass Slipper* by Marcia Brown (Scribner)	
		1955 Honor Books:	
☐	☐	*Book of Nursery and Mother Goose Rhymes* by Marguerite de Angeli (Doubleday)	

List #261 **Caldecott Medal Winners and Honor Books** *(continued)*

Do we have this book?	Have we read it?		Study Ideas / Notes
☐	☐	*Wheel on the Chimney* by Tibor Gergely and Margaret Wise Brown (Lippincott)	
☐	☐	*The Thanksgiving Story* by Helen Sewell and Alice Dalgliesh (Scribner)	
☐	☐	**1954 Medal Winner:** *Madeline's Rescue* by Ludwig Bemelmans (Viking)	
		1954 Honor Books:	
☐	☐	*Journey Cake, Ho!* by Robert McCloskey and Ruth Sawyer (Viking)	
☐	☐	*When Will the World Be Mine?* by Jean Charlot and Miriam Schlein (W. R. Scott)	
☐	☐	*The Steadfast Tin Soldier* by Marcia Brown and M. R. James; a Hans Christian Andersen tale (Scribner)	
☐	☐	*A Very Special House* by Maurice Sendak and Ruth Krauss (Harper)	
☐	☐	*Green Eyes* by A. Birnbaum (Capitol)	
☐	☐	**1953 Medal Winner:** *The Biggest Bear* by Lynd Ward (Houghton)	
		1953 Honor Books:	
☐	☐	*Puss in Boots* by Marcia Brown (Scribner)	
☐	☐	*One Morning in Maine* by Robert McCloskey (Viking)	
☐	☐	*Ape in a Cape: An Alphabet of Odd Animals* by Fritz Eichenberg (Harcourt)	
☐	☐	*The Storm Book* by Margaret Bloy Graham and Charlotte Zolotow (Harper)	
☐	☐	*Five Little Monkeys* by Juliet Kepes (Houghton)	
☐	☐	**1952 Medal Winner:** *Finders Keepers* by Nicolas, pseud. [Nicholas Mordvinoff] and Will, pseud. [William Lipkind] (Harcourt)	
		1952 Honor Books:	
☐	☐	*Mr. T. W. Anthony Woo* by Marie Hall Ets (Viking)	
☐	☐	*Skipper John's Cook* by Marcia Brown (Scribner)	
☐	☐	*All Falling Down* by Margaret Bloy Graham and Gene Zion (Harper)	
☐	☐	*Bear Party* by William Pène du Bois (Viking)	
☐	☐	*Feather Mountain* by Elizabeth Olds (Houghton)	

List #261 **Caldecott Medal Winners and Honor Books** *(continued)*

Do we have this book?	Have we read it?		Study Ideas / Notes
☐	☐	**1951 Medal Winner:** *The Egg Tree* by Katherine Milhous (Scribner)	
		1951 Honor Books:	
☐	☐	*Dick Whittington and His Cat* by Marcia Brown (Scribner)	
☐	☐	*The Two Reds* by Nicolas, pseud. [Nicholas Mordvinoff] and Will, pseud. [William Lipkind] (Harcourt)	
☐	☐	*If I Ran the Zoo* by Dr. Seuss, pseud. [Theodor Seuss Geisel] (Random House)	
☐	☐	*The Most Wonderful Doll in the World* by Helen Stone and Phyllis McGinley (Lippincott)	
☐	☐	*T-Bone, the Baby Sitter* by Clare Turlay Newberry (Harper)	
☐	☐	**1950 Medal Winner:** *Song of the Swallows* by Leo Politi (Scribner)	
		1950 Honor Books:	
☐	☐	*America's Ethan Allen* by Lynd Ward and Stewart Holbrook (Houghton)	
☐	☐	*The Wild Birthday Cake* by Hildegard Woodward and Lavinia R. Davis (Doubleday)	
☐	☐	*The Happy Day* by Marc Simont and Ruth Krauss (Harper)	
☐	☐	*Bartholomew and the Oobleck* by Dr. Seuss, pseud. [Theodor Seuss Geisel] (Random House)	
☐	☐	*Henry Fisherman* by Marcia Brown (Scribner)	
☐	☐	**1949 Medal Winner:** *The Big Snow* by Berta and Elmer Hader (Macmillan)	
		1949 Honor Books:	
☐	☐	*Blueberries for Sal* by Robert McCloskey (Viking)	
☐	☐	*All Around the Town* by Helen Stone and Phyllis McGinley (Lippincott)	
☐	☐	*Juanita* by Leo Politi (Scribner)	
☐	☐	*Fish in the Air* by Kurt Wiese (Viking)	
☐	☐	**1948 Medal Winner:** *White Snow, Bright Snow*, illustrated by Roger Duvoisin; text: Alvin Tresselt (Lothrop)	

List #261 Caldecott Medal Winners and Honor Books *(continued)*

Do we have this book?	Have we read it?		Study Ideas / Notes
		1948 Honor Books:	
☐	☐	*Stone Soup* by Marcia Brown (Scribner)	
☐	☐	*McElligot's Pool* by Dr. Seuss, pseud. [Theodor Seuss Geisel] (Random House)	
☐	☐	*Bambino the Clown* by Georges Schreiber (Viking)	
☐	☐	*Roger and the Fox* by Hildegard Woodward and Lavinia R. Davis (Doubleday)	
☐	☐	*Song of Robin Hood* by Virginia Lee Burton and Anne Malcolmson (Houghton)	
☐	☐	**1947 Medal Winner:** *The Little Island* by Leonard Weisgard and Golden MacDonald, pseud. [Margaret Wise Brown] (Doubleday)	
		1947 Honor Books:	
☐	☐	*Rain Drop Splash* by Leonard Weisgard and Alvin Tresselt (Lothrop)	
☐	☐	*Boats on the River* by Jay Hyde Barnum and Marjorie Flack (Viking)	
☐	☐	*Timothy Turtle* by Tony Palazzo and Al Graham (Welch)	
☐	☐	*Pedro, the Angel of Olvera Street* by Leo Politi (Scribner)	
☐	☐	*Sing in Praise: A Collection of the Best-Loved Hymns* by Marjorie Torrey and Opal Wheeler (Dutton)	
☐	☐	**1946 Medal Winner:** *The Rooster Crows* by Maude and Miska Petersham (Macmillan)	
		1946 Honor Books:	
☐	☐	*Little Lost Lamb* by Leonard Weisgard and Golden MacDonald, pseud. [Margaret Wise Brown] (Doubleday)	
☐	☐	*Sing Mother Goose* by Marjorie Torrey and Opal Wheeler (Dutton)	
☐	☐	*My Mother Is the Most Beautiful Woman in the World* by Ruth Gannett and Becky Reyher (Lothrop)	
☐	☐	*You Can Write Chinese* by Kurt Wiese (Viking)	
☐	☐	**1945 Medal Winner:** *Prayer for a Child* by Elizabeth Orton Jones and Rachel Field (Macmillan)	
		1945 Honor Books:	
☐	☐	*Mother Goose* by Tasha Tudor (Oxford University Press)	

List #261 **Caldecott Medal Winners and Honor Books** *(continued)*

Do we have this book?	Have we read it?		Study Ideas / Notes
☐	☐	*In the Forest* by Marie Hall Ets (Viking)	
☐	☐	*Yonie Wondernose* by Marguerite de Angeli (Doubleday)	
☐	☐	*The Christmas Anna Angel* by Kate Seredy and Ruth Sawyer (Viking)	
☐	☐	**1944 Medal Winner:** *Many Moons* by Louis Slobodkin and James Thurber (Harcourt)	
		1944 Honor Books:	
☐	☐	*Small Rain: Verses From the Bible* by Elizabeth Orton Jones (Viking)	
☐	☐	*Pierre Pigeon* by Arnold E. Bare and Lee Kingman (Houghton)	
☐	☐	*The Mighty Hunter* by Berta and Elmer Hader (Macmillan)	
☐	☐	*A Child's Good Night Book* by Jean Charlot and Margaret Wise Brown (W. R. Scott)	
☐	☐	*Good-Luck Horse* by Plato Chan and Chih-Yi Chan (Whittlesey)	
☐	☐	**1943 Medal Winner:** *The Little House* by Virginia Lee Burton (Houghton)	
		1943 Honor Books:	
☐	☐	*Dash and Dart* by Mary and Conrad Buff (Viking)	
☐	☐	*Marshmallow* by Clare Turlay Newberry (Harper)	
☐	☐	**1942 Medal Winner:** *Make Way for Ducklings* by Robert McCloskey (Viking)	
		1942 Honor Books:	
☐	☐	*An American ABC* by Maud and Miska Petersham (Macmillan)	
☐	☐	*In My Mother's House* by Velino Herrera and Ann Nolan Clark (Viking)	
☐	☐	*Paddle-to-the-Sea* by Holling C. Holling (Houghton)	
☐	☐	*Nothing at All* by Wanda Gág (Coward)	
☐	☐	**1941 Medal Winner:** *They Were Strong and Good* by Robert Lawson (Viking)	

List #261 **Caldecott Medal Winners and Honor Books** *(continued)*

Do we have this book?	Have we read it?		Study Ideas / Notes
		1941 Honor Book:	
☐	☐	*April's Kittens* by Clare Turlay Newberry (Harper)	
☐	☐	**1940 Medal Winner:** *Abraham Lincoln* by Ingri and Edgar Parin d'Aulaire (Doubleday)	
		1940 Honor Books:	
☐	☐	*Cock-a-Doodle Doo* by Berta and Elmer Hader (Macmillan)	
☐	☐	*Madeline* by Ludwig Bemelmans (Viking)	
☐	☐	*The Ageless Story* by Lauren Ford (Dodd)	
☐	☐	**1939 Medal Winner:** *Mei Li* by Thomas Handforth (Doubleday)	
		1939 Honor Books:	
☐	☐	*Andy and the Lion* by James Daugherty (Viking)	
☐	☐	*Barkis* by Clare Turlay Newberry (Harper)	
☐	☐	*The Forest Pool* by Laura Adams Armer (Longmans)	
☐	☐	*Snow White and the Seven Dwarfs* by Wanda Gág (Coward)	
☐	☐	*Wee Gillis* by Robert Lawson and Munro Leaf (Viking)	
☐	☐	**1938 Medal Winner:** *Animals of the Bible, A Picture Book* by Dorothy P. Lathrop and Helen Dean Fish (Lippincott)	
		1938 Honor Books:	
☐	☐	*Four and Twenty Blackbirds* by Robert Lawson and Helen Dean Fish (Stokes)	
☐	☐	*Seven Simeons: A Russian Tale* by Boris Artzybasheff (Viking)	

List #262 Newbery Medal Winners and Honor Books

The Newbery Medal was named for eighteenth-century British bookseller John Newbery. It is awarded annually to the author of the "most distinguished contribution to American literature for children" by the Association for Library Service to Children, a division of the American Library Association.

Do we have this book?	Have we read it?		Study Ideas / Notes
☐	☐	**2007 Medal Winner:** *The Higher Power of Lucky* written by Susan Patron (Simon & Schuster)	
		2007 Honor Books:	
☐	☐	*Penny From Heaven* by Jennifer L. Holm (Random House)	
☐	☐	*Hattie Big Sky* by Kirby Larson (Delacorte Press)	
☐	☐	*Rules* by Cynthia Lord (Scholastic)	
☐	☐	**2006 Medal Winner:** *Criss Cross* by Lynne Rae Perkins (Greenwillow Books/HarperCollins)	
		2006 Honor Books:	
☐	☐	*Whittington* by Alan Armstrong (Random House)	
☐	☐	*Hitler Youth: Growing Up in Hitler's Shadow* by Susan Campbell Bartoletti (Scholastic)	
☐	☐	*Princess Academy* by Shannon Hale (Bloomsbury Children's Books)	
☐	☐	*Show Way* by Jacqueline Woodson (G.P. Putnam's Sons)	
☐	☐	**2005 Medal Winner:** *Kira-Kira* by Cynthia Kadohata (Atheneum/Simon & Schuster)	
		2005 Honor Books:	
☐	☐	*Al Capone Does My Shirts* by Gennifer Choldenko (G.P. Putnam's Sons)	
☐	☐	*The Voice That Challenged a Nation: Marian Anderson and the Struggle for Equal Rights* by Russell Freedman (Clarion Books/Houghton Mifflin)	

List #262 **Newbery Medal Winners and Honor Books** *(continued)*

Do we have this book?	Have we read it?		Study Ideas / Notes
☐	☐	*Lizzie Bright and the Buckminster Boy* by Gary D. Schmidt (Clarion Books/Houghton Mifflin)	
☐	☐	**2004 Medal Winner:** *The Tale of Despereaux: Being the Story of a Mouse, a Princess, Some Soup, and a Spool of Thread* by Kate DiCamillo and Timothy Basil Ering (Candlewick Press)	
		2004 Honor Books:	
☐	☐	*Olive's Ocean* by Kevin Henkes (Greenwillow Books)	
☐	☐	*An American Plague: The True and Terrifying Story of the Yellow Fever Epidemic of 1793* by Jim Murphy (Clarion Books)	
☐	☐	**2003 Medal Winner:** *Crispin: The Cross of Lead* by Avi (Hyperion Books for Children)	
		2003 Honor Books:	
☐	☐	*The House of the Scorpion* by Nancy Farmer (Atheneum)	
☐	☐	*Pictures of Hollis Woods* by Patricia Reilly Giff (Random House/Wendy Lamb Books)	
☐	☐	*Hoot* by Carl Hiaasen (Knopf)	
☐	☐	*A Corner of the Universe* by Ann M. Martin (Scholastic)	
☐	☐	*Surviving the Applewhites* by Stephanie S. Tolan (HarperCollins)	
☐	☐	**2002 Medal Winner:** *A Single Shard* by Linda Sue Park (Clarion Books/Houghton Mifflin)	
		2002 Honor Books:	
☐	☐	*Everything on a Waffle* by Polly Horvath (Farrar Straus Giroux)	
☐	☐	*Carver: A Life in Poems* by Marilyn Nelson (Front Street)	
☐	☐	**2001 Medal Winner:** *A Year Down Yonder* by Richard Peck (Dial)	
		2001 Honor Books:	
☐	☐	*Hope Was Here* by Joan Bauer (G.P. Putnam's Sons)	

List #262 **Newbery Medal Winners and Honor Books** *(continued)*

Do we have this book?	Have we read it?		Study Ideas / Notes
☐	☐	*Because of Winn-Dixie* by Kate DiCamillo (Candlewick Press)	
☐	☐	*Joey Pigza Loses Control* by Jack Gantos (Farrar, Straus, and Giroux)	
☐	☐	*The Wanderer* by Sharon Creech (Joanna Cotler Books/HarperCollins)	
☐	☐	**2000 Medal Winner:** *Bud, Not Buddy* by Christopher Paul Curtis (Delacorte)	
		2000 Honor Books:	
☐	☐	*Getting Near to Baby* by Audrey Couloumbis (Putnam)	
☐	☐	*Our Only May Amelia* by Jennifer L. Holm (HarperCollins)	
☐	☐	*26 Fairmount Avenue* by Tomie dePaola (Putnam)	
☐	☐	**1999 Medal Winner:** *Holes* by Louis Sachar (Frances Foster)	
☐	☐	**1999 Honor Book:** *A Long Way From Chicago* by Richard Peck (Dial)	
☐	☐	**1998 Medal Winner:** *Out of the Dust* by Karen Hesse (Scholastic)	
		1998 Honor Books:	
☐	☐	*Ella Enchanted* by Gail Carson Levine (HarperCollins)	
☐	☐	*Lily's Crossing* by Patricia Reilly Giff (Delacorte)	
☐	☐	*Wringer* by Jerry Spinelli (HarperCollins)	
☐	☐	**1997 Medal Winner:** *The View From Saturday* by E. L. Konigsburg (Jean Karl/Atheneum)	
		1997 Honor Books:	
☐	☐	*A Girl Named Disaster* by Nancy Farmer (Richard Jackson/Orchard Books)	
☐	☐	*Moorchild* by Eloise McGraw (Margaret McElderry/Simon & Schuster)	

List #262 **Newbery Medal Winners and Honor Books** *(continued)*

Do we have this book?	Have we read it?		Study Ideas / Notes
☐	☐	*The Thief* by Megan Whalen Turner (Greenwillow/Morrow)	
☐	☐	*Belle Prater's Boy* by Ruth White (Farrar Straus Giroux)	
☐	☐	**1996 Medal Winner:** *The Midwife's Apprentice* by Karen Cushman (Clarion)	
		1996 Honor Books:	
☐	☐	*What Jamie Saw* by Carolyn Coman (Front Street)	
☐	☐	*The Watsons Go to Birmingham: 1963* by Christopher Paul Curtis (Delacorte)	
☐	☐	*Yolonda's Genius* by Carol Fenner (Margaret K. McElderry/Simon & Schuster)	
☐	☐	*The Great Fire* by Jim Murphy (Scholastic)	
☐	☐	**1995 Medal Winner:** *Walk Two Moons* by Sharon Creech (HarperCollins)	
		1995 Honor Books:	
☐	☐	*Catherine, Called Birdy* by Karen Cushman (Clarion)	
☐	☐	*The Ear, the Eye, and the Arm* by Nancy Farmer (Jackson/Orchard)	
☐	☐	**1994 Medal Winner:** *The Giver* by Lois Lowry (Houghton)	
		1994 Honor Books:	
☐	☐	*Crazy Lady* by Jane Leslie Conly (HarperCollins)	
☐	☐	*Dragon's Gate* by Laurence Yep (HarperCollins)	
☐	☐	*Eleanor Roosevelt: A Life of Discovery* by Russell Freedman (Clarion Books)	
☐	☐	**1993 Medal Winner:** *Missing May* by Cynthia Rylant (Jackson/Orchard)	
		1993 Honor Books:	
☐	☐	*What Hearts* by Bruce Brooks (A Laura Geringer Book, a HarperCollins imprint)	

List #262 **Newbery Medal Winners and Honor Books** *(continued)*

Do we have this book?	Have we read it?		Study Ideas / Notes
☐	☐	*The Dark-Thirty: Southern Tales of the Supernatural* by Patricia McKissack (Knopf)	
☐	☐	*Somewhere in the Darkness* by Walter Dean Myers (Scholastic Hardcover)	
☐	☐	**1992 Medal Winner:** *Shiloh* by Phyllis Reynolds Naylor (Atheneum)	
		1992 Honor Books:	
☐	☐	*Nothing But the Truth: a Documentary Novel* by Avi (Jackson/Orchard)	
☐	☐	*The Wright Brothers: How They Invented the Airplane* by Russell Freedman (Holiday House)	
☐	☐	**1991 Medal Winner:** *Maniac Magee* by Jerry Spinelli (Little, Brown)	
☐	☐	**1991 Honor Book:** *The True Confessions of Charlotte Doyle* by Avi (Jackson/Orchard)	
☐	☐	**1990 Medal Winner:** *Number the Stars* by Lois Lowry (Houghton)	
		1990 Honor Books:	
☐	☐	*Afternoon of the Elves* by Janet Taylor Lisle (Jackson/Orchard)	
		Shabanu, Daughter of the Wind by Suzanne Fisher Staples (Knopf)	
☐	☐	*The Winter Room* by Gary Paulsen (Jackson/Orchard)	
☐	☐	**1989 Medal Winner:** *Joyful Noise: Poems for Two Voices* by Paul Fleischman (Harper)	
		1989 Honor Books:	
☐	☐	*In The Beginning: Creation Stories From Around the World* by Virginia Hamilton (Harcourt)	
☐	☐	*Scorpions* by Walter Dean Myers (Harper)	
☐	☐	**1988 Medal Winner:** *Lincoln: A Photobiography* by Russell Freedman (Clarion)	

List #262 **Newbery Medal Winners and Honor Books** *(continued)*

Do we have this book?	Have we read it?		Study Ideas / Notes
		1988 Honor Books:	
☐	☐	*After the Rain* by Norma Fox Mazer (Morrow)	
☐	☐	*Hatchet* by Gary Paulsen (Bradbury)	
☐	☐	**1987 Medal Winner:** *The Whipping Boy* by Sid Fleischman (Greenwillow)	
		1987 Honor Books:	
☐	☐	*A Fine White Dust* by Cynthia Rylant (Bradbury)	
☐	☐	*On My Honor* by Marion Dane Bauer (Clarion)	
☐	☐	*Volcano: The Eruption and Healing of Mount St. Helens* by Patricia Lauber (Bradbury)	
☐	☐	**1986 Medal Winner:** *Sarah, Plain and Tall* by Patricia MacLachlan (Harper)	
		1986 Honor Books:	
☐	☐	*Commodore Perry in the Land of the Shogun* by Rhoda Blumberg (Lothrop)	
☐	☐	*Dogsong* by Gary Paulsen (Bradbury)	
☐	☐	**1985 Medal Winner:** *The Hero and the Crown* by Robin McKinley (Greenwillow)	
		1985 Honor Books:	
☐	☐	*Like Jake and Me* by Mavis Jukes (Knopf)	
☐	☐	*The Moves Make the Man* by Bruce Brooks (Harper)	
☐	☐	*One-Eyed Cat* by Paula Fox (Bradbury)	
☐	☐	**1984 Medal Winner:** *Dear Mr. Henshaw* by Beverly Cleary (Morrow)	
		1984 Honor Books:	
☐	☐	*The Sign of the Beaver* by Elizabeth George Speare (Houghton)	
☐	☐	*A Solitary Blue* by Cynthia Voigt (Atheneum)	
☐	☐	*Sugaring Time* by Kathryn Lasky (Macmillan)	
☐	☐	*The Wish Giver: Three Tales of Coven Tree* by Bill Brittain (Harper)	
☐	☐	**1983 Medal Winner:** *Dicey's Song* by Cynthia Voigt (Atheneum)	

List #262 **Newbery Medal Winners and Honor Books** *(continued)*

Do we have this book?	Have we read it?		Study Ideas / Notes
		1983 Honor Books:	
☐	☐	*The Blue Sword* by Robin McKinley (Greenwillow)	
☐	☐	*Doctor DeSoto* by William Steig (Farrar)	
☐	☐	*Graven Images* by Paul Fleischman (Harper)	
☐	☐	*Homesick: My Own Story* by Jean Fritz (Putnam)	
☐	☐	*Sweet Whispers, Brother Rush* by Virginia Hamilton (Philomel)	
☐	☐	**1982 Medal Winner:** *A Visit to William Blake's Inn: Poems for Innocent and Experienced Travelers* by Nancy Willard (Harcourt)	
		1982 Honor Books:	
☐	☐	*Ramona Quimby, Age 8* by Beverly Cleary (Morrow)	
☐	☐	*Upon the Head of the Goat: A Childhood in Hungary 1939–1944* by Aranka Siegal (Farrar)	
☐	☐	**1981 Medal Winner:** *Jacob Have I Loved* by Katherine Paterson (Crowell)	
		1981 Honor Books:	
☐	☐	*The Fledgling* by Jane Langton (Harper)	
☐	☐	*A Ring of Endless Light* by Madeleine L'Engle (Farrar)	
☐	☐	**1980 Medal Winner:** *A Gathering of Days: A New England Girl's Journal, 1830–1832* by Joan W. Blos (Scribner)	
☐	☐	**1980 Honor Book:** *The Road from Home: The Story of an Armenian Girl* by David Kherdian (Greenwillow)	
☐	☐	**1979 Medal Winner:** *The Westing Game* by Ellen Raskin (Dutton)	
☐	☐	**1979 Honor Book:** *The Great Gilly Hopkins* by Katherine Paterson (Crowell)	
☐	☐	**1978 Medal Winner:** *Bridge to Terabithia* by Katherine Paterson (Crowell)	

List #262 **Newbery Medal Winners and Honor Books** *(continued)*

Do we have this book?	Have we read it?		Study Ideas / Notes
		1978 Honor Books:	
☐	☐	*Ramona and Her Father* by Beverly Cleary (Morrow)	
☐	☐	*Anpao: An American Indian Odyssey* by Jamake Highwater (Lippincott)	
☐	☐	**1977 Medal Winner:** *Roll of Thunder, Hear My Cry* by Mildred D. Taylor (Dial)	
		1977 Honor Books:	
☐	☐	*Abel's Island* by William Steig (Farrar)	
☐	☐	*A String in the Harp* by Nancy Bond (Atheneum)	
☐	☐	**1976 Medal Winner:** *The Grey King* by Susan Cooper (McElderry/Atheneum)	
		1976 Honor Books:	
☐	☐	*The Hundred Penny Box* by Sharon Bell Mathis (Viking)	
☐	☐	*Dragonwings* by Laurence Yep (Harper)	
☐	☐	**1975 Medal Winner:** *M. C. Higgins, the Great* by Virginia Hamilton (Macmillan)	
		1975 Honor Books:	
☐	☐	*Figgs & Phantoms* by Ellen Raskin (Dutton)	
☐	☐	*My Brother Sam Is Dead* by James Lincoln Collier and Christopher Collier (Four Winds)	
		The Perilous Gard by Elizabeth Marie Pope (Houghton)	
☐	☐	*Philip Hall Likes Me, I Reckon Maybe* by Bette Greene (Dial)	
☐	☐	**1974 Medal Winner:** *The Slave Dancer* by Paula Fox (Bradbury)	
☐	☐	**1974 Honor Book:** *The Dark Is Rising* by Susan Cooper (McElderry/Atheneum)	
☐	☐	**1973 Medal Winner:** *Julie of the Wolves* by Jean Craighead George (Harper)	
		1973 Honor Books:	
☐	☐	*Frog and Toad Together* by Arnold Lobel (Harper)	

List #262 **Newbery Medal Winners and Honor Books** *(continued)*

Do we have this book?	Have we read it?		Study Ideas / Notes
☐	☐	*The Upstairs Room* by Johanna Reiss (Crowell)	
☐	☐	*The Witches of Worm* by Zilpha Keatley Snyder (Atheneum)	
☐	☐	**1972 Medal Winner:** *Mrs. Frisby and the Rats of NIMH* by Robert C. O'Brien (Atheneum)	
		1972 Honor Books:	
☐	☐	*Incident at Hawk's Hill* by Allan W. Eckert (Little, Brown)	
☐	☐	*The Planet of Junior Brown* by Virginia Hamilton (Macmillan)	
☐	☐	*The Tombs of Atuan* by Ursula K. LeGuin (Atheneum)	
☐	☐	*Annie and the Old One* by Miska Miles (Little, Brown)	
☐	☐	*The Headless Cupid* by Zilpha Keatley Snyder (Atheneum)	
☐	☐	**1971 Medal Winner:** *Summer of the Swans* by Betsy Byars (Viking)	
		1971 Honor Books:	
☐	☐	*Knee Knock Rise* by Natalie Babbitt (Farrar)	
☐	☐	*Enchantress From the Stars* by Sylvia Louise Engdahl (Atheneum)	
☐	☐	*Sing Down the Moon* by Scott O'Dell (Houghton)	
☐	☐	**1970 Medal Winner:** *Sounder* by William H. Armstrong (Harper)	
		1970 Honor Books:	
☐	☐	*Our Eddie* by Sulamith Ish-Kishor (Pantheon)	
☐	☐	*The Many Ways of Seeing: An Introduction to the Pleasures of Art* by Janet Gaylord Moore (World)	
☐	☐	*Journey Outside* by Mary Q. Steele (Viking)	
☐	☐	**1969 Medal Winner:** *The High King* by Lloyd Alexander (Holt)	
		1969 Honor Books:	
☐	☐	*To Be a Slave* by Julius Lester (Dial)	

List #262 | Newbery Medal Winners and Honor Books *(continued)*

Do we have this book?	Have we read it?		Study Ideas / Notes
☐	☐	*When Shlemiel Went to Warsaw and Other Stories* by Isaac Bashevis Singer (Farrar)	
☐	☐	**1968 Medal Winner:** *From the Mixed-Up Files of Mrs. Basil E. Frankweiler* by E. L. Konigsburg (Atheneum)	
		1968 Honor Books:	
☐	☐	*Jennifer, Hecate, Macbeth, William McKinley, and Me, Elizabeth* by E. L. Konigsburg (Atheneum)	
☐	☐	*The Black Pearl* by Scott O'Dell (Houghton)	
☐	☐	*The Fearsome Inn* by Isaac Bashevis Singer (Scribner)	
☐	☐	*The Egypt Game* by Zilpha Keatley Snyder (Atheneum)	
☐	☐	**1967 Medal Winner:** *Up a Road Slowly* by Irene Hunt (Follett)	
		1967 Honor Books:	
☐	☐	*The King's Fifth* by Scott O'Dell (Houghton)	
☐	☐	*Zlateh the Goat and Other Stories* by Isaac Bashevis Singer (Harper)	
☐	☐	*The Jazz Man* by Mary Hays Weik (Atheneum)	
☐	☐	**1966 Medal Winner:** *I, Juan de Pareja* by Elizabeth Borton de Trevino (Farrar)	
		1966 Honor Books:	
☐	☐	*The Black Cauldron* by Lloyd Alexander (Holt)	
☐	☐	*The Animal Family* by Randall Jarrell (Pantheon)	
☐	☐	*The Noonday Friends* by Mary Stolz (Harper)	
☐	☐	**1965 Medal Winner:** *Shadow of a Bull* by Maia Wojciechowska (Atheneum)	
☐	☐	**1965 Honor Book:** *Across Five Aprils* by Irene Hunt (Follett)	
☐	☐	**1964 Medal Winner:** *It's Like This, Cat* by Emily Neville (Harper)	

List #262 **Newbery Medal Winners and Honor Books** *(continued)*

Do we have this book?	Have we read it?		Study Ideas / Notes
		1964 Honor Books:	
☐	☐	*Rascal: A Memoir of a Better Era* by Sterling North (Dutton)	
☐	☐	*The Loner* by Ester Wier (McKay)	
☐	☐	**1963 Medal Winner:** *A Wrinkle in Time* by Madeleine L'Engle (Farrar)	
		1963 Honor Books:	
☐	☐	*Thistle and Thyme: Tales and Legends From Scotland* by Sorche Nic Leodhas, pseud. [Leclaire Alger] (Holt)	
☐	☐	*Men of Athens* by Olivia Coolidge (Houghton)	
☐	☐	**1962 Medal Winner:** *The Bronze Bow* by Elizabeth George Speare (Houghton)	
		1962 Honor Books:	
☐	☐	*Frontier Living* by Edwin Tunis (World)	
☐	☐	*The Golden Goblet* by Eloise Jarvis McGraw (Coward)	
☐	☐	*Belling the Tiger* by Mary Stolz (Harper)	
☐	☐	**1961 Medal Winner:** *Island of the Blue Dolphins* by Scott O'Dell (Houghton)	
		1961 Honor Books:	
☐	☐	*America Moves Forward: A History for Peter* by Gerald W. Johnson (Morrow)	
☐	☐	*Old Ramon* by Jack Schaefer (Houghton)	
☐	☐	*The Cricket in Times Square* by George Selden, pseud. [George Thompson] (Farrar)	
☐	☐	**1960 Medal Winner:** *Onion John* by Joseph Krumgold (Crowell)	
		1960 Honor Books:	
☐	☐	*My Side of the Mountain* by Jean Craighead George (Dutton)	
☐	☐	*America Is Born: A History for Peter* by Gerald W. Johnson (Morrow)	
☐	☐	*The Gammage Cup* by Carol Kendall (Harcourt)	

List #262 **Newbery Medal Winners and Honor Books** *(continued)*

Do we have this book?	Have we read it?		Study Ideas / Notes
☐	☐	**1959 Medal Winner:** *The Witch of Blackbird Pond* by Elizabeth George Speare (Houghton)	
		1959 Honor Books:	
☐	☐	*The Family Under the Bridge* by Natalie Savage Carlson (Harper)	
☐	☐	*Along Came a Dog* by Meindert Dejong (Harper)	
☐	☐	*Chucaro: Wild Pony of the Pampa* by Francis Kalnay (Harcourt)	
☐	☐	*The Perilous Road* by William O. Steele (Harcourt)	
☐	☐	**1958 Medal Winner:** *Rifles for Watie* by Harold Keith (Crowell)	
		1958 Honor Books:	
☐	☐	*The Horsecatcher* by Mari Sandoz (Westminster)	
☐	☐	*Gone-Away Lake* by Elizabeth Enright (Harcourt)	
☐	☐	*The Great Wheel* by Robert Lawson (Viking)	
☐	☐	*Tom Paine, Freedom's Apostle* by Leo Gurko (Crowell)	
☐	☐	**1957 Medal Winner:** *Miracles on Maple Hill* by Virginia Sorenson (Harcourt)	
		1957 Honor Books:	
☐	☐	*Old Yeller* by Fred Gipson (Harper)	
☐	☐	*The House of Sixty Fathers* by Meindert DeJong (Harper)	
☐	☐	*Mr. Justice Holmes* by Clara Ingram Judson (Follett)	
☐	☐	*The Corn Grows Ripe* by Dorothy Rhoads (Viking)	
☐	☐	*Black Fox of Lorne* by Marguerite de Angeli (Doubleday)	
☐	☐	**1956 Medal Winner:** *Carry On, Mr. Bowditch* by Jean Lee Latham (Houghton)	

List #262 Newbery Medal Winners and Honor Books *(continued)*

Do we have this book?	Have we read it?		Study Ideas / Notes
		1956 Honor Books:	
☐	☐	*The Secret River* by Marjorie Kinnan Rawlings (Scribner)	
☐	☐	*The Golden Name Day* by Jennie Lindquist (Harper)	
☐	☐	*Men, Microscopes, and Living Things* by Katherine Shippen (Viking)	
☐	☐	**1955 Medal Winner:** *The Wheel on the School* by Meindert DeJong (Harper)	
		1955 Honor Books:	
☐	☐	*Courage of Sarah Noble* by Alice Dalgliesh (Scribner)	
☐	☐	*Banner in the Sky* by James Ullman (Lippincott)	
☐	☐	**1954 Medal Winner:** *...And Now Miguel* by Joseph Krumgold (Crowell)	
		1954 Honor Books:	
☐	☐	*All Alone* by Claire Huchet Bishop (Viking)	
☐	☐	*Shadrach* by Meindert Dejong (Harper)	
☐	☐	*Hurry Home, Candy* by Meindert Dejong (Harper)	
☐	☐	*Theodore Roosevelt, Fighting Patriot* by Clara Ingram Judson (Follett)	
☐	☐	*Magic Maize* by Mary & Conrad Buff (Houghton)	
☐	☐	**1953 Medal Winner:** *Secret of the Andes* by Ann Nolan Clark (Viking)	
		1953 Honor Books:	
☐	☐	*Charlotte's Web* by E. B. White (Harper)	
☐	☐	*Moccasin Trail* by Eloise Jarvis McGraw (Coward)	
☐	☐	*Red Sails to Capri* by Ann Weil (Viking)	
☐	☐	*The Bears on Hemlock Mountain* by Alice Dalgliesh (Scribner)	
☐	☐	*Birthdays of Freedom, Vol. 1* by Genevieve Foster (Scribner)	

List #262 **Newbery Medal Winners and Honor Books** *(continued)*

Do we have this book?	Have we read it?		Study Ideas / Notes
☐	☐	**1952 Medal Winner:** *Ginger Pye* by Eleanor Estes (Harcourt)	
		1952 Honor Books:	
☐	☐	*Americans Before Columbus* by Elizabeth Baity (Viking)	
☐	☐	*Minn of the Mississippi* by Holling C. Holling (Houghton)	
☐	☐	*The Defender* by Nicholas Kalashnikoff (Scribner)	
☐	☐	*The Light at Tern Rock* by Julia Sauer (Viking)	
☐	☐	*The Apple and the Arrow* by Mary & Conrad Buff (Houghton)	
☐	☐	**1951 Medal Winner:** *Amos Fortune, Free Man* by Elizabeth Yates (Dutton)	
		1951 Honor Books:	
☐	☐	*Better Known as Johnny Appleseed* by Mabel Leigh Hunt (Lippincott)	
☐	☐	*Gandhi, Fighter Without a Sword* by Jeanette Eaton (Morrow)	
☐	☐	*Abraham Lincoln, Friend of the People* by Clara Ingram Judson (Follett)	
☐	☐	*The Story of Appleby Capple* by Anne Parrish (Harper)	
☐	☐	**1950 Medal Winner:** *The Door in the Wall* by Marguerite de Angeli (Doubleday)	
		1950 Honor Books:	
☐	☐	*Tree of Freedom* by Rebecca Caudill (Viking)	
☐	☐	*The Blue Cat of Castle Town* by Catherine Coblentz (Longmans)	
☐	☐	*Kildee House* by Rutherford Montgomery (Doubleday)	
☐	☐	*George Washington* by Genevieve Foster (Scribner)	
☐	☐	*Song of the Pines: A Story of Norwegian Lumbering in Wisconsin* by Walter & Marion Havighurst (Winston)	

List #262 Newbery Medal Winners and Honor Books *(continued)*

Do we have this book?	Have we read it?		Study Ideas / Notes
☐	☐	**1949 Medal Winner:** *King of the Wind* by Marguerite Henry (Rand McNally)	
		1949 Honor Books:	
☐	☐	*Seabird* by Holling C. Holling (Houghton)	
☐	☐	*Daughter of the Mountain* by Louise Rankin (Viking)	
☐	☐	*My Father's Dragon* by Ruth S. Gannett (Random House)	
☐	☐	*Story of the Negro* by Arna Bontemps (Knopf)	
☐	☐	**1948 Medal Winner:** *The Twenty-One Balloons* by William Pène du Bois (Viking)	
		1948 Honor Books:	
☐	☐	*Pancakes-Paris* by Claire Huchet Bishop (Viking)	
☐	☐	*Li Lun, Lad of Courage* by Carolyn Treffinger (Abingdon)	
☐	☐	*The Quaint and Curious Quest of Johnny Longfoot* by Catherine Besterman (Bobbs-Merrill)	
☐	☐	*The Cow-Tail Switch, and Other West African Stories* by Harold Courlander (Holt)	
☐	☐	*Misty of Chincoteague* by Marguerite Henry (Rand McNally)	
☐	☐	**1947 Medal Winner:** *Miss Hickory* by Carolyn Sherwin Bailey (Viking)	
		1947 Honor Books:	
☐	☐	*Wonderful Year* by Nancy Barnes (Messner)	
☐	☐	*Big Tree* by Mary & Conrad Buff (Viking)	
☐	☐	*The Heavenly Tenants* by William Maxwell (Harper)	
☐	☐	*The Avion My Uncle Flew* by Cyrus Fisher, pseud. [Darwin L. Teilhet] (Appleton)	
☐	☐	*The Hidden Treasure of Glaston* by Eleanor Jewett (Viking)	
☐	☐	**1946 Medal Winner:** *Strawberry Girl* by Lois Lenski (Lippincott)	

List #262 **Newbery Medal Winners and Honor Books** *(continued)*

Do we have this book?	Have we read it?		Study Ideas / Notes
		1946 Honor Books:	
☐	☐	*Justin Morgan Had a Horse* by Marguerite Henry (Rand McNally)	
☐	☐	*The Moved-Outers* by Florence Crannell Means (Houghton)	
☐	☐	*Bhimsa, the Dancing Bear* by Christine Weston (Scribner)	
☐	☐	*New Found World* by Katherine Shippen (Viking)	
☐	☐	**1945 Medal Winner:** *Rabbit Hill* by Robert Lawson (Viking)	
		1945 Honor Books:	
☐	☐	*The Hundred Dresses* by Eleanor Estes (Harcourt)	
☐	☐	*The Silver Pencil* by Alice Dalgliesh (Scribner)	
☐	☐	*Abraham Lincoln's World* by Genevieve Foster (Scribner)	
☐	☐	*Lone Journey: The Life of Roger Williams* by Jeanette Eaton (Harcourt)	
☐	☐	**1944 Medal Winner:** *Johnny Tremain* by Esther Forbes (Houghton)	
		1944 Honor Books:	
☐	☐	*These Happy Golden Years* by Laura Ingalls Wilder (Harper)	
☐	☐	*Fog Magic* by Julia Sauer (Viking)	
☐	☐	*Rufus M.* by Eleanor Estes (Harcourt)	
☐	☐	*Mountain Born* by Elizabeth Yates (Coward)	
☐	☐	**1943 Medal Winner:** *Adam of the Road* by Elizabeth Janet Gray (Viking)	
		1943 Honor Books:	
☐	☐	*The Middle Moffat* by Eleanor Estes (Harcourt)	
☐	☐	*Have You Seen Tom Thumb?* by Mabel Leigh Hunt (Lippincott)	
☐	☐	**1942 Medal Winner:** *The Matchlock Gun* by Walter Edmonds (Dodd)	

List #262 **Newbery Medal Winners and Honor Books** *(continued)*

Do we have this book?	Have we read it?		Study Ideas / Notes
		1942 Honor Books:	
☐	☐	*Little Town on the Prairie* by Laura Ingalls Wilder (Harper)	
☐	☐	*George Washington's World* by Genevieve Foster (Scribner)	
☐	☐	*Indian Captive: The Story of Mary Jemison* by Lois Lenski (Lippincott)	
☐	☐	*Down Ryton Water* by Eva Roe Gaggin (Viking)	
☐	☐	**1941 Medal Winner:** *Call It Courage* by Armstrong Sperry (Macmillan)	
		1941 Honor Books:	
☐	☐	*Blue Willow* by Doris Gates (Viking)	
☐	☐	*Young Mac of Fort Vancouver* by Mary Jane Carr (Crowell)	
☐	☐	*The Long Winter* by Laura Ingalls Wilder (Harper)	
☐	☐	*Nansen* by Anna Gertrude Hall (Viking)	
☐	☐	**1940 Medal Winner:** *Daniel Boone* by James Daugherty (Viking)	
		1940 Honor Books:	
☐	☐	*The Singing Tree* by Kate Seredy (Viking)	
☐	☐	*Runner of the Mountain Tops: The Life of Louis Agassiz* by Mabel Robinson (Random House)	
☐	☐	*By the Shores of Silver Lake* by Laura Ingalls Wilder (Harper)	
☐	☐	*Boy With a Pack* by Stephen W. Meader (Harcourt)	
☐	☐	**1939 Medal Winner:** *Thimble Summer* by Elizabeth Enright (Rinehart)	
		1939 Honor Books:	
☐	☐	*Nino* by Valenti Angelo (Viking)	
☐	☐	*Mr. Popper's Penguins* by Richard & Florence Atwater (Little, Brown)	
☐	☐	*Hello the Boat!* by Phyllis Crawford (Holt)	

List #262 **Newbery Medal Winners and Honor Books** *(continued)*

Do we have this book?	Have we read it?		Study Ideas / Notes
☐	☐	*Leader by Destiny: George Washington, Man and Patriot* by Jeanette Eaton (Harcourt)	
☐	☐	*Penn* by Elizabeth Janet Gray (Viking)	
☐	☐	**1938 Medal Winner:** *The White Stag* by Kate Seredy (Viking)	
		1938 Honor Books:	
☐	☐	*Pecos Bill* by James Cloyd Bowman (Little, Brown)	
☐	☐	*Bright Island* by Mabel Robinson (Random House)	
☐	☐	*On the Banks of Plum Creek* by Laura Ingalls Wilder (Harper)	
☐	☐	**1937 Medal Winner:** *Roller Skates* by Ruth Sawyer (Viking)	
		1937 Honor Books:	
☐	☐	*Phoebe Fairchild: Her Book* by Lois Lenski (Stokes)	
☐	☐	*Whistler's Van* by Idwal Jones (Viking)	
☐	☐	*The Golden Basket* by Ludwig Bemelmans (Viking)	
☐	☐	*Winterbound* by Margery Bianco (Viking)	
☐	☐	*The Codfish Musket* by Agnes Hewes (Doubleday)	
☐	☐	*Audubon* by Constance Rourke (Harcourt)	
☐	☐	**1936 Medal Winner:** *Caddie Woodlawn* by Carol Ryrie Brink (Macmillan)	
		1936 Honor Books:	
☐	☐	*Honk, the Moose* by Phil Stong (Dodd)	
☐	☐	*The Good Master* by Kate Seredy (Viking)	
☐	☐	*Young Walter Scott* by Elizabeth Janet Gray (Viking)	
☐	☐	*All Sail Set: A Romance of the Flying Cloud* by Armstrong Sperry (Winston)	
☐	☐	**1935 Medal Winner:** *Dobry* by Monica Shannon (Viking)	

List #262 **Newbery Medal Winners and Honor Books** *(continued)*

Do we have this book?	Have we read it?		Study Ideas / Notes
		1935 Honor Books:	
☐	☐	*Pageant of Chinese History* by Elizabeth Seeger (Longmans)	
☐	☐	*Davy Crockett* by Constance Rourke (Harcourt)	
☐	☐	*Day On Skates: The Story of a Dutch Picnic* by Hilda Von Stockum (Harper)	
☐	☐	**1934 Medal Winner:** *Invincible Louisa: The Story of the Author of Little Women* by Cornelia Meigs (Little, Brown)	
		1934 Honor Books:	
☐	☐	*The Forgotten Daughter* by Caroline Snedeker (Doubleday)	
☐	☐	*Swords of Steel* by Elsie Singmaster (Houghton)	
☐	☐	*ABC Bunny* by Wanda Gág (Coward)	
☐	☐	*Winged Girl of Knossos* by Erik Berry, pseud. [Allena Best] (Appleton)	
☐	☐	*New Land* by Sarah Schmidt (McBride)	
☐	☐	*Big Tree of Bunlahy: Stories of My Own Countryside* by Padraic Colum (Macmillan)	
☐	☐	*Glory of the Seas* by Agnes Hewes (Knopf)	
☐	☐	*Apprentice of Florence* by Ann Kyle (Houghton)	
☐	☐	**1933 Medal Winner:** *Young Fu of the Upper Yangtze* by Elizabeth Lewis (Winston)	
		1933 Honor Books:	
☐	☐	*Swift Rivers* by Cornelia Meigs (Little, Brown)	
☐	☐	*The Railroad to Freedom: A Story of the Civil War* by Hildegarde Swift (Harcourt)	
☐	☐	*Children of the Soil: A Story of Scandinavia* by Nora Burglon (Doubleday)	
☐	☐	**1932 Medal Winner:** *Waterless Mountain* by Laura Adams Armer (Longmans)	
		1932 Honor Books:	
☐	☐	*The Fairy Circus* by Dorothy P. Lathrop (Macmillan)	

List #262 **Newbery Medal Winners and Honor Books** *(continued)*

Do we have this book?	Have we read it?		Study Ideas / Notes
☐	☐	*Calico Bush* by Rachel Field (Macmillan)	
☐	☐	*Boy of the South Seas* by Eunice Tietjens (Coward-McCann)	
☐	☐	*Out of the Flame* by Eloise Lownsbery (Longmans)	
☐	☐	*Jane's Island* by Marjorie Allee (Houghton)	
☐	☐	*Truce of the Wolf and Other Tales of Old Italy* by Mary Gould Davis (Harcourt)	
☐	☐	**1931 Medal Winner:** *The Cat Who Went to Heaven* by Elizabeth Coatsworth (Macmillan)	
		1931 Honor Books:	
☐	☐	*Floating Island* by Anne Parrish (Harper)	
☐	☐	*The Dark Star of Itza: The Story of a Pagan Princess* by Alida Malkus (Harcourt)	
☐	☐	*Queer Person* by Ralph Hubbard (Doubleday)	
☐	☐	*Mountains Are Free* by Julie Davis Adams (Dutton)	
☐	☐	*Spice and the Devil's Cave* by Agnes Hewes (Knopf)	
☐	☐	*Meggy MacIntosh* by Elizabeth Janet Gray (Doubleday)	
☐	☐	*Garram the Hunter: A Boy of the Hill Tribes* by Herbert Best (Doubleday)	
☐	☐	*Ood-Le-Uk the Wanderer* by Alice Lide and Margaret Johansen (Little, Brown)	
☐	☐	**1930 Medal Winner:** *Hitty, Her First Hundred Years* by Rachel Field (Macmillan)	
		1930 Honor Books:	
☐	☐	*A Daughter of the Seine: The Life of Madame Roland* by Jeanette Eaton (Harper)	
☐	☐	*Pran of Albania* by Elizabeth Miller (Doubleday)	
☐	☐	*Jumping-Off Place* by Marion Hurd McNeely (Longmans)	
☐	☐	*The Tangle-Coated Horse and Other Tales* by Ella Young (Longmans)	
☐	☐	*Vaino* by Julia Davis Adams (Dutton)	

List #262 **Newbery Medal Winners and Honor Books** *(continued)*

Do we have this book?	Have we read it?		Study Ideas / Notes
☐	☐	*Little Blacknose* by Hildegarde Swift (Harcourt)	
☐	☐	**1929 Medal Winner:** *The Trumpeter of Krakow* by Eric P. Kelly (Macmillan)	
		1929 Honor Books:	
☐	☐	*Pigtail of Ah Lee Ben Loo* by John Bennett (Longmans)	
☐	☐	*Millions of Cats* by Wanda Gág (Coward)	
☐	☐	*The Boy Who Was* by Grace Hallock (Dutton)	
☐	☐	*Clearing Weather* by Cornelia Meigs (Little, Brown)	
☐	☐	*Runaway Papoose* by Grace Moon (Doubleday)	
☐	☐	*Tod of the Fens* by Elinor Whitney (Macmillan)	
☐	☐	**1928 Medal Winner:** *Gay-Neck, the Story of a Pigeon* by Dhan Gopal Mukerji (Dutton)	
		1928 Honor Books:	
☐	☐	*The Wonder Smith and His Son* by Ella Young (Longmans)	
☐	☐	*Downright Dencey* by Caroline Snedeker (Doubleday)	
☐	☐	**1927 Medal Winner:** *Smoky, the Cowhorse* by Will James (Scribner)	
		1927 No Honor Books Recorded	
☐	☐	**1926 Medal Winner:** *Shen of the Sea* by Arthur Bowie Chrisman (Dutton)	
☐	☐	**1926 Honor Book:** *The Voyagers: Being Legends and Romances of Atlantic Discovery* by Padraic Colum (Macmillan)	
☐	☐	**1925 Medal Winner:** *Tales from Silver Lands* by Charles Finger (Doubleday)	
		1925 Honor Books:	
☐	☐	*Nicholas: A Manhattan Christmas Story* by Annie Carroll Moore (Putnam)	
☐	☐	*The Dream Coach* by Anne Parrish (Macmillan)	

List #262 **Newbery Medal Winners and Honor Books** *(continued)*

Do we have this book?	Have we read it?		Study Ideas / Notes
☐	☐	**1924 Medal Winner:** *The Dark Frigate* by Charles Hawes (Little, Brown)	
		1924 No Honor Books Recorded	
☐	☐	**1923 Medal Winner:** *The Voyages of Doctor Dolittle* by Hugh Lofting (Lippincott)	
		1923 No Honor Books Recorded	
☐	☐	**1922 Medal Winner:** *The Story of Mankind* by Hendrik Willem van Loon (Liveright)	
		1922 Honor Books:	
☐	☐	*The Great Quest* by Charles Hawes (Little, Brown)	
☐	☐	*Cedric the Forester* by Bernard Marshall (Appleton)	
☐	☐	*The Old Tobacco Shop: A True Account of What Befell a Little Boy in Search of Adventure* by William Bowen (Macmillan)	
☐	☐	*The Golden Fleece and The Heroes Who Lived Before Achilles* by Padraic Colum (Macmillan)	
☐	☐	*The Windy Hill* by Cornelia Meigs (Macmillan)	